Jeffrey Edwards
Autonomy, Moral Worth, and Right

Kantstudien-Ergänzungshefte

—

Im Auftrag der Kant-Gesellschaft
herausgegeben von
Manfred Baum, Bernd Dörflinger
und Heiner F. Klemme

Band 198

Jeffrey Edwards

Autonomy, Moral Worth, and Right

Kant on Obligatory Ends, Respect for Law, and Original Acquisition

DE GRUYTER

ISBN 978-3-11-065348-9
e-ISBN (PDF) 978-3-11-051740-8
e-ISBN (EPUB) 978-3-11-051611-1
ISSN 0340-6059

Library of Congress Cataloging-in-Publication Data
A CIP catalog record for this book has been applied for at the Library of Congress.

Bibliographic information published by the Deutsche Nationalbibliothek
The Deutsche Nationalbibliothek lists this publication in the Deutsche Nationalbibliografie;
detailed bibliographic data are available on the Internet at http://dnb.dnb.de.

© 2019 Walter de Gruyter GmbH, Berlin/Boston
This volume is text- and page-identical with the hardback published in 2018.
Printing and binding: CPI books GmbH, Leck
♾ Printed on acid-free paper
Printed in Germany

www.degruyter.com

To my mother, Katharine Edwards

Contents

Note on Sources, Abbreviations, and Translations —— XI

Acknowledgements —— XV

Introduction —— 1
    A Prospectus of the Argument —— 6

Part I Obligatory Ends, Material Practical Principles, and Practical Law in Kant's Doctrine of Morals —— 13

Chapter 1
Reason's Lawgiving and Obligatory Ends in the Metaphysics of Morals —— 15
§ 1 Laws of Freedom, Ethical Lawgiving, and the Systematic Division between Kant's Doctrines of Right and Virtue —— 15
§ 2 Obligatory Ends, the End in Itself, and Laws for Maxims of Actions —— 21
§ 3 Own-Perfection and Others' Happiness as Intrinsically Obligatory Ends —— 26
§ 4 Laws for Maxims and the "Dualism" of Morally Practical Reason —— 31

Chapter 2
Obligatory Ends and the Grounding of Maxims: A Key Problem in Kant's Moral Doctrine of Ends —— 35
§ 1 Laws for Maxims of Ends and Empirical Grounds of Maxims —— 35
§ 2 Duty, Self-Constraint, and Objectively Necessary Ends —— 38
§ 3 Ends of Action and the Grounding of Maxims —— 41
§ 4 Material Determining Grounds, the Matter of Universal Laws, and Self-Seeking Ends —— 47
§ 5 Self-Seeking Ends, Own-Happiness, and Universal Lawgiving —— 49

Chapter 3
The Principle of Self-Love and Material Practical Principles in the *Critique of Practical Reason* —— 51
§ 1 Practical Propositions, Maxims, and Practical Laws —— 51
§ 2 Self-Love and Material Practical Principles in Kant's Theorems of Practical Reason —— 52
§ 3 Own-Happiness, Others' Happiness, and Material Conditions of Maxims —— 63

§ 4 Maxims, Practical Laws, and Universal Happiness —— 69
§ 5 A Question of Practical Anthropology? —— 72

Part II Moral Worth and Motivation in Kant and Hume —— 79

Chapter 4
Eudaimonistic Etiology, Own-Perfection, and Moral Worth —— 81
§ 1 Eudaimonistic Etiology and the Happiness of Others —— 81
§ 2 Own-Perfection and Moral Worth —— 85
§ 3 Hume's "Undoubted Maxim" and the Sentimentalist Conception of Actions' Moral Worth —— 92

Chapter 5
Moral Worth and Motivation in Kant's Criticism of Sentimentalist Ethics —— 97
§ 1 Squire Allworthy's Inclinations and the Moral Worth of Actions in Kant's Groundwork for the Metaphysics of Morals —— 97
§ 2 Kant's Anti-Sentimentalist Difficulty with Allworthy-Type Actions —— 105
§ 3 Acting from Respect for Law and the Problems of Prescriptive Regress and Nomothetic Circularity —— 111
§ 4 Dealing with the 'Elephant in the Room': Respect for Law as an Incentive for Action —— 114

Part III Kant's Juridical Theory of Right and the Foundations of Property Law —— 123

Chapter 6
Original Community, Possession, and Acquisition in Kant's Doctrine of Right —— 129
§ 1 Intelligible Possession and the Juridical Postulate of Practical Reason —— 129
§ 2 Acquisition, Occupation, and Original Community —— 135
§ 3 Original Community and Universal Possession —— 142

Chapter 7
Original Acquisition in Kant, Grotius, and Selden —— 149
§ 1 Dominium, Right, and the Reach of the Cannons —— 149
§ 2 Original Community, Prima Occupatio, and the Right to All Things —— 150
§ 3 Kantian Original Acquisition and Material Equality in Distribution —— 160

Part IV Placing Kant in his History of Moral Philosophy —— 171

Chapter 8
Kant's Classification of Material Principles of Morality in the *Critique of Practical Reason* —— 172
§ 1 Epicurus, the Stoics, and "Practical Material Determining Grounds" —— 172
§ 2 Hutcheson, Moral Feeling, and Benevolent Inclination —— 176
§ 3 Material Determining Grounds and Stoic Internal Perfection —— 180

Chapter 9
Hutcheson and Rousseau in the Development of Kant's Doctrine of Morals —— 184
§ 1 "Hutcheson and others", Material Principles of Obligation, and Moral Feeling in 1764 —— 185
§ 2 Moral Feeling and Universal Will in Kant's 1760s Ethics —— 190
§ 3 The Idea of Universal Lawgiving and Rousseau's Anthropology —— 195
§ 4 Rousseau, Self-Love, and the "One-Source View" of Stoic Oikeiôsis —— 197

Chapter 10
Sentimentalist Ethics and Natural Law —— 206
§ 1 Benevolent Inclination and Law in Hutcheson's Account of the Origin of Obligation —— 206
§ 2 Cumberland and Pufendorf in Light of Hutcheson's Criticism —— 213
§ 3 "Kick Not Against the Pricks": Pufendorf and Hobbes on Natural Obligation —— 224
§ 4 Benevolent Inclination and Reason's Lawgiving Function: Kant and Hutcheson as Mirror-Image Counterparts —— 235

Chapter 11
Kant and the Role of the *Honestum* in Sentimentalist and Rationalist Ethics —— 240
§ 1 Retrospectus and Hume's Puzzling Letter to Hutcheson —— 240
§ 2 Cicero's "Proof against the Stoics" and Hume's Undoubted Maxim —— 244
§ 3 The Idea of the Honestum and Cicero's "Proof against the Stoics" in De finibus IV —— 249
§ 4 The Value of the Honestum in Reid's Repudiation of Hume's Undoubted Maxim —— 256

§ 5 The Form of the Honestum and Hutcheson's Account of
Obligation —— 262
§ 6 Kant's Theory of Reason's Autonomy and the Historic Impasse that Need
Never Have Been —— 267

Chapter 12 Natural Right, Material Equality, and the Normative Basis of Acquisition —— 272
§ 1 Ius Utendi, Ius Appropriandi, and the Emergence of the Modern
Conception of Natural Right: Grotius and Ockham on Original
Acquisition —— 273
§ 2 The Right to All Things and Communitas Rerum: Hobbes on the
Conceptual Incoherence of Natural Right-Based Acquisition —— 279
§ 3 Original Acquisition and the Formal Principle of Material Equality in
Distribution: Kant's Surprising Affinity with Both Ockham and
Hobbes —— 289

Conclusion —— 294
Kantian Consequentialism, Equal Right, and a Marxian Principle of
Distributive Justice —— 294
§ 1   Consequentialism in Ethics and Kant's Obligatory Ends —— 294
§ 2   Equal Right, Material Equality, and Marx's Twofold Principle —— 306

Bibliography —— 322
Primary Sources —— 322
Secondary Literature —— 325
Translations: Individual Works and Editions Containing
Translations —— 340

Index —— 343

Note on Sources, Abbreviations, and Translations

(I) Kant is generally cited according to volume, page, and line numbers of *Kants gesammelte Schriften* (the "Academy Edition") in conjunction with the abbreviations listed below. (Excepted are references to Marie Rischmüller's edition of *Bemerkungen in den >>Beobachtungen über das Gefühl des Schönen und Erhabenen<<* and to the *Kritik der reinen Vernunft*.)

AA	*Akademie-Ausgabe*
Anth	*Anthropologie in pragmatischer Hinsicht* (AA 7)
BDG	*Der einzig mögliche Beweisgrund zu einer Demonstration des Daseins Gottes* (AA 2)
BGSE	*Bemerkungen in den "Beobachtungens über das Gefühl des Schönen und Erhabenen"* (edited by Marie Rischmüller, Hamburg 1991; cited by page numbers)
EAD	*Das Ende aller Dinge* (AA 8)
GMS	*Grundlegung zur Metaphysik der Sitten* (AA 4)
GSE	*Beobachtungen über das Gefühl des Schönen und Erhabenen* (AA 2)
KpV	*Kritik der praktischen Vernunft* (AA 5)
KrV	*Kritik der reinen Vernunft* (cited by 1781 [A] and 1787 [B] editions)
KU	*Kritik der Urteilskraft* (AA 5)
MAN	*Metaphysische Anfangsgründe der Naturwissenschaften* (AA 4)
MS	*Die Metaphysik der Sitten* (AA 6)
Op	*Opus postumum* (AA 21–22)
RL	*Metaphysische Anfangsgründe der Rechtslehre* (AA 6)
TL	*Metaphysische Anfangsgründe der Tugendlehre* (AA 6)
NEV	*Nachricht von der Einrichtung seiner Vorlesungen in dem Winterhalbenjahre von 1765–1766* (AA 2)
Refl	*Reflexion* (AA 14–19)
RGV	*Die Religion innerhalb der Grenzen der bloßen Vernunft* (AA 6)
TG	*Träume eines Geistersehers, erläutert durch die Träume der Metaphysik* (AA 2)
TP	*Über den Gemeinspruch: Das mag in der Theorie richtig sein, taugt aber nicht für die Praxis* (AA 8)
UD	*Untersuchung über die Deutlichkeit der Grundsätze der natürlichen Theologie und der Moral* (AA 2)
VAMS	*Vorarbeit zur Metaphysik der Sitten* (AA 23)
VARL	*Vorarbeit zur Rechtslehre* (AA 23)
V-Mo/Collins	*Moralphilosophie Collins* (AA 27)
V-Mo/Mron	*Moral Mrongovius* (AA 27)
V-MS/Vigil	*Die Metaphysik der Sitten Vigilantius* (AA 27)
V-NR/Feyerabend	*Naturrecht Feyerabend* (AA 27)
V-PP/Herder	*Praktische Philosophie Herder* (AA 27)
V-PP/Powalski	*Praktische Philosophie Powalski* (AA 27)
VT	*Von einem neuerdings erhobenen vornehmen Ton in der Philosophie* (AA 8)

(II) For writers other than Kant, references are keyed to two alphabetically arranged lists of author's works (Primary Sources; Secondary Literature) in the bibliography at the end of the book. Works are generally cited by authors' names, publication dates, volumes (if necessary), and page numbers of the corresponding entries in these lists. Excepted are references to works of the following authors, which are here given with the titles, abbreviations, and citation conventions used in my main text and footnotes:

Aristotle:	Pol. = *Aristotelis politica* (Bekker pagination)
Cicero:	*De finibus* = *De finibus bonorum et malorum*
	De officiis
	Tusculanae Disputationes
Cumberland:	*De legibus* = *De legibus disquisitio philosophica* (cited by chapter and section numbers)
	TLN = *A Treatise of the Laws of Nature* (cited by page numbers)
Grotius:	DJB = *De jure belli ac pacis, libri tres* (cited by book, chapter, and [if specified] section numbers)
	DJP = *De jure praedae commentarius* (cited by page numbers of the Hamaker edition)
	ML = *Mare liberum*
Hobbes:	*De cive* (cited by chapter and paragraph numbers)
	Elements = *The Elements of Law* (cited by chapter and paragraph numbers)
	De homine (cited by chapter and paragraph numbers)
	Leviathan (cited by chapter and paragraph numbers)
Hume:	Letters [Grieg] = *The Letters of David Hume*
	EPM = *An Enquiry Concerning the Principles of Morals* (cited by section and paragraph numbers)
	THN = *A Treatise of Human Nature* (cited by book, part, section, and paragraph numbers)
Hutcheson:	ECI = *An Essay on the Nature and Conduct of the Passions and Affections, with Illustrations on the Moral Sense* (cited by page numbers of Aaron Garett's edition)
	IBV = *An Inquiry into the Original of Our Ideas of Beauty and Virtue* (cited by page numbers of Wolfgang Leidhold's edition)
	SMP = *A System of Moral Philosophy* (cited by page numbers of vol. 1)
Marx:	MEGA = *Marx/Engels Gesamtausgabe, Erste Abteilung* (cited by volume, page, and line numbers)
William of Ockham	OND = *Opus nonaginta dierum* (cited by page numbers of *Opera politica*, vol. 4)
Plato:	Rep. = *Platonis rempublicam* (Stephanus pagination)
Pufendorf:	DJN = *De jure naturae et gentium* (cited by book, chapter, and section numbers)
	GW = *Gesammelte Werke* (cited by page numbers of the volumes containing Gerald Hartung's editions of *De jure naturae et gentium* and *De officio hominis et civis*)

Reid: AP = *Essays on the Active Powers of Man* (cited by page numbers of the Haakonssen/Harris critical edition)

Rousseau: OC = *Oeuvres complètes* (cited by volume and page numbers of the Gagnebin/Raymond edition)

CW = *Collected Writings* (cited by volume and page numbers of the Masters/Kelly edition)

(III) I take responsibility for all passages translated into English, although I have made extensive use of the translated works listed at the end of the bibliography. My aim has been to provide, sometimes with stylistic costs to pay, fully literal translations that respect as much as possible the syntax and propositional content of the original sentences. Especially when treating Kant, I have provided in footnotes the original passages for English renderings involving more than one sentence. Where appropriate (given word-count restrictions), I have provided the original passages for paraphrased arguments presented by other thinkers as well. Significant departures from standard translations are discussed or duly noted.

Original passages reproduced in my footnotes regularly contain words or sentences elided from their English translations. I indicate this by repeating, or slightly revising, the corresponding parenthetic reference given in the main text.

Acknowledgements

This book incorporates, with substantial revisions, materials from the following previously published articles and anthology chapters, which I list in chronological order along with the relevant chapters of this book:

1998 (chapters 6 and 7): "Disjunktiv- und kollektiv-allgemeiner Besitz: Überlegungen zu Kants Theorie der ursprünglichen Erwerbung". In: Dieter Hüning/Burkhard Tuschling (Eds.): *Recht, Staat, und Völkerrecht bei Immanuel Kant*. Berlin: Duncker & Humblot, pp. 121–140.

2000 (chapters 3, 8 and 9): "Egoism and Formalism in the Development of Kant's Moral Philosophy". In: *Kant-Studien* 91, pp. 411–432.

2000 (chapter 3): "Self-love, Anthropology, and Universal Benevolence in Kant's Metaphysics of Morals". In: *The Review of Metaphysics* 53, pp. 887–914.

2002 (chapter 11): "Property and *communitas rerum*: Ockham, Suarez, Grotius, Hobbes". In: Dieter Hüning/Gideon Stiening/Ulrich Vogel (Eds.): *Societas rationis: Festschrift für Burkhard Tuschling zum 65. Geburtstag*. Berlin: Duncker & Humblot, pp. 41–60.

2004 (chapters 2 and 4): "Universal lawgiving and material determining grounds in Kant's moral doctrine of ends". In: Marion Heinz/Udo Rameil (Eds.): *Metaphysik und Kritik*. Berlin: De Gruyter, pp. 55–75.

2005 (chapter 11): "Natural Right and Acquisition in Grotius, Selden, and Hobbes". In Dieter Hüning, (Ed.): *Der lange Schatten des Leviathan: Hobbes' politische Philosophie nach 350 Jahren*. Berlin: Duncker & Humblot, pp. 153–178.

2008 (chapters 9 and 10): "Natural law and Obligation in Hutcheson and Kant". In: Ana Marta González, (Ed.): *Contemporary Perspectives on Natural Law: Natural Law as a Limiting Concept*. Aldershot: Ashgate, pp. 87–104.

2011 (chapters 7 and 8): "Original Community, Possession, and Acquisition in Kant's Metaphysics of Morals". In: Charlton Payne/Lucas Thorpe (Eds.): *Kant and the Concept of Community*. Rochester: University of Rochester Press, 2011, pp. 152–182.

2013 (chapter 1 and conclusion): "A Tale of Two Ends: Obligatory Ends and Material Determining Grounds in Kant's *Metaphysik der Sitten*". In: Burkahrd Tuschling/Werner Euler (Eds.): *Kants* Metaphysik der Sitten: *Editorische und Philosophische Probleme*. Berlin: Duncker & Humblot, pp. 147–175.

2014 (chapters 4 and 12): "*Honestum* is as *Honestum* Does: Reid, Hume—and Mandeville?!". In: *The Journal of Scottish Philosophy* 12, pp. 119–141.

2014 (chapter 9): "Self-Love, Sociability, and Autonomy: Some Presuppositions of Kant's Account of Practical Law". In: Steven Hoeltzel/Halla Kim: *Kant, Fichte, and the Legacy of German Idealism*. Lanham, MD: Lexington Books, pp. 1–29.

2014 (chapter 5): "Squire Allworthy's Inclinations and Acting from Duty: On Moral Worth in Kant and Hume". In: Mario Egger (Ed.): *Philosophie nach Kant: Neue Wege zum Verständnis von Kants Transzendental- und Moralphilosophie*. Berlin: De Gruyter, pp. 251–277.

2017 (chapters 4, 10, and 12): "Hume and Hutcheson on Cicero's 'Proof against the Stoics'". In: *The Journal of Scottish Philosophy* 15, 175–195.

I would like to thank Soren Whited for his work on the bibliography, and Chris Fremaux for his compilation of the index entries.

I would also like to express my abiding gratitude to Jerry Schneewind for his work on the history of modern moral philosophy.

Introduction

This book pursues three strands of investigation that stem from the consideration of Kant's last major work in moral philosophy: the *Metaphysics of Morals* of 1797. The first and second of these strands originate in the theory of obligatory ends that systematically grounds the second main part of this work, the Doctrine of Virtue. The third emerges from the account of the normative basis of property law that Kant presents in the Doctrine of Right, which forms the first part of the *Metaphysics of Morals*. Let me provisionally shed light on the paths of inquiry involved in following these strands.

(1) The foundational centerpiece of the 1797 Doctrine of Virtue is provided by Kant's portrayal of one's own perfection and the happiness of others as obligatory ends of morally practical reason. While Kant requires this portrayal in order to ensure the architectonic integrity of his ethics, the concept of end that underlies it—i.e., the concept of an end that is also (*zugleich*) a duty—does not sit easily with some very basic philosophical assumptions that we encounter in Kant critical works on the foundations of morals published prior to the Doctrine of Virtue's introduction. We can tentatively clarify this problem of compatibility by considering the relationship between an end that is also a duty (i.e., an obligatory end) and ends that we are inclined to bring about.

In the context of Kant's 1797 theory of obligatory ends, an end that is also a duty is a matter (*Materie*) or object of the power of choice that furnishes a moral end our actions. As such, it is an end of practical reason that can be set up against the ends of inclination that we may come to have on account of sensible impulse. It is therefore a *material* determining ground (*Bestimmungsgrund*) of the power of choice, but one that "must [...] be given a priori, independently of inclination" (TL 6:381.1–2). Now, despite its independence from inclination, an end that is also a duty seems to be one that we could have because we are inclined to promote it as an empirically given end, i.e., as an end of inclination. If, for example, I am inclined to promote the happiness of others, my end will be empirically given (in Kant's sense) just because it happens to be an end of inclination in addition to being, necessarily, an a priori given end. Thus, it seems that there must be an a priori given end of practical reason that can also be empirically given in the event that I am inclined to promote it. If this is the case, however, then it evidently follows as well that a *maxim* to promote an a priori given end could be empirically grounded in an end of inclination that is a matter or object of the power of choice, provided that such an end is *also* given a priori as an end that is also a duty.

This apparent implication raises a number of puzzling issues when we attempt to bring it into alignment with Kant's earlier treatments of the relationship between maxims, as subjective principles of volition, and the objective laws that satisfy the universality demands of morally practical reason. In particular, it is not obvious to begin with how it can made consistent with the theorematic treatment of practical principles given in the *Critique of Practical Reason* (1788). In the first part of this second *Critique*, Kant insists on the empirical standing of all practical principles, including all maxims, that "presuppose an object as the determining ground of the will" (KpV 5:21.16). For "in such a case the determining ground of the power of choice must be empirical, and so too must be the practical material principle that presupposes it as its condition" (KpV 5:21.29–31). Moreover, he holds in the same context that no principle of this type can furnish a practical law (i.e., a law of duty) because only the "mere *form* of a universal lawgiving" (KpV 5:27.14–15), the "mere lawgiving form of maxims" (KpV 5:28.31), and the "*mere form of law*" (KpV 5:31.12) can supply the determining ground of the will if a maxim is to serve as a universal law in keeping with the "*autonomy*" of pure practical reason" (KpV 5:33.19). So how does a maxim that, as it seems, could be grounded in an end given both empirically and a priori, as a material determining ground and volitional object, go together with Kant's considerations on the strictly formal conditions of practical lawfulness and universal lawgiving that pertain to reason's autonomy?

(2) The second path of inquiry intersects at various junctures with the pathway leading to the puzzling implication just noted. Its primary concern is with the ramifications of Kant's theory of practical reason's obligatory ends for the distinction between acting from inclination and acting from duty that is fundamental to his conception of the moral worth of actions. If, for example, I act to promote others' happiness, my maxim will be able to furnish a practical law in virtue of its fitness for universal lawgiving. But if the end on the basis of which I adopt this maxim is, for me, an end of inclination at the same time as I know it to be one that I ought to contribute to bringing about, just because I know it to be an obligatory end, then I am evidently inclined to promote an end that is also a duty. Does this imply, then, that I act merely in conformity with duty, and not from duty (or from respect for law), when I recognize that I ought to promote the end that I am inclined to bring about? Or does the fact that the matter and determining ground of my power of choice is the same as an end that is both a priori and empirically given indicate that I must be able to act from duty at the same time as I act from inclination—that my action is therefore one that can be from both duty and inclination at once?

It is with regard to questions like these that we need to examine the assumptions underlying Kant's conception of moral worth from the point of view afforded by the Doctrine of Virtue's concept of obligatory end. Specifically, we need to investigate Kant's view of the moral worth of actions from the perspective made possible by Kant's introduction of the concept of an end that is also a duty into his foundational theory of ethics as a doctrine of virtue. For the very thought that any end could be promoted *as* an obligatory end when acting *from* (i.e., not *merely* in accordance with) inclination seems incompatible with at least three crucial features of that view as we find it articulated in works published prior to the *Metaphysics of Morals*. That is, it initially seems incompatible with Kant's position that the "moral content" of a maxim consists in the prescription to perform obligatory actions "not from inclination but from duty" (GMS 4:398.18–20; cf. GMS 4:397.31–398.1, 398.6–7, 4:399.25–26); that actions done from duty are those performed from respect for law as "the sole and also undoubted moral incentive" (KpV 5:78.21–22); and that moral worth, therefore, "must be placed solely in this: that the action takes place from duty, that is, for the sake of the law alone" (KpV 5:81.17–19).

If we maintain, for example, that a maxim to further one's own perfection has no moral content because it does not involve the prescription to act from duty, we are still left with the thought that the *law* which it yields is a practical principle that enjoins the promotion of an end that is also duty. Thus, it seems quite possible for me to act from respect for law while acting on a law-yielding maxim whose content consists in the prescription to further an obligatory end that I am inclined to promote. Consequently, it is far from clear why I should not be acting both from inclination and from duty when I act in this way, even when respect for law is what provides the moral incentive to promote an obligatory end that, for me, is an end of inclination as well. Although the incentive provided by respect for law is only contingently related to every inclination to act, the *end* of inclination is, in this case, necessarily the same as a duty prescribed by a maxim that can yield a practical law. So why should moral worth have to be placed in the performance of actions for the sake of the law *alone* if acting from respect for law requires the promotion of an obligatory end that is *also* a possible end of inclination?

(3) As we will see, the theoretical incentive for setting foot on the third path of inquiry is difficult to discern except against some highly complex historical background in modern natural-law theories of property. The main problem that emerges from the consideration of Kant in view of this background, however, can be characterized quite straightforwardly as follows. Kant requires a conceptually coherent portrayal of original acquisition for his treatment of the foundations of property law in the Doctrine of Right. According to this portrayal, original acquisition must be thought of as appropriation through a unilateral act of first seizure, or *prima occupatio*, undertaken in relation to the originally

common possession (*urprünglicher Gesamtbesitz*; *communio possessionis originaria*) of humankind. Thus, according to Kant, the property-founding act of original acquisition must be considered an act of occupation that any given human agent is entitled to perform upon that which possessed by everyone in common. Yet it must also be understood as a type of act that is congruent with the idea of an "a priori united will" involving "the union of the power of choice of all who can come into practical relations with one another" (RL 6:263.21–23). But why should a *unilateral* act of occupation be authorized by any law of right if, as Kant explicitly acknowledges, its performance on the part of all originally occupying agents unavoidably leads to a condition of universal conflict in which the individual human being's ability to make use of usable things becomes impossible to ensure?

If there is a solution to this problem of original acquisition in the framework of Kant theory of right, then it must be consistent with the principle of innate equality that features in his account of freedom as the innate right of human beings. To satisfy this demand for consistency, however, it seems that original acquisition would have to be represented as taking place in accordance with a formal principle of *material* equality that applies to the distribution of usable things from humankind's originally common possession. But what exactly is the significance of such a principle for a theory of the normative basis of permissible individual appropriation? Specifically, how do we understand, in keeping with the fundamental assumptions of Kant's juridical theory of right, the normative import of that radically egalitarian principle of original material equality for a theory of distributive justice?

I have represented the first two of the main strands of investigation followed in this book as intersecting paths of philosophical inquiry. These are also convergent paths. Indeed, as we will soon see, they are paths that necessarily converge. For the various thickets of problems through which they wend their way all have to do with questions concerning the relationship between duty and inclination that arise when the Doctrine of Virtue's concept of obligatory end is brought to bear on Kant's different treatments of the connections between maxims, practical laws, and incentives or motives for action. Nevertheless, those pathways of inquiry still represent *distinct* strands of investigation. Thus, my strategy of argument and method of presentation will be to keep them separate as long as this is feasible, so that we can properly sort out the systematic ramifications of Kant's employment of the concept of an end that is also a duty. This means that the primary focus of Part I (Obligatory Ends, Material Practical Principles, and Practical Law in Kant's Doctrine of Morals) will be the formal and non-formal properties of maxims and practical laws as *propositions*. I will not become heavily involved, here, with the issues of motivation that lead directly into Kant's work on actions' moral worth. Instead, I will pursue the discussion of those propositional properties, using Kant's late theory of obligatory ends as an anchoring point of reference, to the juncture at which it unavoidably brings us face to face with the subject matter of Part II (Moral Worth and Motivation in Kant and Hume). In this way, we will be in a position to deal with both the systematic significance and the historical import of Kant's doctrine moral worth, especially in relation to competing conceptions of the basis of moral worth and merit that we encounter in eighteenth-century sentimentalist ethics.

As indicated above, considering the historical backdrop to Kant's theory of property is what enables us to discern his problem of original acquisition. Part III (Kant's Juridical Theory of Right and the Foundations of Property Law) therefore examines Kant's account of what it is to possess something as one's own, and to appropriate something external by means of a unilateral act of occupation, in connection with the corresponding features of two early modern natural-law theories of property to which Kant himself refers in the context of his conceptual portrayal of original acquisition. While Kant's references to these theories are one-off and indirect, the historical and logical resources that they provide allow us to pinpoint the crucial systematic difficulty that besets this portrayal.

The historical investigations undertaken in Part IV (Placing Kant in His History of Moral Philosophy) are intended to accomplish two things. First, they show how the laws for maxims of actions at issue in the Doctrine of Virtue, i.e., the laws for duties of virtue grounded in concepts of ends that are also duties, relate to Kant's own assessment of the place of autonomous ethics in the history of moral philosophy. Second, by determining how Kant's theory of the foundations of property law fits into the broader developmental current of theories of property employing the concept of natural right, they show why his Doctrine of Right requires a radically egalitarian principle of permissible individual appropriation if it is to make coherent use of the idea of original acquisition.

The concluding part of this book (Kantian Consequentialism, Equal Right, and a Marxian Principle of Distributive Justice) extends the assessment of the historical significance of Kant's autonomous ethics by showing how the Doctrine of Virtue's theory of obligatory ends undercuts the standard classificatory distinction between consequentialist and deontological ethical theories. It also explores the ramifications of the formal principle of material equality that Kant's theory of original acquisition requires by taking account of a post-Kantian approach to the question of justice in distribution.

A Prospectus of the Argument

The following chapter summaries are repeated below, in expanded form, in the respective introductions to Parts I-IV or at the beginning of individual chapters. Given the scope and complexity of this book's thematic contents, however, it seems appropriate to draw together the main lines of argument for the reader's ease of reference before launching into the main text. As the central issues of chapters 1–2 and 6 have been already been discussed in some detail, the corresponding summary sketches presented here will be relatively brief.

Chapters 1–2: I explain why Kant's theory of the metaphysical foundations of morals requires the concept of an end that is also a duty in order to ground the systematic division between the Doctrine of Right and the Doctrine of Virtue. After explicating this concept, I treat Kant's account of one's own perfection and the happiness of others as the only two promotable ends of action that can be intrinsically obligatory ends. As it is presented in the introduction to the Doctrine of Virtue, this dualistic account seems to allow that there could be an end of inclination that is also an obligatory end of morally practical reason. This appears to entail, in turn, that even an empirically grounded maxim would be able to yield a practical law that presents a duty of virtue. Since this implication is irreconcilable with Kant's standpoint that no empirical or material practical principle can furnish a universal law of the will, we need to ask what condition must obtain if we are to avoid having to draw it.

Chapter 3: I investigate this condition by following up on a clue that Kant offers in the Doctrine of Virtue's introduction. There, in the context of his metaphysical exposition of the concept of obligatory end, Kant takes the position that all ends that provide empirical grounds for the adoption of maxims are self-seeking ends, i.e., ends that we come to have on account of self-love. That Kant in fact assumes this position is supported by the basic principles of practical reason discussed in the opening sections of the *Critique of Practical Reason*, particularly by the theorem which asserts that all material practical principles belong under the general principle of self-love or one's own happiness. Thinking through the systematic consequences of this theorem, however, serves to highlight a fundamental problem for Kant's ethics as a doctrine of virtue based on his dualistic theory of intrinsically obligatory ends: This theory, and consequently Kant's a priori account of the practical laws that present duties of virtue, would have to rely on an empirical tenet that concerns the nature of human motivation if it is to be made consistent with the supposition that no empirically grounded maxim can furnish a universal law.

Chapter 4: This chapter spells out what follows when we combine Kant's theory of obligatory ends with the view of the empirical conditions of motivation at issue in the second *Critique's* self-love theorem. I thus explain what is entailed when we endorse the strategy of argument that takes this theorem as a point of departure and apply it to others' happiness and one's own perfection as ends that are also duties. This enables us to see why the pursuit of this strategy leads, inexorably, to Kant's conception of the moral worth of actions. To prepare the stage for treating this conception (in chapter 5), I consider the basic tenet of an approach to the question of moral worth that Kant opposes. I locate this tenet by examining the account of the merit and moral goodness of actions that David Hume provides in his *Treatise of Human Nature.*

Chapter 5: The discussion turns to Kant's treatment of moral worth in the *Groundwork for the Metaphysics of Morals.* Concentrating on the aspects of this treatment that are opposed to the sentimentalist view of the moral worth of actions, I argue that the way in which Kant establishes his contrasting view gives rise to some basic difficulties for his foundational theory of ethics. First, Kant's anti-sentimentalist approach must implicitly rely on a motivational principle drawn from empirical moral psychology, which threatens to make his theory of the a priori foundations of ethics reliant upon an anthropological explanatory principle. Second, a further anti-sentimentalist tenet of Kant's approach exposes his theory of universal moral prescriptions to a problem of logical regress. Third, this same tenet must make his treatment of autonomous reason's universally lawgiving role non-virtuously circular unless a way can be found to keep Kant from *overreaching* his sentimentalist opponent. The way around all three difficulties, I argue, can be found if we keep the question of incentives for action analytically separate from the question of the formal and non-formal properties of maxims as practical propositions. Paying careful attention to the distinction between incentives and these properties of maxims is what enables us to discern how it is always possible, even on Kant's own terms, to act from respect for law as one's moral incentive even without always making it one's maxim to act from respect for law.

Chapter 6: The focus of discussion now shifts from Kant ethics to his juridical theory of right. After explaining the systematic basis of this theory and its division into Private Right and Public Right, I turn to Kant's account of the foundations of property law. I concentrate on a fundamental problem that stems from Kant's joint employment of two pivotal concepts of his theory of the normative grounds of the external acquisition of things, namely, the idea of 'an a priori united will of all' and the idea of appropriation through first seizure (or *prima occupatio*). The problem is this: Why should first seizure, which is necessarily a unilateral act of occupation, be authorized by any universal law of practical reason when, as Kant insists, its performance on the part of all occupying agents contains the seeds of universal conflict in the use of all things that originally constitute the common possession of humankind?

Chapter 7: The question just posed motivates the investigation of the historical backdrop to Kant's treatment of original acquisition in the Doctrine of Right. Following up on Kant's references to a generative debate in early modern natural-law portrayals of the origins of property, I consider Hugo Grotius's attempt to ground ownership using a concept of subjective natural right in conjunction with a contractualist principle of agreement (*pactum*). I also examine the line of argument by which John Selden drew out a key consequence of Grotius's theory of acquisition—i.e., the implication that the natural right which warrants the unilateral first seizure of things from the originally common property of humankind is in effect a right to all things. After clarifying Selden's proximity to Kant with respect to the role of first seizure and the idea of universal agreement, I show that the solution to Kant's problem of original acquisition has to be consistent with the conception of innate freedom and the innate equality of human beings that underlies his basic view of rights as moral capacities. Accordingly, I argue that the principle of the distribution of usable things at issue in Kant's conceptual determination of original acquisition *ought* to be a formal principle of material equality.

Chapter 8: Chapters 8–12 shed light on Kant's place in the history of moral philosophy by examining his own assessment of his historical forerunners' various approaches to the doctrine of morals. Chapter 8 determines the character of this task by discussing Kant's endeavor, in the *Critique of Practical Reason*, to classify all previously accepted grounding principles for morals as material practical principles. This strategy of classification enables Kant to oppose the historically available collection of these different grounding principles to his supreme formal principle of reason's autonomy. But it is a problematic strategy in two key respects: It is unclear how Kant's classificatory scheme puts him in a position to come to terms with a central tenet of Francis Hutcheson's sentimentalist approach to the foundations of morals. It is also far from evident that this scheme allows for an adequate understanding of the principle of internal perfection which, as Kant himself insists, informs the Stoic approach to those foundations.

Chapter 9: This chapter investigates the pre-critical development of Kant's doctrine of morals in connection with the problematic features just mentioned. The focus of discussion thus moves to Kant's early assessments of perfectionist and sentimentalist ethics that we encounter in published texts and unpublished reflections from the 1760s. I link these assessments to the influence that Jean-Jacques Rousseau had on the emergence of Kant's understanding of autonomous reason's universally lawgiving role. But my primary concern is with another dimension of Kant's relation to Rousseau, namely, Kant's lack of interest in taking full advantage of the conceptual distinction that structures Rousseau's attempts to rethink the relationship between nature-determined sentiment and law-determined action: the distinction between *amour de soi* and *amour propre* as originally different forms of self-love. Why this lack of interest? The most interesting part of the answer has to do with Rousseau's relation to the classic Stoic doctrine of *oikeiôsis* and its role in Stoic-influenced portrayals of the self-perfecting moral agent.

Chapter 10: The opening phase of this chapter treats the account of the relationship between obligation and benevolent inclination by which Francis Hutcheson aimed to provide his sentimentalist alternative to the theories of obligation prevalent in the Grotian natural-law tradition. I concentrate here on the implications of Hutcheson's claim, in his *Inquiry Concerning Moral Good and Evil*, that Richard Cumberland and Samuel von Pufendorf sought to establish the necessary connection between prescriptive natural law and obligation on the basis of self-love. I go on to evaluate Hutcheson's interpretive position by considering the views of natural obligation endorsed by Cumberland and Pufendorf. I then bring to light the conceptual and historical significance of Hutcheson's position by analyzing Pufendorf's criticism of a key argument on the nature of obligation presented by Thomas Hobbes. Finally, drawing together the lines of investigation pursued in chapters 9 and 10, I discuss why Kant would find it reasonable in effect to reverse Hutcheson's approach to the relationship between benevolent inclination (as the crucial affective condition of human moral motivation) and law-determined action when he recognized the systematic ramifications of Rousseau's idea of *volonté générale*.

Chapter 11: I extend the scope of the historical investigations pursued in chapters 9 and 10 by taking account of another element of Stoic moral philosophy that had a decisive impact on modern doctrines of moral worth. Specifically, I consider the Stoic idea of the *honestum* in connection with its influence on eighteenth-century sentimentalist and rationalist ethics. When treating the sentimentalist side of the sentimentalism vs. rationalism divide concerning the question of the moral worth of actions, I build on the treatments of Hume and Hutcheson already provided in chapters 4 and 10. As for the rationalist side, I pay special attention to the role played by the *honestum* in Thomas Reid's criticism of Hume's account of actions' moral worth. In effect, then, I examine the various parts assigned to the idea of the *honestum* in the views on the moral worth of actions held by three major figures of Scottish Enlightenment philosophy. I do this, however, in order to come to grips definitively with the theory of moral worth at issue in Kant's exposition of morally practical reason's obligatory ends.

Chapter 12: In chapter 7, as we have seen, I maintain that the solution to Kant's problem of original acquisition requires a formal principle of *material* equality that applies to the distribution of usable things. This solution, however, demands that *we* forge a link between the Kantian accounts of the innate right of freedom and the normative basis of permissible external acquisition that Kant does not explicitly acknowledge in the systematic context of his theory of private right. Thus, one may well ask why my proposed solution to Kant's problem of original acquisition should be judged plausible, let alone compelling, if it is one that Kant does not expressly acknowledge because it is based on a link-forging interpretive inference that he himself does not draw. I deal with this question in the final section of chapter 12. To set the stage for doing this, I first extend our previous line of historical inquiry into the background conditions of Kant's problem in two directions—first, to the debate concerning the origins of property in which William of Ockham introduced the concept of natural right as a use-warranting subjective attribute; and second, to Hobbes, whose description of the natural condition of humankind calls into question the conceptual coherence of all natural right-based portrayals of original acquisition. Bringing to light Kant's apparently paradoxical affinity with *both* Ockham and Hobbes is what enables us to see why the solution proposed for Kant's problem is not only plausible but also compelling.

Conclusion: My concluding considerations point beyond the central topics covered in Parts I-IV. I begin by linking one of the systematic components of Kant's theory of obligatory ends to the notion of 'Kantian consequentialism', which in recent years has gained traction in contemporary ethical theory. Concentrating on the duty of mutual benevolence treated in the main body of the 1797 Doctrine of Virtue, I argue that Kant's account of ends that are also duties necessarily grounds a consequentialist view of the action-guiding principle that requires us always to promote the happiness of everyone as best we can. I thus show that there is a clear, though restricted, sense in which Kant's theory of obligatory ends makes room for the consequentialist interpretation of a practical law that presents a duty of virtue. After explaining why this kind of interpretation cannot apply to any of the universal laws established in the framework of Kant's juridical theory of right, I return to the solution to Kant's problem of original acquisition put forward in chapter 7 and supported in chapter 10. As indicated above, the principle of distributive equality at issue in Kant's idea of original acquisition must be merely formal even if it requires material equality with respect to all distributable things. How, then, should we understand the relationship between this formal principle of right and approaches to the question of distributive justice that are centrally concerned with unequal human needs and abilities in their accounts of the permissible forms of individual property? To determine at least the point of departure for dealing with this question, I turn to the concept of distribution involved in Karl Marx's twofold principle: from each according to one's abilities, to each according to one's needs. In Kantian terms, both parts of this Marxian principle furnish maxims that satisfy the demands of ethical lawgiving. But can either one of them be consistent with the deontic requirements of Kant's juridical theory, if the innate equality of human beings must provide the basis for the Kantian principle of original acquisition that applies to the individual appropriation of distributable things? Seeing the way to come to grips with this last question, I argue, depends on recognizing that Marx's twofold principle presupposes a purely formal principle of equal right.

Part I Obligatory Ends, Material Practical Principles, and Practical Law in Kant's Doctrine of Morals

This opening phase of our investigations has the following tasks to complete: (1) to explain the architectonic significance of the concept of 'an end that is also a duty' that Kant introduces into his theory of morals in the 1797 introduction to the Doctrine of Virtue; (2) to determine the relationship between the ends that are also duties (namely, one's own perfection and the happiness of others); (3) to lay out the key problem for Kant's metaphysics of morals that comes to light in connection with these obligatory ends of morally practical reason; (4) to explain the solution to this problem apparently offered by the *Critique of Practical Reason's* account of the relationship between empirically conditioned and pure practical reason; (5) to determine the crucial difficulty for Kant's metaphysical project that underlies this initially promising solution.

Chapter 1 is concerned with the first two of these tasks. Beginning with the *Metaphysics of Morals'* systematic portrayal of reason's universally legislative role with respect to duties of right and duties of virtue, I explain why Kant requires the concept of an end that is also a duty if the distinction that he draws between juridical and ethical lawgiving is to ground the basic architectonic setup of his overall doctrine of morals, i.e., its division into a doctrine of right and a doctrine of virtue. Then, after explicating this a priori concept of an objectively necessary end of morally practical reason, I treat Kant's account of one's own perfection and others' happiness as the only two promotable ends of action that can qualify as ends that are also duties, i.e., as intrinsically obligatory ends.

Chapter 2 deals with the third of the aforementioned tasks, which derives from the following consideration: As it is outlined in the Doctrine of Virtue's 1797 introduction, Kant's dualistic theory of obligatory ends seems to leave open the possibility that there is an end of inclination that is *necessarily* an end that is *also* a duty. For that theory involves the idea that own-perfection and others' happiness must be understood as non-formal determining grounds—that is to say: *material* determining grounds—of the power of choice that feature in maxims that are apt for possible universal lawgiving. If this is the case, however, it seems that even an empirically grounded maxim—for example, a maxim that one has because one happens to be inclined to promote others' happiness—should be able to serve as a practical law that presents a duty of virtue. But such a conclusion, of course, calls into question a central tenet of Kant's overall theory of practical reason: the supposition that no empirical or material practical principle can furnish a universal law of the will. So what resource does Kant have at his disposal to block the line of inference just described?

Chapter 3 comes to grips with the fourth and fifth tasks mentioned above by following up on the blocking clue that Kant offers in the context of the Doctrine of Virtue's introduction. This clue is signaled by the claim that all ends that provide empirical grounds for the adoption of maxims are self-seeking ends, i.e., ends that one is inclined to bring about in order to promote one's own happiness instead of the happiness of others or one's own perfection. That Kant in fact accepts this claim is confirmed by reaching back into the opening chapter of the second *Critique*'s Analytic of Pure Practical Reason, where he maintains, as one of the basic theorems of his theory of practical reason, that all material practical principles belong under the general principle of self-love or one's own happiness. Paying close attention to Kant's use of this self-love theorem in the *Critique of Practical Reason*, however, also serves to highlight a deeper problem that will continue to occupy us in subsequent chapters devoted to Kant's ethics as a doctrine of virtue. For to the extent that this doctrine is grounded in Kant's late metaphysical theory of obligatory ends, it must also rely on a motivational tenet belonging to practical anthropology as long as it presupposes that no empirically grounded maxim can be apt for a possible universal lawgiving.

Chapter 1 Reason's Lawgiving and Obligatory Ends in the Metaphysics of Morals

§ 1 Laws of Freedom, Ethical Lawgiving, and the Systematic Division between Kant's Doctrines of Right and Virtue

Kant's doctrine of morals is based on the understanding of moral laws as laws of freedom. He holds that the practical part of philosophy is a *morally* practical doctrine to the extent that it has freedom of the power of choice (*Freiheit der Willkür*) as its theme. The metaphysical theory of morals, which makes up the a priori part of this doctrine, gives a systematic account of the fundamental prescriptive laws by which reason can determine the power of choice in relation to what can be brought about through action. For human beings, the power of choice is free just to the extent that it can be determined by these a priori laws of (pure) practical reason. The choice-determining laws of practical reason are therefore laws of freedom that apply to human agents' ability to bring about objects of the faculty of desire, i.e., to achieve the purposes that such agents set for themselves as ends of action.[1]

The laws of freedom established in the *Metaphysics of Morals* are set forth by means of the examination of the prescriptive role that reason plays with respect to actions. The analysis of this role focuses on what Kant calls "the form of aptness of a maxim of the power of choice to be universal law"[2] (MS 6:214.7–8). Kant's conception of the laws of morally practical reason revolves around this notion of the suitability of subjective principles of action for universal prescription. Only the maxim of my action that satisfies the condition of its aptness for being universal law can furnish a law of freedom; and only a law of freedom can serve for the articulation and exposition of practical reason's universally prescriptive role in relation to the conditions of action in general and the determining grounds of actions.[3] According to Kant, all practical propositions that can be

---

1 On the assertions put forward in this paragraph, see MS 6:213.14–214.30, 6:216.28–218.8, 6:218.10–221.13, 6:226.4–227.9; RL 6:230.7–23, 6:239.4–21; TL 6:379.4–382.5.
2 "die Form der Tauglichkeit der Maxime der Willkür zum allgemeinen Gesetze".
3 "Der positive [Begriff der Freiheit der Willkür] ist: das Vermögen der reinen Vernunft für sich selbst praktisch zu sein. Dieses ist aber nicht anders möglich, als durch die Unterwerfung der Maxime einer jeden Handlung unter die Bedingung der Tauglichkeit der erstern zum allgemeinen Gesetze" (MS 6:213.35–214.4). See also MS 6:214.4–22, 6:221.6–24.

thought of as moral laws are necessarily laws of freedom pertaining to the power of choice (*Willkür*).[4]

As laws of freedom, moral laws are for human beings imperatives that command or prohibit unconditionally. They are, for us, the categorical imperatives of morally practical reason. A categorical imperative, then, is a morally practical law. It is, on Kant's account, a practical proposition that (a) asserts obligation, which Kant defines modally in terms of the necessity of a free action;[5] and (b) presents a duty in as the matter (or content) of obligation (*die Materie der Verbindlichkeit*).[6] The supreme principle of all obligation and all duties—the most basic principle of Kant's entire doctrine of morals—is furnished by the theoretical formula according to which a maxim can be known to satisfy morally practical reason's overarching universality requirement: "act on a maxim that can also hold as a universal law" [7] (MS 6:226.1–2).

This formulation of the supreme principle of the doctrine of morals is found in the general introduction to the *Metaphysics of Morals*. It presents us with the inclusive formulation of the principle of imperation that underlies Kant's conception of morally practical reason and its relation to the conditions of human volition. It thereby provides (according to Kant) the sufficient basis for determining whether a maxim of the power of choice qualifies for a universal lawgiving when one thinks of *oneself* as a being capable of legislating for all rational agents *through* that given maxim.[8] Kant holds that all lawgiving, understood as a procedure of rational prescription, has two essential components.[9] First, there is a law that objectively represents an action as something necessary to perform. Second, there is an incentive (*Triebfeder*) that connects a ground determining an agent's power of choice with the representation of the law in question, this connection being the subjective feature of lawgiving by which the law represented makes a duty the incentive to act. In virtue of the first component of lawgiving, an action is represented as a duty. In virtue of the second component, the *obligation to* that action (or type of action) "is

---

[4] See (again) MS 6:213.37–214.22, 6:221.6–24. On Kant's account of practical propositions, see *KpV* 5:19.7–20.29.
[5] See MS 6:222.3–4.
[6] See MS 6:222.32.
[7] "Der oberste Grundsatz der Sittenlehre ist also: handle nach einer Maxime, die zugleich als allgemeines Gesetz gelten kann" (MS 6:226.1–2; see also MS 6:225.7–8).
[8] See MS 6:225.8–13.
[9] See MS 6:218.11–23.

§ 1 Obligatory Ends, Material Practical Principles, and Practical Law — 17

combined *in* the subject [agent] with a determining ground of the power of choice in general" [10] (MS 6: 218.21–23—italics mine).

It is with reference to the second component of practical reason's lawgiving function that two basic types of morally rational prescription must be distinguished: ethical lawgiving and juridical lawgiving.

Ethical lawgiving involves the type of universally prescriptive thinking that (a) makes an action a duty and (b) connects the obligation to this action with a ground for determining the power of choice by making the duty itself the agent's incentive for acting in conformity with law.[11] Thus, ethical lawgiving makes the rational concept of duty (*die Idee der Pflicht*) the incentive for performing the action that a practical law represents as necessary for any agent to perform. Kant maintains that this sort of lawgiving cannot be external since the idea of duty itself, as distinguished from the particular action or action-type that the law represents as objectively necessary, can only be an internal incentive to action.[12] Ethical lawgiving, then, "includes the internal incentive of the action (the idea of duty) within its law" (MS 6:219.25–26). Ethical lawgiving does this insofar as its law is given *by* the agent *in* whom obligation to action is combined with a ground for determining the power of choice. There can be no external lawgiver for this kind of legislation.[13] Juridical lawgiving, however, does admit an incentive other than the idea of duty. It therefore grants the possibility of external incentives for action. Consequently, juridical lawgiving *can* be external. For this type of lawgiving does not require that an internal incentive to action must be included within the law *as given to* the agent. Juridical lawgiving requires only that a particular law (or laws) for action yielded by practical rea-

---

[10] "Durch das erstere wird die Handlung als Pflicht vorgestellt, welches ein bloßes theoretisches Erkenntniß der möglichen Bestimmung der Willkür, d.i. praktischer Regeln, ist: durch das zweite wird die Verbindlichkeit so zu handeln mit einem Bestimmungsgrunde der Willkür überhaupt im Subjecte verbunden" (MS 6:218.19–23).

[11] This is in keeping with Kant's basic definitional account of duty in MS: "*Pflicht* ist diejenige Handlung, zu welcher jemand verbunden ist" (MS 6:222.31).

[12] Like any concept of reason, the idea of duty is a representation. All representations—whether conceptual or intuitive; and whether a priori or empirical—are internal to a knowing subject. And the idea of duty is the a priori conceptual representation by which the obligation to perform a law-determined action is combined in the practically reasoning subject (i.e., in the agent who can be conscious of the necessity of performing prescribed by practical laws) with a determining ground of the power of choice.

[13] "eben darum, weil die ethische Gesetzgebung die innere Triebfeder der Handlung (die Idee der Pflicht) in ihr Gesetz mit einschließt, welche Bestimmung durchaus nicht in die äußere Gesetzgebung einfließen muß, so kann die ethische Gesetzgebung keine äußere (selbst nicht die eines göttlichen Willens) sein [...]" (MS 6:219.24–28).

son's prescriptive procedure must be consistent with what is demanded by the most general formula of the principle of all categorical imperatives. An external lawgiver is thus possible for this type of legislative enactment.

The main divisions in the architectonic configuration of Kant's doctrine of morals—the Doctrine of Right (*ius*) and the Doctrine of Virtue (*ethica*)—depend on the different ways in which incentives to action are linked to the concepts of practical law and duty in the account of the basic types of reason's lawgiving function.[14] Juridical lawgiving can be external because it does not *require* an internal incentive for the conformity of actions to law. Accordingly, the laws and corresponding duties established by this type of lawgiving—notably, the specifically juridical laws and duties presented and proved in the Doctrine of Right —*can* have their source in an external lawgiver. And because this universally lawgiving source can be external to any particular agent that is subject to juridical laws, the duties that these laws present must be understood as supplying the matter of obligation to external actions. Juridical laws are the practical laws by which the freedom of the power of choice (and hence freedom in action) of each agent can coexist with the freedom of the power of choice of every other agent. Since this form of freedom pertains only to external actions (i.e., to the actions that concern practical relations between different persons), juridical laws are external laws that present duties of outer freedom for every agent. The laws that accord with this description do not, taken by themselves merely as laws, require any agent to make the idea of duty the incentive to action.[15]

Things are more complicated with respect to the laws and duties generated by the other type of lawgiving. In the case of ethical lawgiving, the source of legislation cannot be external to the law-determined agent since the incentive by which obligation is combined with the determining ground of the power of choice must be internal to that agent. This is true even if duties with which ethics is concerned may be *yielded* by juridical lawgiving. All duties, just because they are duties, belong to ethics. But this does not mean that the *giving* of law for all duties is *contained* in ethics.[16] Even if the scope of ethics extends to the external duties that are made known by external laws governing outer freedom, the legislation by which these juridical duties can belong to ethics is entirely distinct from (although, according to Kant, necessarily consistent with) juridical lawgiving. As a doctrine of virtue, ethics is therefore distinguished from the juridical theory of right not so much by the duties that it includes as by the kind of ob-

---

[14] The basis for drawing the distinction between the Doctrine of Right and the Doctrine of Virtue is treated by Esser 2004, pp. 308–312; Gregor 1963, pp. 22–33; Ludwig 2013.
[15] See MS 6:219.17–30, 6:224.7–11; TL 6:406.29–33.
[16] See MS 6:219–31–34. For discussion, see Gregor 1963, pp. 26–28; Schadow 2013, pp. 86–88.

ligation—i.e., the manner, way, or mode of obligation (*die Art der Verpflichtung*)[17] —that is peculiar to it. For what is distinctive about ethical lawgiving is that one is bound to "perform actions just because they are duties and to make the principle of duty itself, wherever duty may come from, the sufficient incentive for the power of choice" [18] (MS 6:220.34–37).

Consider carefully the relation between the duties that we are obligated to perform and the principle of duty itself. In other words, consider the relation between, on the one hand, the actions that we are bound to perform because they qualify as the matter of obligation and, on the other hand, the principle of practical reason that requires us to act on a maxim that can also hold as a universal law. If all duties belong to ethics, then we are in principle obligated to perform every action that can be objectively represented as necessary (i.e., represented as a duty or matter of obligation) *just because* it can be so represented. And we are able to satisfy this obligation because, on Kant's account of ethical lawgiving, the principle of duty itself provides us with the sufficient incentive to action even if we disregard the particular type of incentive that juridical lawgiving allows. Yet precisely because that principle of duty provides such an incentive (i.e., the internal incentive to action denoted by the idea of duty) there must still be something distinctive about the duties presented by practical laws which issue from ethical lawgiving, but which *cannot* issue from juridical lawgiving *because of* the (external) incentive that juridical lawgiving allows.[19] As we have just seen, ethics is distinguished from the juridical theory of right by the kind of obligation that characterizes ethical lawgiving. But even if this kind of obligation extends to all duties, there must be some mark, or marks, by which we can pick out the duties presented by laws that are peculiar to ethical lawgiving. In other words, we must be able to identify the particular properties of the duties made known by laws that are uniquely characteristic of the type of legislation that *is contained* in ethics. Otherwise, Kant's fundamental architectonic division of labor between the juridical theory of right and ethics as a doctrine of virtue could have no adequate grounding in the analysis of the distinctive roles that juridical and ethical lawgiving play with respect to the different sorts of duties that provide the *matter* of obligation, as distinguished from the different kinds (i.e., the *forms*) of obligation itself. While ethics must be able to include all duties as the mat-

---

[17] See MS 6:220.34.
[18] " Denn Handlungen bloß darum, weil es Pflichten sind, ausüben und den Grundsatz der Pflicht selbst, woher sie auch komme, zur hinreichenden Triebfeder der Willkür zu machen, ist das Eigenthümliche der ethischen Gesetzgebung" (MS 6:220.34–37).
[19] That is, there must be something distinctive about the directly ethical duties that are determined by ethical lawgiving even if ethical lawgiving makes all other duties indirectly ethical (see MS 6:221.1–3).

ter of obligation for the type of lawgiving that is contained in ethics, not every duty that belongs to ethics can qualify as a matter of obligation for the type of lawgiving that cannot be contained in ethics on account of the particular incentive to action which juridical lawgiving allows. For if all duties belonged to ethics simply in virtue of being duties, and if every duty belonging to ethics *could* qualify as a matter of obligation for juridical lawgiving, then all of the laws that present us with duties would be able to issue from the type of lawgiving that cannot be contained in ethics because of the sort of incentive that it allows. But this would have the following implication when taken in conjunction with Kant's standpoint that ethical lawgiving cannot be external. It would entail that all practical laws can issue from juridical lawgiving as well as from ethical lawgiving, *although* there must be some practical laws that can issue from ethical lawgiving alone, and not from juridical lawgiving at all, on account of the internal incentive to action that ethical lawgiving requires. How, then, in keeping with that standpoint on ethical lawgiving, does one preclude the possibility of such fundamental systemic inconsistency in a metaphysical theory of morals that depends on the analysis of practical reason's lawgiving function in terms of an essential distinction between different forms of obligation?

Kant addresses the problematic just delineated by specifying essential distinctions between generically different matters of obligation—that is to say: between different types of duty—and by insisting that the kind of obligation essential to ethical lawgiving must be understood in connection with the description of ends of a certain type, namely, the type of ends that furnish duties of virtue (*Tugendpflichten*). The distinction drawn between juridical and ethical lawgiving in terms of different forms of obligation hinges on the conceptual determination of these ends, and thus on the understanding of the ethical obligation to ends (*die ethische Verbindlichkeit zu Zwecken*)[20] that is asserted by the laws of virtue issuing from ethical lawgiving alone. With this, we have arrived at Kant's conception of a "moral (objective) doctrine of ends" (TL 6:385.23–24) and his corresponding definition of ethics as "the system of the *ends* of pure practical reason" (TL 6:381.18–19).

---

20 See MS 6:395.1–2.

§ 2 Obligatory Ends, the End in Itself, and Laws for Maxims of Actions

The general doctrine of virtue presented in Kant's *Tugendlehre* of 1797 revolves around the concept of objectively necessary end.[21] An objectively necessary end is a moral end that is also an end of action. More precisely, it is an end that (pure) practical reason requires us to have by virtue of our obligation to act in accordance with laws for the maxims of our actions, and not just in accordance with laws for actions as such. The objectively necessary ends at issue in Kant's doctrine of virtue are therefore ends that we are to promote and bring about *through* our actions, and not merely to respect or honor as limiting conditions of our freedom to act.[22] According to the arguments presented in the 1797 Introduction to the Doctrine of Virtue, there can be two such objectively necessary ends of morally practical reason: one's own perfection and others' happiness.[23] As an end of action (or actions), each of these ends can furnish a matter of the power of choice, and thus also the matter (or content) of a maxim. Morally practical reason requires us to have ends of this description by binding us to the adoption of maxims to promote them, i.e., by obligating us to make such end-promoting maxims the subjective principles of our action or actions. An objectively necessary end must therefore be conceived as an end that itself furnishes a matter of obligation, i.e., a duty. It is an end that is also a duty (*ein Zweck, der Zugleich Pflicht ist*). It is, for us, an obligatory end that we are to promote through our actions insofar as 'duty' must be understood as designating the type of action that furnishes some matter of obligation. For the imperative that sets forth obligation with respect to action aiming at such an end is necessarily a morally practical law, i.e., a law of freedom.[24] A law of

---

[21] On Kant's account of objectively necessary ends, see Esser 2004, 320–324; Gregor 1963, pp. 80–94; Herman 2007, pp. 254–273; Trampota 2013. See also Denis 2013, pp. 174–179.
[22] See RL 6:354.10–11; TL 6:380.23–25, 6:384.33–385.14, 6:388.32–33, 6:395.15–16. The doctrine of ends presented in the *Tugendlehre* presupposes, of course, that the human being and in general every rational being exists as an end in itself (see, e.g., GMS 4:428.3–431.18, 4:438.8–439.24; KpV 5:87.16–30, 5:131.20–132.5; RL 6:236.24–30; TL 6:390.30–391.3). Moreover, the supreme principle of the doctrine of virtue determines *how* the human being is to be an end for himself as well as for others inasmuch as it prescribes the means by which the human being in general is to be made the end of human beings (see TL 6:395.15–32). For a detailed treatment of this principle and its deduction, see Baum, 1998, pp. 47–49. For related discussion, see Herman 2011 and Hruschka 2006.
[23] See TL 6:385.30–388.30. Cf. Gregor 1963, pp. 86–89; Esser 2004, pp. 318–320; Schadow 2013, pp. 102–105.
[24] See MS 6:222.31–223.5; TL 6:389.12–26, 6:396.24–31, 6:410.21–25.

freedom of this type, however, is one that makes duty, as the matter of obligation, the internal incentive to action.[25] It is therefore a law of inner freedom by which I command myself to make something my end independently of all possibility of external constraint by others.[26]

For Kant, then, an end that is *also* a duty is "an end *that is in itself a duty*" [27] (MS 6:381.14–15). In the context of the Doctrine of Virtue, the term objectively necessary end expresses the concept of being an intrinsically obligatory end of action. It expresses the concept by which I make a duty (*qua* matter of obligation[28]) both the internal incentive to action and the end that I am obligated to promote *through* my action *because* it is an end that all (finite) rational agents are obligated to have as an end *of* their actions.[29] According to this concept, an end-promoting *action* is for me a duty (or matter of obligation) insofar as I make it my maxim to promote an end that everyone is bound to make a matter of the power of choice (*Materie der Wilkür*).[30] Such is the interpretation of 'end' that Kant's formula of the supreme principle of the Doctrine of Virtue presupposes: "act in accordance with a maxim of *ends* that it can be a universal law for everyone to have" [31] (MS 6:395.15–16).

Notice that the Doctrine of Virtue's account of the objectively necessary ends of practical reason differs fundamentally from the treatment of the concept of end in itself given in the 1786 *Groundwork for the Metaphysics*. To explicate this concept, Kant used the distinction between subjective and objective ends. In the context of the *Groundwork*, 'subjective end' denotes the type of end that, as the possible effect of a rational being's action (i.e., as a possible material end), can serve merely as a means to be used by such a being as a matter of preference.[32] By contrast, objective ends are rational beings themselves, i.e., "beings [*Dinge*] the existence of which is in itself an end, and indeed one such that no other end, to which they would serve *merely* as a means, can be put in its

---

25 See MS 6:218.18–19; TL 6:379.25–380.6.
26 See MS 6:214.19–30; TL 6:380.16–18, 6:396.1–24, 6:405.11–22, 6:406.29–407.2.
27 "Daß ich [...] verbunden bin mir irgend etwas, was in den Begriffen der praktischen Vernunft liegt, zum Zwecke zu machen [...]: dieses würde der Begriff von einem Zweck sein, *der an sich selbst Pflicht ist*" (TL 6:381.9–15).
28 See TL 6:222.21–22.
29 More precisely, it is an end that all agents are obligated to have unless there is some agent—notably, a holy being—who cannot be obligated to have such an end because it *necessarily* already has this as the end of its actions. On this, see MS 6:222.3–12.
30 See TL 6:380.22–381.3, 6:389.16–26.
31 "Das oberste Princip der Tugendlehre ist: handle nach einer Maxime der *Zwecke*, die zu haben für jedermann ein allgemeines Gesetz sein kann" (TL 6:395.15–16).
32 See GMS 4:427.19–428.2.

place" (GMS 4:428.27–29).'³³ Since ends of this type are furnished by beings whose nature "limits all power of choice" (BMS 4:428.24),³⁴ the concept of objective end provides the ground of the principle according to which humanity qualifies as "the supreme limiting condition of the freedom of actions of every human being"³⁵ (GMS 4:430.29–431.1). It is by means of this principle that generic humanity (*qua* rational nature) is "represented not as an object that we of ourselves actually make our end, but as an objective end that, whatever ends we may have, ought as law to constitute the supreme limiting condition of all subjective ends"³⁶ (GMS 4:431.7–8).

In the context of the Doctrine of Virtue, however, the specification of the type of end that must figure in a maxim of ends cannot be achieved simply by bringing to bear the classic *Groundwork* distinction between a subjective end of action and the objective end that is represented as something that ought to constitute the supreme limiting condition of all subjective ends. That is because the existence of any end that can serve in a maxim of ends that it can be a law for everyone to have is something that must be representable as a possible effect of our action (or actions), even if it cannot be a merely subjective end. And this is true even if such an effect—that is to say, the possible outcome—is the end at which our action must aim precisely because this is an end that is, in itself, our *duty* to bring about or promote. What Kant's supreme principle of the Doctrine of Virtue presupposes, then, is a concept of duty that picks out the property of being a non-subjective (or at least not-merely-subjective) end of action, a property which in turn furnishes not only a matter of the power of choice but also a "*material* determining ground" (TL 6:381.12–13—italics mine [JE]) of this same essential feature of the faculty of desire.³⁷ Judging from his published

---

33 "Dinge, deren Dasein an sich selbst Zweck ist und zwar ein solcher, an dessen Statt kein anderer Zweck gesetzt werden kann, dem sie bloß als Mittel zu Diensten stehen sollten".
34 "alle Willkür einschränkt". For discussion, see Hruschka 2006, pp. 72–73, 81–82; Herman 2011, pp. 98–111.
35 "die oberste Einschränkenden Bedingung der Freiheit der Handlungen eines jeden Menschen".
36 " [wird nicht] als Gegenstand, den man sich von selbst wirklich zum Zwecke macht, sondern als objectiver Zweck, der, wir mögen Zwecke haben, welche wir wollen, als Gesetz die oberste einschränkende Bedingung aller subjectiven Zwecke ausmachen soll, vorgestellt".
37 The lines in which Kant links the concept of duty to a material determining ground run as follows: "Daß ich aber auch verbunden bin mir irgend etwas, was in den Begriffen der praktischen Vernunft liegt, zum Zwecke zu machen, mithin außer dem formalen Bestimmungsgrunde der Willkür (wie das Recht dergleichen enthält) *noch einen materialen* [italics mine], einen Zweck zu haben, [...] dieses würde der Begriff vonem Zweck sein, der *an sich selbst Pflicht* ist" (MS 6:381.11–13—italics mine). Cf. MS 6:213.14–29, TL 6:389.16–24, 6:395.11–13; GMS 4:427.32–428.1.

works as well as from his lecture transcriptions and handwritten notes, *this* concept of duty is not found in Kant's critical practical philosophy prior to the 1797 Introduction to the Doctrine of Virtue. Before 1797, Kant did not expressly acknowledge that any matter or material ground of the power of choice could supply both an end of action *and* the matter (i.e., the propositional content) of a maxim which could qualify for a universal lawgiving. Nor, by implication, did he explicitly recognize that the maxim to promote such an end could furnish a practical law that makes it a duty for everyone to act in accordance with a maxim of ends. Thus, while the 1797 account of objectively necessary ends is by no means incompatible with the *Groundwork* consideration of objective ends,[38] there is no indication that Kant was willing to make any *deontic* concept of material determining ground a constitutive component of his foundational theory of ethics before he composed the Introduction to the Doctrine of Virtue. The concept of a material determining ground that is both the concept of a promotable end of action and the concept of an end that is also a *duty* (not to mention a matter of the power of choice) is evidently something fundamentally new that emerges in Kant late moral philosophy.[39]

As I mentioned before, Kant argues that one's own perfection and others' happiness are the ends that can be thought of as objectively necessary. The thought that each of us is obligated to further our own perfection and that everyone is obligated to make others happy is, to be sure, nothing at all new to Kant's ethical theory of the late 1790s. The radical novelty of the late moral doctrine of ends lies, instead, in the following. For the purposes of ethics *per se*, Kant speci-

---

38 Kant writes: "Praktische Principien sind formal, wenn sie von allen subjectiven Zwecken abstrahiren; sie sind aber material, wenn sie diese, mithin gewisse Triebfedern zum Grunde legen. Die Zwecke, die sich ein vernünftiges Wesen als Wirkungen seiner Handlung nach Belieben vorsetzt, (materiale Zwecke) sind insgesammt nur relativ; denn nur bloß ihr Verhältniß auf ein besonders geartetes Begehrungsvermögen des Subjects giebt ihnen den Werth, der daher keine allgemeine für alle vernünftige Wesen und auch nicht für jedes Wollen gültige und nothwendige Principien, d.i. praktische Gesetze, an die Hand geben kann" (GMS 4:427.30 – 428.1; cf. also KpV 5:21.14 – 16, 5:22.6 – 8, 5:27.3 – 6, 5:29.14 – 22, 5:39.5 – 41.38). These remarks are consistent with the 1797 definitional account of the objectively necessary ends as ends that are to be effected through action. For such ends are by no means merely subjective; nor are they ends that a rational being proposes according to mere preference (*nach Belieben*) in virtue of its having a specially constituted faculty of desire.

39 The passage from Kant's published works that has perhaps the most direct bearing on this claim is one found in the Preface to the *Religion* of 1793: see RGV 6:3.14 – 4.3 (with note: 6:3.19 – 4.37). What Kant argues there about the relationship between formal and material determining grounds, and about one's own perfection and the happiness of others as ends of action, seems to entail that no matter or material determining ground of the power of choice can furnish a ground that could feature in any concept of duty.

fies the rational concept (*Vernunfbegriff*) of duty *in terms of* the dispositional qualities and states of agents that must be *made* the ends of action; and he holds that human agents are dispositionally capable of making these qualities and states the ends of their actions insofar as they are able to make certain material determining grounds of the power of choice the matter of maxims of ends that furnish laws for maxims of actions. Kant requires such a specification of the concept of duty—a specification that in turn is grounded in the particular interpretation of end-making through law-yielding maxims which I have just described. He requires this kind of specification, thus grounded, in order to clarify how ethical lawgiving can be known to generate its distinctive practical laws and duties, i.e., the particular set of laws and duties that accord with the rational concept of the ethical obligation to ends. Thus, the laws peculiar to ethics as a doctrine of virtue are laws that, in keeping with *this* idea of obligation, present us with duties of virtue. Duties of virtue are distinguishable from all of the duties that can be yielded by juridical lawgiving because they are set forth by practical laws that represent ends of action as objectively necessary ends of practical reason on the basis of the specifically ethical obligation to ends. And the possibility of this kind of obligation rests on the idea that there is a type of material ground which, insofar as it provides for the representation of the matter of maxims of ends, supplies a necessary condition of laws for maxims of actions.

According to Kant, of course, every duty stands in immediate relation to a law. This direct relation between duty and practical law is already indicated by "the formal principle of duty" that the so-called universal-law formula of the categorical imperative contains: "act so that the maxim of your action could *become* a universal law" [40] (MS 6:389.1–3—italics mine [J.E.]). But taken by itself, this strictly formal principle of duty requires nothing *more* than that the maxims on which an agent acts must qualify for a universal lawgiving. It thereby provides the sufficient basis for determining laws for actions that govern everyone's freedom of the power of choice in relation to one another.[41] It cannot, however, deliver the laws for *maxims* of actions that are required by ethics *insofar* as this part of the general theory of morals (*Sittenlehre*) is to offer a theory of

---

[40] "Der Pflichtbegriff steht unmittelbar in Beziehung auf ein Gesetz (wenn ich gleich noch von allem Zweck als der Materie desselben abstrahire); wie denn das formale Princip der Pflicht im kategorischen Imperativ: 'Handle so, daß die Maxime deiner Handlung ein allgemeines Gesetz werden könne' es schon anzeigt'" (TL 6:388.34–389.3). Notice how close this formulation of the formal principle of duty *in* the categorical imperative is to the formula of universal law presented in the *Groundwork:* "handle nur nach derjenigen Maxime, durch die du zugleich wollen kannst, daß sie ein allgemeines Gesetz *werde*" (GMS 4:421.7–8—italics mine).

[41] See TL 6:380.19–381.17, 6:383.1–16, 6:388.34–389.15.

the duties of virtue. That is to say, the purely formal principle of duty supplied by the universal-law formula cannot, by itself, make it a law for an agent to have as *her* maxim precisely the subjective principle of action by which she can freely make a certain matter of the power of choice *her end* in virtue of the internal incentive to action that the idea of duty provides. Laws for maxims of actions can be established only on the additional basis of some representation of an end of action that an agent can have as the matter of the power of choice. But no such representation can refer to a merely subjective end that one may happen to have as such a matter. For the promotion or achievement of an end of action can satisfy the ethical obligation to ends if, and only if, that end itself furnishes a material determining ground that can be represented as objectively necessary, i.e., represented as an end that is *in itself* a duty.

§ 3 Own-Perfection and Others' Happiness as Intrinsically Obligatory Ends

Kant argues that one's own perfection and the happiness of others are the ends of action whose conceptual determination can satisfy the condition just stated.[42] What, then, is the relationship between these intrinsically obligatory ends of morally practical reason? And how exactly do we determine what we are obligated to do when the matter of ethical obligation is supplied by ends that are, in themselves, also duties?

One's own perfection involves two essential features: (a) the cultivation of one's faculties or capacities for furthering all the ends set forth by reason; and (b) the nurturing of one's moral cast of mind (*sittliche Denkungsart*) or, in other words, the cultivation of morality in us (*Kultur der Moralität in uns*).[43] The first facet of own-perfection as an obligatory end provides the law for the maxim to "cultivate your powers of body and mind so that they are fit to realize any ends you might encounter" [44] (TL 392.17–19). The second facet marks "the greatest perfection of a human being", i.e., the cultivated disposition "to do one's duty from duty", whereby "the law is not merely the rule but also the in-

---

[42] See TL 6:384.31–386.14, 6:398 (*Das Schema der Tugendpflichten:* 1 & 2).
[43] See TL 6:386.30–387.5, 391.29–393.10.
[44] "Baue deine Gemüths- und Leibeskräfte zur Tauglichkeit für alle Zwecke an, die dir aufstoßen können".

centive for actions" [45] (TL 6:392.20–23). For the purposes of his moral doctrine of ends, Kant defines happiness as "contentment with one's state as far as one is assured of its lasting" [46] (TL 6:387.26–27). Accordingly, the happiness of others as an end that is also a duty must feature physical welfare (*physische Wohlfahrt*), i.e., strength, health, and well-being in general combined with the external goods needed for prosperous living. Others' happiness must also include their moral well-being (*moralisches Wohlsein*), this being understood in terms of the ability of agents to live conscientiously and without violating the requirements of morally practical reason.[47]

'Perfection' and 'happiness' are not interchangeable terms in the account of ends that are also duties. The perfection of another human being, as a person or moral agent, consists in his achieving the state in which "he *himself* is capable of setting his end in accordance with his own concepts of duty" [48] (TL 6:386.11–12). Thus, it is not possible to require me to make it *my* duty to do something that only another can make it his duty to do. It is, Kant maintains, "a contradiction for me to make another's perfection my end *and* to hold myself obligated to promote it" [49] (TL 6:386.8–10—italics mine [J.E.]). Nor is one's own happiness conceivable as an end that anyone "is obligated to promote with all one's powers" [50] (TL 6:386.7). Kant holds that own-happiness (*die eigene Glückseligkeit*) is an end that all human beings unavoidably have without being constrained to make it their end.[51] All duties, however, involve a concept of necessitation or constraint of free choice through law.[52] Hence (according to Kant) it is self-contradictory to

---

45 "Die größte moralische Vollkommenheit des Menschen ist: seine Pflicht zu thun und zwar aus Pflicht (daß das Gesetz nicht blos die Regel, sondern auch die Triebfeder der Handlungen sei)" (TL 6:392.20–23).
46 "Glückseligkeit, d.i. Zufriedenheit mit seinem Zustande, sofern man der Fortdauer derselben gewiß ist" (MS 6:387.26–27). Cf. KpV 5:12–20, 5:61.18–29; TL 6:480.23–25.
47 See TL 6:394.1–10. The particular components of others' happiness as an obligatory end are thus to be understood in accordance with the concept of natural good that underlies Kant's interpretation of 'highest physical good' and 'highest moral-physical good' (see Anth 7:276.1–277.23; Refl 15:490.8–493.2; cf. EAD 8:335.4–18).
48 "Denn darin besteht eben die Vollkommenheit eines andern Menschen, [...], daß er *selbst* vermögend ist sich seinen Zweck nach seinen eigenen Begriffen von Pflicht zu setzen" (TL 6:386.10–12).
49 "[Es ist] ein Widerspruch: eines anderen Vollkommenheit mir zum Zweck zu machen und mich zu deren Beförderung für verpflichtet zu halten".
50 "Es widerspricht sich also zu sagen: man sei verpflichtet seine eigene Glückseligkeit mit allen Kräften zu befördern" (TL 6:386.6–7).
51 See TL 6:386.1–2.
52 See TL 6:379.15–17, 6:394.24–25.

assert that any human agent is constrained to make his end something that he unavoidably has as an end apart from every deontic constraint.[53]

These arguments, of course, give rise to a number of questions. First, it is not immediately obvious why I cannot self-consistently hold myself obligated to promote the perfection of another agent insofar as I act to bring about the conditions under which human beings can promote their own perfection. Second, there is a significant systematic difficulty that stems from Kant's claim about every human being unavoidably having his own happiness as his end.

Let us take these two issues in reverse order. Consider the claim that each of us unavoidably pursues his own happiness. Kant clearly understands this claim as furnishing a theoretical tenet about what necessarily motivates every human being to act insofar as he has the natural capacity to set his own happiness as an end and to promote it through action. Moreover, it may seem that Kant requires this anthropological tenet if he is to establish conclusively that own-happiness cannot be an end that is also a duty. To be sure, I cannot be constrained to *make* my own happiness my end if it is one that I already have. But it could still happen that such an end will cease to be mine if it is not necessarily my end. And this seems to leave open the possibility that I could be constrained to make my own happiness my obligatory end if I did not *unavoidably* already have it as my end. Now quite apart from any problems that may arise in the attempt to clarify the kind of natural necessity at issue in Kant's unavoidability claim, there seems to be a worrisome systematic implication of Kant's line of argument, at least in the passage in which this claim is advanced.[54] The argument, as presented, makes the metaphysical exposition of what is supposed to be an a priori concept of practical reason—namely, the concept of duty—appear to be dependent on an anthropological assumption. The chief difficulty in this regard, then, lies in the following. According to Kant's conception of practical anthropology, which is a discipline that includes the principles of empirical moral psychology, the truth of such an assumption can be determined only by the empirical investigation of the conditions of motivation that are specific to (though not necessarily unique to) human beings.[55] The metaphysics of morals, however, is not supposed to *rely* on any empirically based description of human motivational conditions, although it allows for the integration of this kind of description with the theory of the a priori concepts and laws of morally practical reason.

---

53 See TL 6:386.3–7.
54 See TL 6:386.1–7.
55 See TL 6:216.28–217.27.

§ 3 Own-Perfection and Others' Happiness as Intrinsically Obligatory Ends — 29

Happily, Kant's overall account of own-perfection and others' happiness contains the resources needed to deal effectively the problems just touched upon. Let me begin with the second problem mentioned. Kant's metaphysical exposition does not really require the anthropological necessity claim just discussed. All that Kant actually needs to do is to bring to bear the basic principle of his standard refutation of ethical egoism, that is, the principle that no maxim of self-love can qualify for a universal lawgiving.[56] In the systematic framework of the Doctrine of Virtue, Kant has merely to establish, and in fact does establish, the following two points. [57] (1) Since no maxim of self-love can qualify for a universal lawgiving, no maxim to promote one's own happiness can be a maxim of *ends* that it can be a universal law for everyone to have. (2) Since no such maxim can be a universal law for everyone to have, own-happiness cannot be an end that is itself also a duty. There will be a good deal more to say about Kant's repudiation of the basis of ethical egoism in the following chapters. The key thing to emphasize at this juncture is this: Kant's line of argument concerning the two points here in question entails that no human agent *could* be constrained to have her own happiness as an intrinsically obligatory end, even in the event that she did not, by nature, have it as one of her ends to begin with.

Notice, however, that this entailment does not at all exclude the principle that we are, each of us respectively, *obligated* to promote our own happiness and not just the happiness of others. For it is by contributing to our own prosperity and general well-being that each of us wards off the temptations that can lead to the non-fulfillment or violation of duty.[58] When we look to our own happiness by reason of this kind of obligation, however, the end that we are bound to pursue is the integrity of character that is essential to the own-perfection of each one of us as a moral agent. To the extent, therefore, that *I* am so *bound*, my end is not (and cannot be) my own happiness. Instead, my end is my own perfection, which I am bound to promote by acting in accordance with a maxim of ends that it can be a universal law for everyone to have.[59] The same considerations apply to any agent who can be bound to promote intrinsically obligatory ends of action. Thus, even if seeking to realize the conditions and elements of one's own happiness is *indirectly* a duty, own-happiness cannot be an *end* that is also a duty for everyone (or anyone at all) to have. It cannot be an end that is in itself a duty if it can only be a means to such an end.

---

56 See KpV 5:25.37–26.33, 5:27.20–28, 5:35.27–38.11. See also GMS 4:421.24–422.36 and RGV 6:36.1–33, 6:45.21–46.37.
57 See TL 6:393.15–23, 450.34–451.19.
58 See TL 6:388.17–20.
59 See TL 6:388.21–30.

Parallel considerations apply to the question of making others' perfection one's end. Even if the perfection of a human person must be understood in terms of an agent's capability of setting her ends in accordance with her own concepts of duty, this hardly keeps me from, in effect, making her perfection my own end when I act to bring about the conditions under which human beings can cultivate their bodily and mental powers as well as their moral cast of mind. Consequently, it is clear that I can make, and do make, make another's perfection my end whenever I seek to put in place the conditions under which human beings can develop their nature-given faculties for achieving ends set forth by reason as well as the disposition to act from duty.[60] (Obviously, we do this sort of thing with our children day-in and day-out. If we didn't, there would be little point to *our* educating *them*.) Yet whenever I make that perfection of another my end in this way, I cannot self-consistently hold myself obligated to promote it by making it my end to do something that only another can make it her duty to bring about. Specifically, I cannot further it as an integral component of my *own* perfection, i.e., the perfection that does qualify as an end that is also a duty for me to bring about by making it my maxim to develop my capacity for realizing ends of reason and by making it my maxim to cultivate my moral cast of mind, this being the greatest perfection of which I am capable. Instead, the obligation that I am under pertains to the duty that I have to promote the physical welfare and the moral well-being of others. That is to say, it pertains (directly) to the happiness of others as an end of action that is also a duty for me to promote. Thus, the *duty* that I have with respect to others' perfection lies in the matter of my obligation to promote the happiness of others. That duty does not lie in the own-perfection that supplies an end that others are obligated to promote. In short: I can make the perfection of others my own end by promoting their happiness (especially their moral well-being), which is for me an end that is also directly a duty; but I cannot possibly make the own-perfection of others my end if perfection is to be such an intrinsically obligatory end *for me*. So even if I can (and in fact self-consistently do) make another's perfection my own end, I cannot hold myself obligated to promote this *as* the perfection that is also a duty for me to promote as my own—namely, the perfection of myself as an agent who can make the perfection of others my end only by promoting others' happiness as a means by which *they* can promote their own perfection.

---

[60] Cf. Sidgwick 1981, pp. 11 (note 1) and 240; Ross 2002, p. 26. Both Sidgwick and Ross understand Kant as asserting that one cannot make the perfection of another one's own end when one acts in such a way that one enables another to promote her own perfection.

§ 4 Laws for Maxims and the "Dualism" of Morally Practical Reason

I have just discussed the relationship between the ends of action that, taken together, furnish the matter of the ethical obligation to ends, and hence the basis for the specification of duties of virtue. Now just what are we obligated to *do* by virtue of this relationship between ends of action whenever we act in accordance with a maxim of ends that it can be a universal law for everyone to have? According to Kant, duties of virtue are duties of wide obligation.[61] They are, in other words, wide duties or imperfect duties since the laws that present us with duties of virtue are laws for *maxims* of actions, not laws for *actions*.[62] Unlike the laws for actions that prescribe juridical duties, all of which are duties of narrow obligation, laws for maxims do not determine the practical necessity of specific actions (or specific courses of action). Thus, all duties of virtue are duties of wide obligation that leave free choice a good deal of latitude in satisfying the demands of the different laws that prescribe them as ends of action. Still, the latitude that wide duties leave to free choice must not be understood as the permission to make *exceptions* to maxims that qualify for universal lawgiving. That latitude may only be regarded as the authorization to "limit" one such maxim by another maxim that satisfies the overarching universality requirement of morally practical reason.[63] Maxims to do well for human beings in general (i.e., maxims pertaining to the practical love of humanity or universal benevolence) may be considered—indeed *must* be considered—in relation to other maxims of other-directed benevolence that can also qualify for universal lawgiving, e.g., maxims pertaining to the care of one's parents and children.[64] Moreover, although wide duties of other-directed benevolence may involve the sacrifice of a part of one's own welfare to that of others, it is impossible to set specific limits on the proper extent of this sacrifice. How far the sacrificing of one's welfare (hence one's own happiness) *should* extend "depends in large part on what each person's true need will be according to his sensibility, which must be left to each to determine for himself"[65] (TL 6:393.27–29). This does not mean, however,

---

[61] See TL 6:390.1–2.
[62] See jointly TL 6:388.32–33, 389.12–26, 390.2–18. For detailed commentary on these points, see Edwards 2018 (forthcoming). See also Schadow 2013, pp. 105–107 and Pinheiro Walla 2017, pp. 732–740.
[63] See TL 6:390.2–12.
[64] See TL 6:390.12, 6:451.21–26, 6:452.1–19.
[65] "Es kommt sehr darauf an, was für jeden nach seiner Empfindungsart wahres Bedürfniß sein werde, welches zu bestimmen jedem selbst überlassen bleiben muß" (MS 6:393.27–29).

that an exception may be made to maxims of actions that, in qualifying for universal lawgiving, furnish the practical laws that present us with duties of virtue. Instead, it means that the particular moral requirement expressed by (or implicit in) a maxim of other-directed benevolence will be counterweighed through consideration of the maxim not to sacrifice the permitted means that are conducive to one's own perfection, and vice versa.

Thus, Kant's interpretation of the ethical obligation to ends in terms of wide obligation demands that a clear distinction be drawn between (a) the (conceptually inadmissible) claim that exceptions may be made to maxims that in virtue of their qualification for universal lawgiving can furnish practical laws and (b) the assertion that the universal prescription contained in one law-yielding maxim of ends is subject to limitation by a corresponding prescription contained in another law-yielding maxim (or other law-yielding maxims) of ends. The latitude left to free choice by duties of virtue derives exclusively from the principle of deliberation at issue in the latter assertion. It represents the field in which the exercise of moral judgment is required for the action-guiding employment of the principles of duty that derive from ethical lawgiving alone.[66] The field itself is quite broad; and the only boundary markers for judgment that can be set in place *from within* this field are those determined by considering different maxims' qualification for universal lawgiving as well the different moral prescriptions contained in the maxims that qualify for such lawgiving.

Kant illustrates this last point by taking account of the relationship between self-sacrifice, own-happiness, the happiness of others, and the basic formal universality requirement of morally practical reason. When considering the degree of demandingness involved in beneficent action under given empirical conditions, we must realize that no self-sacrificing maxim to do well for others can qualify for a universal lawgiving. For "a maxim to promote others' happiness at the sacrifice of one's own happiness, one's true needs, would conflict with itself if it were made a universal law" [67] (TL 6:393.29–32). Thus, if 'I' made it my maxim to sacrifice my own happiness for the sake of others; if 'you' made it your maxim to do this as well; and if 'she' also made it her maxim to do the same, and so forth for everyone, then *no one* could ever be made happy, except perhaps by sheer masochistic bad luck.[68] So it follows that no maxim of material self-abne-

---

[66] See TL 6:390.12, 6:411.10–23.
[67] "Denn mit Aufopferung seiner eigenen Glückseligkeit (seiner wahren Bedürfnisse) Anderer ihre zu befördern, würde eine an sich selbst widerstreitende Maxime sein, wenn man sie zum allgemeinen Gesetz machte".
[68] In which event the appropriate response might be for everyone just to drop dead—assuming, of course, that self-killing for the sake of contentment with one's condition is not a morally per-

gation or misplaced altruism can possibly qualify for a universal lawgiving, and no practical law of other-directed benevolence can require me, or anyone else, to make such a maxim the subjective principle of an action—including any action that *does* involve the sacrifice of own-happiness for the sake of others. While I may not be able to promote the happiness of others without sacrificing (part of) my own happiness, this does not entail that I may, in effect, act on a maxim to make my unhappiness the end of my self-sacrificing action. (That would be incompatible with the duty that I have to promote my own happiness as a permitted means of furthering my own perfection.)

So much for the relationship between obligatory ends and the character of the obligation that has such ends as its matter. Let me draw together the main results of my analysis thus far.

We have seen that Kant's metaphysical theory of morals demands the portrayal of own-perfection and others' happiness as intrinsically obligatory ends of action. This is a portrayal based on the notion that there must be certain *material* determining grounds of the power of choice which, when represented as the matter of maxims of ends, furnish laws for maxims of actions. Yet it is also a portrayal that is fully integrated with Kant's account of the ultimate basis of morality, i.e., freedom. For it is only by inserting the concepts of own-perfection and others' happiness into his foundational account of the free power of choice (*freie Willkür*) that Kant can adequately explain practical reason's universally prescriptive role in relation to the duties that ethical lawgiving *alone* can generate. The practical laws that present us with duties of virtue—that is, the laws for *maxims* of actions that cannot issue from juridical lawgiving as laws for *actions*—are thus laws grounded in the portrayal of own-perfection and others' happiness as a priori specifiable rational ultimate ends.[69] These obligatory ends of morally practical reason are mutually supportive. They are mutually supportive in the sense that each of the concepts of end in question has at least one constitutive feature that cannot be understood (or even identified) without reference to some feature of the other concept. Own-perfection requires the 'cultivation of morality in us', and the disposition to cultivate morality as a

---

missible course of action, at least to the extent that it makes *lasting* contentment with one's condition something rather less than assured.

69 Sidgwick (1981, p. 9) characterizes perfection (or excellence) and happiness as rational ultimate ends. For Kant, however, perfection and happiness can qualify as *ultimate* ends of reason only when specified as own-perfection and others' happiness. (It will be noted here, of course, that such ends of reason are ultimate ends of *action*. The concept of ultimate end (*letzter Zweck*) here at issue has nothing directly to do with an ultimate end of *nature* [cf. KU 5:426.15 – 427.25, 5:429.25 – 434.3, 5:436.14 – 37]).

subjective trait cannot be understood without reference to the capacity of each agent to hold herself obligated to promote the happiness of others. Similarly, others' happiness cannot be coherently entertained in thought without picking out the 'moral well-being' that belongs to the cultivation of morality in every human being that is, by nature, capable of ethical lawgiving. Precisely because of these features of mutual reference, there would be no point to giving either one of the two concepts of rational end at issue theoretical priority over its counterpart in the account of intrinsically obligatory ends. Thus, a certain 'Dualism of the Practical Reason' is built into Kant's foundational theory of ethics by virtue of his understanding of rational ultimate ends of action.[70]

---

[70] Cf. Sidgwick 1981, p. 404. Sidgwick holds, of course, that this dualism leads to a conflict between self-interest and the requirements of duty connected with the happiness of others. For Kant, however, the dualistic foundational doctrine of obligatory ends cannot generate such a conflict as long as this doctrine is clearly distinguished from the account of mere rules of prudence. This is true even if (according to Kant) the sensible nature of human beings makes them unavoidably subject to the conflict between own-happiness and duty.

Chapter 2 Obligatory Ends and the Grounding of Maxims: A Key Problem in Kant's Moral Doctrine of Ends

In the previous chapter, I was concerned to show why Kant's portrayal of the foundations of morals requires the theory of intrinsically obligatory ends that he first presents in the 1797 introduction to the Doctrine of Virtue. I also laid out the key elements of this dualistic theory of practical reason's mutually supportive and objectively necessary ends. I now turn to what I take to be the fundamental problem for Kant's metaphysics of morals that becomes evident when the pivotal concept of such a theory—the concept of an *end* that is *also* a duty—is assertively applied to Kant's understanding of the empirical and non-empirical grounds of maxims as well as to his interpretation of the conditions under which maxims can furnish universal practical laws on account of their aptness for possible universal lawgiving.

§ 1 Laws for Maxims of Ends and Empirical Grounds of Maxims

Kant's Doctrine of Virtue builds on the supposition that there are two basic ways to think of the relation between 'end' and 'duty' with respect to actions and their maxims. This supposition is made explicit at the beginning of the first section of the Doctrine's introduction:

> [O]ne can begin with the end and seek out the *maxim* of actions conforming to duty, or, reversewise, one can begin with the maxims of actions conforming to duty and seek out the end that is also a duty. [71] (TL 6:382.9–11)

The Doctrine of Right (*ius*) takes the first way of approaching the end and duty relation. It starts out from the supposition that a freely willing agent necessarily sets herself *some* end for any given action (or actions).[72] It then proceeds to determine a priori the maxims of right-conforming actions by taking account of the

---

[71] "Man kann sich das Verhältniß des Zwecks zur Pflicht auf zweierlei Art denken: entweder, von dem Zwecke ausgehend, die Maxime der pflichtmäßigen Handlungen, oder umgekehrt, von dieser anhebend, den Zweck ausfindig zu machen, der zugleich Pflicht ist" (TL 382.8–11).
[72] For Kant, it is necessarily true that every action has its end and that having an end of action is an act of freedom. See, e.g., TL 6:384.3–4, 6:389.18–20.

purely formal condition of outer freedom, i. e., the condition that "the freedom of the agent could coexist with the freedom of every other agent in accordance with a universal law" [73] (TL 6:382.14–16). Ethics, which furnishes an account of inner freedom under law, must take the opposite way of determining the relationship between end and duty:

> [Ethics] cannot set out from the ends that a human being may set for himself and in accordance with them have at his disposal maxims that he is to adopt, that is, his duty; for those would be empirical grounds of maxims, which [grounds] yield no concept of duty, a concept (categorical ought) that has its root in pure reason alone.[74] Consequently, if maxims were to be adopted according to those ends (which are all self-seeking), one could not even really speak of the concept of duty.—Hence in ethics the *concept of duty* will lead to ends and will have to ground the *maxims* with respect to ends that we *ought* to set ourselves in accordance with moral principles.[75] (TL 6:382.17–23)

In ethics, then, the concept of duty itself, understood as an a priori concept of pure reason, is what furnishes the theoretical platform for moving from the maxims of actions with which one begins to the ends with reference to which the re-

---

[73] "Es wird jedermanns freier Willkür überlassen, welchen Zweck er sich für seine Handlung setzen wolle. Die Maxime derselben aber ist *a priori* bestimmt: daß nämlich die Freiheit des Handelnden mit Jedes anderen Freiheit nach einem allgemeinen Gesetz zusammen bestehen könne" (MS 382.12–16).

[74] Note well my rendering's substantial divergence from Mary Gregor's Cambridge Edition translation. Gregor writes: "[Ethics] cannot begin with the ends that a human being may set for himself and in accordance with them prescribe the maxims he is to adopt, that is, his duty; for that would be to adopt maxims on empirical grounds, and such grounds yield no concept of duty, since this concept (the categorical ought) has its roots in pure reason alone." But Kant's point here is not that one would adopt maxims on empirical grounds by letting ethics begin with ends that a human being may set for himself and then, accordingly, prescribe his duty in terms of the maxims he ought to adopt. Instead, Kant maintains that ethics cannot begin with the ends that a human being may set for himself because these (contingent) ends are empirical grounds of maxims that, as such, yield no concept of duty as an a priori concept of pure reason.

[75] "Sie [die Ethik] kann nicht von den Zwecken ausgehen, die der Mensch sich setzen mag, und darnach über seine zu nehmende Maximen, d. i. über seine Pflicht, verfügen; denn das wären empirische Gründe der Maximen, die keinen Pflichtbegriff abgeben, als welcher (das kategorische Sollen) in der reinen Vernunft allein seine Wurzel hat; wie denn auch, wenn die Maximen nach jenen Zwecken (welche alle selbstsüchtig sind) genommen werden sollten, vom Pflichtbegriff eigentlich gar nicht die Rede sein könnte.—Also wird in der Ethik der *Pflichtbegriff* auf Zwecke leiten und die *Maximen* in Ansehung der Zwecke, die wir uns setzen *sollen*, nach moralischen Grundsätzen begründen müssen" (TL 6:382.17–25).

quirements of inner freedom under law can be fulfilled. And since the only possible type of end that we ought to set for ourselves is one that is *also* (*zugleich*) a duty, it follows that only such an obligatory end can ground a maxim of ends which can hold as a universal law that presents a duty of virtue.

Now there is a fairly obvious problem that emerges from this view of the direction of fit in the duty-to-end grounding relation that is peculiar to ethics and its account of the duties of virtue. While we may agree with Kant that empirical grounds cannot yield any concept of duty (as 'categorical ought'),[76] the argument provided in support of this position does not seem to establish conclusively that no maxim adopted on empirical grounds—i.e., no empirically grounded maxim —can furnish a principle, and law, that presents a duty. On Kant's account of obligatory ends, 'duty' requires me, for example, to promote the happiness of others as an objective end of morally practical reason. Yet it seems possible for me to act in this way, thus acting in full awareness that I ought so to act, even when the ground of my maxim happens to be empirical. For the happiness of others might be an end that I just *may* set for myself according to my sensible impulses or inclination. So my maxim will be empirically grounded in the sense that it qualifies as a rule that I take as my principle of volition on account of an end that I happen to have.[77] But precisely because others' happiness is also something that I am to promote as an objective end of practical reason—that is, as an end that everyone ought to have—it seems that this same maxim must also fulfill the universality requirement by which it can hold as a practical law that presents a duty of virtue. For it is an end that is given not just empirically but *also* a priori. More precisely, it is an end that *can* be given empirically even when I can know a priori that it *must* be my end. Accordingly, it seems that my empirically grounded maxim should qualify for a universal lawgiving, and should thus be able to hold as a universal law, even if no empirical ground can yield the concept of duty that applies to that end *insofar* as it is an objective end that everyone ought to have.

These last problematizing considerations target the basis of Kant's view of the relation between rational nature and the sensible or affective conditions of action that are characteristic of human beings. They also bear on the distinction that Kant draws between the legality and the morality of actions and, more generally, on his conception of actions' moral worth. We will take up these broad topics in due course—mainly, in the second part of this book. For the purposes of this chapter, however, I will concentrate on bringing to light a single assump-

---

[76] The empirically minded sentimentalist in moral philosophy, of course, will not necessarily be willing to grant this assumption. On this, see chapter 4 (pp. 91–96), chapter 10 (pp. 206– 213), and chapter 11 (pp. 242–247, 262–267).
[77] For the notion of rule at issue here, see MS 6:225.2–3

tion that Kant arguably needs if he is to provide effective support for the position that he takes regarding empirical grounds of maxims and maxims of ends that can serve as universal laws.

§ 2 Duty, Self-Constraint, and Objectively Necessary Ends

In taking up this task, the obvious place to start is with Kant's considerations on how the concept of duty relates to the conditions of action involved in having ends on non-rational grounds. Let us therefore turn to the opening section of the Doctrine of Virtue's introduction.

When clarifying his conception of a doctrine of virtue in this section, Kant begins by characterizing the concept of duty as one that "is in itself already the concept of a *necessitation* (constraint) of the free power of choice through the law" [78] (TL 6:379.15–16). The constraint that features in this concept of duty may be external or self-imposed, but in either case it is made known through the "categorical pronouncement (the unconditional ought)" (TL 6:379.18) issuing from the moral imperative. Although neither external constraint nor self-constraint necessarily applies to rational beings as such, both forms of constraint are in fact normatively necessary for human beings. For "rational *natural* beings" like these are "unholy enough that pleasure can induce them to break the moral law even though they recognize its authority" (TL 6:379.21–23). Moreover, their sensible or affective constitution is such that "even when they obey the law, they do so reluctantly [*ungern*] (with resistance of their inclinations)" (TL 6:379.21–24).[79] Yet despite being subject to constraint on account of its sensible nature, the human being is a free (i.e., moral) being. Thus, when the concept of duty concerns the inner determination of the human will, its restrictive import must be that of self-constraint with respect to the free

---

[78] "Der *Pflichtbegriff* ist an sich schon der Begriff von einer *Nöthigung* (Zwang) der freien Willkür durchs Gesetz; dieser Zwang mag nun (Zwang) der freien Willkür durchs Gesetz; dieser Zwang mag nun ein *äußerer* oder ein *Selbstzwang* sein" (TL 6:379.15–17). For commentary on the notions of the necessitation of or constraint on the free power of choice here at issue, see Gregor 1963, pp. 64–68. See also Baum 2013, pp. 125–136.

[79] "Der moralische *Imperativ* verkündigt durch seinen kategorischen Ausspruch (das unbedingte Sollen) diesen Zwang, der also nicht auf vernünftige Wesen überhaupt (deren es etwa auch heilige geben könnte), sondern auf Menschen als vernünftige Naturwesen geht, die dazu unheilig genug sind, daß sie die Lust wohl anwandeln kann das moralische Gesetz, ob sie gleich dessen Ansehen selbst anerkennen, doch zu übertreten, und, selbst wenn sie es befolgen, es dennoch ungern (mit Widerstand ihrer Neigung) zu thun, als worin der Zwang eigentlich besteht" (TL 6:379.17–25).

power of choice. For it is only in terms of self-constraint that necessitation can be unified with the human being's freedom in exercising the power of choice. Moreover, the concept of duty that underlies this unification must be a specifically ethical duty. It must be distinct from every duty of right, even though ethical lawgiving, which is an internal lawgiving, makes all duties at least indirectly ethical.[80]

In keeping with this initial portrayal of the character of duty-determined action, Kant holds that the "impulses of nature" (TL 6: 380.7) pertaining to human beings must be regarded as

> *hindrances* in the human mind to the fulfillment of duty and (in part powerfully) opposing forces which he [i.e., the human being] must judge himself capable of resisting and conquering by reason, and this not at some time in the future but at once (simultaneously [*zugleich*] with the thought of duty).[81] (TL 6:380.7–11)

Given the forceful quality of these hindrances from the side of our affective constitution, the constraint that features in the rational concept of duty is here linked to the human capacity to resist and overcome natural impulses—i.e., to the capacity that Kant defines as "virtue (*virtus, fortitudo moralis*)" (TL 6:380.15–16).[82]

As we have already seen (in chapter 1), the part of Kant's overall doctrine of morals that deals with virtue and its particular duties is one that has to be sharply distinguished from the juridical theory of right. While Kant's doctrine of right treats merely "the *formal* conditions of outer freedom (the consistency of freedom with itself if its maxim was made universal law)" (TL 6:380.19–21), the additional task of ethics, as a doctrine of virtue, is to provide the account of "a *matter* (an object of the free power of choice): an *end* of pure reason that is also represented as an objectively necessary end, i.e., an end that for humans is also a duty" [83] (TL 6:380.22–25). Since the duty presented by such an objectively nec-

---

[80] See jointly MS 6:220.32–221.3 and TL 6:380.16–18. See also chapter 1, pp. 17–18.
[81] "Die Antriebe der Natur enthalten also *Hindernisse* der Pflichtvollziehung im Gemüth des Menschen und (zum Theil mächtig) widerstrebende Kräfte, die also zu bekämpfen und durch die Vernunft nicht erst künftig, sondern gleich jetzt (zugleich mit dem Gedanken) zu besiegen er sich vermögend urtheilen muß: nämlich das zu *können*, was das Gesetz unbedingt befiehlt, daß er thun *soll*" (MS 6:380.7–12).
[82] Regarding Kant's concept of virtue in the *Metaphysics of Morals*, see Denis 2013; Goy 2013, pp. 184–185, 195–205; Gregor 1963, pp. 70–75. More generally, see Baxley 2010, pp. 48–84; Wood 2008, pp. 142–157.
[83] "Die Rechtslehre hatte es blos mit der *formalen* Bedingung der äußeren Freiheit (durch die Zusammenstimmung mit sich selbst, wenn ihre Maxime zum allgemeinen Gesetz gemacht wurde), d. i. mit dem Recht, zu thun. Die Ethik dagegen giebt noch eine *Materie* (einen Gegen-

essary end belongs to the field of ethics, it involves the self-constraint of the free power of choice through law; and the end connected with this kind of constraint is an a priori given end, i.e., an end given independently of any end to which inclination may lead us:

> For since the sensible inclinations of human beings mislead [*verleiten*] them to ends (as the matter of the power of choice) that can be contrary to duty, lawgiving reason can in turn check their influence only by an opposing moral end, an end that must therefore be given *a priori* independently of inclination.[84] (TL 6:380.25–381.3)

What, then, are the fundamental characteristics of an objectively necessary end as an end given independently of inclination? As "something that lies in concepts of practical reason" (TL 6:381.10), such an a priori given end must be "an object of the power of choice [...] through the representation of which choice is determined to some action to bring about this object" [85] (TL 6:381.10). It must therefore be an end that 'I' come to have as the determining ground of the power of choice by *making* it my end. More particularly, it must be a "*material* determining ground" of the power of choice that I am *obligated* to have in addition to the "*formal* determining ground" at issue in the exposition of the merely formal conditions of outer freedom (TL 6:381.9–14—italics mine [J. E.]).[86]

So much for Kant's opening account of the relationship between the concept of duty as such, the concept of an obligatory end of pure practical reason, and the conditions of action that can present hindrances to the fulfillment of duty. In view of this account, we can see what Kant is driving at when he maintains (see

---

stand der freien Willkür), einen **Zweck** der reinen Vernunft, der zugleich als objective nothwendiger Zweck, d. i. für den Menschen als Pflicht, vorgestellt wird, an die Hand (TL 6:380.19–25)".
84 "Denn da die sinnlichen Neigungen zu Zwecken (als der Materie der Willkür) verleiten, die der Pflicht zuwider sein können, so kann die gesetzgebende Vernunft ihrem Einfluß nicht anders wehren, als wiederum durch einen entgegengesetzten moralischen Zweck, der also von der Neigung unabhängig a priori gegeben sein muß".
85 "Zweck ist ein Gegenstand der Willkür (eines vernünftigen Wesens), durch dessen Vorstellung diese zu einer Handlung diesen Gegenstand hervorzubringen bestimmt wird" (TL 6:381.3–6).
86 "Daß ich aber auch verbunden bin mir irgend etwas, was in den Begriffen der praktischen Vernunft liegt, zum Zwecke zu machen, mithin außer dem formalen Bestimmungsgrunde der Willkür (wie das Recht dergleichen enthält) noch einen materialen, einen Zweck zu haben, der dem Zweck aus sinnlichen Antrieben entgegengesetzt werden könne: dieses würde der Begriff von einem Zweck sein, *der an sich selbst Pflicht ist*" (TL 6:381.10–15). According to the account of the formal conditions of outer freedom given in the Doctrine of Right, any action is right if it can coexist with everyone's freedom in accordance with a universal law, or if on its maxim the freedom of choice of each can coexist with the freedom of everyone in accordance with a universal law (see RL 6:230.29–31).

TL 6:382.17–21), with reference to ends that a human being *may* set for herself, that empirical grounds of maxims yield no concept of duty. For it is empirically evident that sensible inclinations *can* (mis)lead us to ends that are contrary to duty. And, provided that we share Kant's position that the concept of duty is a strictly rational concept that has its "root in pure reason alone" (TL 6:382.21–22), it follows that the influence of ends contrary to duty can be checked by an end that *must* be given a priori, i.e., non-empirically.[87] But this appeal to a priori given ends (i.e., to ends that are also duties) does not cancel the force of the problematizing considerations offered in the first section of this chapter. That is because it is not yet clear why *no* maxim, as a subjective principle of volition, should be able to qualify for a universal lawgiving as long as sensible inclination can lead us to have some end that necessarily is *not* contrary to duty. Consider again the possibility of having the happiness of others as one's end on account of being affectively inclined to do well for them. In this case, the maxim to bring about others' happiness will have its empirical ground in sensible inclination, although the end in question is *also* an a priori given end of practical reason. Why, then, should we hold that no such empirically grounded maxim can satisfy morally practical reason's universality requirement even if we also hold that empirical grounds of maxims cannot yield the a priori concept of duty that applies to the ends that we ought to set for ourselves?

§ 3 Ends of Action and the Grounding of Maxims

Perhaps we can make further headway in dealing with this problem by providing a somewhat more finely tuned analysis of the concept of obligatory end than has been provided thus far. I refer, then, to Kant's discussion of "the basis [*Grund*] for thinking of an end that is also a duty" (TL 6:384.31–32) in the third section of the Doctrine of Virtue's introduction. The main argument there runs as follows:

Every action must have its end, and the end of any action is an object of the *free* power of choice whenever one makes this object one's end. Accordingly, coming to have an object of the power of choice as one's end must be understood as an act of freedom on the part of the acting subject. But the act of freedom by which an agent comes to have an end that is also a duty must be comprehended in terms of "a practical principle that prescribes [*gebietet*] the end itself (and

---

[87] This leaves open the possibility that duty-opposing ends could be checked by other ends to which sensible inclinations lead us—which of course calls into question Kant's claim that ends contrary to duty can *only* be checked by an opposing moral end (see TL 6:381.1). Since this issue is not crucial to my line of inquiry in this chapter, however, I will let it pass unaddressed.

consequently unconditionally)" (TL 6:385.5–6). Given the unconditional character of the prescription that it contains, this principle of free action is "a categorical imperative of pure practical reason, and hence an imperative that connects the *concept of duty* with the concept of an end in general" (MS 6:385.5–9).[88] Thus, it is on the basis of this categorically prescribed connection between end and duty that we can understand why it is necessary for there to be ends of free actions which furnish ends that are also duties:

> Now there must be such an end and a categorical imperative corresponding to it. For since there are free actions, there must also be ends to which, as their objects, these actions are directed. But among these ends there must be some that are also (i.e., by their very concept) duties. For if there were no such ends, then, since no action can be without an end, all ends would hold for practical reason only as means to other ends, and a categorical imperative would be impossible—which would do away with any doctrine of morals.[89] (TL 6:385.10–17)

This way of establishing why there must be obligatory ends raises various questions concerning the relationship between Kant's doctrines of right and virtue.[90]

---

[88] "Eine jede Handlung hat also ihren Zweck, und da niemand einen Zweck haben kann, ohne sich den Gegenstand seiner Willkür selbst zum Zweck zu machen, so ist es ein Act der *Freiheit* des handelnden Subjects, nicht eine Wirkung der *Natur* irgend einen Zweck der Handlungen zu haben. Weil aber dieser Act, der einen Zweck bestimmt, ein praktisches Princip ist, welches nicht die Mittel (mithin nicht bedingt), sondern den Zweck selbst (folglich unbedingt) gebietet, so ist es ein kategorischer Imperativ der reinen praktischen Vernunft, mithin ein solcher, der einen *Pflichtbegriff* mit dem eines Zwecks überhaupt verbindet" (TL 6:385.1–9). Kant here characterizes the *act* of freedom by which the subject comes to have an end that is also a duty as a practical *principle* which unconditionally prescribes an end (and which is therefore an imperative of practical reason). This identification may be thought to raise a number of logical and metaphysical issues concerning the relationship between actions, objects of free choice, acts of freedom, practical principles, and imperatives. But there is no reason to go into these issues here, so I have chosen a weaker characterization of the relationship between act and principle (using 'in terms of' instead of 'as') when presenting the argument in the first paragraph of the third section of Doctrine of Virtue's introduction.

[89] "Es muß nun einen solchen Zweck und einen ihm correspondirenden kategorischen Imperativ geben. Denn da es freie Handlungen giebt, so muß es auch Zwecke geben, auf welche als Object jene gerichtet sind. Unter diesen Zwecken aber muß es auch einige geben, die zugleich (d. i. ihrem Begriffe nach) Pflichten sind.—Denn gäbe es keine dergleichen, so würden, weil doch keine Handlung zwecklos sein kann, alle Zwecke für die praktische Vernunft immer nur als Mittel zu andern Zwecken gelten, und ein *kategorischer* Imperativ wäre unmöglich; welches alle Sittenlehre aufhebt".

[90] If the absence of ends that are also duties implies that *no* categorical imperative would be possible, and consequently that the doctrine of morals would be done away with in its *entirety*, then the argument would seem to entail that the theory of the laws of right as laws of outer free-

§ 3 Ends of Action and the Grounding of Maxims — 43

But here I will concentrate simply on the following two points, which bear directly on the guiding concern of this chapter: (1) Given that every action necessarily has its end, and thus its object, there could be no connection between the categorical ought and *objects* of choice that I can make my ends if there were no ends of actions that are also duties. (2) Consequently, there could be no categorical imperative that applies to the act of freedom by which I make an object of the power of choice the end of my action (or actions).

With this, we can be satisfied that the concept of obligatory end is sufficiently clarified with reference to the description of free action in terms of an act of freedom that presupposes an object of the power of choice. Given this chapter's concern with understanding the relationship between maxims, empirical grounds and obligatory ends, however, this clarification raises a further question: What exactly is it for such an *object*, as the end to which my action is directed, to *ground* the maxim by which I make it my end?

Let us turn to the sixth section of the Doctrine of Virtue's introduction with this question in mind. While highlighting the main features of Kant's argument in this section, I will also spell out its ramifications for the relationship between ethics and his juridical theory of right.

That the concept of duty stands in immediate relation to a law is already indicated by "the formal principle of duty *in* the categorical imperative" [italics mine], i.e., by the principle "so act that the maxim of your action could become a universal law" (TL 6:389.1–3).[91] This direct relation between duty and law ob-

---

dom ultimately depends on the account of the ends of pure reason that furnishes the basis of Kant's account of the duties of virtue. In this case, however, it would also follow that the supreme principle of the of the doctrine of right (which Kant understands as an analytic principle that abstracts from the setting of ends [see TL 6:396.3–28]) is logically dependent on the supreme principle of the doctrine of virtue, i.e., on a synthetic principle of morally practical reason which commands us to "act in accordance with a maxim of *ends* that it can be a universal law for everyone to have" (TL 6:395.15–16). This raises some interesting issues about Kant's understanding of the separateness of *ius* and *ethica*. While there would be no problem in this regard if his use of "doctrine of morals [*Sittenlehre*]" (MS 6:385.25) were simply a reference to ethics (cf. GMS 4:387.16), this is clearly not the reference that Kant intends when he formulates the supreme principle of the doctrine of morals in the general introduction to the *Metaphysics of Morals* (see MS 6:225.31–226.3). At any rate, proper consideration of these issues would require further discussion of how Kant's theory of obligatory ends grounds the architectonic division between *ius* and *ethica* by drawing the distinction between ethical duties that can also be juridical duties and ethical duties that cannot be juridical duties because they are exclusively duties of virtue (on this, see chapter 1, pp. 18–20). I forego this further discussion since it is not essential to the present chapter's argument. See, however, Edwards 2018 (forthcoming).
91 Cf. MS 6:226.1–2.

tains "even if I abstract from all ends, as the matter of law" [92] (TL 6:388.35–389.1). Now in order to specify the laws of outer freedom and their corresponding duties of right, it is necessary that abstraction be made from all such ends, and hence from all matter of law. In the context of the juridical theory of right, then, maxims satisfying the universality requirement contained in the concept of practical law are regarded as "subjective principles that merely *qualify* for a universal lawgiving"[93] (TL 6:389.7–8). And a maxim, *as* a subjective principle, will so qualify as long as it conforms to the basic categorical demand that juridical practical reason makes with respect to maxims. As Kant had already put this point in the introduction to the Doctrine of Right in when formulating the universal principle of right:

> Any action is *right* if it can coexist with everyone's freedom in accordance with a universal law, *or if on its maxim* [italics mine (J.E.)] the freedom of choice of each can coexist with everyone's freedom in accordance with a universal law.[94] (RL 6:230.29–31)

The requirement placed on maxims by this universal principle is purely restrictive since "it cannot be required that this principle of all maxims be itself in turn my maxim, that is, it cannot be required that *I make it the maxim* of my action"[95] (RL 6:231.3–5). Thus (returning to the text of the Doctrine of Virtue), when viewed from the standpoint of juridical lawgiving, the qualification requirement for maxims presented by the formal principle of duty furnishes "a merely negative principle (not to come into conflict with law as such)" (TL 6:389.8–9).[96] Such a principle cannot suffice for ethics. Although it can serve as a fully adequate

---

[92] "Der Pflichtbegriff steht unmittelbar in Beziehung auf ein Gesetz (wenn ich gleich noch von allem Zweck als der Materie desselben abstrahire); wie denn das formale Princip der Pflicht im kategorischen Imperativ: 'Handle so, daß die Maxime deiner Handlung ein allgemeines Gesetz werden könne' es schon anzeigt" (TL 6:388.34–389.3).

[93] "Die Maximen werden hier als solche subjective Grundsätze angesehen, die sich zu einer allgemeinen Gesetzgebung blos qualificiren; welches nur ein negatives Princip (einem Gesetz überhaupt nicht zu widerstreiten) ist" (TL 6:389.6–9).

[94] "Eine jede Handlung ist *Recht*, die oder nach deren Maxime die Freiheit der Willkür eines jeden mit jedermanns Freiheit nach einem allgemeinen Gesetze zusammen bestehen kann".

[95] "daß nicht verlangt werden kann, daß dieses Princip aller Maximen selbst wiederum meine Maxime sei, d. i. daß ich es *mir zur Maxime* meiner Handlung mache".

[96] Accordingly, the positive formula of the universal law of right that governs the use of the power of choice makes no explicit reference to maxims in its statement of the limiting condition that the idea of outer freedom contains—namely: so act externally that the free use of your power of choice can coexist with the freedom of everyone in accordance with a universal law (see MS 6:231.10–12).

and self-contained basis for the derivation of laws of actions as practical principles that specify duties of right, it cannot deliver laws for *maxims* of actions.

According to Kant, as we saw in chapter 1 (pp. 18–26), the laws for maxims of actions can be established only on the basis of the specifically ethical concept of an end that is also a duty. Such a concept can play this grounding role because it offers the way to subordinate the subjective end that everyone has, in any given instance of the free use of the power of choice, to the objective end of action, i.e., to the type of end that everyone ought to have. Thus, while maxims of actions must "contain [*enthalten*]" (TL 6:389.22) the purely formal condition by which they qualify for universal lawgiving, the objective end that everyone ought to have is what makes it a *law* for an agent to have *as her maxim* a principle by which a certain matter of the power of choice is made her end. For "the end that is also a duty can make it a law to have such a maxim, although for the maxim itself the mere possibility of being consonant with a universal lawgiving is already sufficient" [97] (MS 6:389.22–26).

To illustrate Kant's aim in this (highly complex) argument concerning laws for maxims, let us once again take as an example the happiness of others, this time not primarily as an end of sensible inclination, but as a matter of the power of choice and as the end of one's action or actions. As a concept of duty, the representation of this end is employed in the practical proposition (and law) 'You ought to make the happiness of others your end'. The imperative derived from this unconditionally prescriptive statement satisfies the qualification requirement for maxims set forth by the formal principle of duty and actions, i.e., the requirement that the maxim in question be apt for a universal lawgiving.[98] At the same time, though, this imperative "concerns [*geht auf*]" (TL 6:389.17) the matter (i.e., the object) that a freely acting agent wills to bring about by acting on a maxim of ends—in this case, by acting on the maxim of ac-

---

[97] "Da nun keine freie Handlung möglich ist, ohne daß der Handelnde hiebei zugleich einen Zweck (als Materie der Willkür) beabsichtigte, so muß, wenn es einen Zweck giebt, der zugleich Pflicht ist, die Maxime derHandlungen als Mittel zu Zwecken nur die Bedingung der Qualification zu einer möglichen allgemeinen Gesetzgebung enthalten; wogegen der Zweck, der zugleich Pflicht ist, es zu einem Gesetz machen kann eine solche Maxime zu haben, indessen daß für die Maxime selbst die bloße Möglichkeit zu einer allgemeinen Gesetzgebung zusammen zu stimmen schon genug ist" (MS 6:389.18–26).

[98] Kant identifies the formal principle of duty in the categorical imperative as the formal principle of *actions* in the final paragraph of TL *Einleitung* VI: "For maxims of actions can be [preferentially] *arbitrary*, and are subject only to the limiting condition of being apt for a universal lawgiving, which is the formal principle of actions [Denn Maximen der Handlungen können *willkürlich* sein und stehen nur unter der einschränkenden Bedingung der Habilität zu einer allgemeinen Gesetzgebung, als formalem Princip der Handlungen]" (TL 6:389.27–29).

tive benevolence through which her merely subjective ends are subordinated to the objective end of making others happy.[99] Such a maxim is distinguished not only by its qualification *for* a universal lawgiving. It also qualifies *as* a maxim of ends that it can be a universal law for everyone to have.[100]

How, then, does an end that is also a duty ground a maxim by which I make an object of the power of choice the end of my action? It does so on the strength its very concept. It is an essential feature of the concept of this type of end of practical reason that the matter (or object) of the free power of choice is what furnishes the content—i.e., the matter—for maxims of ends which, in virtue of their qualification for universal lawgiving, can yield practical laws that present duties of virtue.[101] For when we think of an end that is also a duty, the matter of the power of choice that this end provides is always one which supplies the matter of a maxim that can become a universal law.[102] This type of end thus grounds its maxim by furnishing an object of the power of choice that is *necessarily* the matter of a practical law.

---

[99] On the maxim of active benevolence, see TL 6:449.16–22, 6:450.16–19, 6:450.31–451.19.

[100] As is demanded by the supreme principle of the doctrine of virtue: "Act in accordance with a maxim of *ends* that it can be a universal law for everyone to have" (TL 6:395.15–16). It is worth noting here that the deduction of this principle in TL *Einleitung* IX could legitimately presuppose that there *are* ends of pure practical reason since Kant argues for the necessity of there being such ends in Section III (TL 6:385.10–18). Nevertheless, the deduction given in section IX does not rely on the soundness of the earlier argument. The supreme principle of the doctrine of virtue applies to maxims of ends that "contain" (TL 6:395.29) ends that pure practical reason *can* prescribe a priori, and its deduction (see TL 6:395.24–32) establishes the following essential point in view of that prescriptive *possibility:* What can be an a priori prescribed end *is* necessarily, on pain of contradiction, an end for pure practical reason just because this a faculty of ends in general (*ein Vermögen der Zwecke überhaupt*). Thus, contrary to what Henry Allison maintains (see Allison 1996, p. 158), the deduction just summarized does not simply assume that there are obligatory ends of pure practical reason. Nor does it purport to derive the necessity of pure reason's practicality with regard to ends that are also duties simply from the assumption that every maxim contains an end. For a discussion of Allison's charges, see Baum 1998, pp. 53–56. Baum criticizes Allison for neglecting to take proper account of the modal distinctions that Kant draws with extreme care when connecting concepts of ends and maxims with the concept of pure practical reason and its laws. Baum also argues that Allison misconstrues Kant's understanding of the relationship between maxims containing ends and pure practical reason as a faculty of ends in general. I find these criticisms convincing.

[101] See TL 6:396.17–31.

[102] On Kant's conception of the matter of maxims, see chapter 3 (pp. 54–55, 57–60, 64–69).

§ 4 Material Determining Grounds, the Matter of Universal Laws, and Self-Seeking Ends

The analyses given in the preceding section—above all, those concerning Kant's conception of laws for maxims of actions—are intended to sort out what it is for an object of the power of choice to ground the maxim by which that object is made one's end in acting. Their particular aim has been to exhibit the way in which an obligatory end, as the object of the power of choice, grounds a maxim of ends that it be a universal law for everyone to have. Does our sorting exercise in this regard provide us with what we need in order to respond effectively to the guiding problem of this chapter?

The general problem, again, is this: When accounting for the direction of fit in the duty-to-end relation that distinguishes ethics from the doctrine of right, Kant does not seem to establish conclusively that no empirically grounded maxim can furnish a law that presents a duty of virtue. Let us see if the preceding line of inquiry shows that Kant can accomplish what needs to be done in this regard.

Our line of inquiry has led to the following result: An obligatory end, i.e., an end that is also a duty, grounds its maxim by furnishing an object of the power of choice which is *necessarily* the matter of a universal law for maxims of ends. Thus, in view of this result, it may initially look as though we should be able to deal once and for all with our guiding problem simply by establishing that a non-obligatory end is an object that is only contingently the matter of such a law. But things are, of course, not that simple. And the reason for this lack of simplicity is straightforward enough, given the background examined thus far: It seems that an end that is also a duty *cannot* contingently be the matter of a universal law, even if it is *also* an end that one happens to have on empirically contingent grounds.

Let us again bring to bear the happiness of others as our working example. As we have seen, this promotable end of action is a matter (or, equivalently, an object) of the power of choice that also supplies a determining ground of this same volitional power. It is, as Kant explicitly states, a *material* determining ground of the power of choice.[103] Yet it is a material determining ground that, by furnishing the matter of a maxim that qualifies for a universal lawgiving, supplies a matter of practical law itself. Moreover, it is a determining ground that is one and the same as the matter of the maxim in question, namely, the maxim of benevolence that pertains to the promotion of others' happiness. As the matter of such a maxim, it is also identical to the matter of the law of pure practical reason

---

103 See (again) TL 6:381.11–12.

that sets forth the duty of beneficence as a duty of virtue.[104] Thus, as long as the happiness of others is a *possible* end that one happens to have according to sensible impulse or inclination, it seems that there can be an empirically grounded maxim that qualifies for a universal lawgiving. And despite this maxim's empirical ground, it looks as though its content (i.e., its matter) will necessarily be the same as that of a principle of duty which requires us to act on a maxim of ends that it can be a universal *law* for everyone to have.[105] Thus, unless some further condition obtains, Kant's account morally practical reason's obligatory ends leaves open the possibility that there is an empirically contingent end—an end of inclination—that is *also necessarily* a duty.

So just what is the further condition that could rule out this possibility? What supposition could be used to pry apart the combined material volitional elements just discussed? Specifically, what theoretical tenet could plausibly put Kant in a position to sever the links between, on the one hand, all possible contingent ends of inclination and, on the other hand, the material grounds of the power of choice that are also necessarily the matter of maxims and practical laws?

As far as I can see, Kant gives only one really clear indication of the needed tenet in the context of the introduction to the Doctrine of Virtue. Fortunately, though, this crucial and most direct clue can be discerned in the hypothetical statement that sums up the argument that first generated our guiding problem in this chapter (see p. 36):

> Consequently, if maxims were to be adopted according to [*nach*] those ends (which are all self-seeking), one could not even really speak of the concept of duty.[106] (TL 6:382.22–24)

Note well Kant's claim that the ends which furnish empirical grounds of maxims are *all* self-seeking ends. It is easy to overlook the significance of this parenthetically embedded claim since it may seem that Kant inserted it as an afterthought (as indeed he may well have done); and I have studiously avoided focusing on it up to this point in my presentation in order to be in a position to clarify its importance for Kant's moral doctrine of ends in the *Metaphysics of Morals*. But let us now come properly to grips with its ramifications for the line of questioning that we have been following.

---

[104] See TL 6:393.11–394.12, 6:448.9–453.33.
[105] Cf. TL 6:388.34–389.3, 6:389.27–29, 6:394.20–395.21.
[106] Gregor translates *nach* as "on the basis of". This reading, which is contextually justified since the self-seeking and contingent ends in question furnish empirical grounds of maxims, lends support to the line of interpretation followed in this section. But I have chosen the weakest feasible rendering ("according to") for the purposes of my argument.

If the ends that furnish empirical grounds of maxims are *all* self-seeking, then Kant can (it seems) justifiably maintain that all empirically grounded maxims are subjective practical principles which relate to the promotion of one's own happiness. Since one's own happiness cannot, on Kant's account, be thought of without self-contradiction as a (direct) duty, it evidently follows that it cannot be thought of as an end that is also a duty.[107] Thus, provided that Kant's account is sound, we can infer that the particular ends of action pursued in order to promote one's own happiness as a general end are ends of inclination that can supply neither the matter of a maxim that can qualify for a universal lawgiving nor, consequently, the matter of any practical law that presents a duty of morally practical reason.[108] And no such matter could be identified as a material determining ground of the power of choice that an agent is obligated to have in addition to the determining ground supplied by the formal principle of duty in the categorical imperative.

§ 5 Self-Seeking Ends, Own-Happiness, and Universal Lawgiving

We can now bring this chapter's argument to a close. Viewed from a first-person perspective, our main topic of concern can be summarized as follows: If an end like the happiness of others furnishes the matter of a maxim that I adopt as mine, then the only condition under which my maxim could fail to qualify for a universal lawgiving (thereby failing to qualify as a maxim of ends that it can be a universal law for everyone to have) would be if this matter could not be an end of inclination that it is also a duty for me to have as an object and material determining ground of the power of choice. For as long as the happiness of others can be an end of inclination as well as an end of pure practical reason, the *maxim* that has this end as its matter *can* have an empirical ground, even if it is necessarily the matter of a maxim that qualifies for a universal lawgiving. Now the concept of duty that pertains specifically to an end of pure practical reason (i.e., to the kind of end that is *also* a duty) is the concept of an end that furnishes (i) the matter of a universal law of morally practical reason as well as (ii) the matter (i.e., the object) of the power of choice and (iii) the material

---

107 See TL 6:386.1–7, 6:387.26–388.30.
108 See TL 6:388.17–30. The grounds of inference here would of course be disputed by an ethical egoist who seeks show that the foundational principles of her theory satisfy the universality requirements of practical laws. Kant, however, elsewhere provides detailed considerations against such an endeavor, and his considerations are arguably compelling (see, e.g., KpV 5:19.14–23, 5:25.14–26.33, 5:28.4–28, 5:35.7–36.8; MS 6:453.5–15).

determining ground of this same volitional power. Consequently, the happiness of others will always provide an end that it is also a duty for an agent to have as a material determining ground of the power of choice whenever the matter to which this power is directed is in fact an end of other-directed benevolent inclination—*unless*, that is, it can be established that such a matter is in reality (despite appearances) the end of predominantly self-benevolent inclination, i.e., one's own happiness.

In keeping with this latter proviso, then, it can be coherently maintained that a maxim containing the happiness of others as its matter cannot be empirically grounded if it is to qualify for a universal lawgiving. To be sure, others' happiness may well *appear* to furnish the empirical ground of this kind of maxim as long as it is an end of inclination. Yet if all such ends are self-seeking, this same ground will in reality be a self-seeking end. Indeed, it will be *the* self-seeking end of predominantly self-benevolent inclination, namely, one's *own* happiness. Thus, provided that no maxim of any self-seeking end can satisfy the conditions for universal lawgiving that apply to the obligatory ends of morally practical reason, there seems to be good reason to think that Kant has at his disposal precisely what he requires in order to establish that no empirically grounded maxim can furnish a universal law that presents a duty of virtue.[109]

Kant's crucial claim that ends providing for the empirical grounding of maxims are all self-seeking accords generally with the descriptions of the relationship between the rational motivating grounds of action and the sensible and empirical conditions of human motivation found in Kant's other writings from the 1780s and 1790s.[110] Even more significantly, that claim is entirely consistent with the central tenets of Kant's account of empirical practical reason in the *Critique of Practical Reason*, where it receives its most explicit formulation in the theorem asserting that that all material (i.e., empirically grounded) practical principles belong under the heading of self-love or one's own happiness (see KpV 5:22.6–8). Thus, to understand whether Kant in fact does dispose over the means of dealing conclusively with the problem that has determined the course of this chapter, let us now turn to the part of the second *Critique* in which the theorem just mentioned plays its systematic role.

---

[109] Mary Gregor put this point as follows: "Kant assumes that apart from obligatory ends, all our maxims will be based on self-love. He implies that even when we make the happiness of others our end on the basis of benevolent inclinations we are, ultimately, seeking the satisfaction of our inclinations" (Gregor 1963, p. 82).

[110] On this, see Edwards 2000a: 411–432; Edwards 2000b: 887–914.

Chapter 3 The Principle of Self-Love and Material Practical Principles in the *Critique of Practical Reason*

§ 1 Practical Propositions, Maxims, and Practical Laws

This chapter is primarily concerned with the four theorems pertaining to practical reason that Kant treats in the first chapter of the *Critique of Practical Reason*. Before getting started on these theorems and their proofs, however, I would like to focus on several patches of terminological and conceptual terrain that I take to be essential to dealing with the issues raised and the tasks presented in the preceding two chapters of this book. Let us consider here the account of the relationship between 'practical principle', 'maxim', and 'practical law' that runs through all of Kant's major works on the doctrine of morals.

Both maxims and practical laws are practical principles. As such, they are propositions. More particularly, they are propositions that contain "a general *[allgemeine]* determination of the will" (KpV 5:19.7–8). It is because it contains this sort of volitional determination that a practical principle, *qua* proposition, supplies a cognizable condition for action. How, then, are we to understand the different ways in which maxims and practical laws supply cognizable conditions for action on account of the general determinations of the will that propositions can contain?

A *maxim*, on Kant's account, is a subjective practical principle. It is subjective in the sense that the condition for action that figures in its propositional content is one that is "regarded by the subject as holding [*gültig*] only for his will" (KpV 5:19.9–10). Accordingly, any maxim must be understood as a subjective principle of volition (*subjective[s] Prinzip des Wollens*—GMS 4:400.34). Every maxim is thus a principle that holds for the will of a particular subject insofar as that same subject regards it as a principle that holds specifically for his (or her, or its) own will, and does not (necessarily) regard it as a principle that holds for the will of any other subject. While a maxim is a proposition that contains a general determination—or indeed a universal determination—of the will, it is also "a rule that the agent himself makes his principle on subjective grounds" (MS 6:225.34–36). Equivalently (for Kant), it is a principle that "the subject himself makes his rule (how he wills to act)" (MS 6:225.34–36).

A practical *law* is "a principle that makes certain actions duties" (MS 6:225.1–2). Any given practical law is therefore a principle of duty, i.e., "a principle that reason prescribes [to a subject] absolutely and so objectively (how he *ought* to act)" (MS 6:225.36–37). Such a prescriptive principle of reason is an objective principle of volition (*objektive[s] Prinzip des Wollens*—GMS 4:400.35). It is objective in the sense that the condition for action which it supplies is one that "is cognized [...] as holding [*gültig*] for the will of every rational being" (KpV 5:19.11–12).

It is our cognition of this prescriptive condition's universal validity (*Allgemeingültigkeit*) which enables us to know that an objective principle of duty "would also serve subjectively as the practical principle for all rational beings if reason had complete control over the faculty of desire" (GMS 4:400.35–36). It is of course not necessarily true that reason has complete control over the faculty of desire of any actually existing rational being.[111] And we know it to be empirically false that reason has complete control over the faculty of desire of all finite rational beings. (We have merely to observe ourselves as human agents in order to know this.) Thus, not every objective principle of duty that reason prescribes necessarily serves *subjectively* as a principle of volition that holds for the will of each rational being—not even when the condition for action that it supplies necessarily holds objectively for the will of every rational being. Nonetheless, the demand that it ought so to serve is precisely what is expressed by practical reason's overarching formula for the objective principle of duty, i.e., by the most general principle of all of the differently specified objective principles that make certain actions duties. In its imperatival formulation, this supreme principle of morally practical reason applies to the actions of every rational agent like a human being simply in virtue of such a being's capacity to act on a subjective principle of volition—that is, to act on a maxim. To quote Kant's 'bare-bones' version of the so-called universal law formula for the categorical imperative: "Act on a maxim that can also hold as a universal law" (MS 6:226.1–2).[112]

§ 2 Self-Love and Material Practical Principles in Kant's Theorems of Practical Reason

The four theorems of Kant's theory of practical reason, as it is treated in §§ 2–8 of the first chapter of his second *Critique*, build upon definitional considerations like those just summarized.[113] The first two theorems present the fundamental

---

[111] The assumption here is that theoretical reason cannot prove the existence of God as *ens perfectissimum*.
[112] "handle nach einer Maxime, die zugleich als allgemeines Gesetz gelten kann".
[113] This statement presupposes that Kant's use of the terms and concepts just considered is consistent during the 1780s (starting with the *Groundwork for the Metaphysics of Morals*) through

tenets of Kant's account of empirically conditioned practical reason.[114] Theorem I states: "All practical principles that presuppose an *object* (matter) of the faculty of desire as the determining ground of the will are altogether empirical and can furnish no practical laws" [115] (KpV 5:21.14–16). According to this first theorem, if a proposition containing a general determination of the will presupposes an object of the faculty of desire as the will's determining ground, then that proposition is an empirical principle. As an empirical principle, such a proposition cannot supply a condition of action that can be cognized as holding for the will of every rational being.

The second theorem of the general account of practical reason given at the outset of the second *Critique* states: "All material practical principles are, as such, altogether of one and the same kind and belong under the general principle of self-love or one's own happiness" [116] (KpV 5:22.6–8). According to this second theorem, every possible practical principle that presupposes an object or, equivalently, some matter of the faculty of desire as the will's determining ground is the type of principle that belongs under the general principle of self-love or one's own happiness.

In view of the problematizing considerations presented in the previous chapter on empirical grounds of maxims and material determining grounds of the power of choice (see pp. 37–38), two quite obvious interpretive questions arise when Kant's basic definitional work on practical principles and propositions is taken in conjunction with what is asserted by Theorems I and II. First, why is it that no material practical principle—that is: no empirical principle that presupposes some matter of the faculty of desire as the general determining ground of the will—can *furnish* (*abgeben*) a practical law? Second, how is it possible to classify *every* material practical principle as one that falls under the general heading of 'principle of self-love or one's own happiness'?

Let us consider Kant's proof of Theorem I in view of the first question just posed. When proving Theorem I (see KpV 5:21.18–22.3), Kant maintains that

---

the 1790s (ending with the *Metaphysics of Morals*). I will not argue the assumption here, however.

114 By 'empirically conditioned' practical reason, I mean reason whose principles of action presuppose the empirically conditioned laws that apply to the sensible nature of rational beings in general. Cf. KpV 5:43.14–16.

115 "Alle praktische Principien, die ein *Object* (Materie) des Begehrungsvermögens als Bestimmungsgrund des Willens voraussetzen, sind insgesamt empirisch und können keine praktische Gesetze abgeben".

116 "Alle materiale praktische Principien sind, als solche, insgesamt von einer und derselben Art und gehören unter das allgemeine Princip der Selbstliebe oder eigenen Glückseligkeit".

when the desire for the reality of an object (*qua* matter of the faculty of desire) is the condition for a given subject's prescription to act, the pleasure that the subject takes in relation to the represented reality of its desired object is what supplies the condition under which that prescription can become a practical principle. He also asserts that this relation of pleasure in the reality of an object is never something that can be cognized a priori. Consequently, he holds that if a principle presupposes this pleasure as the condition under which it can be practical, then it must also be an empirical principle. Furthermore, in keeping with these considerations on the empirical character of material practical principles, Kant affirms that

> a principle that is based only on the subjective condition of receptivity to a pleasure or displeasure (which can always be cognized only empirically and cannot be valid in the same way for all rational beings) can indeed serve as a maxim for the subject who possesses this receptivity, but not as its *law* (because it is lacking in objective necessity, which must be cognized a priori); such a principle can, accordingly, never furnish a practical law.[117] (KpV 5:21.32–22.3)

The line of argument followed in the proof just summarized may well give rise to questions concerning the justification for Kant's apparent acceptance of hedonism as the theoretical platform for his account of sense-based desire (*sinnliche Begierde*).[118] But there is no need to become caught up in this particular issue at this point. To understand better the major issue raised by Theorem I, the following consideration will suffice: Whether or not we hold that Kant's proof of Theorem I relies on hedonistic assumptions, it still does not definitively establish that there is no possible material practical principle that can furnish a practical law. Consider, for example, what follows if the matter of my faculty of desire, i.e., the object whose reality I desire, is either the happiness of others or my own perfection as a physical being and moral agent. According to Kant's general portrayal of practical principles, matters of this sort can provide the contents of maxims that contain general determinations of the will. Such maxims, then, are practical principles that presuppose an object of the faculty of desire as the determining

---

[117] "Da nun [...] ein Princip, das sich nur auf die subjective Bedingung der Empfänglichkeit einer Lust oder Unlust (die jederzeit nur empirisch erkannt und nicht für alle vernünftige Wesen in gleicher Art gültig sein kann) gründet, zwar wohl für das Subject, das sie besitzt, zu ihrer Maxime, aber auch für diese selbst (weil es ihm an objective Nothwendigkeit, die a priori erkannt werden muß, mangelt) nicht zum *Gesetze* dienen kann, so kann ein solches Princip niemals ein praktisches Gesetz abgeben" (KpV 5:21.32–22.3).
[118] 'Sense-based desire' should here be understood as a non-technical rendering of *sinnliche Begierde*.

ground of the will. Yet it is not obvious for this reason that they are principles that cannot furnish practical laws, i.e., objective principles that supply a condition cognized as holding for the will of every possible rational being. On Kant's understanding of practical law, it seems that any maxim to promote others' happiness or to promote one's own perfection (as distinguished from one's own happiness) *must* be a principle that can furnish a practical law. Indeed, it seems that it must be a principle that can furnish such a law whether or not it is based only on the receptivity to pleasure or displeasure as a merely subjective condition for action. That is because every *principle* that prescribes the promotion of others' happiness or one's own perfection seems to be one that can furnish a practical law, and thereby the determining ground of the will, whether or not it presupposes a pleasure-based desire for the reality of such objects.

A principle is a practical proposition whether it is a maxim or a practical law. An object whose reality is desired is the matter of the faculty of desire whether or not it is the determining ground of the will. And whether or not this matter of the faculty of desire is the determining ground of the will for a subject that desires the reality of an object, it seems that a maxim to promote others' happiness or to promote one's own perfection must be a principle that can *furnish* a practical law, i.e., an objective practical principle that should determine the will of every rational being. For any principle to promote the happiness of others or one's own perfection ought to supply a determining ground of the will for all rational beings, including of course those rational beings for whom reason is not exclusively determinative of action.[119]

Perhaps, though, my treatment of Theorem I and its proof has been unduly restrictive. It may be that there is little point in taking this theorem and its supporting argument in isolation from the other theorem that supports Kant's account of empirically conditioned practical reason. Is it not the case, then, that Kant's considerations on Theorem II offer a solution to the puzzling issues just treated?

According to Kant's second theorem, all material practical principles—that is: all principles that presuppose a matter of the faculty of desire as the determining ground of the will—are principles that belong under the general principle

---

[119] It is worth noting here that Kant's ethics would end up lying in ruins if principles enjoining the promotion others' happiness and the furtherance of one's own perfection could not furnish morally practical laws. As we have seen in chapters 1 and 2, the Doctrine of Virtue is grounded in the concepts of others' happiness and own-perfection as intrinsically obligatory ends of morally practical reason, and these ends supply the matter of the practical laws that present duties of virtue. See TL 6:380.19–386.14, 6:388.31–389.32, 6:394.24–396.16.

of self-love or, equivalently, one's own happiness. This suggests that every material practical principle must be interpretable as a specification of an overarching principle—a specification that picks out a way of being motivated by self-love to achieve one's own happiness as one's own end.[120] Thus, if every material principle that can serve as my maxim must be regarded as a specifying interpretation of the own-happiness principle, it seems that we may well be on the way to understanding why no principle of this type can furnish a practical law.

And indeed, as long as the maxim on which I act does presuppose my *own* happiness as the matter of the faculty of desire, it is quite evident that no maxim of this type could furnish such a law. In order for me to think of a maxim of self-love as a practical proposition that can furnish a practical law, the following theoretical requirement would have to be fulfilled: I would have to be able to think of my own happiness as a matter of the faculty of desire that every other rational being can also presuppose for its own maxim as the determining ground of the will. But the own-happiness of each rational being cannot be the own-happiness of any other rational being. That is because the own-happiness of every rational being *is* its own. It is not, and it cannot be, the own-happiness of another. So if any maxim of mine is one that presupposes as its condition my own happiness as a matter of the faculty of desire, then that maxim can only be one that is mine *alone*, even if everyone can (and in fact does) make it a maxim to promote one's own happiness. The self-same own-happiness relation applies to any such maxim of 'yours,' of 'hers', of 'his', and (for that matter) of 'its'. No maxim that presupposes own-happiness as one's *own* object can qualify as a proposition that applies objectively and universally as a law of the will for every possible rational being. That is to say, it cannot possibly be a practical principle that can furnish a practical law. The very thought that a self-consistently self-referential egoistic maxim could furnish a universal law of the will is incoherent.

The argument that I have just presented—which, incidentally, is fully consistent with the refutations of ethical egoism that we find in the second *Critique's* first chapter[121]—does provide support for what Kant asserts in Theorem I. But of course it does so only on one condition. It must be true that all material practical principles are coherently interpretable as maxims of self-love. This condition brings us face to face with the second lead question posed above: *How* is such an interpretation possible?

---

[120] For a concise survey of the historical background of Kant's self-love theorem, see Wilson 2015. Extended discussion of this background, including systematic citation of the relevant primary and secondary sources, is found in Part IV (chapters 8–11) of this book.
[121] See KpV 5:27.20–28.5, 5:35.7–36.6.

Focusing on the idea of pleasure arising from the representation of a thing's existence, Kant's proof of Theorem II expands on the hedonistic portrayal of empirical grounds for action that we have already encountered in the proof of Theorem I. Kant maintains that such sense-based pleasure can be practical only if the feeling of agreeableness that a subject expects from the reality of a represented object is what determines that subject to desire the thing, thus determining its faculty of desire. Thus, since (a) the happiness of a rational being must be understood in terms of its consciousness of pleasure, and (b) the principle of making this happiness the supreme determining ground of the power of choice *is* the general principle of self-love, the following conclusion is evident: "[A]ll material principles, which place the determining ground of the power of choice in the pleasure or displeasure to be felt in the reality of an object, are entirely *of the same kind* insofar as they all belong to the principle of self-love or one's own happiness" [122] (KpV 5:22.21–25).

Let us concentrate on the chief difficulty that Kant's proof presents with regard to our second lead question. The difficulty can be gathered from the following considerations. At least for the sake of argument, I may be willing to accept Kant's point that the happiness of any rational being must be understood in terms of its consciousness of pleasure. Perhaps less controversially, I may also accept his point that the principle of making this happiness of each rational being the supreme determining ground of the power of choice amounts to the general principle of self-love or one's own happiness. Moreover, I may even be prepared to accept (again, for the sake of argument) Kant's conclusion that all material practical principles are of one and the same kind insofar as they belong to the principle of self-love or one's own happiness.[123] Yet none of this entails that I must also hold that all of my maxims (as material practical principles) are of one and the same kind insofar as I feel pleasure or displeasure in the reality of an object (i.e., matter) of the faculty of desire. Take, for example, maxims pertaining to the matters already mentioned: the happiness of others and one's own perfection. If it is my maxim to promote others' happiness or to promote my

---

[122] "Also sind alle materiale Principien, die den Bestimmungsgrund der Willkür in der aus irgend eines Gegenstandes Wirklichkeit zu empfindenden Lust oder Unlust setzen, so fern gänzlich von *einerlei Art*, daß sie insgesammt zum Princip der Selbstliebe oder eigenen Glückseligkeit gehören" (KpV 5:22.21–25).

[123] Indeed, it might seem to be tautologically true that all material practical principles are of one and the same kind insofar as they all belong to this one kind of principle. But Kant clearly means that all such material principles are of one and the same kind *in virtue of* their belonging to (i.e., on account of the *fact that* they belong under) the principle of self-love or one's own happiness.

own perfection as a physical and moral agent, my maxim is *not* to promote my own happiness. This is true whether or not I feel pleasure in promoting (or find displeasure in not promoting) the happiness of others or my own perfection. For if it *is* my maxim to promote either one of these ends, then it is not my maxim to take pleasure in promoting (or to find displeasure in not promoting) either the happiness of others or my own perfection. That is because the matter, i.e., the content, of my maxim cannot be my own pleasure (or the absence of my own displeasure), and therefore my own happiness,[124] as long as this maxim is a *proposition* that contains a general determination of the will. And this is true *whether or not* my maxim presupposes the happiness or the perfection of anyone (or anything, for that matter) as the determining ground of the faculty of desire. Thus, given Kant's fundamental definitional stipulations regarding practical propositions (see above, pp. 51–52), we have as yet found no reason to accept the claim that any practical principle belongs under the general principle of self-love unless one's own happiness is what supplies the propositional content—that is, the matter—of one's maxim.[125]

So much, then, for Theorems I and II, which jointly provide the grounding tenets of Kant's account of empirically conditioned practical reason in the *Critique of Practical Reason*. But there are still the two remaining theorems treated in the first chapter of this work. What about Theorems III and IV, which, taken in conjunction with the fundamental law of pure practical reason ("So act that the maxim of your will could always hold at the same time as a principle in a universal lawgiving" [126] [KpV 5:30.38–39]), provide the corresponding grounding tenets of Kant's theory of morally practical reason in the second *Critique*? Does either one of these theorems allow for an adequate reply to our lead questions?

Theorem III states: "If a rational being is to think of its maxims as practical universal laws, it can think of them only as principles that contain the determining ground of the will not by their matter but only by their mere form" [127] (KpV

---

[124] Given the hedonistic assumptions at work in Kant's proofs of Theorems I and II, the own-happiness of anyone needs to be understood in terms of (consciousness of) one's own pleasure.
[125] Henry Allison has denied that Kant requires a *hedonistic* view of sense-based motivation to establish his self-love theorem (see Allison 1990, pp. 102–103). This may be true. But the fact remains that Kant's proofs of the two theorems in question do not distinguish between egoistic and hedonistic explanatory principles (cf. Beck 1960, pp. 92, 100).
[126] "Handle so, daß die Maxime deines Willens jederzeit zugleich als Princip einer allgemeinen Gesetzgebung gelten könne".
[127] "Wenn ein vernünftiges Wesen sich seine Maximen als praktische allgemeine Gesetze denken soll, so kann es sich dieselbe nur als solche Principien denken, die nicht der Materie, sondern blos der Form nach den Bestimmungsgrund des Willens enthalten".

5:27.2–6). Somewhat elaborated, the proof of this first theorem of Kant's account of morally practical reason (see KpV 5:27.7–19) runs as follows.

Stage 1: The matter of a practical principle—in other words: the content of a proposition that contains a general determination of the will—is the object (*Gegenstand*) of the will. Given this identification, assume that the object of the will is also the will's determining ground. Under this assumption, the rule of the will (i.e., the prescription for action provided by a proposition containing a general determining ground of the will) is subject to an empirical condition. Specifically, it is subject to the condition supplied by the relation of the representation of the object of the will to the feeling of pleasure. Consequently, given the assumption at issue, that rule of the will would not be a universal law.

Stage 2: Now (a) assume that the matter of a practical proposition (which is also the object of the will) is *not* the will's determining ground; and (b) consider what can be the will's determining ground when we think of a practical law (*qua* practical proposition) in abstraction from its matter (i.e., its propositional content). Under this assumption (a), and in keeping with the correlative conceptual task just mentioned (b), all that remains of any practical law is its mere form of universal lawgiving. That is, all that remains of any practical law, once its content is thought away, is its lawgiving form (cf. KpV 5:29.17–20), i.e., its merely formal property of being apt (*tauglich*) for universal lawgiving.

Stage 3: Therefore, if a rational being is to be able to think of its maxims as being at the same time universal laws, then it must accept that what makes its maxims practical laws is nothing other than the mere form of those maxims, which is the property in virtue of which a proposition containing a general determination of the will is apt for a universal lawgiving. In other words (given the fundamental definitional stipulations considered above in the first section of this chapter), if a rational being is to be able to think of its maxims as objective principles, which apply to the determination of the will of every possible rational being, then it must accept that what makes this universally prescriptive thinking possible is a merely formal property common to all of the practical propositions that are apt for universal lawgiving—namely, the property of being prescriptive for all rational beings.

The argument just presented focuses on prescriptivity and universality as formal features of maxims *qua* practical propositions. What, then, does this focus on the formal features of such propositions offer us on our way toward dealing conclusively with our lead questions—especially our question concerning the basis of Kant's claim that no material practical principle can furnish a practical law?

Not much—if indeed that formal focus offers us anything at all. Even if we accept that Theorem III is fully established by the proof that Kant gives, our major sticking point remains as intractable as ever. Why *is* it that no material practical principle can furnish a practical law? As long as we maintain that no egoistic material principle or maxim of self-love can furnish such a law, it is simply not obvious from Theorem III that no material practical principle can be apt for a universal lawgiving. For whether or not my maxim's matter is *for me* a matter of the faculty of desire that is also the determining ground of the will, that maxim *can* be apt for universal lawgiving (provided it is so apt) *only* in virtue of its lawgiving form. After all, the whole aim of Theorem III and its proof is to demonstrate one crucial point: If we are to think of our maxims as universal laws of the will, then our thinking of practical principles must be made independent of any consideration of the non-formal features of the propositions that can furnish those laws.

So what are we left with after all this? What exactly are our prospects for definitively answering our two lead questions? What remains for consideration in this section is the fourth and final theorem of Kant's theory of practical reason. Drawing a fundamental distinction between the autonomy of the will (*Wille*) and the heteronomy of the power of choice (*Willkür*), Theorem IV asserts that the self-legislative function of the will is the sole principle of all moral laws and of the duties that are keeping with them (see KpV 5:33.9–10). What, then, does this assertion provide us with?

The supporting argument for Theorem IV does not offer anything substantively new with respect to Kant's conception of the lawgiving form of maxims. But the first of its two clarifying remarks does provide us with some additional factors to work with. Focusing on the notion of material conditions of practical prescriptions and the corresponding relationship between the matter of practical rules and the subjective conditions for their adoption, Kant argues:

> A practical prescription [*Vorschrift*] that brings with it a material (hence empirical) condition must never be reckoned a practical law. For the law of the pure will [...] puts the will in a sphere quite different from the empirical, and the necessity that a law expresses, since it is not to be a natural necessity, can therefore consist only in the formal conditions of the possibility of a law in general. All the matter of practical rules rests always on conditions which afford it[128] no universality for rational beings other than a conditional one (in case I *desire* this or that, what I would have to do in order to make it real), and they all turn on the principle *of one's own happiness*.[129] (KpV 5:34.2–11)

---

[128] I here follow the wording of the original editions, which refers "*ihr*" to "*Materie praktischer Regeln*" (KpV 5:34.7–8).
[129] "Zum praktischen Gesetze muß also niemals eine praktische Vorschrift gezählt werden, die eine materiale (mithin empirische) Bedingung bei sich führt. Denn das Gesetz des reinen Willens, der frei ist, setzt diesen in eine ganz andere Sphäre als die empirische, und die Nothwen-

§ 2 Self-Love and Kant's Theorems of Practical Reason — 61

Consider here Kant's position that the subjective conditions on which the matter of practical rules rests are conditions that do not afford this *matter* universality with respect to rational beings. Doesn't this position provide Kant with exactly what he needs in order to be able to establish that no material principle can furnish a practical law?

No, it does not. Let it be granted—contrary to fact, one may hope—that there are rational beings who of natural necessity are so constituted that none of their materially (hence empirically) conditioned prescriptions or rules can express the non-natural (i.e., moral) necessity which, as Kant puts it, can consist only in "the formal possibility of the conditions of a law in general". For example, let us assume that there is at least one rational being who by nature is so all-absorbingly self-loving that it is simply incapable of having either the happiness of anyone else or its own perfection as a moral agent as a matter of the faculty of desire[130]—that is, as a matter that could supply a subjective condition of a practical rule that a rational being would be able to adopt. Granted this assumption, we are indeed able to understand how it is *possible* for there to be a subjective condition that affords the matter of a practical rule a merely conditional universality. For if there is a rational being that desires only its own happiness, its rule of self-love will always tell it what it must do in order to make its own happiness real. That is because the matter of its purely egoistic rule of action will necessarily be such that a rational being desiring nothing but its own happiness will always act to promote *only* its own happiness, and never the happiness of another or its own perfection, whenever it acts on its subjectively conditioned rule of self-love. (Notice that this will be true even if the circumstances of own-happiness promoting action happen to be such that a rational being cannot act to promote its own happiness alone except by promoting the happiness of others or its own perfection as well. The practical rule of every exclusively egoistic being can only be furnished by its *maxim* to promote only its own happiness.[131]) The subjective condition of this type of rule will therefore afford the matter of a practical rule

---

digkeit, die es ausdrückt, da sie keine Naturnothwendigkeit sein soll, kann also blos in formalen Bedingungen der Möglichkeit eines Gesetzes überhaupt bestehen. Alle Materie praktischer Regeln beruht immer auf subjectiven Bedingungen, die ihr keine Allgemeinheit für vernünftige Wesen, als lediglich die bedingte (im Falle ich dieses oder jenes *begehre*, was ich alsdann thun müsse, um es wirklich zu machen) verschaffen, und sie drehen sich insgesammt um das Princip *der eigenen Glückseligkeit*".

130 An Epicurean god might be something like this. Or (on a substantially different plane of being) Donald Trump.

131 One implication of this consideration is that an exclusively egoistic being is not necessarily stupid (*stultus*) even if it is unavoidably an idiot (ἰδιώτης).

universality for every rational being in case each rational being can desire only its own happiness as the condition on which it acts. That is, it will afford universality to the content of the purely egoistic rule of action for every rational being who *can* act *only* on the condition just described.[132] But the description of the particular type of subjective condition of rule-determined action here in question by no means rules out the possibility of an opposing description of empirically possible subjective conditions. And according to this opposing description, some practical rules may just rest on subjective conditions that do afford these *rules* unconditional universality for rational beings, even if they do not provide such universality for the *matter* of the same rules.

As an empirically knowable matter of fact, it may well be that not every rational being is by nature capable of adopting practical rules on the basis of subjective conditions that afford universality to the matter of the rules adopted. Yet we can still know—indeed, we can know *a priori*—that there are *possible* subjective conditions which can provide a basis for the adoption of practical rules that necessarily satisfy the formal conditions of the possibility of a law in general. Moreover, we can know this even if that basis in fact happens to be supplied by a subjective condition on which the matter of a practical rule rests. For whether or not the matter of my maxim (*qua* practical rule) rests on my sense-based desire for an object as the subjective condition of my having that maxim, there are some possible matters of the faculty of desire—notably, others' happiness and one's own perfection—the desiring of which *can* be a subjective condition of my (or anyone's) having a maxim that can furnish a practical law. Even if I make it my maxim to promote one of these ends because I am *inclined* to do so on account of sense-based desire, my maxim will necessarily qualify for a universal lawgiving. This is true whether or not everyone else—or indeed anyone else—is so inclined.

It would be beside the point to attempt to derail the argument just presented by pointing out that there may well be rational beings for which the subjective conditions of sense-based desire cannot be conditions for having maxims that satisfy the strict universality requirement of morally prescriptive practical thinking. This would be beside the point because the argument presented relies on nothing more than what is required by the first theorem of Kant's account of *morally* practical reason (i.e., Theorem III of the second *Critique*): If a rational being is to think of its maxims as practical universal laws, then those maxims must be

---

[132] Note well that this is true even if (in keeping with what was argued above) we must accept that no egoistic rule can ever be reckoned a practical law, i.e., a principle that satisfies the strict universality requirement of morally practical reason.

thought of only as principles that contain the determining ground of the will not by their matter but only by their mere form. Whether or not a given maxim rests on subjective conditions that afford its matter universality for rational beings, that maxim will be one that can be thought of as a universal practical law if, and only if, it can be thought of as a principle that contains the determining ground of the will only in virtue of its universally lawgiving form. The contingent conditions of sense-based desire have nothing whatsoever to do with that. And this, after all, is the key tenet of Kant's entire theory of the relationship between empirically conditioned practical reason and the universally prescriptive role of morally practical reason. It is the tenet that makes it possible for the will's autonomy to be the sole principle of all moral laws and of the duties that are in keeping with them.[133]

§ 3 Own-Happiness, Others' Happiness, and Material Conditions of Maxims

In attempting to answer our two lead questions (see, again, p. 53), we have just had recourse to the first of the two clarifying remarks appended to Kant's account of Theorem IV in the eighth section of the second *Critique's* first chapter. As we have seen, the passage quoted above from Remark I does not provide Kant with what he needs in order to establish conclusively that no material principle

---

[133] I should point out here as well that it is beside the point to attempt to refute the arguments that I have presented by pointing to Kant's primary theoretical concern in the first chapter of the *Critique of Practical Reason*—notably, his concern to establish that the laws which determine the supersensible nature of rational beings are laws of causality through freedom (i.e., laws that are independent of any empirically conditioned laws which apply specifically to the sensible nature of those same rational beings). This is indeed the main task of Kant's Deduction of the Principles of Pure Reason (KpV 5:42.1–50.13) in chapter 1 of the second *Critique*. But the way in which Kant takes up this task depends on his *prior* proof that no material practical principle can furnish a practical law. And it is clear from the foregoing that his overall procedure of proof thus far must be judged questionable as long as there can be material principles that necessarily satisfy the strictly formal universality requirement of morally lawgiving reason. While no material principle can furnish a practical law *on account of* its being empirically conditioned, it seems there can still be empirically conditioned principles that furnish practical laws solely in virtue of their aptness for universal lawgiving—that is, solely in virtue of their universally lawgiving form. Kant's proof procedure for his theorems of practical reason has not yet shown us a reason why the objective principles provided by such maxims should not be understood as laws of freedom as long as that same procedure successfully establishes that principles can serve as laws of practical reason's autonomy only on account of their merely formal properties of universality and prescriptivity.

can furnish a universal practical law. But this is of course not to say that we have already exhausted what Kant has to offer in the course of his extended comments on Theorem IV. There are still several arguments presented in these comments that are in need of analysis in view of our lead questions. The final two sections of this chapter focus on these arguments. In this section, I consider the further line of argument that Kant follows in Remark I.

As will be evident from the passage last quoted (see again KpV 5: 5:34.2–11), Kant begins this remark by asserting that no practical precept which presupposes a material condition can ever be counted as a practical law since the necessity expressed by the law of the pure will can "consist" only in the formal possibility conditions of a law in general. He seeks to support this position by making two general claims that are in keeping with Theorems I-III: (1) All the matter of practical rules rests always on subjective conditions which can offer that matter no universality for rational beings. (2) These rules all revolve around (*drehen sich um*) the principle of one's own happiness (or self-love). He then goes on to offer the following extended argument that relates directly to his initial assertion about practical precepts which presuppose material conditions:

> It is indeed undeniable that every volition must have an object and hence a matter; but this matter is not for just that reason the determining ground and condition of the maxim; for if it is, then the maxim cannot be presented in a universally law-giving form [...]. Thus the happiness of other beings can be the object of the will of a rational being. But if it were the determining ground of the maxim, then one would have to presuppose that we find in the well-being of others not only a natural enjoyment but also a need, such as sympathetic sensibility brings with it in human beings. But I cannot presuppose this need in every rational being ([and] not at all in God). Thus, the matter of the maxim can indeed remain; but it must not be the condition of the maxim, for otherwise it would not be fit for a law. Thus, the mere form of a law, which restricts the matter, must at the same time be a ground for adding this matter to the will but not for presupposing it. Let the matter be, for example, my own happiness. Thus, if I attribute it to each (as, in the case of finite beings, I may in fact do), it can become an *objective* practical law only if I include within it the happiness of others. Thus, the law to promote the happiness of others arises not from the presupposition that this law is the object of everyone's power of choice but rather from this: that the form of universality, which reason requires as the condition for giving to a maxim of self-love the objective validity of a law, becomes the determining ground of the will; and so the object (the happiness of others) was not the determining ground of the pure will; this was instead the mere lawful form alone through which I restricted my maxim based on inclination in order to afford it the universality of a law and hence to make it suitable to pure practical reason [...].[134] (KpV 5:34.11–35.2)

---

[134] "Nun ist freilich unleugbar, daß alles Wollen auch einen Gegenstand, mithin eine Materie haben müsse; aber diese ist darum nicht eben der Bestimmungsgrund und Bedingung der Maxime; den ist sie es, so läßt diese sich nicht in allgemein gesetzgebender Form darstellen [...]. So

§ 3 Own-Happiness, Others' Happiness, and Material Conditions of Maxims — 65

Looking beyond the examples used to illustrate his basic position, we can see that Kant here characterizes what he calls the form of practical lawfulness in four distinct (or at least four differently worded) ways: as the universally lawgiving form in which a maxim can be presented; as the mere form of a law that restricts the matter of a maxim; as the form of universality that provides the condition for giving a maxim the objective validity of law; and finally, as mere lawful form through which a maxim founded on inclination is subject to restriction. He does not fully clarify, with reference to each of these general characterizations, the connection between the determining grounds and conditions of maxims and the determining ground of the will. Moreover, keeping in mind what he wants to prove about the relationship between practical laws and the objects of volition and the will, there seems to be considerable terminological imprecision involved in his references to happiness as an objective practical law and to law as *object* of the power of choice. As a result, the thread of argumentation in the passage as a whole is not easy to follow. But the basic position articulated is clearly this: No matter how the happiness of others[135] is made the object of a particular volition and the object of the will, it cannot be presupposed as the determining ground and the material (i.e., non-formal) condition of any maxim that could furnish an objective practical law; nor can it supply the determining ground of the kind of will that is governable by any such law. On the one hand, if the happiness of others is both the matter of my maxim and the object

---

wird fremder Wesen Glückseligkeit das Object des Willens eines vernünftigen Wesens sein können. Wäre sie aber der Bestimmungsgrund der Maxime, so müßte man voraussetzen, daß wir in dem Wohlsein anderer nicht allein ein natürliches Vergnügen, sondern auch ein Bedürfniß finden, so wie die sympathetische Sinnesart bei Menschen es mit sich bringt. Aber dieses Bedürfniß kann ich nicht bei jedem vernünftigen Wesen (bei Gott gar nicht) voraussetzen. Also kann zwar die Materie der Maxime bleiben, sie muß aber nicht die Bedingung derselben sein, denn sonst würde diese nicht zum Gesetze taugen. Also die bloße Form eines Gesetzes, welches die Materie einschränkt, muß zugleich ein Grund sein, diese Materie zum Willen hinzuzufügen, aber sie nicht vorauszusetzen. Die Materie sei z. B. meine eigene Glückseligkeit. Diese, wenn ich sie jedem beilege (wie ich es denn in der That bei endlichen Wesen thun darf), kann nur alsdann ein *objectives* praktisches Gesetz werden, wenn ich anderer ihre in dieselbe mit einschließe. Also entspringt das Gesetz, anderer Glückseligkeit zu befördern, nicht von der Voraussetzung, daß dieses ein Object für jedes seine Willkür sei, sondern blos daraus, daß die Form der Allgemeinheit, die die Vernunft als Bedingung bedarf, einer Maxime der Selbstliebe die objective Gültigkeit eines Gesetzes zu geben, der Bestimmungsgrund des Willens wird, und also war das Object (anderer Glückseligkeit) nicht der Bestimmungsgrund des reinen Willens, sondern die bloße gesetzliche Form war es allein, dadurch ich meine auf Neigung gegründete Maxime einschränkte, um ihr die Allgemeinheit eines Gesetzes zu verschaffen und sie so der reinen praktischen Vernunft angemessen zu machen [...]".
135 Kant's term here is *fremde Wesen*.

of my volition and will, then my maxim must lack the universality of a practical law if it presupposes that matter as its condition. Consequently, as long as this matter is the condition of my maxim as well as the object of my volition and will, my maxim's matter (i.e., its propositional content) cannot supply any determining ground of the will that could make that maxim presentable in a universally lawgiving form, and hence make it fit for being a practical law the form of which restricts the maxim's matter.[136] On the other hand, if the happiness of others is not the material condition of my maxim, but still can be the object of my volition and will, then the form of universality alone supplies a determining ground of the will that enables me to include that object in the matter of a maxim that can be afforded the universality of a practical law.

Let us just grant the soundness of the second stage of Kant's reasoning and concentrate on the pivotal step of the first stage. In the passage quoted, this step is formulated subjunctively as a complex hypothetical statement, whose content I here reformulate in the indicative mood: If the happiness of other beings is the determining ground of a maxim, then (a) we must derive enjoyment from the well-being of others; and (b) we must experience the kind of need that is produced in (some) humans on account of sympathetic sensibility. It is on the basis of this statement that Kant goes on to conclude that the matter of the maxim (i.e., the happiness of other beings) can remain the object of the relevant volition and the will, although it cannot furnish the condition of the maxim in question *if* this maxim is to be suitable for an objective practical law.

Now we can see that the attempt to draw precisely this inference is beset by significant difficulties if we entertain the possibility that others' happiness can be an object (or matter) of the faculty of desire that we are inclined to promote on account of sympathetic need. In shedding light on these difficulties, we may first note the source of one minor irritation: What exactly is the role played by requirement (a) in Kant's further inference? We can assume that Kant thinks the enjoyment derived from the well-being of others results from the satisfaction of a human sympathetic need regarding others.[137] But even granting this assumption, it is still not clear why the object of this apparently other-directed need (i.e., the well-being of others) should not be at least *a* condition of a maxim that can furnish an objective practical law when the need concerns the

---

[136] I suppose here that the matter of the maxim in question is the same as the object of volition and the will, whether or not this object or matter furnishes both the determining ground of the maxim and the determining ground of the will. This supposition is warranted in view of Kant's definitional stipulations in the Analytic of Pure Practical Reason (see KpV 5:19.7–16, 5:21.14–18, 5:27.1–19, 5:28.31–29.1, 5:29.14–22, 5:33.12–13/21–26).

[137] Cf. BDG 2:215.33–216.10, 2:217.26–218.11; GMS 4:413.26–24; MS 6:456.20–33.

§ 3 Own-Happiness, Others' Happiness, and Material Conditions of Maxims — 67

happiness of others in general.[138] Nor is it apparent why the object of the inclination involving this sympathetic need should not be a condition that is *sufficient* for a maxim to have the form of universality, or to be presentable in a universally lawgiving form, as long as one is inclined by sympathetic need to promote the happiness of others.

These difficulties remain, although we may take Kant's cue and endorse the proposition that sympathetic need as such cannot be attributed to all rational beings or, for that matter, to all human beings. For it is simply not evident from these reasons alone that the object of the need and inclination in question should not supply a *condition* of a maxim that can be presented in a universally lawgiving form. There is nothing obvious in the concept of maxims' matter that could keep such a maxim from being so presented.[139] Moreover, there is no immediately apparent reason why a maxim that presupposes the happiness of others as its particular (i.e., non-universal) condition should be unable to furnish an objective practical law as long as the maxim's matter can be restricted (just as Kant maintains it can be) by the mere form of that law as given. Why, then, should the maxim not provide for a law of the will when the need is the result of, or goes hand in hand with, the inclination to promote others' happiness? When a being having that need act from this inclination, the particular condition of her maxim of benevolence will perforce include the happiness of others; and her maxim with its matter (i.e., the happiness of others) can be given the universality of a practical law since, as Kant maintains, the mere form of such a law can restrict the maxim's matter. As a rational agent, then, this being ought to be able to acknowledge that a maxim of other-directed benevolence can provide for a law of the will which morally necessitates action even in the absence of all inclination, and thus quite apart from any condition that presupposes the inclination to bring about others' happiness. But she should also be able to identify

---

138 I assume here that well-being is a necessary but not a sufficient condition of happiness. But I am likely being overly scrupulous since Kant does not draw a clear distinction between the concepts of well-being and happiness in any of the passages that I analyze or cite. Indeed, on at least one occasion he explicitly equates the two concepts when referring to the happiness of others (see TL 6:452.26–27).

139 Kant himself recognizes that each of us has the duty to promote others' happiness by making the morally permissible ends of others our own ends (see TL 6:387.24–388.30, 6:450.30–454.28). Making others' *ends* one's own, of course, is subject to the formal restrictions imposed by reason's universal lawgiving since there are many maxims of ends that cannot be presented in a universally lawgiving form. But the *matter* of a maxim of other-directed benevolence—namely, the happiness of others—is such that this kind of maxim can always be presented in a universally lawgiving form precisely in virtue of its conformity to morally practical reason's the fundamental universality requirement.

this as a law that *necessarily* commands her to act precisely as she is inclined to act whenever the particular condition of her having that maxim of benevolence is in fact the sympathetically attuned inclination to promote the happiness of others. We may well grant, in agreement with Kant, that a rational agent must be moved to act beneficently toward others even without inclination when she understands the restrictive demand placed upon the matters (i.e., the propositional contents) of all maxims by universally lawgiving practical reason. But that does not mean that a human agent will meet this demand only contingently when acting from benevolent inclination on her maxim to promote the happiness of others. Thus, provided that such a maxim's matter can be subject to the restrictions imposed by morally practical reason's universally prescriptive procedure of self-legislative thinking, the maxim will be capable of furnishing a practical law, i.e., a principle containing a determination that holds objectively for the will of every rational being (cf. KpV 5:19.7–12). To be sure, we cannot assume that the maxim presupposes a condition that holds for the will of each given subject—or, for that matter, for the will of any actually existing subject capable of exercising practical reason's universally lawgiving function. Yet, given the basic relation between the matter and the conditions of maxims, the maxim of benevolence in question will still be able to serve as the principle of a universal lawgiving. It will therefore supply an objective principle that prescribes beneficent action as a duty that applies to all rational agents.[140]

We can thus see that the conclusion of the first stage of Kant's argument does not necessarily follow if the happiness of others can be a maxim's particular need-based condition as well as its matter. Or at least that conclusion would not follow if Kant had not already explicitly made it a fundamental theorem of his practical philosophy that all material practical principles derive from the general principle of self-love or one's own happiness. Now the acceptance of this theorem clearly does put Kant in a position to contend that the maxim which presupposes the object of a human sympathetic need as an object of one's volition and will is not one which could furnish an objective practical law. Specifically, it gives him the platform for insisting that this kind of maxim could not be presented in a universally lawgiving form since its particular non-formal (i.e., material) condition can be explained reductively in terms of an intrinsically particularized form of love—namely, self-love understood as predominant benevolence toward oneself. But given the relation between lawgiving form and this kind of condition in the case of maxims founded on sympatheti-

---

[140] These considerations apply *a fortiori* to maxims of universal benevolence, i.e., to maxims the matter of which is the happiness of everyone. On this, see TL 6:450.15–451.19.

cally attuned benevolent inclination, it seems equally clear that Kant should be able to establish conclusively that all material practical principles are *in fact* based on the principle of self-love. For in the context of the second *Critique*, this is the only avenue actually indicated for *preventing* maxims like these from having the universality of a practical law as long as their matter can be restricted by that law's mere form. That is to say: Kant must demonstrate that any maxim founded on sympathetic need involving other-directed benevolent inclination is excluded from the set of maxims which *necessarily* fall under the highest formal practical principle of pure reason (i.e., the moral law). But to do this, his only available option is apparently to suppose that such a maxim is in reality (i.e., despite appearances) a principle founded on the inclination to promote one's own happiness over and above everything else. For at least in view of what Kant has offered thus far, this seems to be the only way to establish that no maxim of other-directed benevolence can fulfill morally practical reason's fundamental universality requirement in case one comes to have it on account of being sympathetically inclined to promote the happiness of others.

Then again, perhaps we have just not gone far enough since we have yet to examine the use to which Kant puts the concept of *universal* happiness in the second explanatory remark to Theorem IV.

§ 4 Maxims, Practical Laws, and Universal Happiness

I refer here to the considerations on the relationship between the concepts of practical law and universal happiness that are meant to buttress the argument of Remark I, which we have just examined. Remark II is primarily intended to show that when one's own happiness is made the determining ground of the will, the result must be the "direct opposite [*Widerspiel*] of the principle of morality" (KpV 5:35.7). But Kant also means to bring out the insurmountable contingency of the connection between all possible maxims yielded by the principle of happiness and the maxims that can be established as universal rules of reason's lawgiving. Insisting on this contingency, he argues that no maxim can serve as a practical law if it is based on the principle of happiness. Specifically, he contends that no such maxim can serve as a law of the will even if it is yielded by the most general interpretation of this eudaimonistic principle:

> The principle of happiness can indeed deliver maxims, but never such as would be fit to be laws of the will, even if one were to make *universal* happiness one's object. For, because cognition of this rests on sheer data of experience, as each judgment about it depends very much upon the opinion of each (which in addition can be very changeable), it can

> give *general* but never *universal* rules, that is, it can give rules that on the average most often hit the mark, but it cannot give rules that must hold always and necessarily; hence no practical *laws* can be based on it Just because an object of the power of choice is here put at the basis of its rule and must therefore precede it, the rule can be referred to and can be based upon nothing other than what one approves [*emphielt*], and so it refers to and is based upon experience, and then the variety of judgment must be endless. This principle, therefore, does not prescribe exactly the same practical rules to all rational beings, even though these rules fall under a common heading—namely, that of happiness. The moral law, however, is thought of as objectively necessary only because it is to hold for everyone who has reason and will.[141] (KpV 5:36.9 – 16).

This argument, too, is not easy to construe with precision since Kant does not spell out the connection between the principle of happiness (*sans phrase*) that can deliver maxims and the cognition of *universal* happiness that can give only general rules. But Kant clearly maintains that our cognition of universal happiness is empirically grounded because it depends on the changeable opinion-based judgments of each. He also holds that not even the cognition of universal happiness can provide for universal rules on account of the endless variety of experience-based judgment. Moreover, it is evident that the Kant's argument hinges on the subjunctively formulated supposition that universal happiness *could* (conceivably) be one's object (and thus, presumably, an object of the power of choice).

Looking back at the line of inquiry pursued in this chapter, the interesting thing about this last pivotal supposition is that it seems, in one fell swoop, to offer us a way of freeing ourselves from the yoke of the two questions that have determined the course of our investigation up to this point. Kant's concessive use of this supposition suggests that not even a maxim of *universal* benevolence can furnish a practical law as long as it is a material practical principle

---

[141] "Das Princip der Glückseligkeit kann zwar Maximen, aber niemals solche abgeben, die zu Gesetzen des Willens tauglich wären, selbst wenn man sich die *allgemeine* Glückseligkeit zum Objecte machte. Denn weil dieser ihre Erkenntniß auf lauter Erfahrungsdatis beruht, weil jedes Urtheil darüber gar sehr von jedes seiner Meinung, die noch dazu selbst sehr veränderlich ist, abhängt, so kann es wohl *generelle*, aber niemals *universelle* Regeln, d. i. solche, die im Durchschnitte am öftersten zutreffen, nicht aber solche, die jederzeit und nothwendig gültig sein müssen, geben, mithin können keine praktische *Gesetze* darauf gegründet werden. Eben darum weil hier ein Object der Willkür der Regel derselben zum Grunde gelegt und also vor dieser vorhergehen muß, so kann diese nicht worauf anders als auf das, was man empfiehlt, und also auf Erfahrung bezogen und darauf gegründet werden, und da muß die Verschiedenheit des Urtheils endlos sein. Dieses Princip schreibt also nicht allen vernünftigen Wesen eben dieselbe praktische Regeln vor, ob sie zwar unter einem gemeinsamen Titel, nämlich dem der Glückseligkeit, stehen. Das moralische Gesetz wird aber nur darum als objectiv nothwendig gedacht, weil es für jedermann gelten soll, der Vernunft und Willen hat".

§ 4 Maxims, Practical Laws, and Universal Happiness — 71

that presupposes the happiness of everyone as the determining ground of the will (cf. KpV 5:21.14–15). Thus, if this suggestion bears weight, it may follow that Kant would not have to rely on his self-love theorem (i.e., Theorem II in his account of empirically conditioned practical reason) in order to prove that *no* maxim that has an object of benevolent inclination as its material condition can qualify for a possible universal lawgiving. For if not even a maxim that has the universal object of happiness-promoting action as its condition can so qualify, then it might be the case that there is no need to establish that *every* material practical principle must belong under the general principle of self-love or one's own happiness. So by all means: let it be granted that universal happiness *can* be a material condition of a maxim as well as the same maxim's matter!

Does the liberating suggestion just mentioned bear weight, though? Does Kant's use of his pivotal supposition concerning universal happiness indicate a way of *not* having to rely on the self-love theorem in order to establish that no material practical principle can furnish a practical law, thus bringing this chapter's line of inquiry to an abrupt (though happy) end?

It does not. For Kant neglects to distinguish between two quite separate issues in the passage under consideration: (1) the question of the derivation of maxims from the principle of happiness as a material practical principle; and (2) the question of the employment of such a principle as the basis for determining what maxims can furnish practical laws on account of their aptness for universal lawgiving.

Kant certainly ought to have addressed the implications of this distinction when arguing his position on the moral law's relation to universal happiness and its empirical cognition. For if the distinction is clearly drawn, then it is quite possible for us to take Kant's position that no practical law can be *based* on any principle of happiness—not even on one that employs the concept of universal happiness—and yet to maintain as well that the connection between the formal requirement of reason's lawgiving and the matter of maxims yielded by the principle of happiness is not in every instance contingent. In other words, even if we hold that no practical law can be grounded in the principle of happiness, we may nonetheless coherently maintain (a) that the principle of happiness (*sans phrase*) can *deliver* maxims which necessarily satisfy the universality requirement of the moral law as a formal principle of duty; and (b) that this formal principle is therefore what grounds such maxims *as* practical laws?

Let us take here as an example a maxim that Kant's concessive supposition concerning universal happiness most obviously suggests—namely, the maxim to promote the happiness of everyone.[142] Kant's use of that supposition does not by itself bring to light any reason why this maxim of universal benevolence should be excluded from the set of maxims that satisfy morally practical reason's formal lawgiving criterion (i.e., universality), even if it is "delivered" by the principle of happiness. For though the maxim's *matter* may be said to derive from the general principle of happiness, its lawgiving form can still provide the determining ground of the will for all rational agents, including those who are inclined to promote the happiness of others as well as those who are not so inclined. Moreover, any agent who *may* be so inclined will necessarily fulfill the requirements of reason's lawgiving whenever she acts on a maxim to promote the happiness of others, and indeed the happiness of everyone. That is because the maxim on which she acts, even when acting on such inclination, just can be presented in a universally lawgiving form. As a practical proposition, it satisfies the demands of universality and necessity at issue in any principle that can serve as a practical law for all rational agents, including those agents who, taken individually, may be positively disinclined to promote the happiness of anyone except themselves. To be sure, agents like these may not have the happiness of others (let alone the happiness of everyone) as a material *condition* of any of their maxims. But any maxim of benevolence that includes others' happiness in its matter will still be able to furnish a principle that holds objectively for the will of all possible rational agents as long as its lawgiving form can provide the determining ground of the will.[143]

§ 5 A Question of Practical Anthropology?

The preceding considerations in this chapter have primarily been intended to clarify the indispensable the role played by the self-love theorem in the second *Critique's* account of the relationship between material practical principles and universal practical laws. In examining this role, I have mainly been concerned to establish the following point: The view of material practical principles at

---

142 Having such a maxim is not (necessarily) to be subject to a delusion of moralistic grandeur. Consider the maxim of benevolence at issue in, say, Jonas Salk's decision to make the polio vaccine available to everyone without the encumbrance of patenting restrictions. Whoever finds oneself in a similar position to act on a maxim of universal benevolence will know what one morally ought to do.

143 This will be true even if the maxim is one of universal benevolence that happens to be founded on the inclination to promote the happiness of others in general, but *not* the happiness of everyone.

§ 5 A Question of Practical Anthropology? — 73

issue in the self-love theorem is what provides the basis upon which Kant can maintain his position that no empirical practical principle, hence no empirically grounded maxim, can serve as a practical law. While attempting to complete this task, however, I have ignored a significant problem for Kant's metaphysics of morals that is implicit in his use of the second *Critique*'s self-love theorem. I already mentioned an aspect of this problem in passing, when discussing the 'worrying systematic implication' (chapter 1, p. 28) of Kant's claim that any human being unavoidably has his own happiness as his end. But it will now be appropriate to address the problem in its entirety.

In his critical metaphysics of morals, Kant insists on keeping the purely rational concepts, laws and principles of moral philosophy strictly separate from the empirical elements of practical anthropology.[144] This is not to say that he treats the a priori part of the doctrine of morals in isolation from empirical psychological concepts and observations about the special nature of human beings. He holds, indeed, that such elements must brought into the formulation of the system of pure morality (*Sittlichkeit*).[145] Still, he maintains that their integration with this system cannot detract from the purity of the highest principles and fundamental a priori concepts of morality themselves, or cast any doubt on the a priori origin of all practical laws in pure reason alone.[146] Within the system of the metaphysics of morals, the pure part of moral philosophy must therefore be logically dissociated from any particular theory of human nature that includes the principles of a specifically human moral psychology. This measure is mandatory if moral philosophy is not to rely on empirical assumptions

---

144 For recent consideration of these elements, see Frierson 2003, pp. 31–37.
145 See, for example, KrV A14–15/B28–29; KpV 5:8.4–9.41; MS 6:216.34–217.18. In Part II of the *Groundwork* Kant does refer to the indispensability of a "completely isolated metaphysics of morals" (GMS 4:410.19). But there his concern is to confirm the architectonic integrity of his metaphysical project by clarifying how it contrasts with the various forms of "mixed moral doctrine" (GMS 4:411.3) favored by popular taste. These doctrines are all "compounded from incentives arising from feelings and inclinations and at the same time from rational concepts" (GMS 4:411.3–5), and they are unable to offer any firm criteria for the proper integration of empirical elements with the systematic treatment of purely rational concepts, laws and principles. Kant's claim is that his method of deriving the fundamental concepts, laws and principles of moral philosophy from their source in pure reason is what allows for this integration.
146 Kant maintains that the principles of morality are to be found "completely a priori, free from everything empirical, simply in pure concepts of reason and nowhere else" (GMS 410.11–13). These concepts, together with the laws that they contain, must be "drawn from pure reason" and presented "pure and unmixed" (GMS 411.18–20). Consequently, the principles of morality may not "be made to depend on the special nature of human reason", but must rather be "derived from the universal concept of a rational being in general because moral laws should hold good for every rational being as such" (GMS 4:411.23–412.1).

about the conditions of human volition when, on the basis of its pure part, it plays its distinctive legislative role for humans beings as rational agents. As Kant states in the *Groundwork for the Metaphysics of Morals*, "all moral philosophy rests wholly upon its pure part, and, when applied to the human being, it borrows not the least thing from the knowledge of that being (anthropology), but rather gives to the human being, as a rational being, laws a priori" [147] (GMS 4:389.26–30). Accordingly, the foundation-laying task of the metaphysical theory of morals must be to investigate the "idea and the principles of a possible *pure* will, and not the actions and conditions of human volition as such, which for the most part are drawn from psychology" [148] (GMS 4:390.34–37). Despite the shift in theoretical emphasis from principles of the will to those of the power of choice that takes place between the *Groundwork* and the *Metaphysics of Morals* itself,[149] Kant's position on this task remains fundamentally unchanged in the latter work. We can discern Kant's consistency in this regard by considering the following important passage from general introduction to the *Metaphysics of Morals*:

> If [...] a system of a priori cognition from concepts alone is called *metaphysics*, a practical philosophy, which has not nature but freedom of the power of choice for its object, will presuppose and require a metaphysics of morals, that is, it is itself a *duty* to *have* such a metaphysics, and every human being also has it within himself, though as a rule only in an obscure way; for without a priori principles how could he believe that he has a giving of universal law within himself? But [...] a metaphysics of morals cannot dispense with principles of application, and we shall often have to take as our object the particular *nature* of human beings, which is cognized only by experience, in order to *show* in it what can be inferred from universal moral principles. But this will in no way detract from the purity of these principles or cast doubt on their a priori source.—That is to say, in effect, that a metaphysics of morals cannot be based upon anthropology but can still be applied to it.
>
> The counterpart of a metaphysics of morals, the other member of the division of practical philosophy as a whole, would be moral anthropology, which would contain only the subjective conditions in human nature that hinder or aid in the *fulfillment* [*Ausführung*] of

---

147 "alle Moralphilosophie beruht gänzlich auf ihrem reinen Theil, und auf den Menschen angewandt, entlehnt sie nicht das mindeste von der Kenntniß desselben (Anthropologie), sondern giebt ihm, als vernünftigem Wesen, Gesetze *a priori* [...]" (GMS 4:389.26–30).
148 "Denn die Metaphysik der Sitten soll die Idee und die Principien eines möglichen *reinen* Willens untersuchen und nicht die Handlungen und Bedingungen des menschlichen Wollens überhaupt, wleche größtentheils aus der Psychologie geschöpft werden" (GMS 4:390.34–37). See also GMS 4:408.12–414.25, 4:425.12–427.18; KpV 5:31.10–33; MS 6:216.28–217.8.
149 I have not paid special attention to this well-known shift, especially as it applies to Kant's change of focus from 'determining grounds of the will' (in the second *Critique*) to 'determining grounds of the power of choice' (in the introduction to the Doctrine of Virtue). I have not done so because nothing in this book's argument depends on dealing with it.

the laws of a metaphysics of morals. [...] It cannot be dispensed with, but it must not precede a metaphysics of morals or be mixed with it [...].[150] (MS 6:216.28–217.18)

In view of what Kant maintains in this passage, the key difficulty that emerges from his use of the self-love theorem is the following: His exclusion of all empirically grounded maxims, and indeed all material practical principles in general, from qualification for possible universal lawgiving and service as practical laws seems to *depend* on the kind of supposition about sensible and empirical grounds that can only belong to practical anthropology. To rely on this supposition, of course, is not tantamount to mixing an anthropological condition with the a priori principles of the metaphysics of morals. But it arguably does amount to making such a condition a presupposition of the latter, if the supposition in question is in fact the basis for establishing that no empirically grounded maxim can qualify for a possible universal lawgiving and that no material practical principle can furnish a practical law.

As far as the *Critique of Practical Reason* is concerned, one may well wish to deflect the force of this argument by maintaining that it unjustifiably places exaggerated emphasis on issues of merely preliminary concern to Kant in the first chapter of the Analytic of Pure Practical Reason. Thus, one may hold that Kant's definitional work on practical principles, maxims, and laws, as well as his proofs of the theorems pertaining to empirically conditioned practical reason, pale in significance when compared with his discussion of Theorems III and IV—not

---

150 "Wenn daher ein System der Erkenntniß a priori aus bloßen Begriffen *Metaphysik* heißt, so wird eine praktische Philosophie, welche nicht Natur, sondern die Freiheit der Willkür zum Objecte hat, eine Metaphysik der Sitten voraussetzen und bedürfen: d. i. eine solche zu *haben* ist selbst Pflicht, und jeder Mensch hat sie auch, obzwar gemeiniglich nur auf dunkle Art in sich; denn wie könnte er ohne Principien a priori eine allgemeine Gesetzgebung in sich zu haben glauben? So [...] wird es [...] eine Metaphysik der Sitten daran nicht können mangeln lassen, und wir werden oft die besondere Natur des Menschen, die nur durch Erfahrung erkannt wird, zum Gegenstande nehmen müssen, um an ihr die Folgerungen aus den allgemeinen moralischen Principien zu *zeigen*, ohne daß jedoch dadurch der Reinigkeit der letzteren etwas benommen, noch ihr Ursprung a priori dadurch zweifelhaft gemacht wird.—Das will so viel sagen als: eine Metaphysik der Sitten kann nicht auf Anthropologie gegründet, aber doch auf sie angewandt werden.

Das Gegenstück einer Metaphysik der Sitten, als das andere Glied der Eintheilung der praktischen Philosophie überhaupt, würde die moralische Anthropologie sein, welche, aber nur die subjective, hindernde sowohl als begünstigende Bedingungen der *Ausführung* der Gesetze der ersteren in der menschlichen Natur, die Erzeugung, Ausbreitung und Stärkung moralischer Grundsätze [...] und dergleichen andere sich auf Erfahrung gründende Lehren und Vorschriften enthalten würde, und die nicht entbehrt werden kann, aber durchaus nicht vor jener vorausgeschickt, oder mit ihr vermischt werden muß [...]".

to mention his presentation of the fundamental law of pure practical reason. Similarly, one may wish to point out that, whatever problematic issues may be raised by Kant's opening treatment of all four of the theorems discussed above, they have no profound impact on what Kant goes on to accomplish in the thematic centerpiece of the Analytic's first chapter, i.e., in the Deduction of the Principles of Pure Practical Reason. One might insist, then, that it is with this deduction that the really distinctive work of a critique of practical reason is taken up. Specifically, one may argue, it is in the context of the deduction of pure practical reason's principles that Kant first gets down to the real work of showing that pure reason can be practical. For only in connection with this deduction does he undertake to establish that the laws of practical reason are laws of causality through freedom, i.e., laws that determine the supersensible nature of rational beings independently of any empirical conditions of volition which apply to such beings' sensible nature (see KpV 5: 42.3–43.34). In brief, one may want to hold that my excessive concern with Kant's account of material practical principles and empirically grounded maxims in the second *Critique* is simply overpowered by Kant's "deduction of freedom as a causality of pure reason" (KpV 5:48.2–3) because I have ignored the crucial concept required for making sense of how pure reason can be practical, namely, "the concept which it [reason] makes of its own causality as noumenon" (KpV 5:49.36–50.1).

I beg to differ. While I have indeed ignored this concept up to the present juncture, I have by no means neglected the condition on which it makes sense for Kant to take up the question of transcendental freedom as it relates to the fundamental concept of his metaphysics of morals: the concept of universal practical law. For the way in which Kant takes up that question depends on his *prior* proof that no material practical principle can furnish a practical law. And it is clear from the investigations undertaken in this chapter that his overall procedure of proof must be judged questionable as long as there can be material principles that necessarily satisfy the strictly formal universality requirement of morally lawgiving reason. While no material principle can furnish a practical law *on account of* its being empirically conditioned, there can still be empirically conditioned principles that furnish practical laws solely in virtue of their aptness for universal lawgiving—that is, solely in virtue of their universally lawgiving form—*unless* it is true that all material practical principles belong under the general principle of self-love or one's on happiness.

Thus, taken apart from its reliance on this principle, Kant's overall proof procedure for his theorems of practical reason does not show us a reason why the apparently objective principles provided by such maxims should not able to furnish practical laws, as long as that same procedure successfully establishes that principles can serve as the laws of practical reason's autonomy only on account of their merely formal properties of universality and prescriptivity. And unless the self-love theorem's view of material practical principles is presupposed by the deduction of pure practical reason's principles, it is unclear why the concept of reason's causality as noumenon should even be specifically relevant to a doctrine of the *laws* of practical reason, i.e., to a doctrine of the laws of freedom of the type that Kant presents in his metaphysics of morals.[151]

The implications of Kant's logical reliance on the anthropological assumptions at issue in the self-love theorem will continue to occupy us, above all when we explore the historical and developmental background of that reliance in Part IV of this book. Bearing it in mind as a problem, then, let us turn to the question of moral worth that emerges from Kant's theory practical reason's obligatory ends.

---

151 As Paul Guyer has made clear (evidently with some rhetorical exaggeration), he considers "Kant's theory that we have a noumenally free will that always allows us to do the right thing no matter what our inclinations" to amount to "a fairy-tale" (Guyer 2012, p. 17). While I generally tend to agree with Guyer's views on noumenal causation (see, e.g., Guyer 2007, pp. 458–462; contrast Allison 2007, 483–487), it may be noted here that nothing that I have argued in the last two paragraphs supports the blanket assessment of Kantian transcendental freedom which is implicit in Guyer's remark. It suffices for this book's argument to show that the way in which Kant broaches the question of transcendental freedom in the second *Critique's* systematic context depends on his establishing that no material practical principle can furnish a practical law.

Part II Moral Worth and Motivation in Kant and Hume

Since chapter 2, we have been following the thread of a problem that arises from Kant's treatment of others' happiness and own-perfection as intrinsically obligatory ends: When accounting for the grounding relation between ends of action and maxims that is distinctive of ethics as a doctrine of virtue, Kant does not seem to be able to establish conclusively that there is no empirically grounded maxim which can furnish a practical law unless he can show that all of the ends providing empirical grounds of maxims are self-seeking ends, i.e., ends that one is inclined to bring about in order to promote one's own happiness. Without this tenet being at least implicitly in play, it is not clear why we should have to hold that there is no possible empirically grounded maxim which can satisfy morally practical reason's universality requirement, even if we *also* hold that empirical grounds of maxims cannot yield the a priori concept of duty that applies to the objectively necessary ends.[1] The happiness of others, for example, is necessarily an end that one ought to seek to bring about. Thus, although an agent's maxim to promote it may happen to be empirically grounded in benevolent sensible impulse or in an inclination to do well for others, such a maxim should be able to furnish a practical law in virtue of its qualification for a universal lawgiving unless some further condition obtains. And the condition, it seems, must be this: The end that the agent seeks to bring about is in reality a self-seeking end of predominantly self-benevolent inclination *just because* her maxim has as its empirical ground in an end she is inclined to promote.

As we have seen in chapter 3, this condition for establishing that no empirically grounded maxim can furnish a universal practical law is entirely consistent with the account of the relationship between reason's lawgiving and material practical principles that Kant offers in the opening sections of the *Critique of Practical Reason*. In fact, the position that Kant takes in the 1797 introduction to Doctrine of Virtue regarding empirical grounds of maxims and self-seeking ends had already implicitly been given theorematic expression in this second *Critique* when Kant asserted that all material practical principles belong under the general principle of self-love or one's own happiness. The second main phase of our investigations in this book therefore begins with the assessment that the key conclusion provisionally drawn in chapter 2 is fundamentally sound: The con-

---

[1] See chapter 2, pp. 40 and 46.

https://doi.org/10.1515/9783110517408-006

ception of material practical principles at issue in the second *Critique's* self-love theorem can be drawn upon to support the portrayal of empirically grounded maxims that Kant provides in the context of his later theory of intrinsically obligatory ends.

Given this assessment, Part II of our project has two main tasks. The first is to show why combining the implications of the self-love theorem with the concepts of others' happiness and own-perfection as obligatory ends necessarily leads to the question of moral worth. The second task is to treat Kant's understanding of the moral worth of actions against the backdrop of an opposing view—specifically, against the view of actions' moral worth at issue in David Hume's theory of morals.

Chapter 4 Eudaimonistic Etiology, Own-Perfection, and Moral Worth

This relatively brief chapter builds a bridge between the problems generated by Kant's theory of obligatory ends in the *Metaphysics of Morals* and the doctrine of the moral worth of actions that furnishes the subject matter of chapter 5. In the first section of the current chapter I examine what follows when the obligatory-end concepts of others' happiness and own-perfection are taken in conjunction with the view of motivation at issue in the second *Critique*'s self-love theorem. Accordingly, I trace the ramifications of Kant's position that maxims adopted according to ends which provide empirical grounds of action are principles of volition whose grounds are all self-seeking ends. In this way I spell out what is entailed when we actually pursue the argument strategy made available by the self-love theorem in order to justify Kant's standpoint that no empirically grounded maxim can furnish a universal practical law. In the second section I clarify how the pursuit of this strategy, as it applies others' happiness and own-perfection as ends that are also duties, leads to Kant's conception of the moral worth of actions. In the third section I set the stage for considering this conception (in chapter 5) by treating a basic tenet of the kind of account of moral worth that Kant diametrically opposes.

§ 1 Eudaimonistic Etiology and the Happiness of Others

In the preface to the Doctrine of Virtue, Kant discusses a general approach to the theory of morals that he explicitly opposes. This competing approach, which shares the view of the empirical motivating grounds of action that underlies the second *Critique*'s self-love theorem, attempts to reduce the principle of duty required by the metaphysics of morals to terms consistent with a doctrine of happiness. In the following passage, Kant lays bare the explanatory circle and logical contradiction that he takes to be part and parcel of this kind of attempt:

> The thinking human being, namely, if he has been victorious over the incentives [*Anreize*] to vice and is aware of having done his often bitter duty, finds himself in a state of satisfaction and peace of mind that could well be called happiness, a state in which virtue is its own reward.—Now the *eudaimonist* says: this bliss, this happiness is the real motive for his acting virtuously. The concept of duty does not *immediately* determine his will; rather, he is moved to do his duty only *by means of* the happiness anticipated.—But since he can look forward to this reward of virtue only from the consciousness of having done his duty, it is clear that the latter must come first; that is, he must find himself bound to do his duty before he even

thinks that happiness will be the consequence of the fulfillment of duty and without thinking of this. With his *etiology* the eudaimonist is involved in a *circle*. That is to say, he can hope to be *happy* only if he is conscious of fulfilling his duty; but he can be moved to the fulfillment of his duty only if he presupposes that he will be made happy by it.—But there is also a *contradiction* in this sophistry. For on the one hand, he ought to fulfill his duty without first asking what effect this will have on his happiness, and so on *moral* grounds; but on the other hand, he can recognize something as his duty only if he can count on happiness to be gained by doing it, and so according to a *pathological* principle. This, however, is the direct opposite of the previous principle.[1] (TL 6:377.18 – 378.7)

Kant's portrayal of the 'eudaimonist' in this passage obviously does not cover what we would ordinarily have in mind today when discussing the various forms of eudaimonistic ethics. He clearly has in mind the eudaimonist of Epicurean provenance, i.e., the eudaimonist for whom the pleasurable state of satisfaction and tranquility of the soul are the key components of happiness as the chief good for human beings.[2] Thus, there is little point in questioning at this juncture whether Kant's criticism of the eudaimonist's explanatory strategy with respect to the relationship between happiness and duty reflects a historically adequate understanding of eudaimonist ethics in general.[3] Let us focus instead on the two tenets that, according to Kant, generate the unavoidable circle in that strategy:

---

[1] "Der denkende Mensch nämlich, wenn er über die Anreize zum Laster gesiegt hat und seine oft sauere Pflicht gethan zu haben sich bewußt ist, findet sich in einem Zustande der Seelenruhe und Zufriedenheit, den man gar wohl Glückseligkeit nennen kann, in welchem die Tugend ihr eigener Lohn ist.—Nun sagt der *Eudämonist:* diese Wonne, diese Glückseligkeit ist der eigentliche Bewegungsgrund, warum er tugendhaft handelt. Nicht der Begriff der Pflicht bestimme *unmittelbar* seinen Willen, sondern nur *vermittelst* der im Prospect gesehenen Glückseligkeit werde er bewogen seine Pflicht zu thun.—Nun ist aber klar, daß, weil er sich diesen Tugendlohn nur von dem Bewußtsein seine Pflicht gethan zu haben versprechen kann, das letztgenannte doch vorangehen müsse; d.i. er muß sich verbunden finden seine Pflicht zu thun, ehe er noch und ohne daß er daran denkt, daß Glückseligkeit die Folge der Pflichtbeobachtung sein werde. Er dreht sich also mit seiner *Ätiologie* im *Cirkel* herum. Er kann nämlich nur hoffen *glücklich* (oder innerlich selig) zu sein, wenn er sich seiner Pflichtbeobachtung bewußt ist: er kann aber zur Beobachtung seiner Pflicht nur bewogen werden, wenn er voraussieht, daß er sich dadurch glücklich machen werde.—Aber es ist in dieser Vernünftelei auch ein *Widerspruch*. Denn einerseits soll er seine Pflicht beobachten, ohne erst zu fragen, welche Wirkung dieses auf seine Glückseligkeit haben werde, mithin aus einem *moralischen* Grunde: andrerseits aber kann er doch nur etwas für seine Pflicht anerkennen, wenn er auf Glückseligkeit rechnen kann, die ihm dadurch erwachsen wird, mithin nach *pathologischem* Princip, welches gerade das Gegentheil des vorigen ist".

[2] On this, see pp. 172–176 of chapter 8.

[3] See, however, Irwin 1996, pp. 67–74; Irwin 2009, vol. 3 pp. 64–76. Cf. also Annas 1993, pp. 52–53, 120–131, 329–333, 426–455; Broadie, 1991, pp. 313–365; Wood 2011, pp. 81–91.

§ 1 Eudaimonistic Etiology and the Happiness of Others — 83

(1) The pleasurable state (i.e., the state of satisfaction and peace of mind) that can be called happiness is what supplies the real motive for acting virtuously.
(2) The happiness of the thinking human being who so acts (i.e., the *own*-happiness of the virtuously acting human being) is therefore what supplies the motive for the fulfillment of duty.

The point of Kant's argument in the passage quoted, of course, is to show that these hedonistic tenets of egoistic eudaimonism cannot provide for a viable theory of properly moral motivation.[4] But let us lay out exactly what follows if, instead of using the principle of duty in general to expose the circular character of the eudaimonist's motivational etiology, we bring to bear the concept of obligatory end that Kant goes on to explicate in the pages immediately following the preface to the Doctrine of Virtue. In other words, let us carefully examine what follows when we use the concept of an *end* that is also a duty, thereby formulating the explanatory circle in egoistic eudaimonism's account of moral motivation with reference to the principle of duty that is distinctive of ethics as a doctrine of virtue, i.e., the principle to "act in accordance with a maxim of *ends* that it can be a universal law for everyone to have" (TL 6:395).[5]

Consider first of all the succinct formulation of the eudaimonist's circle that Kant gives in the passage quoted above:

> He can hope to be *happy* only if he is conscious of fulfilling his duty; but he can be moved to the fulfillment of his duty only if he presupposes that he will be made happy by it.

Taking a first-person perspective, the circle involved in the eudaimonist's etiology can be put in explicitly causal terms as follows:

> (1a) The cause of my (anticipated) own happiness is my (prospective) consciousness of the fulfillment of my duty.
> (2a) At the same time, the cause of my (prospective) consciousness of the fulfillment of my duty is my (anticipated) own happiness.

This formulation of the eudaimonist's circle allows for the following specification if the happiness of others, for example, is thought of as an end that is also a duty and, moreover, as an end to be promoted through action in accordance with a maxim of ends that one is obligated to adopt:

---

[4] The point is made in far greater detail in the criticism that Kant elsewhere delivers against his main contemporaneous eudaimonist target—namely: Christian Garve. On this, see TP 8:281.19–284.8 (cf. also RGV 6:49.34–46.40).
[5] For discussion, see chapter 1, pp. 21–22.

(1b) The cause of my (anticipated) own happiness is my (prospective) consciousness of promoting the happiness of others.
(2b) At the same time, the cause of my (prospective) consciousness of promoting the happiness of others is my (anticipated) own happiness.

Now according to Kant's account of the eudaimonist's explanation of moral motivation, the consciousness of the fulfillment of duty is the same as the pleasurable state caused by that fulfillment; and Kant grants (at least for the sake of argument in this particular frame of reference) that this state of satisfaction and peace of mind is what can be called one's (own) happiness. Consequently, a hedonistic version of the eudaimonist's circle is yielded when the happiness of others is thought of as an end that is also a duty:

(1c) The cause of my (anticipated) own happiness is my (prospective) pleasurable state as caused by the promotion of the happiness of others.
(2c) At the same time, the cause of my (prospective) pleasurable state, as caused by the promotion of the happiness of others, is my (anticipated) own happiness.

Thus, according to the egoistic explanatory principle that underlies the hedonistic eudaimonist's etiology, the cause of my pleasurable state is necessarily my own happiness *even as caused by* the promotion of others' happiness. Or more precisely, *even if* the promotion of others' happiness is the cause of my pleasurable state of satisfaction and peace of mind (i.e., my own happiness), the egoistic principle requires that this cause should be the same as my own happiness as understood in terms of my pleasurable state. The inherent explanatory emptiness of the eudaimonist's project of casual explanation with respect to the fulfillment of duty is therefore evident, especially when the happiness of others as a promotable end that is also a duty is brought into play.

But consider, too, what follows for Kant's theory of obligatory ends if, recognizing the circular character of that project, we attempt to exclude others' happiness from being an end that is also a duty just because it happens to be an end that one has on account of sensible impulse or the inclination to promote it. Even if the causal (i.e., the motivating) ground of my seeking to bring about the happiness of others is in reality my own happiness, my *maxim* to promote others' happiness by making this my end will still qualify for a possible universal lawgiving. For this maxim's *matter* cannot possibly be anything other than an end that is also a duty since it just *is* the happiness of others, and not my own happiness (on this point, see chapter 3, pp. 61–69). This will be true even if it is assumed that the *cause* of my promoting the happiness of others can be nothing other than my own happiness whenever I think to act on my maxim to promote their happiness. And the matter of my maxim will still be an obligatory end, even if that cause turns out to be nothing other than the pleasurable state that I expect to achieve by means of my happiness-seeking action. That is because (according Kant's theory of intrinsically obligatory ends) others' happiness is necessarily an end that is also a duty, although it may also happen to be an end that I promote as a means to achieve my self-seeking end, i.e., the pleasurable state that features in (or constitutes) my own happiness. Thus, even if it is assumed that the only cause of my promoting the happiness of anyone is in reality my own state of satisfaction and peace of mind, the happiness of others must still be an end that I am obligated to bring about. If it were *nothing but* the end that the anticipation of a pleasurable state inclines me to achieve, it could not coherently be thought of as an end that is *also* a duty.

Thus, the egoistic explanation of the motivational basis for bringing about others' happiness turns out to be, at best, simply beside the point as far as it concerns a conceptually coherent account of the promotion of such happiness as an obligatory end. The happiness of others has to be thought of as a self-seeking end if the motivation for seeking it is to be explained (reductively) in terms of one's own happiness. Yet it also has to be thought of as an end that is also a duty whether or not it can be so explained. It therefore makes no difference what the causal ground(s) of the seeking may actually be as long as the happiness of others can be thought of as an objectively necessary end of morally practical reason. And one cannot, consistently with Kant's moral doctrine of obligatory ends, deny that others' happiness *must* be thought of in precisely this way.

§ 2 Own-Perfection and Moral Worth

The upshot of the preceding analysis of the eudaimonist's circle in relation to Kant's theory of intrinsically obligatory ends is this: Even if promoting the happiness of others *can* (or coherently *could*) be reductively explained as the pursuit of a self-seeking end, this kind of explanation would have no relevance for overcoming the difficulty that we have been grappling with since the end of chapter 2 —that is, the difficulty for Kant's account of practical law that arises from the circumstance that some empirically grounded maxims seem to be able to qualify for a possible universal lawgiving. Needless to say, this outcome will no doubt strike us as a dispiritingly meager yield in view of all the complications we have endeavored to work our way through thus far. Far more significantly, however, it is an outcome that calls into question the very basis of Kant's understanding of the relationship between morally practical reason and empirically conditioned action.

Then again, it is also an outcome that we have arrived at by focusing almost exclusively on just one of practical reason's two obligatory ends. So what follows if we shift our theoretical focus from others' happiness to own-perfection as an end that is also a duty?

Such a shift of focus may not appear especially promising to begin with. While own-perfection must be understood as an end that is distinct from and irreducible to its deontic counterpart, its substitution for others' happiness gives rise to the same sort of explanatory circle that we encountered above when we assumed that an end which is also a duty could be promoted on account of sensible impulse or inclination. To avoid unnecessary repetition, let formulate the circle involving own-perfection in view of the last version given above (see p. 84):

> (3c α) The cause of my (anticipated) own happiness is my (prospective) pleasurable state, as brought about by the furtherance of my own perfection.
> (3c β) At the same time, the cause of my (prospective) pleasurable state, as brought about by the furtherance of my own perfection, is my (anticipated) own happiness.

If this is the circle that the eudaimonist's etiology generates when the duty of self-perfection is brought into play, then it seems that we can get no further than the outcome already mentioned. For own-perfection has to be thought of as a self-seeking end if it is to be reductively explained in terms of one's own happiness. And it also has to be understood as an end that is also a duty whether or not it can be so explained. So it makes no difference what the motivating ground of furthering one's own perfection may be. Even if what motivates me to seek my own perfection is in reality my own happiness, the *maxim* that I have to perfect myself will qualify for a possible universal lawgiving simply in virtue of its having as its matter (i.e., its propositional content) an end that is also duty.

Thus, we may well agree that Kant's portrayal of the eudaimonist's etiology implies that the egoistic (and hedonistic) explanation of the motivational basis for the pursuit of one's own perfection must fall prey to circular reasoning if this same basis is used to explain moral motivation in connection with the principle of duty that is distinctive of ethics as a doctrine of virtue. At the same time, though, we must also recognize that demonstrating this circularity does not entail that no empirically grounded maxim of self-perfection can qualify for a possible universal lawgiving. Consequently, it seems that the upshot of our line of inquiry in this second section, thus far, must match the meager outcome that we have already had to face. For *even if* an empirically grounded maxim to perfect oneself can be coherently interpreted as a maxim of (hedonic) self-love, this kind of interpretation is simply irrelevant to resolving the main issue with which we have been concerned since chapter 2: Why *is* it that no empirically grounded maxim can furnish a practical law, even when it should evidently qualify for a possible universal lawgiving? With regard to this inquiry-guiding question, then, we appear to be at an impasse unless we have not yet taken proper account of some essential facet of Kant's treatment of own-perfection and others' happiness as obligatory ends.

Happily, we have not.

Let us turn once again to a topic that was briefly discussed in chapter 1 (see pp. 31–34): Kant's treatment of duties of virtue as wide duties or duties of wide obligation. The exposition of these duties, given in the eighth section of the Doctrine of Virtue's introduction, brings out the symmetry in the essential properties of morally practical reason's obligatory ends. One's own perfection as an end that is also a duty features "*physical*" perfection (TL 6:391.30) as well as the "*cultivation [Kultur] of morality* in us" (TL 6:392.20); and these properties of own-perfection are matched by the "physical welfare" (TL 6:393.12) and the "moral well-being" (TL 6:394.1) in terms of which the happiness of others as an obligatory end must be conceptualized. It is in view of the relation of symmetry exhibited by these sets of constitutive properties that own-perfection and others' happiness are comprehensible as mutually supportive obligatory ends. As an end that is also a duty, own-perfection, for example, requires the cultivation of all our capacities to further ends set forth by reason as well as the fostering of the moral disposition to do our duty. But the self-perfecting development of those capacities and this disposition necessarily involves the promotion of others' happiness as an end that is also a duty. And this includes acting to bring about the conditions under which others can cultivate their capacities for furthering rationally warranted ends in general as well as their dispositions to fulfill the requirements of duty in particular.

Despite the symmetry of the properties treated in Kant's exposition of reason's mutually supportive obligatory ends, however, there is a crucial difference between the laws for maxims that are grounded in these dual ends. While both ends provide the basis for laws that present wide duties, i.e., duties of wide obligation, at least one of the laws pertaining to own-perfection involves a *kind* of demandingness that is not characteristic of the laws requiring the promotion of others' happiness.

To explain, let me begin by considering the nature of the demands involved in the latter. While the duty to promote the happiness of others requires active benevolent concern for their physical welfare, acting to fulfill this deontic requirement has "in it a latitude for doing more or less" (TL 6:393.32–33), depending largely on "what each person's true needs are in view of his sensibility [*Sin-*

nesart]" (TL 6:393.27–28).⁶ Satisfying the categorical demands posed by the obligatory concern for others' happiness also requires promoting their moral well-being by attending to the conditions for their moral contentment. But the wide duty of beneficence that we have to further this form of others' well-being is "only a negative duty" (TL 6:394.3) in the sense that it demands merely that we "refrain from doing anything that, considering the nature of a human being, could tempt him to do something for which his conscience could afterwards pain him, to refrain from what is called giving scandal" (MS 6:394.8–10).⁷

Given the character of the deontic demands linked to the concept of others' happiness, then, the laws for maxims that are based on this concept are not *maximizing* practical principles: They do not require us to promote the greatest happiness of others, much less the greatest happiness of the greatest number of others.⁸ The same sort of consideration seems to apply to laws for maxims pertaining to one's own physical perfection. The demand to further a human agent's natural perfection enjoins the multifaceted development of the skills and talents needed for furthering all manner of rationally warranted ends. Yet, as Kant puts it, "[n]o rational principle prescribes specifically *how* far one should go in cultivating [...] one's capacities" (TL 6:392.11–13).⁹ Moreover, the self-perfecting agent who acts in conformity with the law to cultivate these capacities must take into account the circumstance that "the different situations in which human beings may find themselves make a human being's choice of the kind of occupation for which he should cultivate his talent[s] very much an arbitrary matter" (TL 6:392.13–15).¹⁰ Given reason's inherent lack of specific-

---

6 See chapter 1, pp. 31–32.

7 "Zu verhüten, daß jenen dieser innere Vorwurf nicht verdienterweise treffe, ist nun zwar eben nicht *meine* Pflicht, sondern *seine* Sache; wohl aber nichts zu thun, was nach der Natur des Menschen Verleitung sein könnte zu dem, worüber ihn sein Gewissen nachher peinigen kann, welches man Skandal nennt" (TL 6:394.6–10).

8 These limitations on the prescriptive character and scope of laws for maxims pertaining to others' happiness does not prevent Kant's theory of obligatory ends from grounding a law of universal benevolence that requires the promotion of everyone's happiness. For discussion, see the first section of this book's conclusion.

9 "*Wie* weit man in Bearbeitung (Erweiterung oder Berichtigung seines Verstandesvermögens, d.i. in Kenntnissen oder in Kunstfähigkeit) gehen solle, schreibt kein Vernunftprincip bestimmt vor" (TL 6:392.11–13).

10 "auch macht die Verschiedenheit der Lagen, worin Menschen kommen können, die Wahl der Art der Beschäftigung, dazu er sein Talent anbauen soll, sehr willkürlich". Mary Gregor's Cambridge Edition translation renders this passage as "Then too, the different situations in which human beings find themselves make a human being's choice of the occupation for which he should cultivate his talents very much a matter for him to decide as he chooses". Kant's point is that the contingent circumstances in which a human being chooses the kind of occupa-

ity regarding the extent to which particular human beings should develop their particular talents and skills, combined with the contingencies of human life that furnish the empirical conditions of rational choice, it is far from clear that even the law pertaining to the physical *perfection* of the human agent should be regarded as an unambiguously maximizing practical principle. The agent who acts in conformity with the law for maxims to "[c]ultivate your powers of mind and body so that they are fit to realize any ends you might encounter" (TL 6:392.17–18) does not necessarily have the *greatest* development of these powers as her end when she acts to bring about the kind of perfection that will enable her to realize whatever ends she may end up rationally setting for herself. For she will presumably recognize that acting on the maxim to promote one's powers of body and mind so that *they* are fit to realize any ends one might encounter may well mean choosing to forego their maximal development for the sake of being able to further various ends set forth by reason. (After all, there are only so many waking hours in a day; and we ought not to spend all of them making our end-realizing powers maximally fit while neglecting the ends that reason enjoins us to realize by developing those powers.)

At any rate, there is no question about the unambiguously maximizing import of the categorical demand contained in the law for maxims that applies to the second facet of own-perfection as an obligatory end. To be sure, the law pertaining to the cultivation of morality as a disposition is also one that "prescribes only the *maxim of the action*, namely, that of seeking the basis of obligation solely in the law and not in sensible impulse (advantage or disadvantage)" (TL 6:392.27–29).[11] Yet the maxim, so prescribed, is in this case a principle of volition that demands "[t]he greatest perfection of a human being", which is "to do his duty *from duty* (for the law to be not only the rule but also the incentive of his actions)" (TL 6:393.20–23).[12] Thus, to the extent that furthering one's own per-

---

tion for which he *ought* to develop his talents may be quite accidental. He does not imply here that the choice of the kind of occupation for which one should develop one's talents could be merely a matter of preference. To be sure, Kant does suggest elsewhere (see TL 6:445.28–34) that deciding which physical perfections should take *precedence* when choosing the sort of life one wants to lead is in part a matter of preference. But Gregor's rendering leaves too much room for this kind of suggestion to sneak into Kant's basic exposition of own-perfection as a *duty* of wide obligation.

11 "aber in der That gebietet das Gesetz auch hier nur die *Maxime der Handlung*, nämlich den Grund der Verpflichtung nicht in den sinnlichen Antrieben (Vortheil oder Nachtheil), sondern ganz und gar im Gesetz zu suchen—mithin nicht die *Handlung* selbst" (TL 6:392.26–30)

12 "Die größte moralische Vollkommenheit des Menschen ist: seine Pflicht zu thun und zwar aus Pflicht (daß das Gesetz nicht blos die Regel, sondern auch die Triebfeder der Handlungen sei)" (MS: 6:392.20–23).

fection necessarily requires the cultivation of morality in us, the law that demands this of us is a principle that commands the maximal moral perfection of the human agent. As such, it is the maximizing principle of practical reason that prescribes "not only the *legality* but also the *morality* of every action, that is, the disposition [*Gesinnung*]" (MS 6:392.25).

In keeping with his exposition of duties of virtue as wide duties, Kant insists that this law of greatest perfection does not immediately apply to the "*action itself*" (TL 6:393.30)—in this instance, to the *inner* action itself—even if it pertains to every action that the human agent is capable of performing in order to cultivate the disposition to do one's duty from duty. Given the particular conditions that obtain for human volition, there is (according to Kant) no inner action that can be directly prescribed since this would require the kind of insight into motivating grounds that is simply unavailable to human beings:

> [I]t is not possible for a human being to see into the depths of his heart so as ever to be fully certain, even in but a *single* action, of the purity of his moral intention and the sincerity of his disposition, even when he is not at all doubtful about the legality of the action. Very often he mistakes his own weakness, which counsels him against the venture of a misdeed, for virtue (which is the concept of strength); and how many people who have lived long and guiltless lives may not be merely *fortunate* in having escaped so many temptations? In the case of any deed it remains hidden from the agent himself how much pure moral content there has been in his disposition.[13] (TL 6:392.30–393.2)

As far as the human being's greatest perfection is concerned, then, the limitations intrinsic to human self-knowledge are such that the law in question does not prescribe the "inner action in the human mind itself but only the maxim of the action, to strive with all one's might [*nach allem Vermögen*] that the thought of duty for its own sake is the sufficient incentive for every action conforming to duty" (TL 6:393.5–6).[14] It is in this sense that the duty presented by

---

13 "Denn es ist dem Menschen nicht möglich so in die Tiefe seines eigenen Herzens einzuschauen, daß er jemals von der Reinigkeit seiner moralischen Absicht und der Lauterkeit seiner Gesinnung auch nur in *einer* Handlung völlig gewiß sein könnte; wenn er gleich über die Legalität derselben gar nicht zweifelhaft ist. Vielmals wird Schwäche, welche das Wagstück eines Verbrechens abräth, von demselben Menschen für Tugend (die den Begriff von Stärke giebt) gehalten, und wie viele mögen ein langes schuldloses Leben geführt haben, die nur *Glückliche* sind, so vielen Versuchungen entgangen zu sein; wie viel reiner moralischer Gehalt bei jeder That in der Gesinnung gelegen habe, das bleibt ihnen selbst verborgen".

14 There is of course a difficulty here, since to prescribe the maxim to make the thought of duty the sufficient incentive for all of one's duty-conforming actions is to prescribe the maxim of an inner action. But nothing hinges on dealing with this difficulty at this juncture; and the problem

the law of greatest human perfection must be understood as "the duty to assess the worth of one's actions not by their legality alone but also by their morality (disposition)" (TL 6:393.5–6).[15]

It is thus with the principle of action assessment provided by the law to cultivate morality in us that we at last seem to have come upon a promising theoretical springboard that can be used to get ourselves beyond the impasse noted above (p. 87). Kant's interpretation of that law of greatest human perfection as a principle to assess the worth of one's actions leads to the view that the moral value of our actions is something determined by the cultivated disposition to do one's duty from duty, i.e., to act in such a way that the law of duty is not only the rule but also incentive for acting. Surely, therefore, acting in this way —that is to say: acting on the maxim to strive with all one's might that the thought of duty for its own sake is the sufficient incentive of every action conforming to duty—is to act on a maxim that cannot *possibly* have an empirical ground!

Or can it?

---

that it generates is addressed under the heading of 'prescriptive regress' in chapter 5 (see pp. 111–114).

15 "Also ist auch diese Pflicht, den Werth seiner Handlungen nicht blos nach der Legalität, sondern auch der Moralität (Gesinnung) zu schätzen, nur von *weiter* Verbindlichkeit, das Gesetz gebietet nicht diese innere Handlung im menschlichen Gemüth selbst, sondern blos die Maxime der Handlung, darauf nach allem Vermögen auszugehen: daß zu allen pflichtmäßigen Handlungen der Gedanke der Pflicht für sich selbst hinreichende Triebfeder sei" (6:393.4–10). In his exposition of the duty of moral self-perfection as the duty of wide obligation to assess the worth of one's actions, Kant works with two different versions of the pertinent law of perfection. There is (a) the law of the maxim to seek the basis of obligation solely in the law and not in sensible impulse (advantage or disadvantage); and (b) the law that prescribes the maxim to strive with all one's might that the thought of duty for its own sake is the sufficient incentive for every action conforming to duty. These dual formulas give rise to an apparent interpretive difficulty: In formulating the law that prescribes the greatest human perfection, has Kant formulated two different maxims that pertain to the duty of moral self-perfection? Or has he given two different formulations for one and the same maxim? But this issue need not bother us (any more than it apparently bothered Kant). For in either case the maxims formulated have to be equivalent in what they prescribe as far as the *law* prescribing maximal human perfection is concerned.

§ 3 Hume's "Undoubted Maxim" and the Sentimentalist Conception of Actions' Moral Worth

We have not been able to see exactly why no empirically grounded maxim—hence no material practical principle—should be thought to furnish a universal practical law when it formally qualifies for a universal lawgiving. Yet we have just come face to face with a universally lawgiving maxim that (presumably) cannot be empirically grounded: the maxim to strive, with all the duty-fulfilling capacity available to human beings, to make the (a priori) idea of duty the sufficient incentive for every action conforming to duty. We have also seen that Kant considers the disposition-cultivating duty presented by this maxim's law of greatest perfection to be one of action assessment. It is the duty to assess the worth of one's actions by their morality as well as by their legality (i.e., their mere conformity to duty).

So our investigations in this chapter thus far have yielded the following positive results: (1) Kant's metaphysical system of morals contains a law of greatest human perfection. (2) This law of maximal perfection prescribes a maxim that cannot (one hopes) be empirically grounded. (3) The matter of obligation (cf. MS 6:222.32) presented by the law of this maxim is a duty that demands the assessment of all our actions' worth by their morality. (4) As such, it is the duty to assess our actions according to the value that they have when the thought, or idea, of duty furnishes the sufficient incentive for their performance. In other words, it is the duty to assess our actions in terms of their moral value. More precisely, it is (i) the duty to cultivate our capacity to assess our actions in terms of the moral worth that they can have when the idea of duty itself is their sufficient incentive, and (ii) to act accordingly.

Looking back over the terrain that we have had to cover as well as the obstacles that we have had to deal with in order to get this far, these results may indeed appear to be appallingly meager. But they are by no means dispiritingly paltry. For they propel us toward one of the core components of Kant's ethical thought: his theory of the moral worth of actions. Before going into the key aspects of this theory, I will attempt to bring to light the key tenet of an approach to the question of actions' moral worth to which Kant's theory is opposed. A section from David Hume's *A Treatise of Human Nature* lends itself nicely to this purpose.

At the beginning of the second part of the third book of his *Treatise of Human Nature* (THN), Hume poses the question whether justice is a natural virtue or an artificial virtue. When responding to this question, Hume argues on empirical grounds that we cannot be supposed capable of being moved to act merely from a naturally given "universal affection to mankind" or by "the love of mankind, merely as such" (THN 3.2.1.12). Nor, Hume maintains, is it empirically plausible to claim that "public benevolence […] or a regard to the interests of mankind" can be "the original motive to justice" (THN 3.2.1.13) from which our sense of justice and injustice is naturally derived. Thus, Hume's particular response to his initial query in THN 3.2 is that justice must be understood as an artificial virtue since it does not have as its source any natural determination of the human make—any natural affection or passion—that could furnish an original motive to action. But in order to treat justice within the theoretical framework provided by his distinction between natural and artificial virtues, Hume first gives a general account of the basis of our ascriptions of merit and moral goodness to actions. It is this general account with which I will be concerned in the following.

On Hume's general account, our praise of certain actions depends on our regard to the motives from which they are performed. Accordingly, he holds that all of the actions that we consider praiseworthy are themselves but "signs or indications of certain principles in the mind and temper" (THN 3.2.1.2). In keeping with this standpoint, he asserts that an action's external performance as such has no merit, and he maintains that the moral quality of any action can be determined only by considering its motive.

Hume's position, then, is that an action's merit depends entirely on the motive (or motives) for its performance. Moreover, in keeping with this position, he holds that "the first virtuous motive, which bestows a merit on any action, can never be a regard to the virtue of that action, but must be some other natural motive or principle" (THN 3.2.1.4). Hume takes this assumption regarding the merit-bestowing character of natural motives to be necessary since he holds that the contrary supposition unavoidably leads to a circular explanation of the relationship between the motivational basis for morally good action and the moral goodness of the actions that we are motivated to perform:

> To suppose, that the mere regard to the virtue of the action, may be the first motive, which produc'd the action, and render'd it virtuous, is to reason in a circle. Before we can have such a regard, the action must be really virtuous; and this virtue must be deriv'd from some virtuous motive: And consequently the virtuous motive must be different from the regard to the virtue of the action. A virtuous motive is requisite to render an action virtuous. An action must be virtuous, before we can have a regard to its virtue. Some virtuous motive, therefore, must be antecedent to that regard. (THN 3.2.1.4)

Having exposed what he takes to be the explanatory circle generated by the supposition that an action's virtue could furnish the primary motive that excites its performance and makes it virtuous, Hume insists that the priority of virtuous motives with respect to our regard to actions' virtue (i.e., their moral goodness) is something that "enters into all our reasonings in common life" (THN 3.2.1.5). He seeks to support this view by focusing on why, and how, we come to assess the moral qualities of actions in connection with the affective components of the human constitution and the corresponding dispositional characteristics of human agents.

In the section of the *Treatise* under consideration, Hume illustrates his position on the connection between the merit of actions and motives by considering our assignments of blame in connection with actions having to do with parental obligations:

> We blame a father for neglecting his child. Why? because it shows a want of natural affection, which is the duty of every parent. (THN: 3.2.1.5)

Notice how Hume identifies the affective component in question, understood here as the motivational basis of morally meritorious action, as the *duty* of *every* human parent. For Hume, a father's natural affection for his child must be understood as a deontically salient characteristic of human nature. It is thus a motivational determination of our natural affective constitution that furnishes—indeed, in some sense *is*—the duty that *all* human beings have, in the event that they have offspring. Such a determination is the nature-given feature of the human frame that furnishes the universally shared subjective condition of our awareness of duty with respect to the care of our children. As Hume puts it:

> Were not natural affection a duty, the care of children cou'd not be a duty; and 'twere impossible we cou'd have the duty in our eye in the attention we give to our offspring. In this case, therefore, all men suppose a motive to the action distinct from a sense of duty. (THN 3.2.1.5)

The same kind of account applies to other types of beneficent action, including the actions by which a human agent "extends his bounty even to the greatest strangers" (THN 3.2.1.6). In general, we regard such actions as "proofs of the greatest humanity" (THN 3.2.1.6) insofar as they are motivated by benevolence as a natural affective principle. We hold that this humanity (or fellow-feeling[16]), understood as a trait of the human agent, is what bestows merit on actions concerned with promoting the well-being of others.[17] Moreover, we must also under-

---

[16] Cf. EPM 5.17 (note 19).
[17] For Hume, of course, benevolence of so broad a scope cannot be 'natural' in the same way that parental affection is (cf. THN 3.3.1.14–15; EPM 5.2, 5.42–43; EPM 9.5–9; for relevant discussion, see Debes 2007 and Radcliffe 2004, pp. 641–653.) Nonetheless, such benevolence must still be an antecedent principle of action that is *anchored* in the natural affective constitution

stand that this merit-bestowing trait, grounded in the natural benevolence that motivates us to act, is what provides the antecedent principle of the human affective frame upon which our very regard to actions' merit depends.

Hume formulates the main conclusion that is to be drawn from his illustrative considerations as follows:

> [I]t may be establish'd as an undoubted maxim, *that no action can be virtuous, or morally good, unless there be in human nature some motive to produce it, distinct from the sense of its morality.* (THN 3.2.1.7).

In the paragraphs following the formulation of this basic principle of actions' positive moral value, it becomes apparent that Hume uses "sense of morality" and "sense of duty" (or "regard to moral obligation") as by and large equivalent expressions.[18] Assuming this terminological equivalence, he responds to an obvious objection that can be raised to counter his "undoubted maxim". This is the objection based on the claim that it is possible for the sense of duty (or the sense of morality) to produce an action independently of any other motive for acting— in other words, that it is possible for a human person to act from a sense of duty *alone*. While Hume is quite willing to acknowledge this possibility, he contends that it offers no substantive objection to the doctrine in question:

> But may not the sense of morality or duty produce an action, without any other motive? I answer, It may: But this is no objection to the present doctrine. When any virtuous motive or principle is common in human nature, a person, who feels his heart devoid of that motive, may hate himself upon that account, and may perform the action without the motive, from a certain sense of duty, in order to acquire by practice, that virtuous principle, or at least, to disguise to himself, as much as possible, his want of it [...] But tho', on some occasions, a person may perform an action merely out of regard to its moral obligation, yet still this supposes in human nature some distinct principles, which are capable of producing the action, and whose moral beauty renders the action meritorious. (THN 3.2.1.8)

It is difficult to see exactly how Hume's line of argument in this passage lends support to his dismissive evaluation of the force of the objection at issue. We may well be prepared to grant that it is possible for a person to act from a sense of duty so as to be able, eventually, to act from a virtuous motive that

---

of the human being (or similarly constituted rational agents). If this were not the case, there could be on Hume's account no merit to bestow on actions by which we promote the good of those remote from us (cf. THN 3.2.1.7–12; THN 3.3.1.16–23). For related discussion of this important feature of sentimentalist ethics, see Edwards 2006, pp. 21–30.

18 This is in keeping with Hume's general attitude concerning terminological distinctions that unnecessarily give rise to merely verbal disputes: see EPM Appendix 4.

does not yet furnish a condition on which he is able to act. More controversially, perhaps, we may also be willing to accept that it is possible for a person to act from a sense of duty so that he can disguise from himself his inability to act from a virtuous motive that is distinct from the sort of motive furnished by that same sense or deontic regard. Yet even assuming that such actions are (for us) possible, it is far from clear how a person could ever be motivated to act from a sense of duty *alone* as long as he acts from a sense of duty *in order* to make up for his lack of a virtuous motive, or as long as he acts from a sense of duty *in order* to deceive himself about the affective deficiency that is the source of his moral self-hatred. For anyone who acts in either one of these ways must, it seems, unavoidably be acting from a regard to something other than moral obligation (or duty, or morality), even if he is acting from a sense of duty as well.

Be that as it may, however, the difficulties with Hume's understanding of the enabling conditions of acting from a sense of duty alone do not, by themselves, call into question the key theoretical claim contained in the undoubted maxim of his *Treatise* conception of actions' moral value. Specifically, those difficulties do not affect Hume's claim that the moral goodness of an action depends on some motive for acting that is distinct from the sense of the action's morality, from the awareness of its being a duty in accordance with our sense of duty—or, in other words, from the mere regard to its morally obligatory or meritorious character. For whether or not a human agent really is able to act from the (or a) sense of duty or morality alone if she acts in order to achieve compensatory ends like those just described, Hume's undoubted maxim implies that her very capacity to act from a sense of duty depends on her being subject to an *affective* motivational condition which makes it possible for her to have that sort of sense. This implication, I take it, is what provides the key assumption that supports Hume's general account of the basis of our ascriptions of moral goodness and merit to actions. In particular, it provides the grounding tenet of the theory of the moral worth of actions that is implicit in THN 3.2.1.[19]

Let us move on to Kant's doctrine of moral worth with this tenet in mind.

---

[19] In accepting that this assumption provides the grounding tenet of Hume's sentimentalist theory of moral worth, I am by no means suggesting that it is also the foundational principle of Hume' sentimentalism *per se*. Perhaps there is some template for classifying ethical theories that would make this a reasonable thing to suggest. But if there is such a template, I am not concerned with it in this book.

Chapter 5 Moral Worth and Motivation in Kant's Criticism of Sentimentalist Ethics

This chapter examines the treatment of the moral worth of actions that we find in Kant's *Groundwork for the Metaphysics of Morals*. I begin by considering the aspects of this treatment that are opposed to the sentimentalist view of actions' moral worth, especially as this view is exemplified in Hume's theory of morals. I then argue that Kant's straightforwardly contrasting view gives rise to a number of basic difficulties for his ethics. First, an underlying anti-sentimentalist assumption of Kant's account of actions' moral worth threatens to make his metaphysical theory of the a priori foundations of ethics dependent on an anthropological explanatory principle drawn from empirical moral psychology. Second, to the extent that this first difficulty can be avoided, a further anti-sentimentalist tenet of that account gives rise to a problem of logical regress for Kant's theory of universal moral prescriptions. Third, this same tenet must also make Kant's account of the nomothetic function—the universally lawgiving role—of morally practical reason non-virtuously circular. I go on to argue, however, that all of these difficulties, including the predicaments of prescriptive regress and nomothetic circularity, can be overcome if we properly understand why Kant must do damage to his own position on moral worth when he *overshoots* his sentimentalist target. To achieve this understanding, we have merely to pay attention to a crucial point: It is always possible to act from respect for law as one's *incentive* even without making it one's *maxim* to act from respect for law. To see how this is possible, however, we first have to sort out an array of connections between Kant's account of the moral content of maxims as practical propositions, his view of what it is to have respect for law as an incentive to act, and the method of action assessment at issue in the treatment of his 'canon' for the moral appraisal of action in general.

§ 1 Squire Allworthy's Inclinations and the Moral Worth of Actions in Kant's Groundwork for the Metaphysics of Morals

As is well enough known, Kant begins the first section of the *Groundwork* by specifying the concept of unrestricted good that he takes to underlie common moral understanding. He holds that nothing except a good will can be thought of as good without limitation, and thus as intrinsically and unconditionally good. Accordingly, he undertakes to explicate the concept of a will that is intrinsically and unconditionally good by focusing on the concept of duty. For the concept of duty, according to Kant, "contains [the concept] of a good will though under certain subjective limitations and hindrances" (GMS 4:397.7–8). It is in view of these limitations and hindrances that Kant uses his procedure of conceptual explication, which he combines with illustrations drawn from the consideration of certain types of action, to establish the truth of three propositions that concern the relationship between duty and the grounds of our assessment of the moral worth of actions. The first proposition, though unstated in the particular context of Kant's illustrative considerations, can be formulated as follows:

> (1) Only an action done from duty, not from inclination, is an action that can have genuine moral worth.[20]

The second proposition is explicitly set forth:

> (2) "[A]n action from duty has its moral worth *not in the intent* to be achieved by it but in the maxim in accordance with which it is decided upon [...]"[21] (GMS 4:399.35–36).

---

[20] Henry Allison (2011, pp. 121–125) treats the alternative versions of this 'missing' first proposition that have been put forward in recent years, especially the versions defended in Freudiger 1993; Schönecker 2001 (cf. Schönecker 2012); Timmermann 2007, as well as in Schönecker/Wood 2004 (cf. Schönecker/Wood 2015). I find the reasons that Allison's gives for rejecting these versions to be convincing. My reasons for not endorsing Allison's own proposed version are explained in note 52 of this chapter.—A further interpretation of Kant's first proposition has recently been given by Manfred Baum (2005, pp.183–187). Following the lead indicated in Hermann Andreas Pistorius's 1786 review of the *Groundwork* (cf. KpV 5:8.25–9.3), Baum locates Kant's proposition in the first sentence of the third paragraph of *Groundwork* I: "The good will is not good through what it effects or accomplishes, not on account of its aptness for the attainment of some presupposed end, but through its volition alone, that is, it is good in itself [...]" (GMS 4:394.13–15—Gregor translation substantially altered). I take it that my formulation of proposition 1 is fully consistent with Baum's (and Pistorius's) understanding. It is a formulation yielded by the shift in Kant's explicative focus to the concept of duty (i.e., to the concept which contains the concept of the good will) when "the subjective limitations and hindrances" (GMS 4:397.7–8) that affect human (or human-like) volition are linked to the notion of inclination at issue in the lines which complete the sentence quoted above: "and, regarded for itself, [the good will] is to be valued incomparably higher than all that could merely be brought about by it in favor of some inclination and indeed, if you will, the sum of all inclinations" (GMS 4:397.15–18).

[21] Der zweite Satz ist: eine Handlung aus Pflicht hat ihren moralischen Werth *nicht in der Absicht*, welche dadurch erreicht werden soll, sondern in der Maxime, nach der sie beschlossen wird, hängt also nicht von der Wirklichkeit des Gegenstandes der Handlung ab, sondern blos von dem *Princip des Wollens*, nach welchem die Handlung unangesehen aller Gegenstände des Begehrungsvermögens geschehen ist. (GMS 399.35–400.3)

Kant's third proposition is held to derive from the conjunction of propositions (1) and (2). It, too, is explicitly formulated:

(3) "[D]uty is the necessity of an action from respect for law"[22] (GMS 4:400.18–19).

For the purposes of my argument in this chapter, I will be concerned with the implications of proposition 1 and the *second part* of proposition 2 (i.e., the assertion that an action from duty has its moral worth in the maxim upon which it is decided). I will also be concentrating on the particular interpretation of acting from respect for law that Kant gives in his explanatory considerations on proposition 3. In this regard, I will be especially interested in the view of the relationship between acting from duty, moral worth, and acting on the (or a) maxim of complying with a practical law that underlies the following passage:

> Now, an action from duty is to put aside entirely the influence of inclination and with it every object of the will; hence there is left for the will nothing that could determine it except objectively the *law* and subjectively *pure respect* for this practical law, and so the maxim of complying with such a law even with the infringement of all my inclinations.[23] (GMS 4:400.29–401.2)

I will comment in due course on issues raised by the notion of 'compliance with law' at issue in this passage. But let us now turn to some particulars of Kant's *Groundwork* account of moral worth.

The examples introduced by Kant to illustrate his views on moral worth have been subject to controversy dating back nearly to the *Groundwork's* time of original publication.[24] For the sake of economy in presentation, I will limit my discussion of Kant's illustrative intentions to the example that historically has often been at the center of debates on the Kantian doctrine of moral worth. Let us consider, then, the 'sympathy example' of Section I of the *Groundwork*.

---

22 Den dritten Satz als Folgerung aus beiden vorigen würde ich so ausdrücken: *Pflicht ist die Nothwendigkeit einer Handlung aus Achtung fürs Gesetz*. (GMS 400.17–19)

23 "Nun soll eine Handlung aus Pflicht den Einfluß der Neigung und mit ihr jeden Gegenstand des Willens ganz absondern, also bleibt nichts für den Willen übrig, was ihn bestimmen könne, als objectiv das *Gesetz* und subjectiv *reine Achtung* für dieses praktische Gesetz, mithin die Maxime, einem solchen Gesetze selbst mit Abbruch aller meiner Neigungen Folge zu leisten".

24 For historical orientation and influential contemporary discussion, see Allison 1990, pp. 108–120; Guyer 1993, pp. 335–356; Herman 1993. See also Ferguson 2012; Guyer 2000, 287–329; Henson 1979; Schaller 1987; Wilson 2015; Weber 2007; Wood 2008, pp. 24–42; Wood 2014, pp. 21–31.

To support his view of the relation between benevolent inclination (understood as a feature of the human affective constitution) and duties of beneficence, Kant introduces three stock characters that have regularly played their assigned roles in debates over the *Groundwork* ethics for the past two centuries and more.[25] First, there is the sympathetically attuned person of good-natured temperament who acts from inclination in order to do well for others by spreading joy around, and who in so acting takes delight in the satisfaction of others insofar as this is his own work. Second, there is the same good-natured man who, because of the distressing circumstances of his life, has become sorrowful, and thus acts beneficently from duty but without sympathetically reverberant benevolent inclination.[26] Finally, there is the man of cold and indifferent temperament who lacks the capacity for sympathetic sentiment, but who also can and does act beneficently from duty. The sensibility of a man of this third sort is shaped by nature in such a way that, although he is reliably disposed to doing well for others, he wills to do this utterly without benevolent inclination.[27] As Kant insists that the joy-spreading action of the first person—the annoyingly amiable, if harmless, do-gooder—has no genuine moral worth, the second and third figures must end up looking a good deal better as far as moral appraisal is concerned. It is with the depressed character lacking benevolent inclination that we first encounter an action that has moral worth. And it is only with the emotionally unresponsive disposition of the final figure described that we can properly speak of the worth of character that is "moral and incomparably the highest" (GMS 4:399.1).

It may be noted that the approach here taken by Kant to the basis of the moral worth of actions is directly opposed to the corresponding sentimentalist approach entailed by the 'undoubted maxim' of Hume's *Treatise of Human Nature* that we considered at the end of chapter 4.[28] While Hume explicitly acknowl-

---

[25] For closely related discussion of this example in connection with Francis Hutcheson, see Edwards 2006, pp. 17–36 (especially pp. 27–30).
[26] See GMS: 4:398.20–27.
[27] See GMS: 4:398.27–399.2.
[28] To preclude misunderstanding, let me emphasize the following: I am not in any sense suggesting that the *Groundwork* passage under consideration reflects a reading of Hume's *Treatise* on Kant's part. My intention is merely to indicate a way in which Kant's approach to a basic issue in ethics is opposed to the corresponding sentimentalist approach taken by Hume. At any rate, given the availability of its contemporaneous German translation, the *Enquiry concerning the Principles of Morals* provides a more plausible source text for interpreting the historical background of the *Groundwork's* sympathy example (see, e.g., EPM 5.2.39–43). Moreover, Francis Hutcheson arguably played a far more significant role in Kant's reception of 18th century British sentimentalist ethics than did Hume (or Shaftesbury). For discussion, see chapter 11.

edges that "the sense of morality or duty" (THN 3.2.1.8) can provide a motive to act virtuously without any other motive being in play, he also insists that a person who acts *only* from such a sense must be someone who acts to compensate for the deficiency of his affective constitution. Hume therefore holds that the possibility of acting from "a regard to moral obligation" (THN 3.2.1.8) does no damage to the view of moral motivation (hence moral worth) at issue in his undoubted maxim. For that possibility always presupposes, according to Hume, the efficacy of affective motivational conditions that are distinct from the regard paid to the obligatory character of actions. Kant, on the other hand, must reject each one of these points if he is to remain faithful to the argument of the *Groundwork*'s sympathy example. Even if he is in a position to grant, for the sake of psychological plausibility, that his third figure's emotional frame is seriously defective, he could never self-consistently concede that the moral worth of this figure's actions (not to mention character) is distinct from the consciousness of what it is to act *from* duty.

Obviously, Kant's line of argument in the illustrative passage under consideration gives rise to many questions, especially when it is compared with the type of approach to actions' moral worth that is implicit in Hume's *Treatise*. There will be occasion, in Part IV of this book, to go into the ramifications of Kant's argument against its historical backdrop. But the question of specific interest to the argument of this chapter can be gleaned from Kant's treatment of the type of action performed by first of the three figures discussed, i.e., the sympathetically attuned agent who acts from benevolent inclination:

> To be beneficent where one can is a duty; and besides, there are a good many souls so sympathetically attuned that, even without any other motive of vanity or of self-interest [*des Eigennutzes*], they find an inner enjoyment in spreading joy around them and can take delight in the contentment of others, in so far as this is their work. But I claim that in the case of an action like this, however dutiful and however amiable that action may be, it has no true moral worth. Rather, it is on a par with [actions proceeding from] other inclinations—for example, the inclination to honor, which, if it does by a stroke of luck hit upon that which is indeed of public utility [*gemeinnützig*] and dutiful, and consequently honorable, deserves praise and encouragement, but not esteem; for the maxim lacks moral content [*Gehalt*], namely, to do such actions not from inclination but *from duty*.[29] (GMS 4:398.8–20)

---

[29] "Wohlthätig sein, wo man kann, ist Pflicht, und überdem giebt es manche so theilnehmend gestimmte Seelen, daß sie auch ohne einen andern Bewegungsgrund der Eitelkeit oder des Eigennutzes ein inneres Vergnügen daran finden, Freude um sich zu verbreiten, und die sich an der Zufriedenheit anderer, so fern sie ihr Werk ist, ergötzen können. Aber ich behaupte, daß in solchem Falle dergleichen Handlung, so pflichtmäßig, so liebenswürdig sie auch ist, dennoch keinen wahren sittlichen Werth habe, sondern mit andern Neigungen zu gleichen Paaren gehe, z. E. der Neigung nach Ehre, die, wenn sie glücklicherweise auf das trifft, was in der

Kant's position here is threefold. First the sympathetically attuned agent's beneficent action has no true moral worth because the maxim on which he acts has no moral content. Second, one's maxim must lack moral content (*Gehalt*) if it is a maxim to perform a beneficent action on account of one's inclination to do well for others (in this case, by bringing joy to them). Third, no maxim—not even a maxim of beneficent action—can have moral content unless it prescribes the performance of an action from duty. Or more precisely: no maxim can have moral content unless its content consists in a prescription to perform an action (in this case, a beneficent action) from duty, and not from inclination.

Given Kant's fondness and respect for Henry Fielding, one might be tempted to discern the moral of the sympathy example's overall narrative in a message that can be crafted (without all that much exaggeration) from the satirical representations of contemporaneous moral philosophy found in the novel *Tom Jones*. In this literary frame of reference, I have in mind the message that a sympathetically attuned 'Squire Allworthy', depicted as someone who just likes to resonate over the landscape doling out prodigious quantities of joy-producing pleasure to people he happens to meet, ends up on the wrong end of the moral stick when compared to Kant's cold-fish character number three (who, as luck would have it, bears a striking resemblance to Monsieur de Wolmar of Rousseau's novel *Julie*).[30] To be sure, taking this kind of message literally would land us in the midst of unfounded speculation about hidden literary allusions in a major text of the history of philosophical ethics. Still, there is nothing to hinder us from making good use of such speculation as long as we are clear that it amounts to nothing more than just that: speculation that is unsupported (and perhaps unsupportable) by serious textual scholarship. Thus, for the purposes of further illustration, let us now overcome the temptations of belletristic conjecture by the simple expedient of giving in to them. Specifically, let us take a little liberty with the facts of European literary geography, not to mention chronology, by transporting one of the leading figures in Fielding's cast of characters —the aforementioned Squire Allworthy—to the Kantian domain of actions' moral

---

That gemeinnützig und pflichtmäßig, mithin ehrenwerth ist, Lob und Aufmunterung, aber nicht Hochschätzung verdient; denn der Maxime fehlt der sittliche Gehalt, nämlich solche Handlungen nicht aus Neigung, sondern *aus Pflicht* zu thun".

30 See *Julie, ou la nouvelle Heloïse*, in: Rousseau OC II 489–493/CW 275–276 (cf. *Les confessions de J. J. Rousseau*, in: Rousseau OC I 326–327/CW 401–405). To imply that Squire Allworthy ends up on the wrong end of the moral stick when compared with Monsieur de Wolmar is not to suggest, of course, that the amiable squire is attached to one and the same stick as are both Mr. Square (the hypocritical family tutor in Fielding's *Tom Jones*) and the sadistic, whip-wielding Reverend Thwackum.

worth.³¹ (For the time being, we will leave M. de Wolmar behind where he belongs—in Julie's garden.³²)

We can readily understand why the maxim of our sympathetically attuned philanthropist must lack moral content *if* it is true that every maxim must be lacking in moral content as long as it is a principle of volition that an agent comes to have on account of some inclination to act—even if its content as a practical proposition consists in the prescription to act from benevolent inclination.³³ Moreover, we can also understand why no such maxim to act can have moral content *if* it is true that a maxim's moral content consists in, or depends upon, its having the prescriptive content of a principle to act from duty, and not from inclination. But are both of these conditions actually satisfied? Indeed, is either one of them satisfied?

Any defender of Kant's theory of actions' moral worth must incorporate, or presuppose, the following sort of consideration when responding to the questions just posed: No maxim of action that we *may* have *simply because* we are inclined to act in a certain way is a subjective principle of volition that can furnish a practical law.³⁴ That is to say, no volitional principle can furnish a universal law of the will *merely* on account of some component of our affective constitution. For it is not necessarily true that every rational being—or every human being, for that matter—is capable of acting on a law-furnishing maxim because what moves it to act is some sensible impulse that inclines it to act on such a subjective principle.

There is, however, a crucial difficulty in defending Kant's position on moral worth on the basis of this sort of consideration *alone*. The difficulty is this: While it is indeed not necessarily true that every rational being—or even every human being—is capable of acting on maxims in the manner just described, it also seems to be false that *no* maxim that we may have because we are inclined to act is one that can furnish a practical law, i.e., a universal law of the will. That is because there just are, it seems, some maxims that can furnish practical

---

31 To a certain extend the wider landscape for this kind of uprooting move lies (curiously) ready and waiting. See Jacobi 1776 (Eduard Allwill) and 1779 (Woldemar).
32 We will encounter him again at the end of chapter 11. In the meantime, see Starobinski 1971, pp. 102–148 (especially pp. 137–139); Gauthier 2006, pp. 79–106 (especially pp. 84–88).
33 In this chapter, I rely primarily on the definitional accounts of 'maxim' and 'practical law' that Kant provides in the following passages: GMS 4:400.34–37; KpV 5:19.7–12; TL 6:225.1–5. See pp. 51–52 in chapter 3.
34 See, e.g., GMS 4:400.19–29, 4:402.1–15, 4:434.7–30; KpV 5:19.14–19, 5:21.10–22:3, 5:27.3–19, 5:72.28–32, 5:80.25–33.

laws, as objective principles of duty, *whether or not* they are founded on inclinations.

Needless to say, this difficulty is nothing new to us since it was the source of all the major problems investigated in Part I of this book. But for the sake of thoroughness, let me explain it with reference to the maxim suggested by the *Groundwork's* sympathy example, i.e., the maxim to do well for others. More particularly, let us take here as an example the maxim to promote the happiness of others (which, as we know, one may do by furthering the conditions of others' physical and moral well-being).[35] As Kant himself repeatedly emphasizes, such a maxim of beneficence (or active benevolence) necessarily satisfies the fundamental universality requirement of morally practical reason.[36] Yet it seems that exactly the same sort of maxim will necessarily satisfy this very same requirement *although* it is founded on one's inclination to do well for others. For taken simply as a maxim of beneficence, its content consists in the prescription to promote others' happiness; and *this* content, as the matter of such a maxim, is precisely what is universally enjoined by the practical law that makes the happiness of others our duty to promote.[37] Moreover, the universal law that commands us to promote others' happiness will prescribe precisely this content as our duty, whether or not the maxim on which one acts when promoting the happiness of others happens to be founded on other-directed benevolent inclination (i.e. happens to be a maxim that one comes to have on account of one's inclination to do well for others). Thus, the *fact* that a maxim is or is not founded on inclination, in the sense of 'founded' just indicated, seems to make no difference to that maxim's aptness for universal *prescription* as a practical law (i.e., to its qualification for a possible universal lawgiving). That is because the prescriptive content of any given maxim will remain just what it is whether or not that same maxim (*qua* practical proposition) also has the formal property of being capable of universal prescription.[38] In short, it looks like the maxim to promote others' happiness should necessarily have a *moral* content precisely in virtue of its having this property, even in the event that it is founded on an inclination to do well for others.

Kant, of course, seems to deny precisely this sort of claim in his *Groundwork* account of the moral worth of actions when he argues that no maxim founded on

---

[35] See TL 6:393.11–394.12; cf. GMS 4:423.16–35; 4:430.18–27.
[36] It would tedious to cite here all relevant passages in Kant's works and lectures from the 1760s onwards. But in addition to the references provided in the previous note (35), see TL 6:449.30–450.19, 6:452.15–453.15.
[37] See, e.g., KpV 4:19.14–23, 4:20.6–13, 4:27.7–8; MS 6:452.2–30.
[38] Or more precisely: exhibits the formal features of universality and prescriptivity.

inclination—not even one founded on benevolent inclination—can have moral content. But how can such a value negating move be validated if, as would seem to be the case, it is *false* that no maxim which we can have because we are inclined to act is one that can furnish a practical law? There are but two initially promising paths of argument that Kant can take in order to support his position on the moral content of maxims and benevolent inclination as long as the focus of our inquiry is restricted to the properties of maxims as propositions. The first of these supporting pathway options has to do with Kant's understanding of the relationship between inclination and maxims of self-love. Kant's second option lies in his notion of 'compliance with law' that we have already encountered in his explanatory comments on proposition (3) in Section 1 of the *Groundwork*. I will explore these options in the order just indicated.

§ 2 Kant's Anti-Sentimentalist Difficulty with Allworthy-Type Actions

Let us bring out the underlying import of Kant's observation (GMS 4:398.8–12) that there are "souls so sympathetically attuned that, even without any *other* motive of vanity or self-interest, find an inner enjoyment in spreading joy around them and can take delight in the contentment of others, *insofar as this is their work*" (italics mine [J. E.]). This observation from the *Groundwork's* sympathy example suggests that Kant can consider the joy-distributing actions performed by a sympathetically attuned agent—by our Squire Allworthy, as it were—to be actions motivated by predominantly *self*-directed benevolence.[39] Moreover, although this sort of benevolence provides the *only* motive of vanity or self-interest evidenced by such actions, the delight that the sympathetically attuned agent can take in the contentment of others seems to arise from the efforts by which the agent himself brings about others' contentment. Thus, it is reasonable to suppose that the enjoyment which our Squire Allworthy derives from effecting the contentment of others is what furnishes the motive for his joy-distributing action(s). On this reading, then, it is the egoistic motive of vanity or self-interest that provides a sufficient condition for a sympathetically attuned agent to bring joy and contentment to others. More generally, it is plausible to read Kant as proposing that even actions which appear to be genuinely beneficent must be understood as actions taking place from self-serving intent (*aus selbstsüchtiger Ab-*

---

[39] For Kant's notion of 'predominant benevolence toward oneself' (i.e., self-love), see KpV 5:73.12–13.

sicht—GMS 4:397.18–19) if benevolent inclination is what furnishes their motivational condition.⁴⁰ No matter how subtly self-serving actions like these may be, they will still be actions motivated by predominantly self-directed benevolence.

The type of reading just indicated shows several distinct advantages as far as the interpretation of Kant's doctrine of morals is concerned. First, it is certainly consistent with the treatment of the other three examples that Kant brings into the *Groundwork's* first section in order to illustrate his view of actions moral worth. In particular, it is consistent with a crucial point that Kant wants to make when discussing these examples—that is, his point that acting from self-regarding inclinations makes our actions self-interested, and indeed self-serving, as long as we do not act from duty.⁴¹ Third, looking beyond the 1785 *Groundwork* itself, our suggested reading seems to be required by one of the key theorems of Kant's theory of the determining grounds of the will and of the power of choice. I have in mind here of course (see chapter 3, pp. 52–58). Theorem II of Kant's analytic of pure practical reason in the second *Critique*, i.e., the theorem according to which every material (i.e., empirically grounded) practical principle must be interpretable as a specification of an overarching principle of self-love or (equivalently) one's own happiness.

Given these advantages, the proposed reading of the lines in question (GMS 4:398.8–12) enables us to regard Kant's sympathetically attuned agent—*our* Squire Allworthy—as someone who acts on a maxim of self-love when spreading joy around him and seeking to bring contentment to others. Thus, if I pull on our worthy squire's estate-walking shoes and choose to resonate across my (Baltic) fields of plenty in a joy-scattering manner, I can readily recognize that I will be acting on maxims such as the following:

(a) to find my inner enjoyment by spreading joy to as many of my cottagers as I can catch; or

(b) to take delight in my self-gratifying activity of causing the contentment of others; or

(c) to obtain the self-satisfying pleasure that results from my bringing about the contentment of others; or, more generally,

(d) to promote my own happiness by endeavoring to obtain the self-satisfying pleasures of self-contentment that result from my causing the contentment of others.⁴²

---

40 See Edwards 2000b for more detailed discussion of these points.
41 See GMS 4:397.14–398.7, 4:399.3–34 in conjunction with GMS 4:422.3–14, 4:422.20–31, 4:423.16–31; cf. KpV 5:82.18–83.2.
42 This final maxim, of course, could hardly be formulated by anyone lacking philosophical training. But we can reasonably assume that our Squire Allworthy has had sufficient leisure

Now, if my maxim of self-love is in fact *founded* on my inclination to act with one of these self-regarding aims in mind, then arguably the maxim on which I act will not be one that can satisfy the fundamental universality requirement of *morally* practical reason. That is because there is no possible self-referencing maxim of self-love that can furnish a practical *law*.[43]

This point was already made in chapter 3 (see pp. 61–62), but I will elaborate on it here in view of the problem of the moral content of maxims that is raised by the *Groundwork's* sympathy example. Let us consider, then, a maxim as a practical principle whose propositional content consists in the prescription to promote one's own happiness. If I am supposed to think of such a maxim as principle of volition that can furnish a practical law, then the following requirement of intelligibility would have to be fulfilled: I would have to be able to think of my *own* happiness as supplying the content of a maxim that can serve as a *subjective* principle of volition for *every* rational being.[44] That is to say, I would have to be able to think of my own happiness not only as the happiness that supplies the prescriptive content of my own maxim of self-love, but also as the content of a maxim that every *other* rational being could have as its own. But this is impossible. It is impossible because the own-happiness of each rational being is necessarily its own and not the happiness of another. Thus, *my* own happiness cannot be the own-happiness of any being other than myself. And if any maxim of mine is one that has my own happiness (or my own enjoyment, my own pleasure, my own contentment, my own well-being, etc.) as its content, then that maxim can only be one that is mine *alone*.

Thus, my own happiness cannot possibly supply the content of *anyone's* maxim (*qua* proposition) unless I make it my maxim to promote the happiness of someone as *my* own happiness. And this someone, whose own-happiness I make it my maxim to promote, can be none *other* than me. There cannot be another whose own-happiness I make it my maxim to promote as long as my maxim is to promote my own happiness as my own, and not to promote the happiness of someone else as the happiness of another. It is therefore not possible for me to think of my maxim of self-love as a subjective principle of volition which I could will that it become a practical law, i.e., a universal law of the will for all rational beings, including every rational being apart from myself.

---

to combine his study of Shaftesbury with that of Kant's 'eudaimonist' (on which, see chapter 4, p. 83 [note 4].
43 In accordance with the definitions of 'practical law' provided at KpV 19.7–12 and MS 6:225.1–2.
44 See GMS 4:400.34; KpV 5:19.9–10; MS 6:225.34–36.

The very thought that a self-referencing maxim of self-love could hold objectively as such a law for all possible rational beings is an incoherent thought.[45]

In sum, if I make it my maxim to promote my own happiness, then promoting my own happiness is exactly what I am doing when I act on this maxim of self-love; and promoting my own happiness is all that I make it my maxim to do when I so act. While it is indeed possible for me to think of what I am doing as acting on the maxim to promote the own-happiness of myself (alone), this does not entail that you can be acting on a maxim of self-love if you have made it your maxim to promote the happiness of me, and not the own-happiness of you. Nor does it entail that I (or anyone else) can be acting on such a subjective principle of volition if my maxim is to promote the happiness of you, and not the own-happiness of me. *This* is obvious, which only serves to underscore the incoherence of thinking that a self-referencing maxim of self-love could hold as a universal law. For the formal property of universality that is constitutive for Kant's concept of practical law cannot provide a feature of the concept of a maxim of intrinsically particularized self-love.

So far, so good as far as Kant's first supporting option is concerned (see pp. 104–105). While it may not be obvious that *no* maxim founded on benevolent

---

[45] One might attempt to put an end to this line of argument by pointing out that there is a very obvious sense in which one can intelligibly be said to promote, indirectly, the own-happiness of another whenever one acts on a maxim to promote the happiness of someone else. For it is precisely by acting on this sort of maxim that one endeavors to bring about conditions under which others can seek to achieve their own happiness. (Think of what we do for our children, for example, day-in and day-out.) Thus, by parity of reason, it seems that it ought to be *possible* for everyone to do the same for me by making it everyone's (shared) maxim to promote the own-happiness of me alone. *Why* anyone—apart from 'me'—would want to do this is here beside the point since the purpose of the conceptual exercise at issue is to show that a maxim of self-love *can* furnish a practical law. And it looks like we just might have hit upon such a maxim. Yet this cannot be the case for the following reasons. First, the own-happiness that one undertakes to promote when acting on one's maxim to promote the happiness of another (or others) cannot be one's *own* own-happiness, which is what a maxim of self-love would have to contain in the event that its content is supplied by the own-happiness of anybody at all. Second, the maxim on which one acts when *indirectly* promoting the own-happiness of someone else is not a maxim of self-love at all since it is not the maxim to promote one's own happiness (or one's own pleasure, one's own enjoyment, one's own contentment, etc.). Instead, it is the maxim of an action that has doing well for another as its aim. To the extent, then, that one can sensibly be said to be promoting the own-happiness of someone else, one cannot be acting on a maxim of self-love. One has to be acting on a maxim of other-directed beneficence. In instances of the type of action in question, one has to be acting on the maxim to promote another's happiness, which one does by bringing about conditions under which someone else can act to achieve her own happiness as a morally permissible end.

inclination can have moral content, the *Groundwork's* sympathy example still indicates an at least initially plausible way of denying the moral worth of actions performed by our Squire Allworthy: If it is true that (a) a maxim can have moral content only in virtue of its aptness for universal prescription; that (b) no maxim of self-love is so apt; and that (c) our squire always acts on a maxim (or maxims) of self-love when he acts to further the joy and contentment of others, then it must also be true that Allworthy-type actions will have no true moral worth, no matter how sympathetically attuned our squire may be to the feelings, the needs, the desires, or the preferences of others.

There is just one problem that arises in pursuing the Kantian option just portrayed. Despite the promise of support that it initially seems to offer, this option does not yet put us in a position to establish that a sympathetically attuned person's action can have no moral worth when she acts on a maxim to promote the happiness of others *because* she is inclined to act on such a maxim of beneficence.

To spell out why this is so, let us discard the caricature of the Squire Allworthy figure that I have been playing upon thus far. Thus, let us consider what happens if we challenge Kant's apparently egoistic description of the sympathetically attuned agent's motives for acting. Specifically, let us consider these two assumptions:

> (1) A sympathetically attuned agent is quite capable of acting on the maxim to promote the happiness of others, even if she is *also* inclined to promote her own happiness.
>
> (2) The maxim that such an agent has when she acts to promote the happiness of others is a practical principle that happens to be founded on *other*-directed benevolent inclination (i.e., on the agent's inclination to do well for others, as distinct from the inclination to do well for herself alone).

Now let us ask what condition must be satisfied if the maxim of this same sympathetically attuned agent is *not* to have a moral content when she makes it *her* maxim to promote the happiness of others.

In accordance with the assumptions put forward, there is but one way to establish that the happiness-promoting maxim of *this* sympathetically attuned agent could fail to have a moral content: One would have to be able to establish that this agent's maxim to promote the happiness of others is in reality, despite appearances, a maxim of self-love, i.e., a maxim that the agent has because she is moved to act on account of predominant benevolence toward herself. Completing this task, however, is a tall order. First, there is the difficulty presented by the fact that the prescriptive content of our agent's maxim just *is* her maxim's prescription to promote the happiness of others (see p. 104). Thus, as we have already seen when discussing Kant's account of the eudaimonist's circle in chapter 4 (see pp. 84–85), a maxim may qualify for a possible universal lawgiving whether or not it is empirically grounded in own-happiness as an end of inclination. For it will, or will not, so qualify solely in virtue of the prescriptive content that enables it to have a universally lawgiving form. Second, even in the event that this first issue *could* be successfully addressed by showing, somehow, that no empirically grounded maxim can be apt for universal lawgiving, Kant must still be able to do the following. He must be able to demonstrate that *every* sympathetically attuned agent's maxim to promote the happiness of others is in reality, despite appearances to the contrary, a maxim of self-love *insofar* as it is a maxim that such an agent has on account of her inclination to act. To do this, however, Kant has no choice but to maintain that there is no human agent—not even a sympathetically attuned human agent acting on the maxim to promote the happiness of others—who can act from any inclination whatsoever *except* predominantly self-benevolent inclination in the event that her maxim is founded on any sort of inclination at all. Otherwise, he cannot establish that there is no inclination-founded maxim that can have a moral content.[46]

As we have had ample opportunity to observe above in Part I (pp. 47–50, 55–58), Kant in fact does endorse the essential elements of the type of egoistic explanatory scheme just mentioned in the broader context of his work on the metaphysics of morals.[47] But we have also discussed what follows if this kind of metaphysical project must rely on the explanatory program that incorporates these elements (see chapter 3, pp. 72–77). According to Kant's conception of practical anthropology, which is a discipline that includes empirical moral psychology, the principles underlying this type of view have to be established by means of an investigation of the empirically cognizable conditions of motivation that are specific to (though not necessarily unique to) human beings. As Kant repeatedly emphasizes, however, the metaphysical theory of morals may not *presuppose* any anthropological explanatory tenet.[48] The metaphysics of morals may therefore not rely on a particular description of specifically human motivational conditions, although it must allow for (and indeed demands) the integration of this kind of description with the theory of the a priori concepts and laws of morally practical reason. Yet the main upshot of our explorations on Kant's

---

46 At least he cannot not establish this on the basis of his preferred conception of the relationship between inclination and maxims of self-love.
47 See, e.g., KpV 5:22.4–26.40, 5:39.5–41.38. Cf. GMS 441.25–443.27; TL 6:377.13–378.22; Refl 19:118.26–119.30, 19:121–122.7; V-Mo/Collins 27:252.7–255.28; V-Mo/Mron 27:1404.22–1406.22; V-MS/Vigil 27:646.12–651.13.
48 See, e.g., GMS 4:390.8–391.15; MS 6:216.28–217.27.

first supporting option is this: If Kant has no alternative to this option, then the *Groundwork* account of actions' moral worth would unavoidably depend on such a description and the egoistic anthropological tenet that this sort of description generates.

The theoretical costs that emerge from Kant's first supporting option for his *Groundwork* treatment of actions' moral worth are extremely high—too high, in fact, if we insist on being in a position to take seriously his metaphysically foundational project in moral philosophy. I conclude that the pathway of support explored thus far is a dead end, no matter what Kant may have thought of the psychologically egoistic account of the empirical conditions of human motivation that evidently underlies the *Groundwork's* sympathy example. Let us turn, then, to the remaining pathway mentioned above, which starts with the notion of compliance with law that we have already seen Kant address at GMS 4:400.29 – 401.2.

§ 3 Acting from Respect for Law and the Problems of Prescriptive Regress and Nomothetic Circularity

In the above quoted gloss on the nature of acting from duty as acting from respect for law (see p. 99), Kant maintains this: To act from duty is to put aside entirely the influence of inclination, so that nothing is left to determine the will except the maxim of complying with a practical law. In other words, he maintains that to act from duty is to act on the maxim of complying with a practical law, even if acting on this maxim infringes on *all* of one's inclinations.

If we are willing to grant this point, then we will indeed be in a position to uphold the view that a maxim with moral content can only be *the* maxim of complying with a practical law (even with the infringement of all one's inclinations). And this, in turn, should make it feasible to rule out the notion that any maxim founded on any sort of inclination could furnish a practical law. Thus, to use our previous example: if I act on a maxim to promote the happiness of others, my action will have no genuine moral worth unless the maxim on which I act is that of complying with the sort of practical principle that makes promoting others' happiness the duty of everyone, including myself. This maxim of *compliance*, however, is just the maxim to comply with the fundamental universality requirement of morally practical reason. It is *not* the maxim to promote the happiness of others, which one may or may not have as the result of one's inclination to do well for others. Nor can it be such a maxim since no maxim to comply with a universal law of morally practical reason can contain a prescription to do what one *may* be *inclined* to do, or not.

The line of argument just pursued may well accomplish what Kant needs to have done in order to support the particular position that he takes on the moral content of maxims. Yet if it does accomplish this, the theoretical costs that fall upon Kant's ethical theory are, once again, arguably far greater than any philosophic theory can plausibly be expected to bear. For whether or not my maxim has moral content whenever I act on the maxim to promote others' happiness, it is necessarily true (according to the fundamental assumptions involved in Kant's definitional account of practical law[49]) that my maxim can *furnish* the practical law that prescribes the promotion of others' happiness as the duty of everyone. Moreover, it is also true (according to those same fundamental assumptions) that that very same maxim of mine can furnish precisely this universal law, even if it is not the same as my maxim to *comply* with the practical law that prescribes the promotion of others' happiness. So why should my maxim of complying with such a law provide my action with its moral worth if the law that it is my maxim to comply with is one furnished by a maxim that *may or may not* be founded on an inclination to act?

This question has some interesting ramifications for Kant's view of the universally prescriptive role of morally practical reason. I will address these ramifications presently. But first let me say something about the general problem of prescriptive regress that emerges from Kant's *Groundwork* conception of the moral content of maxims. The problem is as follows.

In the explanatory gloss under consideration, Kant evidently holds, in effect, that a maxim's moral content is not supplied by its own prescriptive content (e. g., by the prescription to promote others' happiness), but is instead supplied by the second-order prescription to comply with that same content insofar as it can be universally enjoined in the form of a practical law. It follows from this that only the maxim of complying with such a law can be a maxim with properly moral content. But if this entailment holds, then it seems to follow as well that only the maxim of complying with such a maxim of compliance can have moral content. And so forth for all possible morally contentful prescriptions in ever ascending (or, if you will, descending) order. For if it is true that no maxim has its moral content simply in virtue of its *own* prescriptive content as a practical proposition, but only in virtue of being a maxim to comply with a practical law,[50] then it must also be true that the prescription to comply with a practical law cannot supply the *moral* content of a maxim unless one's maxim is to comply with a

---

[49] See chapter 3, pp. 51–52.
[50] More precisely: only in virtue of having the formal property of being the maxim to comply with a practical law.

§ 3 Respect for Law, Prescriptive Regress, and Nomothetic Circularity — 113

maxim whose content is supplied by the maxim of complying with a practical law.[51] And so on, uninterestingly, if not *ad nauseam*.[52]

While this might not amount to empty formalism, it does seem to involve a theory of the possible deontic content of practical propositions that is implicitly hyper-charged by the spurious infinite.[53] And even if Kant's theory of moral worth can effectively respond to the general regress problem just delineated, it still involves a very puzzling loop-generating implication when we bring it face to face with the *Groundwork's* basic imperatival formulation of the moral law itself. [54] The categorical imperative, after all, enjoins each one of us to act

---

[51] Notice that this implication holds even if dutifulness is *built into* a maxim's prescriptive content (see note 52). Let my maxim be, for example, 'to promote the happiness of others from duty' or 'to promote others' happiness from respect for law'. If a maxim has its moral content only in virtue of its being a maxim to comply with a practical law, then not even my maxim to promote the happiness of others *from duty* will have a moral content unless I make it my maxim to comply with a maxim whose content is supplied by the maxim of complying with a practical law. And so on.

[52] This, I take it, is the snare that threatens to entrap Henry Allison's preferred version of proposition 1 (see note 20 in this chapter). Allison writes: "[M]y proposal is that Kant's missing first proposition be expressed as follows: '"A good will under human conditions is one whose maxims have moral content', by which is understood one for which the dutifulness of a course of action is contained in (incorporated into) its maxim as a condition of its adoption" (Allison 2011, p. 125). Allison goes on to claim that this interpretation has the advantage of enabling us "to understand how an agent may act 'under the idea of duty,' as it were, without acting directly *from* duty" (Allison 2011, p. 125). That may well be so. But as long as the moral content of maxims is linked to the idea of acting from *duty*, it does not seem possible for Allison's proposal to escape the regress spiral just indicated unless some further condition can be brought to bear in Kant's account of law-compliant maxims. And *this* condition is not clarified by maintaining that a good will is one for which the dutifulness of a course of action is *contained in* a maxim as the condition of its adoption. To be sure, we must always bear in mind that (in the context of Kant's doctrine of morals) a maxim is a proposition that has a prescriptive content, i.e., a matter which consists in a prescription to act. It is also clear, according to Kant, that the prescriptive content of a maxim furnishes a condition for its adoption. Yet the moral quality or standing (*Gehalt*) of such a content is not explained by proposing, in effect, that the moral content of a maxim consists in compliance with the condition supplied by compliance with the moral content of a maxim. This is true even if the content is that of a universally prescriptive maxim, i.e., a maxim that qualifies for a possible universal lawgiving.

[53] I allow myself here the circumspect use of some Hegelian expressions.

[54] Paul Guyer as argued that Kant's basic conception of the moral worth of an *agent* consists "in making respect for duty itself one's fundamental maxim" (Guyer 2000, p. 379). Regrettably, however, taking this position provides no basis for resolving the regress problem in question, which concerns the *maxims* of the agent whose character has (or does not have) moral worth. Even if an agent has the cultivated disposition to make it her *fundamental* maxim to act from duty, it follows from Kant's *Groundwork* argument that this maxim's moral content must be

only in accordance with that maxim through which one can at the same time will that it become a universal law.⁵⁵ It does not enjoin any one of us to act only in accordance with that maxim to act only in accordance with that maxim through which one can at the same time will that it become a universal law. And even if it did, then what sort of maxim could *that* maxim possibly be apart from a maxim through which one can at the same time will that it become a universal law—a maxim to promote the happiness of others, for example, whether it is founded on inclination or not?

In sum, the particular account of compliance with law that Kant offers in his initial *Groundwork* explanation of acting from duty, as we have explored it thus far, seems not only to generate a not obviously resolvable problem of regress for the theory of universal moral prescriptions.⁵⁶ Perhaps even more significantly, it by no means sits easily with the specific interpretation of the nomothetic function—the universally lawgiving role—of morally practical reason that forms the very basis of Kant's own ethical theory.

§ 4 Dealing with the 'Elephant in the Room': Respect for Law as an Incentive for Action

Up to this point, I have attempted to deal with Kant's *Groundwork* conception of moral worth by paying close attention to the propositional properties of the practical principles that figure in Kant's account of universal lawgiving. My considerations thus far have therefore assiduously disregarded what the reader familiar with that conception will no doubt deem to be the proverbial 'elephant in the room'. By this I mean a crucial factor in Kant's discussion of moral worth that

---

that supplied by the maxim of complying with a practical law. For Kant implies that a maxim can have a *morally* prescriptive content only in virtue of being a maxim to comply with a practical law. Yet it seems to follow from this, in turn, that only a maxim of complying with such a maxim of compliance can have a moral content. And so on.

55 See GMS 4:421.6–8; cf. MS 6:226.1–3; TL 6:388.34–389.3.

56 In order for this general regress problem to be avoidable, it would have to be true that no *possible* maxim can have the formal property of being capable of universal prescription (i.e., of being a maxim that can qualify for a universal lawgiving) *in virtue of* the particular prescription for action that it contains. But this is obviously false, even on Kant's own terms. Kant emphatically insists that the contents of *some* maxims *necessarily* furnish the contents of prescriptions that qualify as practical laws. On this, see Kant's examination of the relationship between maxims of ends and practical laws in his portrayal of others' happiness and one's own perfection as necessary ends of morally practical reason (TL 6:685.30–689.30, 6:395.15–32), as treated in the first chapter of this book.

cannot credibly be ignored, namely, his understanding of the necessary connection between actions' moral worth and acting from respect for law. Yet I trust that the clarifying advantages of my procedure of presentation will soon become apparent as our concentration now shifts from the relation between maxims and the formal features of universal lawgiving to Kant's idea of acting from respect for law as an incentive.

Consider again the core contents of the three propositions linked to Kant's account of actions' moral worth in the first part of the *Groundwork*:

Proposition 1: An action has genuine moral worth if, and only if, it is done from duty.

Proposition 2: An action has its moral worth in the maxim in accordance with which it is decided upon.

Proposition 3: Duty is the necessity of an action from respect for law.[57]

As was mentioned above, Kant holds (GMS 4:400.17) that the third of these propositions follows as a consequence of the first two. In view of this intended derivation, he holds that acting from duty—hence acting in such a way that one's action has genuine moral worth—is understandable as the determination of the will by "the maxim of complying with a practical law even with the infringement of all my inclinations [*selbst mit Abbruch aller meiner Neigungen*]" (GMS 4:400.33–401.2).

Let us ignore here whatever difficulties there may be in pinning down all facets of the logical linkage between the three propositions at hand.[58] For if we ac-

---

57 There is an important point to bear in mind concerning the notion of duty mentioned in Proposition 1 and specified in Proposition 3: Kant is working here with what comes very close to being a subjectively reduced definition of the concept of duty. In focusing on the subjective aspect of duty—the necessity of an action from *respect for law* (which is an *incentive* for action—see below)—Kant is giving a definitional account that effectively downplays duty's objective aspect, which elsewhere in the *Groundwork* is characterized as, simply, the "practical unconditional necessity of [an] action" (GMS 4:425.16) and as the "objective necessity of an action from obligation" (GMS 4:439.33–34). Kant's way of treating the concept of duty in his *Groundwork* portrayal of actions' moral worth raises a number of issues. As I see it, the main problem is this: Because it does not offer an adequate conceptual platform for distinguishing between (i) duties of right (*Rechtspflichten*) and (ii) ethical duties that cannot be duties of right, the concept of duty at issue in the *Groundwork* treatment of moral worth does not allow for the distinction between different types of practical law that grounds the fundamental systematic division of Kant's metaphysics of morals—namely, the division presupposed by the juridical theory of right (*ius*) and ethics as a doctrine of virtue (*ethica*). On this, see MS 6:218.10–221.3; RL 6:232.2–23; TL 6:379.15–75, 6:383.18–20, 6:388.34–389.26, 6:394.24–32, 6:396.2–34.
58 Henry Allison maintains that there are two models for understanding Kant's claim that the third proposition in question is a "consequence of [*Folgerung aus*] the two preceding" (GMS

cept that an action has genuine moral worth only if it is done from duty (proposition 1), and if we also accept that duty is the necessity of an action from respect for law (proposition 3), then it is evident that the maxim required for an action to have moral worth (proposition 2) must be *a* maxim by which one is able to act from the practical necessity of respect for law. Consequently, it also seems plausible to hold that this must be *the* maxim of complying with a practical law even with the infringement of all one's inclinations. Whatever the nature of the argument may be that is construable from Kant's three propositions, we can therefore discern that acting on *this* maxim is just what it is to act from duty when 'duty' is understood as the necessity of an action from respect for law.

So far, so good. The constructive interpretation just offered establishes the initial consistency and coherence of Kant's *Groundwork* (Section I) considerations on the moral worth of actions. Not so good is the fact that even the most charitable interpretation of these considerations ultimately leaves Kant exposed to the related charges of prescriptive regress and nomothetic circularity that I have attempted to explain in the preceding section of this chapter. And there is a further related difficulty that I have not yet explicitly considered. It is that the *Groundwork* account of moral worth cannot be derived from the fundamental principle of Kant's method for the moral assessment of actions.

Regarding this further difficulty, consider the portrayal of the method of action assessment that Kant gives in the second part of the *Groundwork* as the re-

---

4:400.17)—namely, "(a) the deductive model, where the first and second propositions are premises from which the third is a logical consequence; or (b) the combinatory model, in which the third proposition is viewed as a combination or synthesis of the first two" (Allison 2011, p. 134). Favoring the combinatory model (properly interpreted), Allison considers model (a) to be "a non-starter" that to his knowledge "no interpreter has advocated" (Allison 2011, p. 134). He thus evidently overlooks the possibility that a proposition which combines or synthesizes elements of two other propositions can be understood as following (in keeping with rules of deductive inference) from these propositions if they are taken in conjunction with one another and regarded as premises. To be sure, Kant does not spell out the nature of the argument involving the three propositions presented in *Groundwork* I. But it does not follow from this that there is in principle no (syllogistic) argument to construe from the propositions that he presents when he asserts that one of them is a consequence of the other two combined. (Kant is certainly no stranger to the type of construal here in question. For a far more intricate instance of it, see RL 6:258.28–259.11. I discuss this instance in chapter 7, pp. 136–137.) In my view, then, the non-starter is an approach to the relationship between Kant's three propositions that begins by setting up an unwarranted opposition between two models for understanding Kant's claim concerning the derivation of proposition 3. While my considerations in this paragraph are in keeping with the combinatory model, I do not mean to suggest that a deductive approach to interpreting that relationship is inherently implausible.

sult of his *in concreto* representation of categorically prescriptive law as a law of nature:[59]

> One must *be able to will* that a maxim of our action become a universal law: this is the canon of the moral appraisal of action in general. Some actions are so constituted that their maxim cannot even be *thought* without contradiction as a universal law of nature, much less could one will that it *should* become such. In the case of others that inner impossibility is indeed not to be found, but it is still impossible to *will* that their maxim be raised to the universality of a law of nature [...].[60] (GMS 4:424.1–9)

Kant's canonic principle of action assessment is here explicated in view of three possibility conditions of coherent volition that apply to acting on maxims: (1) the possibility of thinking (without contradiction) a maxim of an action as a universal law of nature; (2) the possibility of willing that a maxim should become a universal law of nature; and (equivalently to this second condition) (3) the possibility of willing that a maxim be raised to the status of a universal law of nature.

Taken by itself, any maxim that satisfies *at least* the second or (equivalently) the third of these possibility conditions of coherent willing ought to be one that fulfills the fundamental deontic requirement asserted by the formulation of the moral law in question.[61] Thus, if I act on the maxim to promote the happiness of others, my maxim will fulfill the fundamental requirement for rationally coherent volition just because it *is* a maxim that satisfies two equivalent conditions for universal prescription on its *in concreto* interpretation in terms of natural law: (a) I can act as if the maxim of my action should become, by my will, a universal law of nature; and (b) I can act as if such a maxim of mine is one that I can will that it be raised to the universality of a law nature.

Now the contingent fact that I happen to *have* my maxim on account of being inclined to act benevolently is simply immaterial to the question of whether my maxim to promote others' happiness satisfies the fundamental deontic re-

---

[59] That is, its presentation in accordance with the notion of a 'typic' of morally practical judgment. See, jointly, GMS 4:421.4–20, 4:424.3–10; KpV 5:69.12–70.1.
[60] "Man muß *wollen können*, daß eine Maxime unserer Handlung ein allgemeines Gesetz werde: dies ist der Kanon der moralischen Beurtheilung derselben überhaupt. Einige Handlungen sind so beschaffen, daß ihre Maxime ohne Widerspruch nicht einmal als allgemeines Naturgesetz *gedacht* werden kann; weit gefehlt, daß man noch *wollen* könne, es *sollte* ein solches werden. Bei andern ist zwar jene innere Unmöglichkeit nicht anzutreffen, aber es ist doch unmöglich, zu *wollen*, daß ihre Maxime zur Allgemeinheit eines Naturgesetzes erhoben werde [...]".
[61] Namely, the so-called formula of the law of nature, which commands: "act as if the maxim of your action were to become by your will a *universal law of nature* [handle so, als ob die Maxime deiner Handlung durch deinen Willen zum *allgemeinen Naturgesetze* werden sollte]" (GMS 4:421.18–20).

quirement on the basis of which Kant explicates the meaning of his canonic principle of moral action assessment. But if this is so, then we must ask what additional basis there is for Kant's stance that my happiness-promoting action can have genuine moral worth (i.e., can be a morally good or morally meritorious action) only if I act on the maxim of complying with a practical law, even when my acting on this maxim of compliance with law infringes upon *all* my inclinations.

There is, of course, no question about what Kant's position in fact is. He is quite explicit in his insistence that an action from duty—that is, an action performed on account of the moral necessity of acting from respect for law—is one for which respect for law itself furnishes the *incentive* for that action. As Kant puts this point in the second part of the *Groundwork* at the end of his summary presentation of the line of argument leading up to the statement of the principle of autonomy as the supreme principle of morality:[62]

> We have shown [...] above how neither fear nor inclination but simply respect for law is that incentive which can give actions a moral worth. Our own will insofar as it would act only under the condition of a possible universal lawgiving through its maxims—this will possible for us in idea—is the proper object of respect [...].[63] (GMS 4:440.5–10)

This passage points all the way back to the account of actions' moral worth given in the *Groundwork's* first part. But let us consider it specifically in connection with the possibility conditions of rationally coherent volition at issue in the canon for the moral assessment of actions set forth in *Groundwork* II. It should be noted in this connection that these conditions are specified *solely* in view of a maxim's aptness for a possible universal lawgiving (in accordance with the formula "act as if the maxim of your action were to become by your will a *universal law of nature*"). Such a specification, to be sure, does entail that I must comply with a practical law to the exclusion of doing what I am inclined to do if not infringing upon all my inclinations would involve acting in a way inconsistent with the possibility of my willing that my maxim should become a universal law (or, in other words, in a way inconsistent with my acting as if my maxim were to become by my will a universal law of nature). Yet it does not entail that I must act

---

62 See GMS 4:437.5–440.13.
63 "Auch haben wir [...] gezeigt, wie weder Furcht, noch Neigung, sondern lediglich Achtung fürs Gesetz diejenige Triebfeder sei, die der Handlung einen moralischen Werth geben kann. Unser eigener Wille, so fern er nur unter der Bedingung einer durch seine Maximen möglichen allgemeinen Gesetz|gebung handeln würde, dieser uns mögliche Wille in der Idee ist der eigentliche Gegenstand der Achtung [...]".

on the *maxim* of complying with such a law *even if* it is possible for me to will, without infringing upon *all* my inclinations, that a different maxim—the maxim to do well for others, for example—should become a universal law. We can therefore see that Kant's method of action assessment, as it is presented in the second part of the *Groundwork*, leaves open the following possibility. Insofar as our (including my) own ideally possible lawgiving will *is* the proper object of respect, my respect for law *can* be the incentive for my acting on the maxim to promote the happiness of others even when I am inclined to act on *this* maxim, and consequently do not act on the maxim of complying with a practical law even to the exclusion of everything that I might be inclined to do. Thus, even if complying with my maxim does not infringe upon all my inclinations, I am still able to act from respect for law as my incentive for acting. And I am able to do so whether or not I am inclined so to act whenever I act on my maxim to promote others' happiness rather than on the maxim of complying with a practical law. For neither my ability nor my inability to act from inclination when I act on a maxim excludes the possibility of my acting from respect for law as my incentive (as distinguished from my maxim), especially if I can will that the maxim on which I am acting is one that should become a universal law. It is, after all, a constitutive feature of Kant's very concept of morally practical reason that any rational agent must be able to act from respect for law as its incentive *even if inclined* to act in a certain way.[64] In my capacity as a rational agent, then, I must be able to act from the incentive furnished by my respect for law *whenever* I can will that my maxim should become a universal law. And I must be able to do this even when I do not act on the maxim of complying with a practical law even to the exclusion of all my inclinations.

Whatever claims Kant may make concerning the impossibility of acting from *both* duty and inclination,[65] such claims are not supported by the *Groundwork* account of his method for the moral assessment of actions. While Kant's canon for moral action assessment is fully consistent with the view that the concept of duty involves the necessity of acting from respect for law, it does not support the assumption that I am *always* to act in such a way that I must exclude my acting from inclination if I am to act from duty, or if I am to act from respect for law as my incentive for acting. It does not support this assumption because it is always possible for me—or for any other finite rational agent—to act from respect for law as my *incentive* without making it my *maxim* to act from respect for law,

---

64 See, e.g., KpV 5:78.20–82.12.
65 See e.g., KpV 5:83.17–22; VARGV 23:100.19–20, 23:119.31–120.1.

even if I can will that the maxim on which I am acting is one that should become a universal law.

How is this possible? According to Kant, an incentive (*elater animi*) is a subjective motivational feature of our constitution that pertains to, or presupposes, feeling (*Gefühl*) even when it is something brought about through the efficacy of reason (as is the case with moral feeling *qua* feeling of respect for the moral law).[66] A maxim, however, is a type of proposition: the sort of proposition that contains a prescriptive rule for reason-guided, or indeed reason-determined, action.[67] Thus, since having the incentive to act from respect for law cannot be the same thing as making it one's maxim to act from respect for law as one's incentive, I (like any other finite rational agent) may perfectly well be able to act from respect for law even without infringing upon whatever inclination I might have to do what is commanded by a practical law. And in the event I am able to act in this manner, then making it my maxim to act from respect for law will not be the same as making it my maxim to comply with a practical law even with the infringement of all my inclinations. I will simply be making it my maxim to act from respect for law as my incentive for acting. Or more precisely, if less simply, I will be making it my maxim to act from respect for law as my incentive for complying with *a* law that I may be inclined to comply with—which is not the same as making it my maxim to comply with a practical law as my incentive, much less the same as making it my maxim to comply with a practical law even to the exclusion of all my inclinations. Moreover, I will be *able* to act from respect for law as my incentive even if I do not make it my maxim to act from respect for law and, moreover, even if I am not inclined to act in this way. For it may well be that I am acting on another maxim that satisfies the condition for a possible universal lawgiving while my incentive, if not my inclination, is to act from respect for law (as such). Just because I am a rational agent, respect for law can *always* be my incentive to act. It makes no difference whether I am or am not *inclined* to act from respect for law as my incentive as long as it is possible for me to act as if the maxim of my action were to become by my will a universal law of nature.

In sum: Kant's stated method for the moral assessment of actions provides no sufficient theoretical basis for excluding the *possibility* of my acting from respect for law *insofar* as I act on a maxim that I happen to have on account of my being inclined to act, even when acting on a maxim that is apt for a universal

---

[66] See, e.g., GMS 4:401.15–25; KpV 5:75.6–76.23; MS 6:387.12–23, 6:399.1–400.20; VAMS 23:389.9–13. For discussion of various problems involved in Kant's account of respect for law in relation to moral feeling, see Stratton-Lake 2000, chapters 2–4. See also Baum 2006; Baxley 2011, pp. 145–171; Esser 2004, pp. 329–339; Goy 2013; Guyer 2010.
[67] See chapter 3, pp. 51–52.

lawgiving. And while the *Groundwork* (I) position on the moral worth of actions evidently requires the exclusion of this possibility, the actual costs of exclusion— spuriously infinite prescriptive regress and non-virtuous nomothetic circularity— leave Kant dangling and without the theoretical resources needed to offer an effective argument against the type of counter-position that we encounter in the 'undoubted maxim' of Hume's *Treatise*. Thus, the effective Kantian response to this sentimentalist counter-position should arguably not be to maintain this (which is what Kant in effect maintains in *Groundwork* I):

> No action done from inclination can have genuine moral worth *because* only actions done from duty even to the complete exclusion of inclination can have such worth.

Instead, it seems that the basis for an adequate Kantian response, in keeping with Kant's explicated method of assessing the moral qualities of actions, should lie in the following revised position:

> An action can have genuine moral worth *only if* one can will that its maxim should become a universal law, and *even if* acting on its maxim infringes upon all of one's inclinations— *including* every inclination that one might have, but in fact does not have, to act on that maxim *insofar* as one can will that it should become a universal law.

Needless to say, this revised position involves an approach to the question of actions' moral worth that is *prima facie* far less straightforward, and is indeed intrinsically rather more complex, than the approach leading from the first. Its great advantage, though, is that it actually provides the theoretical platform for delivering an effective response to anyone who, like Hume, would insist that no action performed from the sense of duty *alone* can have genuine moral worth. It provides this platform because it allows us to establish that respect for law can *always* be one's incentive for acting on a maxim that is apt for a universal lawgiving, whether or not one is *inclined* to act on such a maxim.

If the theoretical platform just characterized holds up, then we will do well to ask exactly what we have been arguing about for the past two centuries, and more, whenever we have taken opposing positions that stem from eighteenth-century ethics in order to intervene in an ongoing debate on the moral worth of actions. We will take up this task below, in chapter 11, when we broaden the scope of the discussion of moral worth to include the Stoic idea of the *honestum* and its significance for eighteenth-century sentimentalist and rationalist ethics. The concluding task of the present chapter is to prepare the way for this broadening discussion by linking my suggestion for revising Kant's *Groundwork* position to the considerations on moral worth and the law of greatest human perfection that were offered in chapter 4.

At the end of the second section of chapter 4 (see pp. 90–91), I called attention to Kant's interpretation of this law of perfection as a principle of action assessment according to which we have the duty to appraise the worth of all our actions. I pointed out that this interpretation involves the view that the worth of our actions is a function of a human agent's capacity to do his duty from duty, even though "in the case of every deed it remains hidden from the agent how much pure moral content there has been in his disposition [*Gesinnung*]" (TL 6:393.1–3). Given this limitation placed on self-knowledge with respect to the moral content of any human agent's disposition or set of mind, Kant understands his law of greatest human perfection to be one that presents a duty of action assessment that pertains to the cultivated disposition to make duty the incentive for acting. Accordingly, he holds that this law prescribes the maxim "to *strive* with all one's might that the thought of duty for its own sake is the sufficient incentive for every action conforming to duty" (TL 6:393.8–10—italics mine [J. E.]).

At the very end of my considerations on Kant's law of greatest perfection, I claimed that to act on the maxim so prescribed must 'surely' be to act on a principle of volition that cannot possibly have an empirical ground. I made this claim primarily in view of Kant's denial that we can know the extent of our disposition's pure moral content when acting. But I also immediately called it into question in anticipation of the investigations that would be undertaken up to this point. Thus, I here pose that question once again, this time in conjunction with two queries about the platform provided by the suggested revision of Kant's *Groundwork* position on the moral worth of actions: (1) Can this platform bear the weight of a theory of moral worth that incorporates Kant's account of reason's obligatory ends as material determining grounds of the power of choice. (2) Can such a theory of moral worth, using this this platform, accommodate an empirically grounded maxim of moral self-perfection. We will return to these questions in Part IV, after completing the historical and conceptual framework needed for a proper response.

Part III Kant's Juridical Theory of Right and the Foundations of Property Law

We now come to grips with the first main division in the *Metaphysics of Morals:* the Doctrine of Right, which treats the laws of freedom that present duties of right as matters of juridical obligation. As is the case in the Doctrine of Virtue, the juridical laws of Kant's theory of the metaphysical first principles of right are established by examining the role that reason plays with respect to actions. But our focus now shifts to a fundamentally different type of reason's nomothetic function than we have encountered thus far when dealing with issues concerning the relationship between maxims and practical laws that arise in connection with Kant's moral doctrine of obligatory ends. Specifically, we move from Kant's conception of ethical lawgiving and its account of ends that are also duties to the consideration of juridical lawgiving, which involves the kind of universally prescriptive thinking that does not make the idea of duty the incentive for performing actions that practical laws represent as necessary to the agent. That is, our focus shifts to the type of lawgiving which, unlike ethical lawgiving, "does not include the incentive of duty in the law and so admits an incentive other than the idea of duty itself" (MS 6:219.3–6).

Juridical lawgiving, then, "does not require that the idea of duty, which is internal, itself be the determining ground of the agent's power of choice" (MS 6:219.18–20). Accordingly, the matters of obligation for which it is responsible are "external duties" (MS 6:219.17–18). And because juridical lawgiving, like ethical lawgiving, still requires "an incentive suited for laws", the kind of incentive that it "connects with law" can only be an external one (MS 6:219.20–21). Thus, the external duties (i.e., the duties of external action) with which juridical lawgiving is concerned are the matters of obligation connected with "external constraint [*der äußere Zwang*]" (MS 6:220.4) or coercion.

In keeping with the external character of the duties, and incentives for action at issue in the theory of right, Kant holds that the laws which present duties of right are those for which an external lawgiver, and thus an external lawgiving, is possible. For unlike its ethical counterpart, juridical lawgiving yields laws that are not necessarily thought of as laws of "*your* own will" but of "will in general, which could also be the will of others" (TL 6:389.4–5).

Generally speaking, the doctrine of right (*ius*) as a whole is "the sum [*Inbegriff*] of those laws for which an external lawgiving is possible" (RL 6:229.5–6).[1]

---

[1] Comprehensive treatments of Kant's doctrine of right are provided in Byrd/Hruschka 2010;

Included in this definition are both positive right, when there has actually been an external lawgiving, and "the immutable principles for any giving of positive law" (RL 6:229.15). The foundational part of the doctrine of right, i.e., the part that deals with such immutable first principles, is Kant's general theme in the first division of the *Metaphysics of Morals*. Thus, the 1797 Doctrine of Right concerns the concept of right to the extent that it has to do with three metaphysically fundamental relations that feature in Kant's idea of reason's external lawgiving: first, "the external, and indeed practical, relation of one person to another, insofar as their actions, as deeds [*facta*], can have (direct or indirect) influence on each other" (RL 6:230.9 – 11); second, "a relation […] to the other's *power of choice*" (RL 230.14 – 15), i.e., the reciprocal relation between the powers of choice of different persons whose actions are reciprocally related; and third, this same reciprocal relation of volitional powers, but only insofar as "no account at all is taken of the *matter* of the power of choice that is, the end that each [person] has in mind [*zur Absicht hat*] with the object that he wants" [2] (RL 6:230.15 – 17). It is in view of this exclusion of the matter of the power of choice, as it applies to the practical relation of persons, that Kant formally defines "right" as "the sum of the conditions under which the power of choice of one can be united with the power of choice of another in accordance with a universal law" [3] (RL 6:230.24 – 26).

When treating the conditions of unity for the law-conforming reciprocal relation of persons' powers of choice, Kant is concerned with conditions of the free use of these powers. Consequently, the universal principle that applies to this

---

Kersting 1993; Gregor 1963. See also Ludwig 1986, pp. XII-XL for a brief account of the developmental history and contemporary impact of Kant's juridical doctrine.

2 "Der Begriff des Rechts, sofern er sich auf eine ihm correspondirende Verbindlichkeit bezieht, (d.i. der moralische Begriff desselben) betrifft *erstlich* nur das äußere und zwar praktische Verhältniß einer Person gegen eine andere, sofern ihre Handlungen als Facta aufeinander (unmittelbar oder mittelbar) Einfluß haben können. Aber *zweitens* bedeutet er nicht das Verhältniß der Willkür auf den *Wunsch* (folglich auch auf das bloße Bedürfniß) des Anderen, wie etwa in den Handlungen der Wohlthätigkeit oder Hartherzigkeit, sondern lediglich auf die Willkür des Anderen. *Drittens*, in diesem wechselseitigen Verhältniß der Willkür kommt auch gar nicht die *Materie* der Willkür, d.i. der Zweck, den ein jeder mit dem Object, was er will, zur Absicht hat, in Betrachtung, z.B. es wird nicht gefragt, ob jemand bei der Waare, die er zu seinem eigenen Handel von mir kauft, auch seinen Vortheil finden möge, oder nicht, sondern nur nach der Form im Verhältniß der beiderseitigen Willkür, sofern sie bloß als frei betrachtet wird, und ob durch die Handlung eines von beiden sich mit der Freiheit des andern nach einem allgemeinen Gesetze zusammen vereinigen lasse" (RL 6:230.7 – 23).

3 "Das Recht ist also der Inbegriff der Bedingungen, unter denen die Willkür des einen mit der Willkür des andern nach einem allgemeinen Gesetze der Freiheit zusammen vereinigt werden kann" (RL 6:230.24 – 26).

use must be that "[a]ny action is *right* if it can coexist with everyone's freedom in accordance with a universal law' (RL 6:230.28–31). This overarching juridical principle of freedom, however, is only a principle of *external* actions and the conditions that apply to them. For as long as "my action or my condition [*Zustand*] in general can coexist with the freedom of action of everyone in accordance with a universal law" (RL 6:231.32–33), it cannot be demanded of me that I make the universal principle of right the *maxim* of my action, even if it is a "principle of all maxims" (RL 6:231.4)—i.e., a principle that holds for all of the subjective principles of volition that I might adopt when pursuing the ends that I may have in mind with the objects that I want. Thus, the universal law here in question (namely, the law in accordance with which an action is right if it can coexist with everyone's freedom) must be one that takes account of the limited scope of the deontic requirement that applies to external action:

> [T]he universal law of right, so act externally that the free use of your power of choice can coexist with the freedom of everyone in accordance with a universal law, is [...] a law that lays an obligation upon me, but it does not expect, far less demand, that I *myself should* restrict my freedom just for the sake of this obligation; instead, reason says only that freedom *is* restricted to those conditions in conformity with the idea of it and that it may be actively restricted by others.[4] (RL 6:231.10–17).

The universal law of right, then, is the encompassing law that applies to all specifying laws for external actions that present particular duties of right. It does not apply to any laws for maxims of actions, although all laws for maxims must also be consistent with the laws for external actions (on this, see chapter 1, pp. 18–19).

Accordingly, the concept of right contained in Kant's universal principle and universal law of right is that of a "completely external" right (RL 6:232.17). It is the concept of a "strict right" (RL 6:231.13)—i.e., a right that is "not mingled with anything ethical", and is thus "not mixed with any precepts of virtue" (RL 6:232.13–16). As such, it is a deontic concept that includes external coercion as an essential feature. For whatever is contrary to right, i.e., whatever is juridically wrong (*unrecht*), is a hindrance to freedom in accordance with universal

---

4 "Also ist das allgemeine Rechtsgesetz: handle äußerlich so, daß der freie Gebrauch deiner Willkür mit der Freiheit von jedermann nach einem allgemeinen Gesetze zusammen bestehen könne, zwar ein Gesetz, welches mir eine Verbindlichkeit auferlegt, aber ganz und gar nicht erwartet, noch weniger fordert, daß ich ganz um dieser Verbindlichkeit willen meine Freiheit auf jene Bedingungen *selbst* einschränken *solle*, sondern die Vernunft sagt nur, daß sie in ihrer Idee darauf eingeschränkt sei und von andern auch thätlich eingeschränkt werden dürfe" (RL 6:231.10–17).

laws; and the use of coercive force in opposition to this kind of hindrance must be consistent with freedom in accordance with those same laws. That is to say: external coercion must be right if it is the "*hindering* of a *hindrance to freedom*", from which it follows that "there is connected with right by the principle of contradiction the authorization [*Befügnis*] to coerce someone who infringes upon it"[5] (RL 6:231.31–34). Thus, given the analytic relation between right and external coercion, strict right can be straightforwardly represented as "the possibility of a fully reciprocal use of coercion that is consistent with everyone's freedom in accordance with universal laws"[6] (RL 6:232.2–4). Kant develops his theory of the normative basis for all laws of right in view of this representation of strict right.[7]

The foundational account of the laws of right provided in the *Metaphysics of Morals* is itself divided into two main parts: Private Right (*das Privatrecht, ius privatum*) and Public Right (*das öffentliche Recht, ius publicum*). The theory of private right establishes laws pertaining to what is "externally mine and thine in general" (RL 6:245.7). These are laws that must be thought of as having universally prescriptive import even when taken in abstraction from the conditions of civil society by which they are secured. The basic laws of private right are therefore the a priori laws of practical reason that ought to be obeyed by everyone in accordance with the rational idea of a state of nature. That is "why right in a state of nature is called private right" (RL 6:242.19). The theory of public right treats laws that provide the normative framework of the "civil condition (*status civilis*)", i.e., the state of "a society subject to distributive justice" (RL

---

[5] "wenn ein gewisser Gebrauch der Freiheit selbst ein Hinderniß der Freiheit nach allgemeinen Gesetzen (d.i. unrecht) ist, so ist der Zwang, der diesem entgegengesetzt wird, als Verhinderung eines Hindernisses der Freiheit mit der Freiheit nach allgemeinen Gesetzen zusammen stimmend, d.i. recht: mithin ist mit dem Rechte zugleich eine Befugniß, den, der ihm Abbruch thut, zu zwingen, nach dem Satze des Widerspruchs verknüpft" (RL 6:231.28–34).

[6] "*Das* **stricte** *Recht kann auch als die Möglichkeit eines mit jedermanns Freiheit nach allgemeinen Gesetzen zusammenstimmenden durchgängigen wechselseitigen Zwanges vorgestellt werden*" (RL 6:232.2–5). On the analytic connections between the concepts of right and compulsion or constraint, see the critical discussion of Reinhardt Brandt, Wolfgang Kersting, and Bernd Ludwig in Friedrich 2004, pp. 12–17, 55–57, 69–71, 174–181. See also Pinheiro Walla 2014.

[7] The Doctrine of Right makes room for the consideration of two rights that do not belong to the theory of strict right: equity and the right of necessity *(ius necessitatis)* (see RL 6:230.30–236.16). But these are only ambiguously (or equivocally) rights since "[t]he first admits a right without coercion, [and] the second coercion without a right" (RL 6:234.3–5). Kant's aim in placing these ambiguous rights in the appendix of the introduction to his juridical doctrine is thus to explain why they cannot be elements of the theory of *ius strictum*. For systematic discussion of Kant's aim in conjunction with his account of the relationship between commutative and distributive justice in the Doctrine of Right as a whole see Byrd/Hruschka 2010, pp. 214–231.

6:306.21–22). Since the laws of private right (i.e., the laws governing the juridical state of nature) are universally prescriptive even when considered apart from the civil condition structured by the laws of public right, Kant holds that the systematic account of the latter "contains no further or other duties among human beings than can be conceived in the former state" (RL 6:306.31–32). Thus, maintaining that "the matter of private right is the same in both", he infers that "[t]he laws of the condition of public right [...] concern only the juridical form of their [i.e., human beings'] association (constitution)" (RL 6:306.32–34).[8]

Given Kant's understanding of the relationship between matter and form that applies to the systematic division between private and public right, Part III of this book will be concerned with the material aspect of the doctrine of right's metaphysical foundations. That is, I will be concerned with duties among human beings that furnish the matter of both private and public right. More particularly, I will examine the components of the overall account of these duties and their corresponding laws by which Kant lays out the normative basis for understanding what it is to have an external thing as one's own and to acquire something external that one does not have to begin with. In brief, I will be dealing exclusively with Kant's theory of the foundations of property law, especially as it pertains to the possession and acquisition of external things.

My reasons for restricting our thematic concern to Kant's treatment of possession and the normative grounds of acquisition will be fully clarified only in chapter 12, where I discuss the significance of various theories of original acquisition in connection with the ideas of natural right and material equality in distribution. The task of chapters 6 and 7 is therefore essentially preparatory. There is just one further point to which I want to draw our attention at this juncture, before launching into Kant's theory of the foundations of property law.

As noted above, Kant's metaphysical doctrine of right takes no account of the *matter* of the powers of choice of persons who, directly or indirectly, exist in a relation of reciprocal influence in virtue of their free use of these volitional powers. When discussing this kind of matter, Kant makes it abundantly clear that the theory of strict right brackets out all questions of need such as those that arise in connection with "actions of beneficence or callousness" (RL 6:230.13–14). It is also important to note, however, that this crucial bracketing

---

[8] "Man kann den ersteren und zweiten Zustand den des *Privatrechts*, den letzteren und dritten aber den des *öffentlichen Rechts* nennen. Dieses enthält nicht mehr oder andere Pflichten der Menschen unter sich, als in jenem gedacht werden können; die Materie des Privatrechts ist eben dieselbe in beiden. Die Gesetze des letzteren betreffen also nur die rechtliche Form ihres Beisammenseins (Verfassung), in Ansehung deren diese Gesetze nothwendig als öffentliche gedacht werden müssen" (RL 6:306.29–35).

operation does *not* amount to a decision that there is no doctrine of positive right which could be consistent with Kant's foundational treatment of strict right if it *does* take full account of human needs.[9] Indeed, as we will ultimately see, Kant's treatment of *ius strictum* does not necessarily exclude the possibility that a coherent theory of distributive justice must address the question of human needs on the *basis* of a formal principle of material equality which applies to the acquisition of external things.

But this is already to go well beyond the preparatory work that has to be undertaken Part III. Let us turn to Kant portrayal of the foundations of property law.

---

[9] For the bearing that Kant's foundational juridical doctrine has on the question of social welfare, see Kaufman 1999, pp. 1–35; Rosen 1993, 173–208. More generally, for discussion of the relationship between Kant's theory of the state and contemporary forms of liberalism, libertarianism, and socialist theory, see Wood 2008, pp. 192–205; Wood 2014, pp. 83–89; Ripstein 2009, 232–299.

Chapter 6 Original Community, Possession, and Acquisition in Kant's Doctrine of Right

As noted, Kant's theory of private right treats the conditions under which external objects of the power of choice can be rightfully "mine and yours". It is divided into three main parts, all of which concern the principles that ought to govern the power of choice in relation to anything that can be acquired as externally mine or yours.[1] The first part, the doctrine of possession (§§ 1–9), determines the general conditions under which one can have something external as "one's own [*das Seine*]". The second part, the doctrine of acquisition (§§ 10–35), establishes the way in which something external may be rightfully acquired. The third part—"Of Subjectively Conditioned Acquisition through Decision by a Public Court of Justice" (§§ 36–42)—gives an a priori account of basic contractual relations and other normative factors in keeping with which the public administration of justice should take place. In this chapter, I discuss the doctrine of possession in connection with the portion of the doctrine of acquisition in which Kant establishes the principles by which corporeal objects can become property (*Eigentum* or *dominium*). I therefore focus on the concepts of possession and acquisition as they apply to the law of things (*Sachenrecht*).[2] The primary item of interest is the role played by the idea of an original community of possession, or original possession in common, in Kant's theory of acquisition.

§ 1 Intelligible Possession and the Juridical Postulate of Practical Reason

The doctrine of possession revolves around two systematic factors: the exposition of the concept of intelligible possession; and the argument by which Kant establishes the universal validity of the juridical postulate of practical reason. In this section, I will clarify these factors in the order just mentioned.

---

[1] See RL 6:245.5. For general discussion of the structure and systematic character of the theory of private right, see Fulda 1998, pp.141–156; Kersting 1993, pp. 225–321. See also Guyer 2002, pp. 23–64.

[2] On the relationship between *Sachenrecht* and the theory of property in Kant, see Friedrich 2004, 89–95. On modern theories of property and their developmental background, see Brandt 1974; Brocker 1992; Buckle 1991; Edwards 2002; Tierney 1997; Tierney 2001. For a general account of Kant's theory of property, see Gregor 2006. See also Ripstein 2009, pp. 86–106; Westphal 1997.

Kant defines what is "rightfully mine" (*meum iuris*) as something with which "I am so connected that another's use of it without my consent would wrong me"³ (RL6:245.9–11). In view of this definition, he stipulates that the subjective condition under which I can make use of anything is possession; and he holds that the possibility of my possessing (and hence using) something as rightfully mine presupposes that a clear distinction can be drawn between two basic meanings of possession.⁴ It is necessary to distinguish between sensible or physical possession and intelligible or merely rightful possession (*bloß rechtlicher Besitz*).⁵ These different meanings correspond to a distinction that underlies our thinking of objects, a distinction implicit in the expression 'external to me'. It is the distinction between an object conceived as something 'merely distinct from me' as a subject and an object regarded as something located in another position in space or existing in another time. The type of possession that corresponds to the first sense of externality—intelligible possession—is possession taken without limiting reference to the conditions under which something exists apart from me in space or time.⁶ Since (according to Kant) these conditions are all sensible, intelligible possession leads to the understanding of rightful possession as purely rational possession (*Vernunftbesitz*).

Interpreted as intelligible or rational possession, rightful possession is not merely non-sensible. It is also non-empirical. Possession is empirical when a subject's relation to objects depends on the spatial and temporal limitations that are characteristic of physically having some object in hand or at hand.⁷ As Kant puts this point: "Intelligible possession (if such is possible) is possession *without holding* (*detentio*)" (RL6:245.27–246.2).⁸ Accordingly, the possibility of intelligible possession, as rational possession, has fundamentally to do with our capacity to abstract from the conditions of physical possession. As rational beings, we must be able to disregard the set of sensible conditions under which 'empirical possession' denotes a subject's phenomenal relation to certain objects

---

3 "Das rechtlich Meine (*meum iuris*) ist dasjenige, womit ich so verbunden bin, daß der Gebrauch, den ein Anderer ohne meine Einwilligung von ihm machen möchte, mich lädiren würde" (6:245.9–11).

4 See RL 6:245.13–21.

5 Whenever appropriate, I translate *rechtlich* with 'rightful'. Ordinarily, though, I use 'juridical'. This accords with Kant's own use of the cognate adjective when he refers to *juridische Gesetzgebung* and *juridischer Naturzustand*, and it avoids Gregor's circumlocutionary renderings (e.g., 'postulate of practical reason with regard to rights' for *rechtliches postulat der praktischen Vernunft*), which on occasion can be misleading.

6 See RL 6:245.23–27.

7 See RL 6:245.16–27.

8 "Ein *intelligibler* Besitz (wenn ein solcher möglich ist) ist ein Besitz *ohne Inhabung* (*detentio*)".

of choice (i.e., *possessio phaenomenon*). Intelligible possession must therefore denote a noumenal possessive relation to such objects (*possessio noumenon*), and the practical proposition that grounds the juridical possibility of intelligible (or non-physical) possession is one which presupposes that *all* conditions of empirical possession in space and time can be set aside. For only in this way can possession without holding, i.e., intelligible possession, be affirmed as "necessary for the concept of something externally mine and yours" (RL6:250.13–14).[9]

The practical proposition just referred to is the juridical postulate of practical reason. This postulate is given its primary formulation in § 2 of the Doctrine of Right.[10] The postulate states:

---

9 "Dagegen geht der Satz von der Möglichkeit des Besitzes einer Sache *außer mir* nach Absonderung aller Bedingungen des empirischen Besitzes im Raum und Zeit (mithin die Voraussetzung der Möglichkeit einer *possessio noumenon*) über jene einschränkende Bedin|gungen hinaus, und weil er einen Besitz auch ohne Inhabung als nothwendig zum Begriffe des äußeren Mein und Dein statuirt" (RL 6:250.9–14). For commentary covering the relationship between intelligible and empirical possession, see Byrd (2010; Byrd/Hruschka 2010, pp. 107–142; Flikschuh 2000, pp. 121–134; Friedrich 2004, pp. 95–134; Gregor 2006, pp. 125–131.

10 As has long been widely acknowledged, the Doctrine of Right's § 6 ("Deduction of the Concept of the Merely Rightful Possession of an External Object [*possessio noumenon*]") was flawed by the insertion of a piece of text the content of which belongs to Kant's reflections on original acquisition. Bernd Ludwig, in his *Philosophische Bibliothek* edition of Kant's *Rechtslehre* (1998), has maintained that the faulty insert should be replaced by transferring the entire text of § 2 to § 6. This is not the place to examine the extensive controversy in the secondary literature that has arisen in the wake of Ludwig's editorial work and publications relating to the textual reconstruction of the Doctrine of Right. While not insisting on the sanctity of the original text, however, I should at least state here my reasons for rejecting Ludwig's approach (especially since the recent Cambridge Edition of the *Metaphysics of Morals* follows it): (1) I find that removing the faulty insert leaves no logical gap in the argument of § 6. (2) Because Kant asserts in § 6 that the possibility of non-physical possession is the immediate consequence of the juridical postulate (see RL 6:252.17–21), the deduction of the concept of non-empirical possession (in § 6) presupposes the soundness of the argument by which Kant establishes the juridical postulate. Transferring this argument from its original location (in § 2) to the middle of § 6 threatens to make Kant's deduction of the concept of merely rightful possession circular and question-begging. (I owe this point to Rainer Friedrich [2004, p. 104].) (3) The argument of § 2 grounds the juridical postulate by appealing to the formal coherence of the concept of external freedom, and by determining pure practical reason's lawgiving role in relation to the use of external objects of the power of choice. It makes no reference to the concept of non-empirical or non-physical possession, i.e., the type of possession whose possibility Kant holds to be an immediate consequence of the juridical postulate as a synthetic a priori practical proposition. Thus, even if there is a logical gap in § 6, we cannot fill it or bridge it by transferring § 2 from one textual location to another. In sum: apart from removing the considerations belonging to the doctrine of acquisition from the doctrine of possession, I see no plausible reason for assenting to any conjectural rerouting of Kant's line of argument in the Doctrine of Right.

> It is possible for me to have any [*einen jeden*] object of my power of choice as mine; that is, a maxim by which, if it were to become a law, an object of the power of choice would *in itself* (objectively) have to become something *belonging to no one* (*res nullius*) is contrary to right.[11] (RL 6:246.5–8)

Kant argues that this juridical postulate provides us with a permissive law (*lex permissiva*): a law that authorizes each of us to put all other rational agents under an obligation that they would not otherwise have, namely, the obligation to "refrain from the use of certain objects of our power of choice because we were the *first* to take them into our possession [italics mine]"[12] (RL 6:247.2–6). He maintains further that the possibility of intelligible (i.e., non-physical) possession must be "inferred" from the juridical postulate as an *immediate* consequence of the latter.[13] As we will see, the combination of these two factors—the interpretation of the juridical postulate as a permissive law that grounds obligation through first possession; and the view that intelligible possession is grounded as a direct implication of the same postulate—determines the character of Kant's theory of the foundations of property law. But first we need to understand these factors in the context of the doctrine of possession in which they are introduced.

Since the juridical postulate asserts that *any* object of my power of choice is something that is possibly mine, we can see that physical possession cannot be the defining mark of the rightful possession that correlates with the notion of rightfully mine.[14] Thus, if rightful possession is to be possible, the spatio-temporal conditions that limit physical (or empirical) possession must be set aside. And if this is true, we can readily understand how the possibility of rightful possession (as intelligible possession) is anchored directly in the categorical requirement of practical reason expressed by the juridical postulate. What is not so

---

[11] "Es ist möglich, einen jeden äußern Gegenstand meiner Willkür als das Meine zu haben; d.i.: eine Maxime, nach welcher, wenn sie Gesetz würde, ein Gegenstand der Willkür *an sich* (objectiv) *herrenlos* (*res nullius*) werden müßte, ist rechtswidrig".

[12] "Man kann dieses Postulat ein Erlaubnißgesetz (*lex permissiva*) der praktischen Vernunft nennen, was uns die Befugniß giebt, die wir aus bloßen Begriffen vom Rechte überhaupt nicht herausbringen könnten: nämlich allen andern eine Verbindlichkeit aufzulegen, die sie sonst nicht hätten, sich des Gebrauchs gewisser Gegenstände unserer Willkür zu enthalten, weil wir zuerst sie in unseren Besitz genommen haben" (RL 6:247.1–6).

[13] See RL 6:252.17–21.

[14] Kant defines "object of choice [*Gegenstand der Willkür*]" as "something that I have physically in my power [*Macht*] to use" (RL 6:246.9–10). Thus, the concept of 'rightfully mine' at issue in the juridical postulate applies to any object (and indeed to all objects) that I *can* have physically in my power to use irrespective of the limitations of my actual physical possession of any particular object (or objects) that is (or are) spatially distinct from me at any given point of time.

§ 1 Intelligible Possession and the Juridical Postulate of Practical Reason — 133

readily apparent, however, is how this grounding relation fits together with the interpretation of the juridical postulate as a law that authorizes me (or anyone else) to obligate others to refrain from making use of some object of my power of choice because I was the first to take it into my possession.[15] To better understand this problematic, let us turn to §§ 8–9 of the Doctrine of Right, where Kant treats the concept of provisional rightful possession in connection with his account of the juridical and civil condition (*Zustand*).

In the sections just cited, Kant establishes that a subject can be in the state of having something external as her own only if she exists in a juridical condition (*rechtlicher Zustand*) with respect to other subjects, that is, in a civil condition (*bürgerlicher Zustand*) involving a publicly legislative power. Such a power requires a civil constitution that conforms to the universal principle and a priori laws of right set forth as principles of natural law in the Doctrine of Right.[16] This civil constitution is what represents the juridical condition in which everything that belongs to each person is secured for every single person respectively as his own. Kant thus takes the civil constitution to be the fundamental guarantee of right with respect to everything that is externally mine and yours. At the same time, though, he insists that this guarantee *presupposes* a normatively valid possessive relation, and he links this presupposition to the assumption that something externally mine and yours must be possible even apart from the condition under which it is guaranteed:

---

[15] Kant holds that the authorization to place such an obligation on others cannot be obtained "from mere concepts of right" (RL 6:247.2–3)—i.e., from the fundamental understanding of right as "the sum of the conditions under which the power of choice of one can be united with the power of choice of another in accordance with a universal law of freedom" (RL 6:230.24–26). This standpoint is fully consistent with Kant's position that the juridical postulate furnishes a synthetic a priori proposition that cannot be derived analytically from the universal principle or the universal law of right, even though the proof of practical reason's capacity to lay down synthetic a priori propositions "can […] in a practical respect, be adduced in an analytic way" (RL 6:255.20–21). (Regarding this position, see further RL 6:230.29–31, 6:231.10–11, 6:249.30–250.17, 6:251.37–252.30, 6:255.13–20; TL 6:396.4–11.) But just why should the *possibility* of my having any object of my power of choice as something rightfully mine warrant the exclusion of others from the use of an object because I *was* the first to take possession of it? In other words, the question is why the juridical postulate (as the synthetic a priori practical proposition that asserts the possibility of the merely rightful possession of external objects) does not necessarily abstract from the temporal priority of possession-taking acts if we must set aside all conditions of empirical possession.
[16] On the significance of Kant's account of private right for natural-law theory, see, e.g., RL 6:242.3–19, 6:256.22–35, 6:257.14–19.

> Any guarantee, then, already presupposes that something belongs to someone (to whom it secures it). Thus, prior to the civil constitution (or in *abstraction* from it), something externally mine or yours must be assumed as possible, and with it also a right to compel everyone with whom we could have any dealings to enter with us into a constitution in which what is externally mine and yours can be secured.[17] (RL 6:256.30 – 35)

We thus arrive at the interpretation of rightful possession that furnishes the centerpiece of the description of the state of nature relevant to the theory of private right. Apart from the civil constitution, anything that can be thought of as externally mine and yours must be understood as a merely provisional rightful possession.[18] In a provisional sense, possession can be rightful even for agents who are thought of as existing in a state of nature. Possession in this natural condition can be rightful in the sense that it permits anyone to resist those who are unwilling to enter into the civil condition and who would interfere with what one has come to possess. But this way of portraying what it is to have something as one's own in the state of nature must still be characterized in terms of *physical* (or *empirical*) possession. It qualifies as rightful possession only in a derivative sense: It has in its favor "the rightful presumption" that it will be *made* rightful possession "through unification with the will of all in a public lawgiving" (RL 6:257.14 – 18). Thus, by treating the relationship between the different meanings of rightful possession, Kant brings to light the necessary connection between the concepts of rightful possession and universal will. But he also acknowledges, as a crucial component of his theory of private right, a "prerogative of right arising from empirical possession" (RL 6:257.20).

Now consider again the problem addressed above, which concerns the interpretation of the juridical postulate as a permissive law by which the obligation-founding character of first possession is determined. In keeping with Kant's considerations thus far, we can understand first possession-taking (*Bestiznehmung*) as the type of act that gives rise to empirical possession. We can also accept that the empirical possession achieved through first possession-taking has to be consistent with the deontic requirements of right which are developed from Kant's concept of universal will. On these assumptions, we are presumably in a position to grasp how possession-taking can establish a prerogative of right that necessa-

---

[17] "Alle Garantie setzt also das Seine von jemanden (dem es gesichert wird) schon voraus. Mithin muß vor der bürgerlichen Verfassung (oder von ihr abgesehen) ein äußeres Mein und Dein als möglich angenommen werden und zugleich ein Recht, jedermann, mit dem wir irgend auf eine Art in Verkehr kommen könnten, zu nöthigen, mit uns in eine Verfassung zusammen zu treten, worin jenes gesichert werden kann".
[18] See RL 6:256.35 – 257.6.

rily correlates with the obligation of others (or more precisely: with the obligation to be placed on others) to refrain from using objects of our powers choice *because* we were, each of us respectively, the first to take them into our possession. To see whether these conjectures bear out, however, we must move beyond Kant's treatment of rightful possession to his account of the possibility conditions for rightful acquisition. We thus turn to the theory of original acquisition.

§ 2 Acquisition, Occupation, and Original Community

A fully detailed analysis of Kant's arguments on rightful acquisition as they pertain to the law of things (*Sachenrecht*) is beyond the scope of this study.[19] My considerations on the doctrine of acquisition will therefore presuppose that Kant effectively substantiates the following points in the course of his reflections on the principles of private right. *First*, whoever wants to claim that he has a thing (*Sache*) as his own must be *in* possession of an object; for otherwise he could not be wronged by another's use of any object without his consent, and such use would for that reason not be contrary to right.[20] *Second*, the fundamental principle of external acquisition in general is fully consistent with the universal law of right, the juridical postulate of practical reason, and the juridical requirements of practical reason that are contained in the concept of universal will.[21] *Third*, only corporeal things can be originally acquired.[22] *Fourth*, the basic argument presented in the second paragraph of § 12 of the Doctrine of Right is sound. That is to say: Kant successfully establishes that first acquisition of a thing can only be thought of in terms of the acquisition of land if it is to have foundational significance for the law of things.[23] *Finally*, the possibility of originally acquiring an external object of the power of choice is the immediate consequence of the juridical postulate of practical reason.[24]

---

[19] See, however, Byrd/Hruschka 2010, pp. 119–142; Friedrich 2004, pp. 134–156; Gregor 2006, pp. 131–138.
[20] See RL 6:247.10–13.
[21] "The principle of external acquisition is as follows: that is mine which I bring under my control [*Gewalt*] (in accordance with the law of outer *freedom*); which, as an object of my power of choice, is someting that I have the capacity [*Vermögen*] to use (in accordance with the postulate of practical reason); and which, finally, I *will* that it is to be mine (in conformity with the idea of a possible united will)" (RL 6:258.22–27).
[22] See RL 6:258.22–25.
[23] See RL 6:262.1–10; cf. Marx (*Grundrisse*) 1974, pp. 391–392.
[24] See RL 6:263.12–19.

How exactly are we to understand the concept of original acquisition in accordance with the assumptions just stated, especially given Kant's position that the possibility of original acquisition is the *immediate consequence* of the juridical postulate? If, in keeping with this postulate, I am to acquire anything originally, then what I acquire must be something external that is not originally mine. For nothing external to me can be mine originally;[25] and whatever I can acquire originally *as* mine cannot be something acquired from anything that belongs to someone else as anyone's own, since all acquisition from another person or persons is derivative, and so cannot be original.[26] Consequently, if original acquisition is to be possible as a rightful act, then two things must obtain. I must not only be able to think of myself as a subject that can relate itself to something external. I must also be able to think of this external something as a thing that can be neither originally mine nor possessed by another subject as something that is her own. According to Kant, thinking jointly in these ways is possible only if the following conditions are satisfied. Acquisition must take place through the act of bringing something corporeal under my control. The control-seizing act (*Bemächtigung*) by which things are brought under my control must be the result of *unilateral* choice. Yet such a unilaterally performed act of seizure, or occupation (*occupatio*), must be able to take place consistently with the understanding of universal will as an *omnilateral* will—that is, it must be compatible with the idea of a will that is "united not contingently but a priori and therefore necessarily, and because of this is the only will that is lawgiving"[27] (RL 6:263.26–27).

It is in view of the relation between action proceeding from unilateral choice and action performed in conformity with the idea of an omnilateral will that Kant articulates the three aspects or 'moments' (*Momente*) of original acquisition through seizure or occupation: (a) the apprehension (*apprehensio*) of an object that belongs to no one, which is effected by a subject's taking possession of

---

25 According to Kant, everything that is originally mine (or yours) falls under the heading of "inner mine and yours (*meum vel tuum internum*)". It is therefore a feature of freedom understood as the single innate right of human beings. As such, it cannot be a systematic component of the account of acquired right to which the theory of private right belongs. See RL 6:237.13–32; cf. VARL 23:295.33–296.18, 23:297.10–20, 23:302.27–303.30, 23:309.4–7.

26 See RL 6:256.1–11, 6:259.17–20.

27 "denn der einseitige Wille (wozu auch der doppelseitige, aber doch *besondere* Wille gehört) kann nicht jedermann eine Verbindlichkeit auflegen, die an sich zufällig ist, sondern dazu wird ein *allseitiger*, nicht zufällig, sondern *a priori*, mithin nothwendig vereinigter und darum allein gesetzgebender Wille erfordert; denn nur nach dieses seinem Princip ist Übereinstimmung der freien Willkür eines jeden mit der Freiheit von jedermann, mithin ein Recht überhaupt, und also auch ein äußeres Mein und Dein möglich" (RL 6:263.23–30).

an object of choice in space and time, and which therefore results in *possessio phaenomenon*; (b) the designation (*declaratio*) of the possession of this object as mine and of my act of choice to exclude everyone else from it; and (c) appropriation (*appropriatio*) conceived as an act performed in conformity with the idea of an externally and universally lawgiving will, whereby everyone is bound to agree with my choice.[28] Kant understands the connections between these different aspects of original acquisition in terms of the stages of syllogistic inference. The descriptions given for apprehension and designation provide, respectively, the contents of the major and minor premises. The conclusion asserts that what I possess by virtue of the acts described under (a) and (b) is merely rightful possession (or *possessio noumenon*).[29] Thus, the movement of thought from the first to the last conceptual moments of original acquisition makes the transition from empirical possession (*possessio phaenomenon*) to intelligible possession by an inference of reason. This inference is meant to demonstrate how, in accordance with the universality requirements of practical reason, "abstraction can be made from the empirical conditions of possession, so that the conclusion, 'the external object is mine', is correctly drawn from sensible to intelligible possession"[30] (RL 6:259.8–10).

But here, of course, we must ask how anything that I come to possess empirically as the result of unilateral choice could be something that I *can* possess in conformity with the idea of an omnilateral will. Kant formulates this specific problem of original acquisition as follows:

> Original acquisition of an external object of the power of choice is called *seizing control* [*Bemächtigung*] (*occupatio*), and it can take place only with respect to corporeal things (substances). When it takes place, what it requires as the condition of empirical possession is priority in time to anyone else who wills to seize control of a thing [*Sache*]. [...] As original, it is only the result of unilateral choice [...]—Still, if an acquisition is *first*, it is not yet for that reason *original*. For the acquisition of a public juridical condition by the union of the will of all for universal lawgiving would be an acquisition such that none could precede it,

---

[28] RL 6:258.28–259.4. For discussion, see Kersting 1993, pp. 264–267, Ludwig 1988, pp. 127–133.
[29] RL 6:259.4–7.
[30] "Die Gültigkeit des letzteren Moments der Erwerbung, als worauf der Schlußsatz: der äußere Gegenstand ist *mein*, beruht, d.i. daß der Besitz als ein *bloß rechtlicher* gültig (*possessio noumenon*) sei, gründet sich darauf: daß, da alle diese Actus *rechtlich* sind, mithin aus der praktischen Vernunft hervorgehen, und also in der Frage, was Rechtens ist, von den empirischen Bedingungen des Besitzes abstrahirt werden kann, der Schlußsatz: der äußere Gegenstand ist mein, vom sensibelen auf den intelligibelen Besitz richtig geführt wird" (RL 6:259.4–11).

yet it would be derived from the particular wills of each and would be *omnilateral*, whereas original acquisition can proceed only from a unilateral will.[31] (RL 6:259.12–18)

Thus, the specifically Kantian problem of original acquisition has to be understood in view of the following requirements of intelligibility. First, original acquisition has to be thought of as taking place only in connection with a condition of empirical possession, namely, the temporal priority of the act by which one wills to seize control of—occupy—corporeal entities. Second, original acquisition is conceivable only as the result of unilateral choice in keeping with this temporal condition. Third, because of its conceptual link to such a condition of empirical possession, the act by which original acquisition takes place must somehow be made consistent with the act to which it may seem to be most radically opposed: We must be in a position to hold that the unilaterally acquisitive act of choice, i.e., the act by which a particular acquiring agent aims to seize control of (or occupy) things, is compatible with the omnilaterally unifying and universally lawgiving act by which a public juridical condition is to be established.

By this point, then, we can see how Kant clarifies the concept of original acquisition by explicating the notion of *occupatio* (*Bemächtigung*). We can also see how this explicatory work enables him to formulate the problem of original acquisition so as to make it the systematic centerpiece of the law of things. But the considerations on original acquisition summarized thus far do not yet provide an adequate platform from which to address the problem of obligation that emerges from the interpretation of the juridical postulate as a permissive law, i.e., from the interpretation of this postulate as the law that authorizes me (or anyone) to hold that everyone else *ought* to refrain from using some object of my power of choice *because* I was the first to take possession of it. Those considerations do, of course, confirm one of the conjectural assumptions mentioned above: If taking possession of an object of choice represents the initial aspect (or moment) of original acquisition, and if priority in time with respect to the oc-

---

[31] "Die ursprüngliche Erwerbung eines äußeren Gegenstandes der Willkür heißt Bemächtigung (*occupatio*) und kann nicht anders, als an körperlichen Dingen (Substanzen) statt finden. Wo nun eine solche statt findet, bedarf sie zur Bedingung des empirischen Besitzes die Priorität der Zeit vor jedem Anderen, der sich einer Sache bemächtigen will (*qui prior tempore potior iure*). Sie ist als ursprünglich auch nur die Folge von einseitiger Willkür [...]—Indessen ist die erste Erwerbung doch darum sofort nicht die ursprüngliche. Denn die Erwerbung eines öffentlichen rechtlichen Zustandes durch Vereinigung des Willens Aller zu einer allgemeinen Gesetzgebung wäre eine solche, vor der keine vorhergehen darf, und doch wäre sie von dem besonderen Willen eines jeden abgeleitet und allseitig: da eine ursprüngliche Erwerbung nur aus dem einseitigen Willen hervorgehen kann" (RL 6:259.12–28).

cupying will of others provides the condition for empirical possession, then we are surely justified in regarding first possession-taking as the act that gives rise to empirical possession. Consequently, as long as it can be demonstrated that the achievement of empirical possession through first possession-taking is necessarily consistent with the categorical prescriptions of right involved in the concept of universal will, we should be able to grasp how this kind of acquisitive action establishes a prerogative of right corresponding to the obligation placed on others by the juridical postulate. The ground of this purported consistency, however, is precisely what is not yet evident. Indeed, the contrast that Kant brings out between (i) the necessarily unilateral character of the initial moment of the procedure of original acquisition and (ii) the union of the will of all for universal lawgiving serves to highlight the problem of obligation that issues from the interpretation of the juridical postulate as a use-excluding permissive law. So just how is this problem to be solved in the context of a doctrine of acquisition that takes the possibility of original acquisition to be the immediate consequence of the juridical postulate of practical reason?

Kant holds that original acquisition, regarded as the result of unilateral choice, is possible as a rightful act because the original possession of an external object can *only* be possession in common.[32] Accordingly, he maintains that first possession-taking can be thought of as an act performed in agreement with the law of the external freedom of everyone only if it is conceived in connection with an "original possession in common [*ursprünglicher Gesamtbesitz*] (*communio possessionis originaria*) whose concept is non-empirical and independent of temporal conditions" (RL 6:262.28 – 30). If one accepts, with Kant, that first acquisition must be thought of as the acquisition of land, it follows that the relationship between the subjects who possess something in common must be represented in terms of what Kant calls the "original community of land in general" (RL 6:262.13 – 14).[33] Moreover, because the earth's surface is spherical, this community must extend to "the possession of the land of the entire earth" (RL 6:267.4 – 5). This conception of the universal scope of original community is yielded when we take account of a fundamental material factor that conditions

---

32 See RL 6:258.9 – 14.
33 See also RL 6:268.3 – 4. It is natural to think of *Ursprünglicher Gesamtbesitz* as the term to use when referring to the object possessed in common (that is, when referring to the relation of possessors *to* their common object). It is also natural to think of *Gemeinschaft des Bodens* as the expression for the mutual relations that possessors have to one another on account of their relations to that common object. Kant, however, seems to use the two terms interchangeably. In any event, nothing in his arguments on original acquisition hinges on the distinction just mentioned.

human existence on earth: the unending finitude, as it were, of the terrestrial globe's surface makes it physically impossible for human beings to be dispersed to the extent that they exist beyond the limits of possible community with one another.[34]

By specifying the notion of original possession in common in terms of the universal community of land, Kant introduces "a practical rational concept that contains a priori the principle in accordance with which alone human beings can use a place on earth in accordance with laws of right" (RL 6:262.32–34). He thus bases his theory of rightful acquisition on the idea of "the possession of all human beings on earth that precedes every rightful act of theirs", a possession that is "constituted by nature itself"[35] (RL 6:262.26–28). By employing the idea of the original community of land, Kant seeks to explain how it is possible to think of first possession-taking as an act by which I (or anyone else) can come to use, in accordance with laws of external freedom, things that I *already* possess in common with all others. By means of his conception of original community, then, Kant wants to show that the act of physically taking possession of something (*apprehensio physica*) furnishes an "empirical title" of acquisition that correlates directly, and necessarily, with "the title to an intellectual possession-taking [*intellektuelle Besitznehmung*] (setting aside all empirical conditions of space and time)" (RL 6:264.9–14). The latter serves as a principle of entitlement that authorizes my (or anyone's) control-seizing activity with respect to objects that can only be thought of as belonging to *everyone* once all *empirical* conditions of space and time are set aside. As such, it provides for "the rational title of acquisition" that "can lie only in the idea of the will of all united a priori" (RL 6:264.17–18).

The analysis of this concept of universal will thus yields the warranting principle by which external acquisition is authorized. Accordingly, we can say that the idea of universal will must be presupposed as an indispensable condition for *all* external acquisition. For all external acquisition must accord with the requirements of reason developed from the concept of the unified will of everyone if the control-seizing activity that proceeds from a unilateral will is to place upon others the obligation to refrain from using the things which one has taken into

---

[34] See RL 6:262.20–26.
[35] "Der Besitz aller Menschen auf Erden, der vor allem rechtlichen Act derselben vorhergeht (von der Natur selbst constituirt ist), ist ein *ursprünglicher Gesammtbesitz (communio possessionis originaria)*, dessen Begriff nicht empirisch und von Zeitbedingungen abhängig ist, [...] sondern ein praktischer Vernunftbegriff, der *a priori* das Princip enthält, nach welchem allein die Menschen den Platz auf Erden nach Rechtsgesetzen gebrauchen können" (RL 6:262.26–34).

one's possession and designated as 'one's own'.³⁶ Otherwise, the rightful quality of derivative acquisition could have no strictly rational ground; and the possession-taking act required by original acquisition could not be consistent with the formal requirements set by practical reason's universal lawgiving in the domain of external freedom of action.³⁷ With reference to this domain, the idea of original community is a conceptual representation that furnishes the material correlate of the idea of universal will. The employment of this idea of will in conjunction with its correlate leads to the theoretical insight that something external can be rightfully acquired only if its way of acquisition conforms to the specific requirements of the juridical or civil condition: *Anything* external that I can have as mine must be acquired "in conformity with the idea of a civil condition" (RL 6:264.24). For Kant, this means that whatever one chooses to seize (i.e., occupy) as one's own from the originally common possession of humankind must be something acquired *with a view to* the realization of the civil condition, but prior to its establishment. Original acquisition is therefore necessarily provisional.³⁸ And anything originally acquired in keeping with laws of external freedom must be thought of in terms of the provisional acquisition of land through occupation.³⁹

In Kant's doctrine of acquisition, then, reference to the global unity of the earth's surface, i.e., to the physically insurmountable unity exhibited by the universal object and material substrate of all possible originally acquirable particular things, puts us in a position to regard possession-taking as the type of act that can be performed in conformity with the idea of an a priori united will. Kant introduces the notion of "the unity of all places on the face of the earth as a spherical surface" (RL 6:262.22–23) as an essential feature of the rational concept of an original community of possession. He employs this idea to show how every subject's possession-taking acts can be conceived as ultimately grounded in an authorization to occupy that fulfills the universality requirements of practical reason's external lawgiving. The idea of an original community of land thus furnishes an a priori conceptual representation that structurally corresponds to, and combines with, the idea of universal will as an omnilateral will. Although this rational concept of original community is non-empirical and independent of temporal conditions, its correlation with the idea of universal

---

36 See RL 6:264.17–22, 6:265.19–30.
37 See RL 6:259.17–20, 6:260.33–261.14.
38 If it were thought of as acquired at the same time as or subsequent to the establishment of the civil condition, it would have to be understood as a derivative acquisition. It would depend on a type of acquisition that cannot be original. On this, see RL 6:259.23–28, 6:264.23–28.
39 See RL 6:264.29–35.

will allows for the determination of certain sensible conditions–specifically, the spatial conditions–for everyone's original external possession as well as the conditions under which empirical possession is established through a unilateral will to occupy:

> We have found the *title* of acquisition in an original community of land, and thus among the spatial conditions of an external possession. The *way of acquisition* [*Erwerbungsart*], however, we have found in the empirical conditions of an external possession-taking (*apprehensio*), joined with the will to have the external object as one's own[40]. (RL 6:268.3–7).

There will be a good deal more to say below about the connection between original community and the spatial conditions for external possession. At this juncture, the major item of interest lies in the connection that Kant discerns between the empirical conditions of external possession-taking and the naturally given unity exhibited by the universal object of possible acquisition.

§ 3 Original Community and Universal Possession

To clarify further the notion of the community of possession that the latter connection presupposes, I refer here to several passages from Kant's preliminary work on private right, as published in volume 23 of the Academy Edition.[41] In these passages, Kant is concerned with two different views of universality involved in the idea of original possession in common. He distinguishes between disjunctively (or distributively) universal possession and collectively universal possession.[42] We must think of the earth as the disjunctive-universal possession (*disjunktiv-allgemeiner Besitz*) of humankind when we take account of the physical fact that the earth's spherical surface, and hence its finite magnitude, sets all of the earth's inhabitants in a relation of thoroughgoing reciprocal possible influence (*ein Verhältnis des durchgängig-wechselseitigen möglichen Einflusses*). By virtue of this relation of possible causal reciprocity, every human being is poten-

---

[40] "Wir haben den *Titel* der Erwerbung in einer ursprünglichen Gemeinschaft des Bodens, mithin unter Raums-Bedingungen eines äußeren Besitzes, die *Erwerbungsart* aber in den empirischen Bedingungen der Besitznehmung (*apprehensio*), verbunden mit dem Willen, den äußeren Gegenstand als den seinen zu haben, gefunden". See also RL 6:263.4–12.
[41] See Loose Leaf 58, especially the following passages: VARL 23:320.19–321.8, 23:323.26–324.2.
[42] Regarding Kant's conception of the relationship between distributive and collective universality, see KrV A582/B610, A643/B671-A644/B672; MAN 4:526.15–18, 4:563.39–564.9; RL 6:256.8–10; Refl 14:287.1–288.2; 17:397.7–12, 17:442.10–23, 17:570.26–571.2, 17:703.7–11; Refl 18:238.26–28, 18:366.28–29, 18:528.6–9; Op 21:586.8–24, 21:603.4–9.

tially in possession of any place on the earth's surface. Each human agent is therefore "in a potential but only *disjunctive-universal* possession of all places on the earth's land" (VARL 23:320.22–23).[43]

Regarded from this distributive viewpoint, i.e., from the point of view by which each human inhabitant of the earth is considered in relation to what any given agent can individually possess, the original community of possession is something more than a merely spatial relation of human beings. It has to be understood as a spatial relation of possible causal community between all agents, i.e., as a universal relation of possible reciprocal influence. We must therefore think of it in terms of the dynamical community—the *commercium*—of all originally possessive agents, and not just in terms of the spatial juxtaposition (*communio spatii*) of separate human entities.[44] Now because the possible reciprocal causal relation between these agents extends to their possessive relations to all places on the earth's surface, the relation of community between the earth's inhabitants must itself be thought of in terms of a universal community of possession. Moreover, the form and scope of the relation of possessors is such that this community of possession must be regarded from a collective point of view as well as from the distributive point of view just characterized. Specifically, it must be thought of as the

> possession in common which, as *collective*-universal possession through resistance in occupying the space that everyone on earth requires, makes a rightful act possible and practically, i.e., objectively, necessary—an act by which the possession of each is *distributively* [italics mine (J.E.)] determined [...].[45] (VARL 23:320.30–31)

Thus, the universal community of possession, the form of which consists in the relation of possible reciprocal influence between all of the earth's inhabitants, puts anyone in a position to possess any place on earth, which is what it means to say that the earth is originally possessed in common. But this is precisely why

---

43 "er ist in einem potentialen aber nur *disjunctiv allgemeinen* Besitz aller Plätze des Erdbodens [...]".
44 These terms are, of course, taken from the *Critique of Pure Reason*'s Third Analogy of Experience (see KrV A213/B260; cf. RL 6:352.6–22). For discussion, see Edwards 2000, pp. 20–21, 37–43.
45 "Dieser Gesammtbesitz der als collectiv-allgemeiner Besitz durch den Wiederstand in Einnehmung des Raumes den ein jeder auf der Erde bedarf macht nun einen rechtlichen Act möglich und practisch d.i. objectiv nothwendig wodurch der Besitz einem jeden *distributiv* bestimmt werde [...]" (VARL 23:320.30–31).

> this possession must also be regarded as *collectively* universal, i.e., as the common possession of the human species to which corresponds an objectively united will or will that is to be united; for without a principle of distribution (which can only be found in the united will as law) the right of human beings to be anywhere at all would be entirely without effect and would be destroyed by universal conflict."[46] (VARL 23:323.30 – 324.2)

Taken from the standpoint of its disjunctive universality, then, humankind's original community of possession represents a state of nature. Since the juridically salient feature of this natural condition is its potential for universal conflict, the specification of the properties of the disjunctive-universal possession makes evident practical reason's demand for a principle of distribution by which the possession of each can determined as rightful possession. According to Kant, the practical rational ground of this principle can lie only in the idea of an a priori united will that corresponds to the collective view of the originally common possession of all humanity.

Let us return to the published text of the Doctrine of Right. The considerations on disjunctively universal and collectively universal possession just treated are fully congruent with what Kant argues in his metaphysical exposition of the concept of the original acquisition of land (§ 16 of the Doctrine of Right). Given that all human beings are originally in common possession of the land of the entire earth, and assuming that each has the will to use this land, it follows that the "naturally unavoidable opposition of the power of choice of one in relation to another" would "do away with all use of it [the land] if that will to use it did not also contain the law by which a *particular possession* can be determined" [47] (RL 6:267.7–11). This law—the distributive law of mine and yours with respect to land (*das Austeilende Gesetz des Mein und Dein eines jeden am Boden*)—can issue only from the a priori united will that normatively underlies, and is realized in, the civil condition. Still, the account of the juridical state of nature as a condition of unavoidable opposition between human agents' powers

---

[46] "so muß dieser Besitz auch als *collectiv*-allgemein d.i. als Gesammtbesitz des menschlichen Geschlechts dem ein objectiv vereinigter oder zu vereinigender Wille correspondirt angesehen werden weil ohne ein Princip der Vertheilung (die nur dem vereinigten Willen als Gesetz zukommen kann) das Recht der Menschen irgend wo zu seyn ohne allen Erfolg seyn und durch den allgemeinen Wiederstreit vernichtet werden würde".

[47] "Alle Menschen sind ursprünglich in einem *Gesammt-Besitz* des Bodens der ganzen Erde (*communio fundi originaria*) mit dem ihnen von Natur zustehenden Willen (eines jeden) denselben zu gebrauchen (*lex iusti*), der wegen der natürlich unvermeidlichen Entgegensetzung der Willkür des Einen gegen die des Anderen allen Gebrauch desselben aufheben würde, wenn nicht jener zugleich das Gesetz für diese enthielte, nach welchem einem jeden ein *besonderer Besitz* auf dem gemeinsamen Boden bestimmt werden kann (*lex iuridica*)" (RL 6:267.1–11).

of choice must include the "rightful capacity [*Vermögen*] of the will of everyone to recognize the act of possession-taking and appropriation as valid, even though it is only unilateral"[48] (RL 6:267.19 – 21). That is because original acquisition, understood as the provisional acquisition of land, "requires and has the favor of the law (*lex permissiva*) in view of the determination of the limits of rightful acquisition" [49] (RL 6:267.24 – 26). This favor (*Gunst*) of the law in question (i. e., the favor of the permissive law by which the obligation-founding character of first possession-taking is determined) does not reach beyond the point at which the juridical condition is established. In other words, it obtains only with a *view to* the achievement of the condition in which the limits of rightful acquisition on the part of each agent are determined in accordance with the principle of distribution that proceeds from an a priori united will of all. Nonetheless, that favor of law carries with it "all the effects of acquisition in conformity with right" (RL 6:267.31).

It is essential to note that the favor extended by *lex permissiva* with respect to external acquisition cannot derive from any consideration of need or equity that may pertain to the distribution of some good. This type of material consideration can play no grounding role in a doctrine of acquisition that is consistent with the general account of strict right (*ius strictum*) at issue in the Doctrine of Right as a whole. As noted above (p. 124), this account concerns *only* the conditions under which the power of choice of one can be united with the power of choice of another in accordance with a universal law of freedom. Within the systematic framework of the theory of these conditions, the concept of right "has to do solely with the external and practical relations of one person to another, insofar as their actions [...] can have (direct or indirect) influence on each other" (RL 6:230.9 – 11). It concerns the "reciprocal relation of powers of choice" in which "no account at all is taken of the *matter* of choice, that is, of the end that each has in mind with the objects he wants" (RL 6:230.16 – 17). The theory of the metaphysical foundations of right therefore treats only the formal conditions under which the relation of possible influence between subjects whose powers of

---

[48] ‚In diesem Zustand aber, d.i. vor Gründung und doch in Absicht auf denselben, d.i. *provisorisch*, nach dem Gesetz der äußeren Erwerbung zu verfahren, ist *Pflicht*, folglich auch rechtliches *Vermögen* des Willens jedermann zu verbinden, den Act der Besitznehmung und Zueignung, ob er gleich nur einseitig ist, als gültig anzuerkennen [...]" (RL 6:267.17– 21).

[49] "Eine solche Erwerbung aber bedarf doch und hat auch eine *Gunst* des Gesetzes (*lex permissiva*) in Ansehung der Bestimmung der Grenzen des rechtlich-möglichen Besitzes für sich [...]" (RL 6:267.24 – 26).

choice are reciprocally related can be in accordance with practical reason's universally prescriptive lawgiving role.[50]

The strict formalism of Kant's foundational juridical position entails that this lawgiving role of reason, as clarified by means of the concept an a priori united will,[51] furnishes the only possible basis for limiting the scope of original acquisition by occupation. To clarify this thought, Kant employs the idea of an original contract in conformity with which the juridical or civil condition is to be established. By introducing this conceptual device, Kant wants to show how a given agent's authorization to occupy land unilaterally is necessarily subject to restriction, given the deontic requirements developed from the concept of the united will of all. This restriction on the scope of original acquisition, however, is itself subject to a crucial qualification. According to Kant, it is not possible to specify, either quantitatively or qualitatively, the limits of what *can* be originally acquired unless the conditions that feature in the idea of the original contract actually apply to the whole human species:

> The indeterminacy with regard to quantity as well as quality of the external object that can be acquired makes this problem (of the sole, original acquisition) the hardest of all to solve. Still, there must be some original acquisition or other of what is external since not all acquisition can be derived. So this problem cannot be abandoned as insoluble and intrinsically impossible. But even if it is solved through the original contract, such acquisition will always remain provisional unless this contract extends to the whole human race.[52] (RL 6:266.28–37)

What follows from the qualification just stated?

It is essential to bear in mind here that the contractualist idea at issue in this passage must in any event apply normatively to the entire human species, whether or not all acquisition is merely provisional. So the implication of Kant's qualifying claim must be this: No definite limits can be placed upon the unilateral act of occupation by which original acquisition occurs as long as the juridical con-

---

[50] Which is *not* to say that this theory disregards the force of moral requirements derived in view of need, or that it assigns no place to the determination of equity in the public administration of justice. See RL 6:235.6–11, 6:235.16–236.7.
[51] Regarding this concept and its historical background, see Byrd/Hruschka 2006.
[52] "Die Unbestimmtheit in Ansehung der Quantität sowohl als der Qualität des äußeren erwerblichen Objects macht diese Aufgabe (der einzigen ursprünglichen äußeren Erwerbung) unter allen zur schwersten sie aufzulösen. Irgend eine ursprüngliche Erwerbung des Äußeren aber muß es indessen doch geben; denn abgeleitet kann nicht alle sein. Daher kann man diese Aufgabe auch nicht als unauflöslich und als an sich unmöglich aufgeben. Aber wenn sie auch durch den ursprünglichen Vertrag aufgelöset wird, so wird, wenn dieser sich nicht aufs ganze menschliche Geschlecht erstreckt, die Erwerbung doch immer nur provisorisch bleiben".

§ 3 Original Community and Universal Possession — 147

dition of humanity as a whole is not *realized*. Apart from the universal realization of a juridical condition in accordance with the idea of an original contract that extends to the entire human species, original acquisition through unilateral occupation cannot be understood as the type of act that is subject to specific distributive restriction.

This interpretation follows from Kant's understanding of the relationship between the juridical state of nature and the civil condition. It is a required interpretation because the laws of juridico-practical reason prescribe the realization of the right-conformable condition of humanity, and because these laws therefore maintain their prescriptive force for human beings, as rational beings, no matter what the condition may be in which their powers of choice are in fact reciprocally related.[53] At the same time, though, that interpretation sheds light on a fundamental problem for Kant's theory of private right. Let me formulate this problem with reference to the disjunctively universal quality of the originally common possession of humankind and the dynamical nature of the original community of possession. According to Kant, *all* acquisition must satisfy one of two demands: Either it must take place in view of the determination of the limits of rightful possession (that is, it must be thought of as taking place with a view to the establishment of the juridical condition), or it must occur in accordance with the distributive law of mine and yours that is actually operative in a universally realized juridical condition. But if this is true, why should original acquisition receive the favor of *any* law of right if we have to think of it as following from a unilaterally appropriative act of possession-taking—that is, if we have to think of it as something achieved by an act of occupation that *can* generate a condition of universal conflict in virtue of the nature-given form of the causal community of all human possessors? As we have seen, this is a condition characterized by the unavoidable opposition of the powers of choice of all appropriating agents; and this opposition is such that it would do away with *all use* of things already possessed in common if the will of each to use such things did not "contain" (in other words, were not capable of conforming with) a law by which the particular possession of each can be determined. We have also seen that the quantitative and qualitative indeterminacy of the object of external acquisition is what makes original acquisition a problem to be solved by means of the idea of an original contract. Why, then, should we accept that the type of act which gives rise to such indeterminacy with respect to particular possession is compatible with the categorical requirements of right that demand, in keeping

---

[53] See chapter 7 note 96.

with the contractualist idea, the realization of a universal juridical condition in which all indeterminacy of possession is overcome?

To address this problem, we need to consider Kant's account of original acquisition in relation to its historical background in early modern natural law theory. This is the theme of the next chapter.

Chapter 7 Original Acquisition in Kant, Grotius, and Selden

§ 1 Dominium, Right, and the Reach of the Cannons

In view of the problem just posed at the end of chapter 6, let us consider several passages from two sections of the doctrine of acquisition in which Kant concretely treats empirical conditions of external possession-taking. At the beginning of the remarks appended to the main argument in RL § 15, which establishes the provisional status of all acquisition in the state of nature, Kant writes:

> The question arises, how far does the authorization to take possession of land extend? As far as the capacity for having it under one's control extends, that is, as far as whoever wills to appropriate it can defend it—as if the land were to say, if you cannot protect me, you cannot command me. This is also how the dispute over whether the sea is *free* or *closed* would have to be decided; for example, within the range of cannon fire no one may fish, haul up amber from the ocean floor, and so forth along the coast of a territory that already belongs to a certain state.[54] (RL 6:265.1–10)

And in a similar vein, Kant puts forward the following claims in his remarks on the deduction of the concept of original acquisition in RL § 17:

> My *possession* extends as far as I have the mechanical capacity, from where I reside, to secure my land against encroachment by others (e.g., as far as cannon reach from the shore) and up to this limit the sea is closed (*mare clausum*). But since it is not possible to *reside* on the high seas themselves, possession also cannot extend to them and the open seas are free (*mare liberum*).[55] (RL 6:269.31–36)

---

[54] "Es ist die Frage: wie weit erstreckt sich die Befugniß der Besitznehmung eines Bodens? So weit, als das Vermögen ihn in seiner Gewalt zu haben, d.i. als der, so ihn sich zueignen will, ihn vertheidigen kann; gleich als ob der Boden spräche: wenn ihr mich nicht beschützen könnt, so könnt ihr mir auch nicht gebieten. Darnach müßte also auch der Streit über das *freie* oder *verschlossene* Meer entschieden werden; z. B. innerhalb der Weite, wohin die Kanonen reichen, darf niemand an der Küste eines Landes, das schon einem gewissen Staat zugehört, fischen, Bernstein aus dem Grunde der See holen u.dergl.".

[55] "So weit ich aus meinem Sitze mechanisches Vermögen habe, meinen Boden gegen den Eingriff Anderer zu sichern (z. B. so weit die Kanonen vom Ufer abreichen), gehört er zu meinem *Besitz*, und das Meer ist bis dahin geschlossen (*mare clausum*). Da aber auf dem weiten Meere selbst kein Sitz möglich ist, so kann der Besitz auch nicht bis dahin ausgedehnt werden, und offene See ist frei (*mare liberum*)".

Both of these passages refer to a dispute in modern international law concerning the permissibility of acts and policies that would establish exclusive *dominium* in the seas. Hugo Grotius and John Selden set the terms of the dispute in the early seventeenth century. In order to determine with precision how Kant relates to these particular figures, it would be necessary to investigate various references (direct or indirect) to the *mare liberum* vs. *mare clausum* controversy found in the eighteenth-century compendia on natural jurisprudence that Kant used in connection with his lectures on natural law.[56] But we need not be concerned here with the philological details. For the dispute between Grotius and Selden was of fundamental importance for the whole development of modern natural-law theories of property, and Kant makes it quite clear that he addresses an issue of international maritime law only because it pertains to a basic question of his general theory of original acquisition. In keeping with Kant's concern with this question about the limits of occupation, I will discuss Grotius and Selden in view of the problem of original acquisition that underlies the *mare liberum/mare clausum* controversy.[57]

Selden's treatise against Grotius–*Mare clausum*–is intended to establish that the high seas are just as much subject to exclusive appropriation and use as landed territory. Selden's argument is based on an account of the principally unrestricted scope of the unilateral act of occupation. While Selden directly opposes Grotius on the question of *dominium* in the seas, his account of occupation makes use of the key elements of the theory of original acquisition that Grotius constructs in his *Mare liberum* and in *De iure belli ac pacis*.[58] Given our primary concern with Kant, Selden's critical employment of these elements will be the primary item of interest in this section. But before turning to this employment, a brief consideration the Grotian theory of the origins of property is in order.

§ 2 Original Community, Prima Occupatio, and the Right to All Things

Grotius presents most of the key elements of his doctrine of original acquisition in the chapter of *De iure praedae commentarius* first published separately in 1609

---

[56] See, e.g., AA 19:425 (Achenwall, *Iuris naturalis pars posterior* § 231). On Kant's relation to Achenwahl, see Byrd/Hruschka 2010, pp. 15–22, 45–48, 122–126, 132–135, 146–149, 171–184, 236–239, 261–264, 270–272, 286–288, 290.
[57] For more extensive treatment of both Grotius and Selden, see Edwards 2005.
[58] For a succinct account of the complicated, and exceptionally interesting, publication histories of the works mentioned in this paragraph, see Tuck 1993, pp. 169–170, 190–192, 211–214.

under the title of *Mare liberum*.⁵⁹ But this doctrine is given its main systematic formulation in *De jure belli ac pacis*.⁶⁰ As is evident especially in the latter work, Grotius supposes that there is a subjective attribute in virtue of which a human agent is warranted in acquiring external things. Ascribing this attribute to the human subject as a natural quality or faculty, he understands right (*qua* faculty) as the moral quality of a person.⁶¹ Accordingly, he maintains that the faculty by which a human agent is able to acquire external things as his own must be thought of as the subjective natural right by which the human being can both use and establish *dominium* in those things. In keeping with his account of this particular meaning of right (*ius*), Grotius makes use of a concept that was also employed by his Spanish contemporary, Francisco Suarez. It is the concept of a 'dominative' natural right.⁶²

In the fifth chapter of *Mare liberum*,⁶³ Grotius begins his account of the origins of property ownership by postulating a state of nature in which all men have common *dominium* in all things. But he immediately qualifies his use of *dominium* with reference to this natural condition. Grotius explains that the term must not be taken in anything like its standard juridical employment. According to this standard employment, *dominium* denotes either individual or joint private ownership. As applied to the originally common word of external objects, however, the term abstracts from all positive characteristics of property

---

59 I cite *Mare liberum* (here abbreviated as ML) according to the page numbers of the Latin text published together with Magoffin's English translation in Grotius 1916 (1608). The references in brackets following these numbers are to the corresponding pages in H. G. Hamaker's 1868 edition of *De jure praedae* (DJP).

60 All references to this work (here abbreviated as DJB) are to the 1646 edition of the Latin text, as reproduced in Grotius 1913. I cite according to book, chapter, section and (if specified) paragraph numbers.

61 This understanding is required by Grotius' basic definition of *ius* in its subjective and strict sense ("quo sensu ius est, Qualitas moralis personae, competens ad aliquid iuste habendum vel agendum. [...] Qualitatem autem moralis perfecta, Facultas nobis dicitur [...]" [DJB I 1.4]).

62 I borrow the term *ius dominativum* from Suarez, who uses the expression *de iure naturali dominativo* when characterizing the natural right of a subject (specifically, the *facultas moralis* of a human subject) that grounds *dominium*. (See Suarez 1971, Book II Chapter 14 §16.) I will therefore use 'dominative right' as a convenient term of art for the purposes of my discussion of Grotius and Selden. It should be noted that I do not claim that Grotius' concept of dominative natural right is taken from Suarez. The historical network of influences connecting the two thinkers is far more complicated—not to mention philosophically far more interesting—than that. For useful discussions of the broader historical context, see Tierney 1997, especially pp. 194–342, and Brett 1997.

63 In what follows, I refer to this title instead of *De iure praedae* since it designates the text that John Selden used for his critical commentary.

ownership. Thus, the natural power that each subject has to make warranted use of the things belonging to the originally common *dominium* of humankind denotes nothing more than a "faculty of not unjustly using [*facultas non iniusta utendi*]" them (ML 23 [DJP 214].⁶⁴

Grotius maintains that the exercise of this power or faculty upon things that are consumed through use (e.g. food and clothing) must be understood as an act of first seizure or occupation.⁶⁵ He recognizes, of course, the distinction between the mere use of something and the use of something with the aim of making it one's own. He therefore acknowledges that it is possible to distinguish conceptually between a subject's *facultas utendi* and the dominative faculty or power (i.e., the right) by which an agent first makes things his own. He is also well aware of the uses to which this conceptual distinction had historically been put.⁶⁶ Still, Grotius in effect contends that the conceptual distinction in question is not specifically relevant to the account of *original* acquisition.⁶⁷ For any act of using a consumable thing not already possessed by another is a unilaterally possessive act, i.e., an act of first seizure or occupation. As such, it amounts an act of appropriation that is capable of extension beyond the physical limitations of direct use.⁶⁸

Hence we encounter the problem of juridical obligation that is intrinsic to the Grotian conception of the basis of acquisition—and that is indeed inherent in any account of the normative foundations of property that employs the concept of a natural right in order to make the idea of *prima occupatio* the pivotal notion in the theory original acquisition. This problem of obligation can be for-

---

64 Compare Samuel Pufendorf's characterization of Grotius' *communio primaeva* as *communio negativa* in Pufendorf DJN IV.4.9/GW 4.1:363. (Citation explained at the beginning of this book on pp. X–XI.)
65 See ML 24/DJP 215–216.
66 In particular, he refers obliquely to the fourteenth century debate over property and mendicant poverty that took place between William of Ockham and Pope John XXII. Grotius indirectly acknowledges Ockham's employment of that distinction as the basis of his argument against the papal position on property. We will return to this important point in chapter 12.
67 For further discussion of this point, see Edwards 2002, pp. 53–55.
68 Grotius argues (ML 24–25/DJP 216) that the ownership-establishing act of seizing consumable things extends to arable lands and pastures. Although these immovable objects of appropriation are not them selves consumed through use, their use is nonetheless necessary for consumption. For it is by means of that use that consumable things are produced. Consequently, property in the earth's substance came to be originally established as the result of the act of first seizure or occupation. ("Repertae proprietati lex posita est, quae naturam imitaretur. Sicut enim initio per applicationem corporalem usus ille habebatur, und proprietatem primum ortam diximus, ita simili applicatione res proprias cuiusque fieri placuit. Haec est quae dicitur occupatio, voce accommodatissima ad eas res quae ante in medio positae fuerant [...]"). We will return to this account of the extension of ownership in chapter 12 (see pp. 273–274).

§ 2 Original Community, Prima Occupatio, and the Right to All Things — 153

mulated as follows. How does one account for *anyone's* obligation to restrict the scope of his unilaterally appropriative activity as long as it is assumed that each human agent by nature satisfies the necessary and sufficient condition for engaging in exactly the same kind of activity—i.e., as long as it is assumed that *every* human agent has by nature the same *facultas utendi?*

Grotius does not indicate any clear way of answering this question in *Mare liberum*.[69] This picture seems to change, however, when we turn to the passage in his major later work on the law of war and peace—*De iure belli ac pacis* (DJB)— where he introduces the idea of universal agreement into his doctrine of original acquisition:

> At the same time we learn how things came to be property. It was not by an act of the mind alone; for some could not know what others wanted to have their own so as to abstain from it, and many might want one and the same thing. Rather, it was by some agreement [*pactum*]—an agreement either expressed, as by division, or tacit, as by occupation. For it must be supposed that as soon as community was no longer satisfactory, and before any division was instituted, all agreed to this: that which anyone had occupied he should have as his own.[70] (DJB II.2.2)

In the paragraphs leading up to this passage, Grotius begins his portrayal of the origins of property by presenting the notion of an originally common world of things in which every man arbitrarily seizes (*arripere*) for his own use whatever may offer itself for consumption. In the natural condition of humankind, then, such universally permissible primitive use takes the place of property. For to deprive anyone of what he had thus seized and brought into his physical possession cannot, according to Grotius, amount to anything but an injury to the possessing subject. Property as such arises only when that primitive use is replaced by productive activity requiring the distribution of livestock and land.[71] Notice, however, that the idea of universal agreement at issue in the passage just quoted is not linked to the primitive use of things for the satisfaction of human needs *or* to the fruits of human labor and productive activity in general. While the required supposition of universal agreement presupposes that the condition of original community has come to be unsatisfacto-

---

[69] Nor is an answer to be found in the other parts of the manuscript of *De iure praedae*.
[70] "Simul discimus quomodo res in proprietatem iverint: non animi actu solo; neque enim scire alii poterant, quid alii suum esse vellent, ut eo abstinerent; et idem velle plures poterant: sed pacto quodam aut expresso, ut per divisionem, aut tacito, ut per occupationem. Simulatque enim communio displicuit, nec instituta est divisio, censeri debet inter omnes convenisse, ut quod quisque occupasset id proprium haberet".
[71] See DJB II.2.2.1–4.

ry, the *principle* to which everyone agrees is simply this: what anyone *had* occupied should be had as one's own.⁷²

To be sure, Grotius's underlying aim in employing this principle of first seizure is to establish two things: first, that each agent has the natural right to take what is needed from the world of things; and second, that this right can ground ownership with respect to things that are useful for the production of goods. This twofold aim is discernible in an assumption Grotius implicitly makes in order to get his description of original acquisition off the ground—i.e., the assumption that depriving (or dispossessing) an agent of what he had already seized from the common stock of unoccupied things self-evidently qualifies as an injury to that agent.⁷³ But even if we accept the implied self-evidence claim here in question, it is still not obvious why any *unilateral* act of occupation should *originally* be subject to obligatory restriction as long as it must be supposed that everyone agrees to act in accordance with the principle of seizure linked to the Grotian idea of universal agreement (i.e., the principle of *prima occupatio*). For according to Grotius's depiction of the condition of original community, the first seizure of *anything* should be able satisfy the requirement of consumptive utility in case it can serve as a means for the production of consumable things. So why exactly should 'I' by nature be bound not to make originally unrestricted use of *everything* that I have a mind to make use of, as long as I agree that what anyone *had* occupied should be possessed as his own—provided, of course, that I am the *first* to seize whatever it is I might have in mind to use for the purpose of consumption?

I emphasize, again, that this line of questioning runs counter to Grotius's own aim. Grotius wants to show that original acquisition through first seizure leads to limited appropriation for productive use. Nevertheless, his linking the idea of universal agreement to the principle of *prima occupatio* serves highlight the problem of obligation that arises when an originally unrestricted right of appropriation is accepted as the cornerstone of a natural-law theory of the normative foundations of external property: Despite Grotius's restrictive aim, his theory of acquisition does not clearly provide a way of understanding the grounding of

---

72 Bernd Ludwig (2001, pp. 69–104) argues that Locke's "labor theory of property" was meant to supplement rather than replace the type of account of the origins of property found in Grotius. I find Ludwig's interpretation convincing, which is why I also think that the line of questioning pursued in the next paragraph applies, *mutatis mutandis*, to Locke's theory of property in the *Second Treatise of Government*. I note this merely in passing, though.

73 Grotius appeals to the authority of Cicero and Quintilian to support the correctness of this assumption. The textual sources cited (see DJB II.2.2.5) are intended to underscore the self-evident impermissibility of depriving anyone of the fruits of first seizure.

§ 2 Original Community, Prima Occupatio, and the Right to All Things — 155

obligation with respect to originally acquisitive acts and the limitation of their appropriative scope.[74] This is where John Selden enters our story.

In the second (1631) edition of *De jure belli ac pacis*, Grotius appeals to an argument found in Selden's *Mare clausum*.[75] Grotius makes this appeal to support his position that first seizure or occupation serves as the foundation of the original acquisition of property.[76] It is certainly understandable that Grotius would refer to Selden's argument since the reference is to the textual location in *Mare clausum* where Selden quotes with glowing praise the passage from the treatise on the law of war and peace in which Grotius introduces an idea of universal agreement into his account of the law of things.[77] Yet Grotius also interestingly neglects to call attention to the fact that Selden employs this idea in order to draw conclusions about the permissible scope of exclusive appropriation that are diametrically opposed to the aim that Grotius himself had in mind when constructing his doctrine of original acquisition. In the following considerations on Selden's corresponding doctrine, then, I will be primarily concerned to clarify the significance of the anti-Grotian consequences that Selden draws from Grotius's use of the idea of universal agreement.

Selden's systematic portrayal of the origins of property is found in the fourth chapter of *Mare clausum*. He combines under the heading of common *dominium* two different conceptions of the natural condition of humankind with respect to externally acquirable things.[78] On the one hand, he refers to the view of primitive community found in Roman literary descriptions of humanity's golden age. On the other hand, he discusses in detail the biblical view of the divine act of donation by which Adam, and afterwards Noah and his sons, received *dominium* over and in the world. Selden holds that these views are fundamentally congru-

---

[74] Even less obviously, of course, does it furnish the theoretical basis upon which to establish that the sea should not be subject to partition and exclusive appropriation, which is a central aim of Grotius' theory of property.
[75] See Tuck 1999, pp. 94–102 for discussion of the differences between the two editions.
[76] See the reference to Selden contained in the first note of DJB II.2.2.5.
[77] See Selden 1726, p. 1198 (2nd column). Selden quotes from the first (i.e., the 1625) edition of *De jure belli ac pacis*.
[78] Selden gives his definitions of common and private *dominium* at the beginning of Book I, chapter IV ("Dominium, quod est jus utendi furendi, alienandi, libere disponendi, aut omnium hominum, poro indiviso possidentium, commune est, aut aliquorum tantum privatum, id est, inter universitates singulares, principes, personas qualescunque, privatim ita tributum, ut libertas utendi fruendi allis aut intercludatur aut saltem minuatur" [Selden 1726, p. 1195 (2nd column)]).

ent.[79] He understands this congruity as furnishing an indication that the theory of property must begin by supposing that all things were at first given to all humans in common, and that the earth and its products therefore constituted the originally common property of humankind.

Proceeding from this starting point, Selden maintains that the natural condition of community could not be of long duration, and that distinct ownerships (*dominia*) came into being consistently with natural law in its permissive sense (i.e., in keeping with its interpretation as *ius permissiva*). Like Grotius, he uses the idea of universal agreement (or accord) to explain how private property came to be distributively established:

> In territories thus distributed, there intervened an accord, if you will, of the body or universality of humankind (by the interposition of a compact of trust [*interposita fide*], which would obligate their posterity) for departing from the common or pristine right in things that were thus ceded to individual owners: not otherwise than when partners or co-heirs divide among themselves any things they hold undivided. As for the things remaining, however, which are in no wise possessed in several [*distributim*] nor expressly retained in common [*pro indiviso retentis*], that is, the things which have remained vacant or deserted—what is to be said? Among the more illustrious peoples it has truly held as a custom of old, and holds even to this time, that things vacant come to belong to the occupiers [*ea fieri occupantis*]; as is usually said of no one's property [*nullius in bonis*].[80] (Selden 1726, p. 1197 [2nd column])

Thus, when it came to the division of the earth into particular territories, there intervened an accord (*consensus*), as it were, for exiting the condition of common possession with its originally common right (*ius pristinum*) in things—things that by virtue of such a universal consensual act (or more precisely: in conformity with the *idea* of such a consensual act) came to be ceded to individual owners (*domini*). Accordingly, the emergence of private property must be understood

---

[79] Selden (1726, p. 1195 [2nd column]) treats ancient pagan views concerning the common use of things in humankind's primitive condition with reference to the descriptions of the golden age found in Virgil, Seneca, and Tibellus. He then appeals to the authority of Lactantius in order to establish what he takes to be the underlying congruity between the pagan Roman and the Judeo-Christian portrayals of the original natural condition.

[80] "In territoriis ita distribuendis, consensus veluti humani generis corporis seu universitatis (interposita fide, quae etiam posteros obligaret) intervenit, ut a communione seu pristino jure eorum, quae ita distributim signulis dominis cederent, plane discederetur: non aliter ac ubi socii seu cohaeredes partes aliquas rerum pro indiviso possarum inter se dividunt. At vero de reliquis, neutiquam distributim possessis, nec pro indiviso expressim retentis, id est, quae vacua seu derelicta mansere, quid dicendum. Obtinuit sane antiquitus in gentium illustriorum moribus, atque etiamnum obtinet, quae vacua sunt, ea fieri occupantis; scilicet, ut dici solet, nullius in bonis".

§ 2 Original Community, Prima Occupatio, and the Right to All Things — 157

as a consensually grounded transition undertaken by all of humankind. This kind of transition must be thought of in the same way as when partners or joint heirs come to divide up among themselves the things given to them in common. Everything else, i.e., each thing neither individually distributed nor left undivided, qualifies as vacant, i.e., as *res nullius*. As such, it lies open to the acquisitive act of occupation.

Two facets of this description of humankind's natural condition must be underscored. First, the description shows that the originally common *dominium* must be understood positively. It may not be interpreted in keeping with Grotius's negative characterization of the primitive condition of community, which abstracts from the characteristics of established property in terms of which ownership can be thought of as a right to exclude others from the use of what one seizes from the common stock of things. In keeping with his abstractive account (see pp. 151–152), Grotius maintains at least a conceptual distinction between a human subject's non-dominative *facultas utendi* and this same subject's *dominium*-founding power to seize or occupy. Selden, however, evidently has no use for such a distinction; and his conception of common *dominium* is consequently far removed from the notion of a merely negative community of things that is suggested by the Grotian conception of the community of things.[81] For Selden, the original possessors are *eo ipso* owners in just the same way that joint heirs are owners of a common estate.[82] Thus, the use that any one of these possessors makes of anything belonging to the common stock of things is necessarily the seizing of something that is already that possessor's own simply in virtue of his nature-given relation to the common *dominium*.

The second facet to emphasize is the following one. On Selden's view, there has never been a time in which the entire earth and its products were not (i) the common *dominium* of all humanity or else (ii) either exclusively owned or unoccupied. Selden's general argument in *Mare clausum* is meant to establish, on the basis of an idea of universal consent, that the latter sub-classification for things (i.e., the division of things into exclusive *dominium* and *res nullius*) must apply to

---

[81] See the reference to Pufendorf in note 64.
[82] Or to extend Selden's analogy: in the same way that the residents of an English village were joint owners of the local commons before enclosure (cf. Tuck 1999, p. 117). It should be noted here, incidentally, that Selden's conception of positive community should not be confused with Pufendorf's basic interpretation of *communio positiva* (see DJN IV.4.2–3/GW 4.1: 354–356; cf. notes 19 and 28). For Pufendorf, *communio positiva* implies the exclusion of others from things that are said to be in common, just as ownership implies their exclusion from things that are said to be one's own. On Selden's account of universal positive community, however, no one is originally excluded in this way.

the sea as well as to all available land after the universal relinquishment of the common right to all things that make up the originally common *dominium* of humankind. Selden strategy in presenting his general argument is to show that this inclusion follows from the key assumptions Grotius's theory of property.

It is in keeping with this strategy that Selden explicitly links his considerations on original acquisition to the idea of universal agreement that we have already encountered in Grotius's *De jure belli ac pacis*. (As I indicated at the beginning of this section, this is the textual connection to which Grotius refers when he appeals to Selden's *Mare clausum* in the second edition of DJB.) The crucial passage for understanding the implications of Selden's table-turning strategy is found at the end of the fourth chapter of *Mare clausum*. [83] Paraphrased, its argument runs as follows:

> If all people were originally owners (*domini*) of what was given to everyone in common, then it seems that they must have retained their community of ownership with respect to anything not subject to distribution in the first partition of things through universal consent. Yet, although it is true that all humans must be regarded as joint owners of what was given to everyone in common prior to the first partition, we must still conclude that the original common title and right to things given to everyone in common was renounced in a way that any individual might become the owner of what remained vacant (i.e., undistributed) after that accord-based partition. This accords with a parity of sound reason (*parilis sane ratio*). For if we accept, with Grotius, that each should retain as his own whatever he *had* come to possess before this partition, then we also have reason to conclude that anyone may occupy anything that was afterwards left vacant as *res nullius*.

---

[83] "Jam vero si communiter & pro indiviso fuere universi domini ante partium aliquot distributionem, earum quae in distributionem non venerant, ut manerent pariter universi, quemadmodum ante, pro indiviso domini, necessum est ut existimemus; nisi pactum aliquod intervenerit, quo pristino omnimodo communionis titulo jurique ita renunciatum fuerit, ut deinceps eorum, quae vacua manerent, seu in distributionem non venirent, domini fierent singulares quicunque primo animo possidendi, insistendi, utendi furendi, corporaliter occuparent. Neque aliter in cassua sociorum aut cohaeredum (quales in rerum communione homines fuisse videntur universi) fingi potest, quomodo ea quae in distributionem non veniant, non ut antea maneant communia. Itaque pactum ejusmodi primariis dominii privati initiis intercessisse, [...]. Adeo ut non minus de distributione per assignationem, quam de occupatione rerum derelictarum ad libitum, pactum universale, sive verbis difertis sive tacite ex morum usu, initum esse decernamus. Quod ipsum sane amplecti videtur V. C. Hugo Grotius: *Res*, inquit, *in proprietatem* (de cujus exordio loquitur) *ibant, non animi actu soli (neque enim scire alii poterant, quid alii suum esse vellent, ut eo abstinerent; et idem velle plures poterant) sed pacto quodam aut expresso, ut per divisionem, aut tacito, ut per occupationem. Simulatque enim communio displicuit, nec instituta est divisio, censeri debet inter omnes convenisse, ut quod quisque occupasset id proprium haberet*. Parilis sane ratio etiam ejus quod quisquam postea, ex eo quod derelictum erat, occuparet" (Selden 1726, pp. 1197 [2nd column]-1198 [1st column]).

§ 2 Original Community, Prima Occupatio, and the Right to All Things — 159

Note well the implication of Selden's 'parity of reason' argument: *All* components of the originally common stock of things are subject to exclusive appropriation by way of first seizure or occupation. Exactly this is the lesson that Selden is concerned to draw from the link that Grotius forges between the concepts of universal agreement and *occupatio*. For Selden, the unilateral act of occupation performed subsequent to the partition of humanity's common *dominium* is (*qua* act) conceptually indistinguishable from such an act performed beforehand. Thus, there is no reason to employ a principle of universal agreement (or accord) in order to restrict the quantitative or qualitative scope of occupation after the dissolution of the common *dominium* while not placing any explicit restriction on it prior to this dissolution. For the same universality principle that allows an agent to retain what he had seized prior to dissolution must apply to all things not owned by particular subjects afterwards. (This is the underlying point of Selden's parity of reason claim.) And there is, according to Selden, no basis whatsoever for restricting the scope of anyone's unilateral act of occupation prior to everyone's agreement that whatever anyone had occupied should be something that one has as one's own.

Selden holds, then, that every agent is entitled unilaterally to occupy any given thing from the common stock of things available to humankind. The *ius commune pristinum*, as Selden designates it, determines the character of the human agent's possessive relation to things seized before the first partition. It also determines this agent's possible appropriative relation to everything afterwards left vacant. Thus, with regard to both the originally common *dominium* and all things that can qualify as *res nullius* subsequent to the dissolution of the original community, Selden's *ius commune* serves as the rational ground for unrestricted appropriation. It is, in effect, *ius commune in omnia*: a right of all to all things—at least to those things not previously subject to exclusive occupation and particularized distribution.[84]

It is on the basis of his doctrine of acquisition that Selden seeks to refute Grotius's arguments against the permissibility of exclusive appropriation of the world's oceans. In his most telling counterargument, Selden maintains that Grotius fails to comply with what is entailed by his own crucial claim, i.e., the claim that the seas do not present a proper object of acquisition.[85] Grotius insists that the seas are not, and never have been, subject to exclusive appropriation. Yet he also concedes that it is possible to establish *dominium* in certain parts of the

---

[84] For discussion of Selden in connection with Thomas Hobbes's account of natural right and the state of nature, see Richard Tuck 1999, pp. 16–50.
[85] See Selden 1726, p. 1274 (2nd column).

maritime world (stretches near the shore, bays, and the like). As Selden points out, this concession implicitly reduces the whole problem of the permissibility or impermissibility of the oceans' exclusive appropriation to an empirical question about the pragmatically feasible reach of occupation—which is in fact to miss the philosophic import of the point in question. This point, after all, concerns the juridical possibility of unilateral occupation; and a coherent doctrine of acquisition—even one that takes its key elements from Grotius's own theoretical arsenal—must allow for the possibility of the unilateral and *global* occupation of the oceans. Selden grants, of course, that this global occupation would be an exceedingly difficult act to carry out unilaterally. But if such an act of occupation *could* be successfully performed, then the object of acquisition—the oceans and, indeed, the entire globe for that matter—would become part of the occupant's *dominium*.[86] And this would be entirely consistent with the requirements of natural law in its permissive sense.[87]

§ 3 Kantian Original Acquisition and Material Equality in Distribution

So much for the historical background to Kant's references to the *mare liberum v. mare clausum* debate. Having explored a bit of this background territory, we can see how Kant's claims regarding the extent of the seas' occupation are in keeping with the position that Grotius wanted to defend. It might be an interesting exercise to investigate the extent to which Kant actually understood his doctrine of acquisition as offering support for Grotius's attempt to set limits on the appropriation of the world's oceans. Our interest in this particular issue in international maritime law, however, extends only as far as it sheds light on a basic problem in Kant's theory of original acquisition. The problem, again, is this: Why should acquisition through unilateral occupation receive the favor of any law of right if it represents the type of control-seizing act that can generate a condition of universal conflict on account of the dynamical community of all possessive agents? In view of this question, the focus of our interest in Grotius's and Selden's doctrines of acquisition has been the connection between the concepts of occupation and community of possession. Thus, in assessing the significance of those doctrines

---

[86] "Et sane ut occuparetur totius oceanus, nemo existimare potest non esse difficillimum. Si tame occuparetur, ut fretum aut finus, ut totus orbis veteribus occupari a principibus dictus est, aeque etiam in dominium occupantis posset transire" (Selden 1726, p. 1274 [2nd column]).
[87] Selden lays out his conception of universal permissive natural law (*ius permissiva*) in chapters 5–7 of *Mare clausum*.

for Kant's theory of original acquisition, we need to bear in mind the following considerations.

The conceptions of common *dominium* found in Grotius's and Selden's doctrines fall under the Kantian heading of primitive community (*uranfängliche Gemeinschaft*).[88] According to Kant, the concept of primitive community, or primitive possession in common, underlies the quasi-historical and unavoidably fictional (*gedichtet*) descriptions of humankind's natural condition that Grotius and others put forward in order to depict the beginnings of property and juridical relations among human beings.[89] It is an empirical concept that depends on temporal conditions.[90] The theory of original acquisition, however, is not concerned with temporal conditions that underlie the description of supposed historical (or pre-historical) states of affairs. Rather, this theory aims to determine *a priori* the necessary conditions for all rightful acquisition. To achieve this aim, it requires a concept of the community of possession, but this must be a rational practical concept whose application in no way depends on empirically specifiable temporal conditions. No empirical concept of the community of possession can qualify as such a concept of reason, and the narrative portrayals of the beginnings of property that rely on this kind of empirical concept cannot satisfy the conceptual demands of the theory of original acquisition.

This Kantian criticism of traditional doctrines of acquisition certainly applies to Grotius's portrayal of the origins of property relations.[91] It also applies to Selden, at least to the extent that he follows Grotius in giving a historicizing depiction of the state of nature and the dissolution of primitive community. But we should notice as well an interesting implication of the parity of reason argument that Selden directs against the Grotian doctrine of acquisition (see p. 158). Selden contends that the contractualist principle of universal agreement can furnish no ground for restricting the quantitative or qualitative scope of unilateral occupation after the dissolution of primitive community if it does not place any explicit restriction on this occupation beforehand. But if this is true, then (*parilis sane ratio*) it must also be the case that there can be no such restriction on the scope of occupation prior to that dissolution either. This follows for two reasons: first, because there is no basis for restricting the scope of anyone's unilateral act

---

[88] See RL 6:258.14–21, 6:262.26–34.
[89] See RL 6:251.1–13. Regarding this passage's underlying references to Grotius and Pufendorf, see Edwards 1998, pp. 126–127.
[90] See RL 6:262.28–31.
[91] For extended discussion of the medieval and modern background relevant to pre-Kantian doctrines of acquisition and theories of property, see Brett 1997; Brocker 1992; Edwards 2002, pp. 41–60; Tierney 1997; Tierney 2001; Robinson 2013, pp. 285–295.

of occupation apart from some principle of agreement to do so; and second, because the whole point of employing the principle of universal agreement is to establish that each occupying agent should have as his own whatever he had occupied prior to everyone's (tacit or expressed) agreement to restrict each agent's unilaterally occupying acts to those things not already occupied by another.

Selden himself does not bring out this implication regarding the unrestricted scope of occupation prior to universal agreement. As we have seen, his main line of attack against Grotius in *Mare clausum* leads him to concentrate instead on the temporal conditions under which the dissolution of primitive community leaves a world full of objects (including all the seas) that have *yet* to be occupied. But if the further inference step is taken, then the general upshot of Selden's parity of reason argument against Grotius becomes clear: Apart from the determination of an occupying act's priority in the *order* of time, the specification of temporal conditions is not relevant to a theory of acquisition that employs a contractualist principle of universal agreement. As long as an agent's unilaterally occupying act is thought of as performed prior to the corresponding act of another, it makes no difference whether occupation occurs before or after the point in time at which universal agreement is supposed (imagined or stipulated) to take place. For the relevant conditions to account for in a theory of *original* acquisition are those by which all occupying agents are set in community with one another in virtue of the relation of each of these agents to all of the outer objects that are subject to unilateral occupation.

It is (logically, if not historically) but a short further step to link the conceptual representation of the sum and the material substrate of these spatial conditions to the potential for universal conflict and the naturally unavoidable opposition of occupying agents' powers of choice. But it is precisely in view of this potential and this opposition that we must again consider the passages from RL § 15 and § 17 quoted at the outset of this chapter.[92] The general question that Kant poses is the question of the extent to which one is authorized to take possession of unoccupied land. His response, which is keyed to the *mare liberum vs. mare clausum* controversy, is in keeping with his standpoint that the theory of original acquisition must not rely on the substantive specification of particular conditions of empirical possession apart from the condition of temporal priority in possession-taking. But notice that his treatment of the permissible extent of occupation under actual empirical conditions of possession-tak-

---

[92] A more thorough discussion of the historical background covered thus far will of course have to consider Kant in relation to Hobbes as well as Hobbes's relation to Grotius and Selden. On this, see chapter 12.

ing is entirely unilluminating as far as the pivotal task of that theory is concerned. To put the matter in terms as blunt as Kant's own: settling the permissible spatial scope of possession-taking (hence occupation) by calculating the range of one's weapons is unhelpful if the theoretical task is to clarify how the will of each to use humanity's originally common possession can lead to unilaterally possession-taking acts that are necessarily in keeping with the universality requirements of juridico-practical reason. That is because the insurmountable global unity of this object of possible use is such that the weapons of each *can* be within the range of everyone else's weapons, in which case the nature-given will of each to use the originally common object can give rise to a condition of universal conflict in which no one's use of that object is possible.

It will hardly do to think that an indispensable systematic component of Kant's doctrine of right depends on empirical assumptions about the limitations on human beings' technical capacity for the use-prohibiting mutual infliction of physical damage. There must be something still missing from our treatment of original acquisition. It is certainly not the possible existence of the cannon, which nowadays are real enough in any event.

§ 17 of the Doctrine of Right gives Kant's "Deduction of the Concept of Original Acquisition" (RL 6:268.2). The overall argument of the doctrine of acquisition prior to this deduction leads to the following results, which Kant summarizes in the passage translated above at the end of the second section of chapter 6. The title of acquisition (*Title der Erwerbung*) is found in the original community of land, and thus "among the spatial conditions of external possession". The way of acquisition (*Erwerbungsart*), however, is found by taking account of empirical conditions of external possession-taking, and by conceptualizing how these conditions connect up with the will to have external objects as one's own. The remaining task—the actual deduction of the concept of original acquisition—is to "develop *acquisition* itself, i.e., the external mine and yours [...] from the principles of pure practical reason" (RL 6:268.8–11). Perhaps, then, we can find the way to complete the pivotal task of the theory of original acquisition by carefully examining this deduction.

In the second paragraph of RL § 17,[93] Kant explicates the concept of intelligible possession (*possessio noumenon*), showing that it contains as one of its fea-

---

[93] "Der *Rechtsbegriff* vom *äußeren* Mein und Dein, so fern es *Substanz* ist, kann, was das Wort außer mir betrifft, nicht einen anderen *Ort*, als wo ich bin, bedeuten: denn er ist ein Vernunftbegriff; sondern, da unter diesem nur ein reiner Verstandesbegriff subsumirt werden kann, bloß etwas von mir *Unterschiedenes* und den eines nicht empirischen Besitzes (der gleichsam fortdauernden Apprehension), sondern nur den des *in meiner Gewalt Habens* (die Verknüpfung desselben mit mir als subjective Bedingung der Möglichkeit des Gebrauchs) des äußeren Gegen-

tures a representation that denotes "the connection of an external object with me insofar as this connection is the subjective condition of the possibility of the object's use" (RL 6:268.18–19). Since it features in a concept of pure practical reason, this representation must itself be both non-empirical and intellectual. Specifically, it must be the *a priori* conceptual representation that signifies the circumstance of *"having* an external object *under my control"* (RL 6:268.18–20). Even as applied to sensible objects, the concept of having here at issue is one that abstracts from the sensible conditions by which possession appears as "a relation of person to objects that have no obligation" (RL 6:268.22–23). Now when these sensible conditions of concept application are disregarded, possession proves to be "nothing other than the relation of a person to persons, all of whom are subject to the first person's *will* to *bind*" (RL 6:268.23–28) to the extent that this first person's will accords with the principles of juridico-practical reason and the idea of the universally lawgiving function of the united will of all. In sum, the deduction of the concept of original acquisition involves the specification of the concept of intelligible possession in terms of having an external object under one's control; and this specification is what furnishes the particular concept of having that we can employ to explain how one person's will to bind can actually place an obligation upon all other persons with respect to certain objects of the power of choice. By means of that specification, then, Kant wants to show how the concept of having that plays so central a role in the doctrine of possession also provides the key to understanding the justificatory basis of original acquisition.

Is Kant successful in this endeavor? The analytic procedure of RL § 17 clearly does show the way to think of the possession of objects as a relation of obligation between persons, instead of merely as a physical relation of persons to objects. It therefore sheds considerable light above all on the culminating aspect (or 'moment') of original acquisition mentioned above in chapter 6 (see pp. 136–137). (In particular, it allows for a proper understanding of what Kant means in § 10 when he asserts that appropriation is "the act of an externally and universally lawgiving will (in idea) through which everyone is bound to

---

standes, welcher ein reiner Verstandesbegriff ist, bedeuten. Nun ist die Weglassung oder das Absehen (Abstraction) von diesen sinnlichen Bedingungen des Besitzes als eines Verhältnisses der Person zu *Gegenständen*, die keine Verbindlichkeit haben, nichts anders als das Verhältniß einer Person zu *Personen*, diese alle durch den *Willen* der ersteren, so fern er dem Axiom der äußeren Freiheit, dem *Postulat* des Vermögens und der allgemeinen *Gesetzgebung* des *a priori* als vereinigt gedachten Willens gemäß ist, in Ansehung des Gebrauchs der Sachen zu *verbinden*, welches also der *intelligibele Besitz* derselben, d.i. der durchs bloße Recht, ist, obgleich der Gegenstand (die Sache, die ich besitze) ein Sinnenobject ist" (RL 6:268.12–30).

agreement with my choice" [RL 6:259.2–4].) Given its focus on an a priori concept of *having*, however, it is far from obvious that Kant's procedure in § 17 can even address what is fundamentally at issue in the required account of original acquisition, as long as acquisition as such must be understood as an act of *acquiring* things in order to be in the state of having them. With regard to the use of these things, Kant's aim in § 17 is to show how all persons can be bound by the will of a first person, i.e., by the will of a unilaterally control-seizing agent who was the first to take possession of an object. The argument is that all persons are so bound *insofar* as that first person's will to have something under her control accords with the universality requirements of juridico-practical reason, and hence conforms with "the universal *lawgiving* of the will that is thought as united *a priori*" (RL 6:268.25–26). Yet it remains entirely unclear how we are to go about determining the extent to which the way of acquisition (*Erwerbungsart*) can be in conformity with this universally prescriptive role of the *a priori* united will of all as long as that way of acquiring things is to be found in the empirical conditions of possession-taking that are joined with a person's will to have objects under her control.

The full import of this line of questioning becomes evident when we consider three things that Kant establishes in the sections that prepare the terrain for the deduction of the concept of original acquisition in RL § 17. As we have seen, Kant argues in RL §15 and §16 that (a) taking possession of objects from the originally common possession of all human beings gives rise to quantitative and qualitative indeterminacy with regard to particular possession (*besonderer Besitz*); that (b) each human being's nature-given will to use that common possession is unavoidably faced with the opposition of human powers of choice; and that (c) this opposition would do away with all use of the common possession unless that will to use contained the law by which the particular possession of each can be determined. What, then, is the determining ground of the will that this law expresses? Kant makes it quite clear, of course, that the law itself must derive from the *idea* of an *a priori* united will of all. Consequently, the ground in question obviously cannot be found in empirical conditions of possession-taking. But neither the expository work on the concept of original acquisition that Kant undertakes prior to his deduction of this concept nor the deduction itself provides for the explanation of any non-empirical ground (or condition) by which the particular possession of each can be *determined*.

There is but one remaining path to take if we are to discover this kind of ground. It is the path that leads from the title of acquisition, not from the empirical conditions of an external possession-taking. Let us therefore examine more closely the "spatial conditions" (RL 6:268.3) that feature in the *a priori* concept of the original community of land that furnishes the title of acquisition. This is best accomplished with reference to the considerations on disjunctively universal and collectively universal possession found in Kant's preliminary work on the doctrine of right. As we have seen (in chapter 6, pp. 142–144), the thought that the earth furnishes the disjunctive-universal possession of humankind takes account of a physical factor that conditions human existence: The spatial properties of the earth's surface are such that all of the earth's inhabitants stand in a relation of possible reciprocal influence or possible dynamical community (*commercium*). In virtue of this relation, each human being is *always* potentially in possession of any place among *all* places on the earth's surface, which is what requires the collective view of the universal dynamical community of possession. The explication of this collective view shows both the possibility and the practical necessity of a rightful act "by which the possession of each is determined distributively" (VARL 23:320.36). Regarded from the collective point of view, the common possession of the human species must therefore be thought of as something whose particularized distribution *can* coincide with "an objectively united will or will that is to be united". Apart from the consideration of this possible structural overlap, there is no way to ground the principle that warrants the distributive determination of possession, i.e., the principle of distribution without which "the right of human beings to be anywhere at all would be entirely without effect and would be destroyed by universal conflict" (VARL 23:323.31–324.2).

All this is in keeping with the argument presented in the published version(s) of the Metaphysical Foundations of the Doctrine of Right. Yet Kant's concern to highlight the causal features of the universal spatial community of possession allows us to discern the import of a key requirement of practical reason that is not readily apparent in the published text. On its collective view, the original community of possession may not be understood *simply* in terms of the reciprocal causal relation of all persons that can emerge from their possessive relation to usable objects. For in addition to its representing a universal relation of persons to persons, that original community must also be thought of as representing the relation of all persons to all possible objects that are subject to original acquisition by virtue of the circumstance that all such objects are constitutive components of the common possession of all human beings. It is this collective causal relation of *persons to objects*—that is, the possessive relation that persons have to usable objects of the power of choice on the basis of their possible reciprocal causal relations to the powers of choice of all other persons—that must be constituted in conformity with a principle of distribution that derives from the idea of a united and universally lawgiving will of all persons.

Now as regards acquired rights, all lawgiving in accordance with this idea of practical reason is subject to a fundamental requirement. It has to be consistent with a basic principle of juridico-practical reason involved in Kant's understanding of freedom as "the only original right belonging to every human being by virtue of their humanity" (RL 6:237.32–33). That principle—the principle of innate freedom—is one that contains innate equality, i.e., "independence from being bound by others to more than one can also reciprocally bind them" (RL 6:237.34).[94] Kant's theory of private right, and hence his account of original acquisition, presupposes the practical objective validity of this idea of independence. The principle of distribution that applies to original possession in common, i.e., to the original community of land, must therefore accord with the constraint against the non-reciprocal imposition of obligation in terms of which the innate freedom and equality of human beings is defined.[95] With respect to the conditions of original acquisition, then, what Kant calls the "rightful capacity [*Vermögen*] of the will to bind everyone" (RL 6:267.19–20) must be governed by a principle that recognizes this essential limitation: *No* person's unilateral act of possession-taking and appropriation can bind other persons to more than that first person can be bound by them. Thus, with regard to all things that can be acquired for use, the principle of distribution here in question allows for indefiniteness or indeterminacy from the point of view of disjunctive-universal possession (i.e., from the point of view according to which every human being is potentially in possession of any arbitrarily chosen place on earth because of the possible dynamical community—the *commercium*—of all the planet's inhabitants). Yet Kant's understanding of original possession in common is such that the principle of distribution contained in the idea of the united will of all must be a principle of *equality* in distribution. For even if I am (originally) the first to *take* possession of something that I already possess in common with all others, I would violate the constraint against the non-reciprocal placement of obligation

---

94 "*Freiheit* (Unabhängigkeit von eines Anderen nöthigender Willkür), sofern sie mit jedes Anderen Freiheit nach einem allgemeinen Gesetz zusammen bestehen kann, ist dieses einzige, ursprüngliche, jedem Menschen kraft seiner Menschheit zustehende Recht.—Die angeborne *Gleichheit*, d.i. die Unabhängigkeit nicht zu mehrerem von Anderen verbunden zu werden, als wozu man sie wechselseitig auch verbinden kann; mithin die Qualität des Menschen sein *eigener Herr* (*sui iuris*) zu sein, imgleichen die eines *unbescholtenen* Menschen (*iusti*), weil er vor allem rechtlichen Act keinem Unrecht gethan hat; endlich auch die Befugniß, das gegen andere zu thun, was an sich ihnen das Ihre nicht schmälert, wenn sie sich dessen nur nicht annehmen wollen; [...]—alle diese Befugnisse liegen schon im Princip der angebornen Freiheit und sind wirklich von ihr nicht (als Glieder der Eintheilung unter einem höheren Rechtsbegriff) unterschieden" (RL 6:237.29–238.11). For commentary pertaining to this passage and considerations on its historical significance, see Byrd/Hruschka 2010, pp. 77–93; Friedrich 2004, pp. 73–87; Gregor 1993; James 2016; Ripstein 2009, pp. 30–56.
95 Which is not to say that this principle can be *derived* from Kant's account of the innate notion of freedom.

unless I limited the extent of my possession-taking in accordance with the following precept: We may place upon all others an obligation to refrain from using certain objects of our powers of choice because we were (each of us respectively) the first to take possession of these objects—but *only insofar* as this does not bind all others, in their use of objects, to refrain from *more* than we are reciprocally bound by all of them to refrain from using.

However quantitatively or qualitatively indeterminate the object of acquisition may turn out to be under empirical conditions of possession-taking, the consideration of the collective relation of all persons to the universal object and material substrate of all possible external acquisition gives rise to the following demand. The principle of distribution at issue in the conceptual determination of original acquisition must be a principle of equality. It must be the principle (or law) through which the a priori determinable condition of possession-taking is *specified as* the ground of equality in the distribution of things. This is the only way to establish that the will of each to use the originally common possession of humankind is necessarily consistent with the universal lawgiving at issue in the idea of an a priori united will of all. The normative basis for all derivative acquisition therefore lies in a distributive principle of original equality in use. This principle must retain its objective validity and prescriptive necessity with respect to all conditions of possession-taking. That is to say: it must retain its universally prescriptive force independently of the extent to which the outcome of the unilaterally control-seizing activity of human beings in fact satisfies the imperative of reason that such a principle of equality yields.

We should bear in mind, again, that the principle in question furnishes a law of practical reason that belongs to the theory of *ius strictum*. This is a law of right that concerns merely the reciprocal relations of person's powers of choice. As repeatedly noted above (see pp. 124–128, 145–146), its derivation does not in any way depend on considerations equity, desired ends or human needs;[96] and it takes no account of the matter of choice, i.e., the end that one may have in mind with whatever object one might want to have. The principle of distribution in question is therefore a strictly formal principle of equality. Nonetheless, it is a principle of *material* equality as far as the acquisition of objects is concerned. Only if it incorporates a formal principle of material equality can Kant's theory of original acquisition provide a coherent normative basis for property law.[97]

---

[96] In this regard, the position that I take on what is required by Kant's doctrine of original acquisition may well differ significantly from Paul Guyer's approach to the same set of issues. See Guyer 2000, pp. 253–58; Guyer 2002, pp. 273–292; Guyer 2005, pp. 237–242.

[97] After considering the relationship between Kant's conception of innate equality and the idea of originally common possession, David James has recently insisted on "Kant's failure to establish the

§ 3 Kantian Original Acquisition and Material Equality in Distribution — 169

Needless to say, this conclusion is hardly what one would expect to get from a classic modern theory of the foundations of property, and I hasten to emphasize that Kant himself by no means draws it in the Metaphysical Foundations of the Doctrine of Right. Yet there seems to be no defensible alternative conclusion —unless, that is, we are prepared to accept that a person's will to use and rightfully to have objects need not be in keeping with practical reason's *exeundum* prescription, that is, with its commandment to go forth from the juridical state of nature and leave it behind.[98]

We will return to the idea of a formal principle of material equality in chapter 12, where my proposed solution to Kant's problem of original acquisition is discussed in connection with the emergence of the modern conception of natural right.

---

rightful nature of provisional forms of ownership that simply need to be transformed into a legal right of private property in the transition to the civil condition" (James 2016, p. 318). Accordingly, James infers that what is really required is "a system of property rights that is determined by decisions regarding the distribution of land and other resources reached on an ongoing basis with the aim of securing the independence of all citizens after some kind of deliberative process" (p. 318). Yet it is unclear why such a system should not be grounded by a Kantian theory of original acquisition that would incorporate a formal principle of material equality. There will be a good deal more to say about this point in the concluding chapter of this book.

[98] Marcus Willaschek (2002, pp. 65–87) has argued that Kant denies the prescriptive character of the laws of right (or juridical laws). According to Willaschek, "we are forced to the paradoxical conclusion that, in a Kantian framework, juridical laws cannot be prescriptive in the sense that they do not issue in prescriptions meant to direct the behaviour of their addressees" (p. 71). While juridical laws are normative in the sense that they define a nonfactual standard of rightness, "they cannot *prescribe, command,* or *require* that their addressees act in accordance with that standard" (p. 71). Thus, in adhering to Kant's theory of *ius strictum*, we end up with "a purely non-prescriptive conception of Right" (p. 85) that makes no room for categorical imperatives of right. I find this anti-prescriptivist interpretation of Kant's juridical laws remarkably interesting, especially since it represents a frontal assault on the type of interpretive approach taken in the last two chapters. It seems to me, however, that Willaschek's approach stems from a failure to take proper account of how Kant's crucial distinction between laws for *actions* and laws for *maxims* of actions relates systematically to the ways in which Kant differentiates between juridical and ethical lawgiving, internal and external lawgiving, internal and external actions, and "the law of *your* own will" and "the law of will in general, which could also be the will of others" (see MS 6:219.17–221.3 and TL 6:388.32–389.11). My detailed criticism of Willaschek's anti-prescriptivist approach can be found in in the final endnote (number 57) of Edwards 2011b.

Part IV Placing Kant in his History of Moral Philosophy

Needless to say, ascertaining Kant's place in *the* history of moral philosophy would be an exceedingly lavish undertaking. For our purposes, it would also amount to an exercise in historiographic pretentiousness unless the scope of the placing project can be in keeping with this book's thematic limitations, which are determined by the Doctrine of Virtue's theory of reason's obligatory ends, on the one side, and by the Doctrine of Right's theory of original acquisition, on the other. Thus, in this final main phase of our investigations, I propose to dig deeper into the historical subsoil of the systematic terrain that we have already covered in Parts I through III. In chapters 8–11, I examine Kant's own views on how his predecessors in moral philosophy relate to his work on the foundations of the doctrine of morals. In chapter 12, I extend the line of inquiry previously followed when discussing Kant's relation to early modern theories of original acquisition.

Chapter 8 Kant's Classification of Material Principles of Morality in the *Critique of Practical Reason*

In this very brief, though pivotal, chapter I will be primarily concerned with a strategy of classification that Kant follows in the *Critique of Practical Reason* in order to make systematic sense of the history of moral philosophy prior to the establishment of the principle of reason's autonomy. I will consider this strategy as it applies to what Kant calls practical material determining grounds in the principle of morality. In doing this, I will examine Kant's concern to interpret his predecessors' different grounding principles for the theory of morals as material principles of morality, and thus as belonging under the general principle of self-love or one's own happiness.

As this examination will show, Kant's strategy may be plausible for most of the representative figures that he lists in connection with his typology of material determining grounds. Yet it demands the kind of interpretation of both Francis Hutcheson's sentimentalist approach and classic Stoic perfectionism that is, at least on the face of things, quite surprising. For one thing, it is unclear how Kant's classificatory game plan can avoid falling prey to the arguments that Hutcheson had already leveled against reductively egoistic accounts of actions motivated by benevolent inclination. For another, it is far from evident that Kant's historical view of Stoic moral philosophy can do proper justice to the principle of internal perfection that Kant himself holds to be the central tenet of the Stoics' approach to the foundations of morals. It is in view of these two exceptionally problematic components of Kant's historiographic scheme that we will go on, in chapter 9, to consider several key aspects of the development of Kant's doctrine of morals in the 1760s. Those same components will also serve as guideposts for the historical investigations pursued in chapters 10–11, where I discuss Hutchesons's account of the origin of obligation in relation to modern natural law theories as well as the role played by the Stoic idea of the *honestum* in modern sentimentalist and rationalist ethics.

§ 1 Epicurus, the Stoics, and "Practical Material Determining Grounds"

The lines of argument followed in Parts I and II of this book lead to the conclusion that Kant's basic understanding of practical law and the moral worth of ac-

§ 1 Epicurus, the Stoics, and "Practical Material Determining Grounds" — 173

tions may well allow for a substantially revised conception of the relationship between, on the one hand, the sensible or affective conditions of action to which rational agents may be subject and, on the other hand, the concepts and action guiding principles of morally practical reason. We can see the special relevance of this conclusion if we consider Kant's own classificatory schemes for comparing the foundational principles of morality endorsed by his historical predecessors with the strictly formal principle of morality provided by the principle of the autonomy of the will (i.e., the principle: "So act that the maxim of your will could always hold at the same time as a principle in a universal lawgiving" [KpV 5:30]). I refer here to the various templates that Kant provides for classifying the material grounding principles of the different types of heteronomous ethics. We find these templates in Kant's published writings, unpublished reflections, and lecture records from the 1770s through the 1790s.[1] I will comment on the template presented in the first chapter of the *Critique of Practical Reason*, in the context of Remark II to Theorem IV of Kant's theory of practical reason.

We have already examined a significant facet of this remark when discussing Kant's treatment of universal happiness in connection with material conditions of maxims (see chapter 3, pp. 69–72). Our focus here is on the account of "[a]ll possible determining grounds of the will" (KpV 5:39.11) that Kant gives in the final paragraphs of this remark. In these paragraphs, Kant provides a comprehensive list of the possible types of "practical material determining grounds in the principle of morality" (KpV 5:40). The list, structured according to subjective and objective as well as internal and external determining grounds of the will, is supposed to furnish a table for the classification of practical principles (see KpV 5:40) in which "all possible cases are exhausted except the one formal principle" (KpV 5:39.8–9). Kant's intention is thus to provide for a systematic classification of all historically competing foundational principles for the theory of morals by showing how all principles apart from his own principle of the autonomy amount to "*material* principles of morality" (KpV 5:39.6–7). Given what the second theorem of his moral doctrine asserts about material principles— namely, that all material practical principles belong under the general principle of self-love or one's own happiness—the clear implication of Kant's classificatory strategy is this: the various grounding principles for the theory of morals that were endorsed by his predecessors in the history of Western moral philosophy must be regarded as specifying interpretations of the same general own-happiness principle. It is in keeping with this implication that Kant means to show the historical import as well as the historiographic plausibility of his claim

---

[1] For references, see note 3 of this chapter.

that only the "*formal* supreme principle of practical reason (as that of the autonomy of the will)" (KpV 39.5–6) can be "the *sole* principle that can *possibly* be fit for categorical imperatives, that is, practical laws (which make actions duties), and in general for the principle of morality both in assessment and in application to the human will in determining it" [2] (KpV 5:41.34–38).

The basic division in Kant's classification of material principles of morality is between two types of material determining grounds of the will. There are (i) subjective or empirical material determining grounds and (ii) objective material determining grounds, i.e., material determining grounds that are based on the rational concept of perfection as it is employed for the determination of ends of action. According to Kant, the first of these types is exemplified by the material grounds contained in the founding tenets of the moral theories of Michel de Montaigne, Bernard Mandeville, Epicurus, and Francis Hutcheson. Referring to his preceding analysis of empirically conditioned practical reason and the account of its relation to the principles of pure practical reason, Kant holds that no principle involving such subjective grounds is qualified to be the universal principle of morality. Things are rather more complicated when we come to the material determining grounds at issue in Kant's second division, i.e., the grounds drawn from the rational concept of perfection that gives rise to the moral theories exemplified by Christian Wolff and the Stoics as well as to the versions of theonomous moral doctrine advocated by Christian August Crusius and others. As Kant acknowledges, we are indeed confronted with *objective* practical determining grounds when dealing with either the Stoic conception of the human being's internal perfection or with the idea of divine perfection at the core of the theonomous approach. So it may seem that the principles incorporating these grounds as conditions of action should be able to furnish practical laws that hold for the will of every rational being. But Kant's strategy is to show that not even a principle based on the concept of perfection can be strictly objective and purely rational since it can only serve as a principle of the doctrine of happiness. The key to making this strategy work lies in the argument that

---

[2] "so folgt *erstlich*, daß alle hier aufgestellte Principien material sind, *zweitens*, daß sie alle mögliche materiale Principien befassen, und daraus endlich der Schluß: daß, weil materiale Principien zum obersten Sittengesetz ganz untauglich sind (wie bewiesen worden), das *formale praktische Princip* der reinen Vernunft, nach welchem die bloße Form einer durch unsere Maximen möglichen allgemeinen Gesetzgebung den obersten und unmittelbaren Bestimmungsgrund des Willens ausmachen muß, das *einzige mögliche* sei, welches zu kategorischen Imperativen, d.i. praktischen Gesetzen (welche Handlungen zur Pflicht machen), und überhaupt zum Princip der Sittlichkeit sowohl in der Beurtheilung, als auch der Anwendung auf den menschlichen Willen in Bestimmung desselben tauglich ist" (KpV 5:28–37).

there is no firm criterion for drawing a fundamental distinction between, on the one hand, the practical material determining grounds that underlie the two types of perfectionist principle of morality in question and, on the other hand, the kind of material determining ground at issue in the principle of Epicurean eudaimonism.[3]

According to Kant, then, all of the foundational principles of the theory of morals that derive from various descriptions of practical material determining grounds in the principle of morality, including even the principles based on the rational concept of perfection, can be interpreted as falling under the general principle of self-love or one's own happiness—as is plainly required by Theorem II of Kant's theory of practical reason in the second *Critique*. Since subsuming such material grounding principles under this self-love theorem is also fully consistent with the second *Critique*'s overall account of the relationship between empirically conditioned practical reason and pure practical reason, the crucial question that remains to be asked is this: Just how plausible is Kant's classificatory scheme as a historically well-founded account of the competing principles that he brings into play?

From a straightforwardly historiographic point of view, it may well be uncontroversial for Kant to imply that the moral theories of Montaigne, Mandeville, and Epicurus are grounded in specifications of the general principle of self-love or one's own happiness.[4] Moreover, by taking the same approach to the eudaimonistic perfectionism of Wolff as well to Crusius's theonomous employment of the idea of the divine will, Kant offers an interpretation of these thinkers' moral doctrines that can lay claim to textual support.[5] But Kant's strategy of clas-

---

[3] See KpV 5:41.15–28. See also RGV 6:111.18–112.26; V-PP/Powalski 27:100.31–101.14, 103.5–7, 104.1–105.21, 107.5–19, 109.33–110.33; V-Mo/Collins 27:249.14–252.5, 253.11–15, 254.10–255.28; V-Mo/Mron 27:1401.25–1404.20, 1405.16–22, 1406.9–42. For discussions of Kant's relation to Epicurean and Stoic principles, see Irwin 1998, pp. 63–76, 79–84; Schmucker 1961, pp. 310–316; On Kant's relation to Wolff and Crusius, see Hartung 1999, pp. 168–172; Henrich 1963, 404–431; Kain 2004, pp. 271–280; Schneewind 1998, pp. 501–518, 521.

[4] For a different view of Mandeville's account of the foundations of morals, however, see Edwards 2014, 135–138.

[5] See C. Wolff 1969 [1733], §§ 42–62; Crusius 1969 [1744], §§ 133, 173–176. In an influential article on the development of Kant's ethics, Dieter Henrich maintains that Kant's subsumption of the Wolffian internal principle of perfection under the heading of an "explicit ethics of self-love" is without any foundation in Wolff's theory of morals (see Henrich 1963, pp. 424, 428). But Henrich does not consider the argument that Kant offers in KpV to justify his classification of Wolff; and he does not take into account the fact that the first premise of this argument (i.e., Kant's claim that "the concept of *perfection* [...] can become the determining ground of the will only if ends are previously given to us" [KpV 5:41.15–18]) is already in evidence in 1763 (see DBG 2:108.23–109.3). More on Kant's KpV argument presently.

sification raises especially significant questions when it is applied to both Hutcheson's sentimentalist theory of the foundations of morals and classic Stoic perfectionism. For it is not obvious—at least not to begin with—that either one of these last-mentioned theories is grounded in a material principle of morality that can plausibly be understood as a specifying interpretation of a general principle of self-love.

We will be centrally concerned with Kant's relation to Hutcheson as well as with some key components of Stoic moral philosophy in chapters 9 and 10. At this juncture, I will limit my comments to the aspects of this relation that bear specifically on the classificatory scheme at work in the *Critique of Practical Reason*.

§ 2 Hutcheson, Moral Feeling, and Benevolent Inclination

As just indicated, a major difficulty with Kant's classification is to understand exactly how Kant thinks it applies to Hutcheson. This difficulty is especially pressing for our line of inquiry since Hutcheson's entire approach to the foundations of morals requires a moral psychology that allows some actions to proceed from benevolence as an impulse arising from the affective constitution of the soul.[6] Moreover, Hutcheson's theory of virtue quite explicitly presupposes the repudiation of all egoistic explanations of moral motivation and makes the principle of other-directed benevolent inclination its central pillar.[7] How, then, can Kant's classificatory strategy credibly be thought to apply to Hutcheson's sentimentalist approach to the theory of morals?

Let us consider here the paragraph in the second *Critique* that immediately precedes Kant's classification of all material practical principles. Although it is unclear that the chief target of Kant's critical comments in this paragraph is Hutcheson himself—it could just as well be Shaftesbury, for example—these comments are still directly relevant to the reading of Hutcheson's moral doctrine that is demanded by the self-love theorem of the Kantian account of empirically conditioned practical reason.[8] Kant's main interest is to argue that the "concept of

---

[6] See Hutcheson IBV 108–112, 114–115, 122, 148–150; ECI 5, 8, 28, 33–34, 130, 142, 188; SMP 1–2, 8–10.
[7] See Hutcheson IBV 123–128, 132–144, 176–178, 180–182, 186; ECI 5, 105–106, 188, 192–194; SMP 50, 74–78, 255–257.
[8] Cf. MS 6:376.34–378.7. Regarding the implicit reference to *both* Shaftesbury and Hutcheson, see V-PP/Herder 27:4.16–5.15, 15.14–25; V-PP/Powalski 27:107.31–34; V-Mo/Collins 27:253.15–19;

§ 2 Hutcheson, Moral Feeling, and Benevolent Inclination — 177

morality and duty" (KpV 5:38.23) must precede any appeal to the feeling of satisfaction involved in the morally good agent's performance of dutiful actions or to the dissatisfaction involved in the transgression of duty. But his assessment of the underpinnings of moral sentimentalism is fully evident as well:

> More refined [...] is the pretense of those who assume a certain special moral sense which, instead of reason, would determine the moral law; and according to which the consciousness of virtue would be immediately bound up with satisfaction and enjoyment, while the consciousness of vice would be so bound to mental uneasiness and pain. And so everything would still be ceded [*aussetzen*] to the hankering after one's own happiness.[9] (*KpV* 5:38.12–17)

We may wish to contend that this criticism does damage to someone like Shaftesbury.[10] But even the most fleeting acquaintance with Hutcheson's theory will give us pause concerning its broader application, which Kant here clearly intends.[11] For it is not obvious that the type of criticism advanced by Kant can withstand the countering arguments that Hutcheson had already leveled against it on the basis of the elementary distinction between the desire of an object or event and the sensations of uneasiness or delight that are accessory to the desire.[12] Given this distinction, the uneasy sensation *accompanying* any object-directed desire cannot be prior to the "Desire itself", and so "cannot be a Motive to that Desire which it presupposes" (ECI 24). Nor, according to Hutcheson, can the pleasant sensation expected to *attend* the future satisfaction of a desire give rise to the desire of any object or event that could be judged morally preferable to another on account of its connection with that pleasant sensation. This is true especially when the object of desire happens to be the happiness of others, for "[t]his Expectation of the *Pleasure of gratified Desire*, would equally excite us to desire the *Misery* of others as their Happiness; since the *Pleasure* of *Gratification* might be obtained from both Events alike" (ECI 24).

V-NR/Feyerabend 27:1325.4–38. See also VT 8:390.25–34, 395.1–396.24; V-MS/Vigil 27:497.35–498.14, 500.19–23, 580.5–17.
9 "Feiner noch [...] ist das Vorgeben derer, die einen gewissen moralischen besondern Sinn annehmen, der, und nicht die Vernunft, das moralische Gesetz bestimmte, nach welchem das Bewußtsein der Tugend unmittelbar mit Zufriedenheit und Vergnügen, das des Lasters aber mit Seelenunruhe und Schmerz verbunden wäre, und so alles doch auf Verlangen nach eigener Glückseligkeit aussetzen".
10 See Shaftesbury 2003 [1713], pp. 200–213.
11 See the passages cited in note 7.
12 See, e.g., IBV 106–107; ECI 23–27. (Citation of Hutcheson's works is explained at the beginning of this book on p. X.)

In keeping with these considerations, Hutcheson maintains that an agent can disinterestedly desire the good of others even if it is granted that the successful promotion of others' happiness always yields the "Pleasures of Self-Approbation" (ECI 25) anticipated to attend the satisfaction of the desire. The prospect of obtaining these pleasures cannot afford a purely self-interested incentive to act for the sake of others merely in order to further an agent's own happiness since others' happiness could not possibly be an event that satisfies a desire if their happiness were pursued as nothing more than a means to the agent's private good. This is supposed to follow from the general conceptual point that Hutcheson makes about self-love's relation to the existence of a desired event as distinguished from its relation to the desire of an event:

> That alone which raises in us from *Self-Love* the Desire of any Event, is an *Opinion* that *that Event* is the *Means* of private Good. As soon as we form this Opinion, a Desire of the Event immediately arises: But if *having the Desire or Affection* be imagined the *Means* of private Good, and not the *Existence of the Event desired*, then from *Self-Love* we should only desire or wish to have the *Desire* of that Event, and should not desire the Event itself, since the *Event* is not conceived as the *Means* of Good. [...]
>
> [H]ad we no Affection distinct from *Self-Love*, nothing could raise our *Desire of the Happiness of others*, but conceiving their Happiness as the Means of ours. An Opinion that our having *kind Affections* would be the Means of our private Happiness, would only make us desire to have those Affections. (ECI 25)

It seems, then, that Kant would need to contest at least the positions just summarized if he is credibly to integrate Hutcheson with the scheme of material practical principles that fall under the second *Critique's* the self-love theorem.[13] Yet it is not

---

[13] The challenges facing Kant in his reading of Hutcheson are obviously compounded by the fact that he tacitly equates principles of egoism and hedonism in the second *Critique* (see, e.g., KpV 5:22.9–25). But there is no need for this to detain us, since the criticism here presented would apply even if Kant did not do this. For the sake of simplicity, I therefore concentrate on the broader question of (motivational) egoism even where Kant emphasizes the hedonistic dimension of the question. Regarding the equation of egoistic and hedonistic principles, I follow here the venerable lead of Beck (1960, pp. 92, 100 [cf. Irwin 1998, pp. 66–68]) and oppose Henry Allison (1990, pp. 102–103). Allison denies that Kant understands all non-moral motivation in terms of self-interest and that he requires a hedonistic view of such motivation in order to establish his theorem of self-love. But we can accept the point that the egoistic and hedonistic theses are distinct without denying (as Allison seems to do) that Kant's proof of his self-love theorem equates them. Moreover, we can accept that point without disregarding what the theorem itself actually asserts. In my view, to overlook this is to miss the crucial point of Kant's treatment of empirically conditioned practical reason in the second *Critique*.

evident where the contesting argument is to be found in the second *Critique*.¹⁴ This apparent lack of argument becomes especially perplexing when we consider the various classifications of material principles of morality that Kant had worked out prior to 1788. None of these expressly assumes the reductive reading of the central assumptions of Hutcheson's moral psychology that the self-love theorem of 1788 demands.¹⁵ Indeed, when commenting on the classificatory scheme adopted several years earlier in the *Groundwork for the Metaphysics of Morals*, Kant plainly seeks to discriminate between the egoistic principle of private happiness and the particular principle of moral feeling with which he associates the name of Hutcheson.¹⁶ To be sure, he holds in the *Groundwork* that both principles must be counted together under the general principle of happiness. But there is no evidence that their common subsumption under this principle of happiness (*sans phrase*) presupposes that the sentimentalist notion of moral feeling is ultimately intelligible only in terms of refined self-interest, and thus exclusively in terms of one's own happiness. As Kant states with explicit reference to Hutcheson in the note keyed to *Groundwork's* classificatory scheme:

> I attribute the principle of moral feeling to that of happiness, because every empirical interest promises a contribution to well-being merely from the agreeableness that something affords—whether this happens *immediately and irrespectively of advantages*, or else with a view to these.¹⁷ (GMS 4:442.32–34 [italics mine (J. E.)])

We may wish to assert that this attribution of principle already assumes the type of criticism of Hutcheson demanded by the second *Critique's* classificatory scheme since the well-being that is linked to moral feeling is evidently nothing more than the *own* well-being of the agreeably affected agent. Yet nothing written

---

14 The proper context for this would have been the chapter on the incentives of pure practical reason (see especially KpV 5:74.1–76.23, 78.20–79.19; cf. MS 6:376.10–378.18).
15 See Refl 19:118.24–119.30, 19:121.27–122.7; GMS 4:441.32–443.2; V-PP/Herder 27:3.1–5.33; V-PP/Powalski 27:107.1–110.33; V-Mo/Mron 27:1404.22–1406.42. This reading, indeed, is not even *explicit* in Kant's 1793–94 lectures on the metaphysics of morals (see V-MS/Vigil 27:497.3–500.23). Kant's criticism of the sentimentalist approach, however, is fully consistent with the one offered in the preface to the Doctrine of Virtue in connection with his repudiation of eudaimonism in general; and this repudiation, as we have seen (chapter 4, pp. 81–85), clearly does rely on the interpretation of material practical principles in terms of one's own happiness (compare V-MS/Vigil 27:497.35–498.17 and 27:500.19–21 with TL 6:376.34–378.14 and 6:382.17–24).
16 See GMS 4:442.6–443.2.
17 "Ich rechne das Princip des moralischen Gefühls zu dem der Glückseligkeit, weil ein jedes empirische Interesse durch die Annehmlichkeit, die etwas nur gewährt, es mag nun unmittelbar und ohne Absicht auf Vortheile, oder in Rücksicht auf dieselbe geschehen, einen Beitrag zum Wohlbefinden verspricht [...]".

in the note containing the lines just quoted definitively supports this claim. Moreover, as Kant goes on to point out in the *Groundwork*'s main text, the principle of moral feeling is closer to morality than the principle of one's own happiness, given that moral feeling at least does virtue the honor of "ascribing to her *immediately* the liking [*Wohlgefallen*] and high esteem felt for her, and does not, as it were, say to her face that it is not her beauty but merely advantage that attaches us to her" [18] (GMS 4:442.30 – 443.2). While the allusion to what is *not* said in virtue's face brings Kant's position within striking distance of the interpretation of sentimentalist ethics implicit in the second *Critique*'s self-love theorem, there is no indication in these lines that the immediate liking openly ascribed to virtue is attached *merely* to the advantage that it brings to the virtuous agent. Accordingly, Kant could perfectly well accept (at least in the context of the *Groundwork*) that the satisfaction immediately bound up with the consciousness of virtue does not force the sentimentalist to cede everything to the hankering after one's own happiness.

Our guiding question with respect to Hutcheson is thus as yet unanswered: How can Kant plausibly maintain that Hutcheson's foundational notion of benevolence as an original affective determination of the human constitution could be explicated in terms of self-love?

§ 3 Material Determining Grounds and Stoic Internal Perfection

As we saw in the first section of this chapter, Kant's classificatory strategy with regard to both Stoic and theonomous moral philosophy involves the argument that there is no firm criterion for drawing a basic distinction between the type of material determining ground that underlies perfectionist approaches to the foundations of morals and the type of ground at issue in Epicurean eudaimonism. The argument itself is presented in the following passage:

> The concept of perfection in the *practical* sense is the fitness or adequacy of a thing for all sorts of ends. This perfection, as a *characteristic* of the human being and so as internal, is nothing other than *talent* and what strengthens or completes this, *skill*. The supreme perfection in *substance*—that is, God—and so as external (from a practical point of view) is

---

[18] "dagegen das moralische Gefühl [...] dennoch der Sittlichkeit und ihrer Würde dadurch näher bleibt, daß er der Tugend die Ehre beweist, das Wohlgefallen und die Hochschätzung für sie ihr unmittelbar zuzuschreiben, und ihr nicht gleichsam ins Gesicht sagt, daß es nicht ihre Schönheit, sondern nur der Vortheil sei, der uns an sie knüpfe" (GMS 5:442.22 – 443.2).

the adequacy of this being to all ends in general. Now if ends must first be given to us, in relation to which alone the concept of *perfection* (whether internal in ourselves or external in God) can be the determining ground of the will; and if an end as an *object* which must precede the determination of the will by a practical rule and contain the ground of the possibility of such a determination—hence as the *matter* of the will taken as its determining ground—is always empirical; then it can serve as the Epicurean principle of happiness but never as the pure rational principle of the doctrine of morals and of duty (so too talents and their development only because they contribute to the advantages of life, or the will of God if agreement with it is taken as the object of the will without an antecedent practical principle independent of this idea, can become motives of the will only by means of the happiness we expect from them) [...].[19] (KpV 5:40.9 – 29)

Let us here concentrate on Kant's view of the principle of the internal perfection of the human being that lies at the foundation of Stoic moral philosophy.[20] Given that Kant understands perfection in its practical sense as a thing's fitness or adequacy for all kinds of ends, he wants to show that the Stoics' concept of internal perfection cannot furnish an adequate basis for the pure rational principle of duty that the doctrine of morals requires. Kant's argument against the Stoics thus breaks down as follows:

(1) Assume that ends must first be given to us in relation to which alone the concept of perfection can be the determining ground of the will.

(2) Assume also that an end is always empirical if (i) it must precede the will's determination by a practical rule and (ii) it must contain the ground of the possibility of the will's determination by such a rule. In other words: assume that an end (as the object or matter

---

[19] "Der Begriff der Vollkommenheit in *praktischer* Bedeutung aber ist die Tauglichkeit oder Zulänglichkeit eines Dinges zu allerlei Zwecken. Diese Vollkommenheit als *Beschaffenheit* des Menschen, folglich innerliche, ist nichts anders als *Talent* und, was dieses stärkt oder ergänzt, *Geschicklichkeit*. Die höchste Vollkommenheit in *Substanz*, d.i. Gott, folglich äußerliche, (in praktischer Absicht betrachtet) ist die Zulänglichkeit dieses Wesens zu allen Zwecken überhaupt. Wenn nun also uns Zwecke vorher gegeben werden müssen, in Beziehung auf welche der Begriff der *Vollkommenheit* (einer inneren an uns selbst, oder einer äußeren an Gott) allein Bestimmungsgrund des Willens werden kann, ein Zweck aber als *Object*, welches vor der Willensbestimmung durch eine praktische Regel vorhergehen und den Grund der Möglichkeit einer solchen enthalten muß, mithin die *Materie* des Willens, als Bestimmungsgrund desselben genommen, jederzeit empirisch ist, mithin zum *Epikurischen* Princip der Glückseligkeitslehre, niemals aber zum reinen Vernunftprincip der Sittenlehre und der Pflicht dienen kann (wie denn Talente und ihre Beförderung nur, weil sie zu Vortheilen des Lebens beitragen, oder der Wille Gottes, wenn Einstimmung mit ihm ohne vorhergehendes, von dessen Idee unabhängiges praktisches Princip zum Objecte des Willens genommen worden, nur durch die *Glückseligkeit*, die wir davon erwarten, Bewegursache desselben werden können) [...]".
[20] The defender of Crusius may well want to resist Kant's criticism. But I will not treat the nature of Crusius's voluntarism in this book.

of the will that is also the will's determining ground) is something that is always empirical, i.e., is always an empirically given end.

(3) It follows that an end which (*qua* object or matter of the will) contains the ground of the will's possible determination must be one that can serve as the Epicurean principle of the doctrine of happiness. As such it can never serve as the pure rational principle required by the doctrine of morals and duty.

Needless to say, Kant's second premising assumption raises questions when taken in conjunction with his later account of own-perfection as a material determining ground of the power of choice and as an a priori given obligatory end of morally practical reason (see chapter 1, pp. 26–30). But for the sake of sorting out the argument at hand, let us push this broader issue to the side and concentrate on the particular difficulties that arise from Kant's attempt to show that the end at issue in the Stoic concept of internal perfection—i.e., human perfection considered as an object that contains the ground of the possibility of the will's determination—is one that plays its proper role in the principle of happiness that underlies Epicurean eudaimonism. I take it that there are two major difficulties that Kant must be a position to address if this Epicurean assimmilation of the Stoic principle of internal perfection is to be successful.

First, even if the formal principle of the will's automomy provides the "the *sole* practical principle that can *possibly* be fit [...] in general for the principle of morality" (KpV 5:41.34–36), it does not obviously follow that there is *no* principle of the human agent's internal perfection which "can *possibly* be fit for categorical imperatives, that is, practical laws (which make actions duties)" (KpV 5:41.34–35). Put differently: we may agree with Kant that the principle of autonomy is what furnishes the formal *supreme* principle of pure practical reason; but agreeing to this does not by itself commit us to holding that no concept of internal perfection[21] can ground a principle or rule of perfection that can furnish a practical law. For if one makes it one's rule to perfect oneself by developing one's talents and skills, then such a rule to further one's own perfection ought to be fit for a categorical imperative precisely because it is apt for a universal lawgiving. And it is apt for universal lawgiving insofar as the concept of internal perfection *necessarily* denotes a matter (or object) of the will that ought to be developed in accordance with what the principle of autonomy demands.[22] So why

---

[21] That is, no concept of internal perfection denoting a "*matter* of the will taken as its determining ground" (KpV 5:41.20–21).
[22] If this were not the case, of course, then a considerable portion of the system of ethical duties based on Kant's MS account of obligatory ends would be reduced to smoking ruins. But let us keep this issue in the periphery of our present concern with Kant's classificatory scheme.

shouldn't there be *a* practical law (or laws) grounded in a concept of internal perfection, as long this matter can supply a determining ground of the will in keeping with what is prescribed by the sole practical principle that can be fit *in general* for the principle of morality?

The second difficulty stems from Kant's claim about what results when one's own (physical) perfection is taken as both a matter and determining ground of the will. Even if we accept that the *Epicurean* must hold that the perfecting of our talents and skills can furnish motives of the will only on account of the happiness that we expect from it, it is not apparent why the *Stoic* should have to take this Epicurean position. For as long as the Stoic can sensibly hold that the perfecting of a human agent's talents and skills provides a volitional matter that is also the will's determining ground, it is simply not clear why she should have to agree with the Epicurean that talents and skills are to be developed *only* because they contribute to such an agent's advantages in life.[23] In other words: we may accept, with Kant, that the Epicurean eudaimonist must maintain that a human agent can be motivated to further her own perfection as her end only because of the happiness which she herself expects to achieve by developing her talents and skills; but it is still unclear why the Stoic should have to accept that the practical concept of internal perfection is tied to the principle of one's own happiness in the *way* that the Epicurean implies that it is. To be sure, it may well be that the Stoic, just as the Epicurean (or anyone else, for that matter), must maintain that one's own happiness requires the development of one's talents and skills. Moreover, the Stoic may also have to accept that the prescription to perfect oneself by means of the development of these human characteristics is a rule that serves as a material practical principle. But none of this entails that no such principle— i.e., no rule to perfect oneself by developing one's talents and skills—can possibly be fit for *a* categorical imperative. And if this is true, then we have an instance of a material practical principle that can furnish a practical law, even if the principle of the will's autonomy furnishes the formal practical principle of pure reason that serves as the supreme principle of morality.

This last implication, of course, will by now hardly be surprising, especially when taken against the backdrop of the considerations on material determining grounds, material practical principles, and the concept of practical law offered above in Parts I and II. But when taken in conjunction with Kant's highly complex relation to Hutcheson, the Stoic concept of perfection targeted in Kant's classificatory scheme provides us with a second historical guidepost for the investigations that we will pursue in chapters 9–11.

---

23 Cf. Long 1996, pp. 143–145.

Chapter 9 Hutcheson and Rousseau in the Development of Kant's Doctrine of Morals

This chapter investigates a crucial developmental phase of Kant's doctrine of morals prior to the emergence of his critical philosophy. It does this in view of the problematic implications of Kant's understanding of Hutcheson and Stoic perfectionism that were just discussed. Broadly speaking, our focus now moves to Kant's early view of a principle of perfectionist ethics and, more significantly, to the assessment of the sentimentalist approach to the foundations of morals that we find in Kant's 1764 *Inquiry*, i.e., the *Inquiry Concerning the Distinctness of the Principles of Natural Theology and Morality*. Moving forward from this work, I go on to consider several related 1760s texts and series of reflections in connection with the influence that Rousseau had on Kant's theory of the autonomy of reason. Then, after duly noting the well-known impact of Rousseau's idea of *volonté générale* on Kant's portrayal of reason's universally lawgiving function, I turn to a further aspect of Kant's relation to Rousseau. By this, I have in mind Kant's evident lack of interest in exploiting a key conceptual distinction involved in Rousseau's attempt to rethink the relationship between nature-determined sentiment and law-determined action—namely, the distinction between *amour de soi* and *amour-propre* as originally and fundamentally different forms of self-love.

Why this apparent lack of interest on Kant's part? One part of the answer, I argue, is that already by the mid-1760s Kant was by and large satisfied with a traditional explanation of the affective conditions of human motivation. Another part of the answer has to do with Rousseau's relation to the theoretically decisive aspect of ancient Stoic and modern Stoic-influenced portrayals of the self-perfecting moral agent—notably, the use of the classic Stoic doctrine of *oikeiôsis* to link together two morally salient dimensions of the human developmental pursuit of one's own perfection: (a) self-love and the instinctually anchored drive for self-preservation; and (b) natural sociability and the practical love of human beings.[24]

---

[24] I call attention here to Jean Barbeyrac's early 18th century editions and translations of the natural law treatises of Hugo Grotius and Samuel Pufendorf. Barbeyrac's annotations and commentary are especially valuable for understanding the aspect of the history of moral philosophy here at issue. See, for example, the notes to Section VI in the preliminary discourse to Grotius's *De jure belli ac pacis*. (A readily available English translation is found in Grotius 2005,

§ 1 "Hutcheson and others", Material Principles of Obligation, and Moral Feeling in 1764

I will discuss Rousseau in relation to Stoic *oikeiôsis* doctrine in due course. In the first three sections of this chapter I will be concerned with the 1764 *Inquiry* and related textual sources of mid-1760s.

As we saw in chapter 8, Kant comes to view modern sentimentalist ethics as well as the perfectionist theories of "Wolff and the Stoics" (KpV 5:40) as resting on egoistic foundations. The reductive strategy of interpretation that this view involves is especially noteworthy if we compare it with the assessment of Hutcheson and Wolff that informs Kant's first systematic treatment of the foundations of morals. Kant takes up the question of our knowledge of these foundations in the second section of the fourth part of the 1764 *Inquiry*.[25] Focusing on the need to clarify "the primary concept of obligation" (UD 2:298.5), he holds that a viable theory of practical cognition must acknowledge a basic distinction between, on the one hand, first formal rules of obligation and, on the other hand, material practical principles that that are based on feelings of the good. The basic formal rules of obligation are principles of commission and omission that prescribe perfection-promoting actions. Taken jointly, they comprise what Kant calls the "supreme rule of all obligation" (2:299.1). Kant understands this principle of obligation as a two-pronged rule of perfection that governs free actions: "Do the most perfect thing that is possible through you [...]; omit doing that by which the greatest possible perfection is hindered" (UD 2:299.10 – 13).[26] Kant takes his perfection-maximizing principle of obligation quite directly from "the universal rule of free actions" that underpins Wolff's ethics.[27] There is no suggestion on Kant's part, however, that the strictly formal rules of commission and omission included in his perfectionist principle are prescriptions pertaining to the self-perfecting agent's promotion of own-happiness as the object of the faculty of desire. Kant's account of the first *formal* grounds of obligation is in effect divested of precisely the type of eudaimonistic connection that lends plausibility to the egoistic read-

---

pp. 79 – 81.) For a general account of Stoic influences on modern moral philosophy, see Brooke 2012.
25 See UD 2:298.1 – 301.33
26 "Thue das Vollkommenste, was durch dich möglich ist [...]. Unterlasse das, wodurch das grösstmögliche Vollkommenheit verhindert wird".
27 Wolff's formulation of this universal rule—"*Thue was dich und deinen oder anderen Zustand vollkommener machet; Unterlass, was ihn unvollkommener machet*"—is found in chapter 1, § 12 of the *Vernünfftige Gedancken von der Menschen Thun und Lassen*.

ing of Wolff's perfectionist approach that we encounter in the *Critique of Practical Reason*.

Parallel considerations apply to Kant's early treatment of material practical principles. In the 1760s *Inquiry*, Kant understands material principles of practical cognition primarily as principles by which we know that actions exhibit perfection insofar as they are immediately cognized as good on the basis of feeling or sensation pertaining to the good. To be sure, these sense-based principles of practical cognition are immediately subsumed under the basic formal rules of commission and omission presented by the perfectionist supreme principle of all obligation. Nevertheless, they are essential components of the account of moral obligation since we could not know *what* actions tend to promote or hinder the greatest perfection that we are capable of bringing about if we did not possess principles that are grounded in "feelings [*Empfindungen*] of the good" (UD 2:299.29). For we require such feelings (or sensations) in order to cognize the categorical necessity of perfection-maximizing actions; and a sense-based cognition of this sort of necessity is itself "an indemonstrable material principle of obligation" (UD 2:300.1–2).[28]

In keeping with the conception of material principles of moral cognition just summarized, Kant holds that accounting for the obligation-founding role and the action-guiding character of material practical principles demands a sufficiently developed description of the affective dimension of the human agent's cognitive constitution. The theory of the "first foundations of morals [*die ersten Gründe der Moral*]" (UD 2:298.2) must therefore be set up in such a way that it can portray the affective features of the mind that underlie our capacity to know the particular types of action we are morally bound to perform. In calling for the clarification of the foundations of morals, then, Kant has in mind an inquiry that must include the investigation of the sensible conditions of human moral agency as conditions for our knowledge of material principles of moral obligation. He holds that only an investigation of this type can provide for the systematic treatment of principles of obligation as action guiding precepts. Kant thereby envisages a way of completing the type of foundational theory of moral philosophy that he supposed was offered by "Hutcheson and others" who "under the name of

---

[28] Kant's idea is that, without the material principles of obligation provided by cognitions of the good grounded in feeling or sensation, we would not be able to know any "specifically determined obligation [*besonders bestimmte Verbindlichkeit*]" (UD 2:298.16). That is, we would not be able to know what actions we ought to perform, even if we are aware (in virtue of our cognition of the supreme principle of obligation and the formal grounds of obligation that it contains) that we are bound to bring about the greatest perfection of which we are capable.

moral feeling made a beginning to fine remarks" (UD 2:300.24 – 25) concerning material principles of practical cognition.

Contrary to what Kant would come to maintain in the second *Critique*, the reference to Hutcheson (and implicitly to Shaftesbury and Hume as well[29]) carries with it no indication that he regarded the sentimentalist approach to the doctrine of morals as being, in effect, a form of closet egoism inconsistent with the requirements of morally practical reason. To the contrary, Kant is quite explicit, in the 1764 *Inquiry*, that no account of moral obligation (hence no account of the practical laws that present the ethical duties comprising the matter of obligation) is feasible unless it includes sense-based material practical principles. For no such theory can provide a supportable account of our knowledge of what we are morally bound to do unless it incorporates material principles that complement the purely formal deontic rules contained in the perfectionist version of supreme principle of all obligation. In other words, unless it incorporates material practical principles, the theory of moral obligation based on purely formal rules of perfection will amount to nothing more than an empty formalism in ethics.

So what happened to Kant's view of the relationship between empirically conditioned practical reason and morally practical reason between the mid-1760s and the 1780s? As we will see, the main thing that happened can be summed up in one word: Rousseau. But there are still some paving stones to account for if Kant's road to Rousseau is to be properly (even if very quickly) surveyed.

As indicated above, Kant ends his assessment of the relation between the formal rules and grounds of obligation and the first material practical principles with an explicit reference to Hutcheson's concept of moral feeling. Apart from mentioning Hutcheson's name, the reference is quite vague, and its implications are far from clear. It is therefore not possible to determine definitively the extent to which Kant intends his portrayal of the affective components of practical cognition to incorporate the central tenets of the sentimentalist approach to the foundations of morals.[30] Nevertheless, we can confidently say that he does suppose the following: (1) An adequate understanding of the foundational role of material practical principles in moral philosophy requires a properly developed account of moral feeling. (2) "Hutcheson and others" have provided an interest-

---

[29] On this, see Kant's lecture notice for Winter Semester of 1765 – 1766: NEV 2:311.10 – 212.7.
[30] On the longstanding controversies in the secondary literature regarding Kant's relation to the British moralists, see Forschner 1974, pp. 76 – 95; Henrich 1957 – 58, pp. 49 – 51; Schmucker 1961, 117 – 128.

ing starting-point for considering the question of moral feeling.³¹ Let us consider Kant's remarks on moral feeling in the *Observations Concerning the Feeling of the Beautiful and the Sublime* (1764) in view of the theoretical task suggested by these suppositions.³² In the second section of the *Observations* Kant maintains that true virtue can only be supported by universal principles. These are not, however, speculative rules. They are rather the "consciousness of a feeling that is alive in every human breast and reaches much further than the particular grounds of sympathy and complaisance [*Wohlgefälligkeit*]" (GSE 2:217.12–15). At issue here is the "feeling for the beauty and dignity of human nature" (GSE 2:217.16–17). While the latter aspect of this "universal moral feeling" (GSE 2:217.27) is the "ground of universal respect", the former constitutes the "ground of universal kindly affection [*Wohlgewogenheit*] toward the human species" (GSE 2:217.7–8, 218.18–19). Since it encompasses both of these grounds, universal moral feeling provides for the recognition of a principled standpoint from which we are able to regulate our inclination toward acts of sympathy and complaisance in conformity with our "whole duty [*gesammte Pflicht*]" (GSE 2:216.11), and hence to act in accordance with the "strict duty of justice" (GSE 2:216.3–4). But due to the weakness of human nature, moral feeling requires certain "auxiliary impulses as supplements to virtue", impulses that "move some to perform beautiful actions even without principles" (GSE 2:217.27–30). We are thus providentially furnished with the kindly sentiments of sympathy and complaisance that incite us to the performance of actions that "would perhaps have been stifled altogether by the predominance of crude self-interest" (GSE 2:217.33–34). These sentiments are not, however, "immediate grounds of virtue" (GSE 2:217.34–35). They must therefore fall under the heading of "adopted virtues" (GSE 2:217.37), even though they are quite similar to the genuine virtues in the sense that they too "contain the feeling of immediate pleasure in [an] kind and benevolent actions" (GSE 2:218.7–8).³³

---

31 As already noted (see p. 187), the 'others' in question are presumably Shaftesbury and Hume. In the announcement of the program of his lectures for the winter semester of 1765–66, Kant maintains that the "attempts of *Shaftesbury, Hutcheson* and *Hume*, though incomplete and defective, have nonetheless reached furthest in the quest for the first grounds of all morality" (NEV 2:311.25–28).

32 The manuscript of the *Observations* (GSE) was finished by October of 1763. The published text was available at the beginning of 1764. On the relationship between GSE and UD, see Forschner 1974, pp. 86–88; Schmucker 1961, pp. 110–118.

33 Kant's employment of the terms "feeling"' "sensation", "impulse" and "virtue" in the text under consideration is quite loose, and my reconstruction of his argument does not seek to make his usage conceptually more precise than it is.

§ 1 Material Principles of Obligation in 1764 — 189

As we can gather from the preceding, Kant is not expressly concerned in the *Observations* to clarify the relationship between formal and material practical principles. Nevertheless, his arguments are consistent with a moral theory built on the supposition that there is a necessary connection between formal and material first principles of practical cognition and obligation.[34] Moreover, his considerations on moral feeling in the *Observations* represent a number of quite significant theoretical refinements when compared with the portrayal of our cognition of the good in the 1764 *Inquiry*. First, his emphasis on the universal scope of the feeling allows him to define moral feeling proper in terms of its application to a single fundamental value: the value of human nature.[35] This in turn permits him to offer a more unified account of moral feeling than the *Inquiry*'s sketch of the multiplicity of feelings for the good could sustain. Second, the sharp distinction that he draws between moral feeling proper and the auxiliary impulses or feelings puts him in a position show how a comprehensive theory of the moral sentiments is consistent with a doctrine of obligation which gives pride of place to the strict duty of justice. The theoretical groundwork for making that distinction, which underlies the subsequent phases in the development of Kant's metaphysics of morals, is not laid out in the 1764 *Inquiry*.[36]

Finally, Kant's conception of the universal scope of moral feeling proper enables him to offer a portrayal of practical love based on the affective dimension of human nature. Immediately after his characterization of the feeling for the beauty and dignity of human nature he writes:

> [I]f this feeling had its greatest perfection in any human heart, then this human being would indeed also love and esteem himself, but only in so far as he is one among all of those to whom his extensive and noble feeling expands to cover. Only by subsuming one's particular inclination under such an extended inclination can our kindly impulses be applied in proper proportion and bring about the noble sense of decorum [*Anstand*] that is the beauty of virtue.[37] (GSE 2:217.19–25)

---

34 Forschner 1974, pp. 86–88 and Schmucker 1961, pp. 111–114 came to similar conclusions about what Kant must have had in mind in the *Observations* concerning the connection between formal and material principles. I find both interpretive attempts plausible, but there is no need here to go into further detail. My argument hinges merely on the claim that the *Observations* contain nothing *inconsistent* with a theory that accepts a necessary connection between the two types of principle.

35 On the significance of this point for Kant's concept of human nature as an end in itself, see Schmucker 1961, pp. 115–118. See also Forschner 1974, pp. 82–88.

36 See Schmucker, 1961, pp. 105–110, 114–115. Regarding the ultimate systematic ramifications of that distinction, see, e.g., TL 6:390.1–391.25, 6:396.1–397.2, 6:456.17–458.19.

37 "wenn dieses Gefühl die größte Vollkommenheit in irgend einem menschlichen Herzen hätte, so würde dieser Mensch sich zwar auch selbst lieben und schätzen, aber nur in so fern

As we have already seen in the *Observations*, Kant does connect a "feeling of immediate pleasure" with the performance of kind and benevolent actions. Nevertheless, he clearly does not think this logically compels acceptance of the psychological tenets that we found to underlie the interpretation of Hutcheson in the *Critique of Practical Reason*.

§ 2 Moral Feeling and Universal Will in Kant's 1760s Ethics

A sea-change is detectable in Kant's orientation toward moral feeling in the handwritten remarks found in Kant's copy of the *Observations*.[38] These reflections, which I will here refer to as the *Remarks*, exhibit the results of his careful study of Rousseau's critical theory of society and morality. Scholarship has underscored above all the strong influence of *Émile* as well as Kant's endeavor to utilize, for the purposes of his foundational theory of morals in general, the cornerstone of Rousseau's juridical theory of right, namely, the idea of the *volonté générale*. We will take up both of these factors in due course.[39] At present, I will limit my comments to developments in the conception of moral feeling. From our vantage point, one of the most striking features of the *Remarks* is Kant's tendency to concentrate his analysis of the affective dimension of moral experience on the participatory (*teilnehmende*) sentiments and instincts. The sentiment of sympathy, which, as we have just seen, plays an important auxiliary role in the depiction of the grounds of moral virtue in the *Observations*, is singled out for extensive treatment in the *Remarks*. Echoing a similar assessment on Rousseau's part, Kant emphasizes the idle or merely wishful quality of sympathy not commensurate with an agent's actual power to do good or not regulat-

---

er einer von allen ist, auf die sein ausgebreitetes und edles Gefühl sich ausdehnt. Nur indem man einer so erweiterten Neigung seine besondere unterordnet, können unsere gütige Triebe proportionirt angewandt werden und den edlen Anstand zwege bringen, der die Schönheit der Tugend ist".

38 These notes were probably composed between January 1764 and the end of 1765. On the relevant dating criteria, see Marie Rischmüller's introduction to her edition of the *Remarks:* Her edition: BGSE pp. xii-xvii.

39 Kant's reception of Rousseau has been discussed quite extensively. Scholarly debate has generally centered on the question of the degree to which the crucial tenets and systematic contours of Kant's mature autonomous ethics are already discernible in the *Observations*. See, e.g., Forschner 1974, pp. 102–135; Henrich 1965–1966, pp. 259–260; Henrich, 1963, pp. 430–431; Schmucker 1961, pp. 143–144, 172–176, 184–199, 245–261; Velkley 1989, pp. 1–8, 12–14, 32–39, 44–84; Piché 1990, pp. 625–635. See also, very helpfully, Rischmüller's editorial commentary in BGSE: 151–152, 194, 205–211 and Schneewind 1998, pp. 487–492.

ed by the requirements of reason.⁴⁰ He couples this with the depiction of the illusory character of sympathy that purports to be of universal scope.⁴¹

Kant's assessment of sympathy correlates with his endeavor to make "freedom in the real sense [...] the highest *principle* of all virtue and also of happiness" (BGSE: 29).⁴² This goes hand in hand with the emergence of a concept of moral feeling that looks forward to the corresponding concept employed in the later critical system. In the *Remarks*, moral feeling has come to be the "feeling of the perfection of the will", whereby the will is perfect "so far as it is the greatest ground of the good in general in accordance with the laws of freedom" (BGSE: 102).⁴³ Though Kant has not yet clarified the core tenets of his autonomous ethics, we can nonetheless recognize a decisive move toward the interpretation of moral feeling as something that presupposes the causality of reason to determine the sensibility in accordance with strictly rational principles.⁴⁴

Two closely linked passages are especially important for understanding why this move occurs. Notice in them Kant's concern to establish that (a) the *immediate* pleasure or enjoyment taken in the well-being of others derives from the anticipation of the exercise of our power to promote it; that (b) moral feeling must therefore be defined in terms of the pleasure intrinsic to the exercise of the free power of choice in the performance of beneficent actions; and that (c) the particular participatory "instincts" of sympathy and kindness are themselves effects of the self-approval, and thus the self-caused enjoyment or self-gratification, produced by that exercise of one's own power:

> The ability to recognize something as a perfection in others does not at all produce the effect that we ourselves feel enjoyment [*Vergnügen*] in it. But if we have a feeling of finding enjoyment in it, we will also be moved to desire it and to apply our powers to it. The question is whether we immediately feel enjoyment in the well-being of others or whether the immediate pleasure lies in the possible use of our power to promote it. Both are possible, but which is real? Experience teaches that in the simple condition a human views the happiness of others with indifference. But if he has promoted it, it pleases him infinitely more. The ill-being [*Übel*] of others is commonly indifferent. But if I have caused it, then it grieves; likewise if another has done it. And as far as the participatory instincts of sympathy and

---

40 On the similarities between Rousseau's and Kant's assessments of sympathy, see Rischmüller's commentary in BGSE: 151. See also Schmucker 1961, pp. 188–192 for the passages in Rousseau's writings corresponding to Kant's considerations.
41 See BGSE: 46, 101, 108. For specific references to Rousseau linked to the reflections here cited, see Rischmüller's notes in BGSE: 151, 168, 249. For contextual analysis, see Schmucker 1961, pp. 185–194.
42 See also BGSE: 46, 52–53, 68, 70–71, 102, 103–104, 107–109.
43 See also BGSE: 46, 52–53, 62, 102, 103–104, 107–109.
44 Regarding this move, see Schmucker 1961, pp. 197–199.

> kindness are concerned, we have cause to believe it is merely great efforts to relieve the suffering of others deriving from the soul's self-approval which produces these sensations.
> We take enjoyment in certain of our perfections, but far more if we ourselves are the cause. Most of all when we are the freely effective cause. To *subordinate* all to the power of choice is the greatest perfection. And the perfection of the free power of choice as a cause of possibility is far greater than all the other causes of the good even if they should bring forth the reality.⁴⁵ (BGSE: 107–108)

> The feeling of pleasure and displeasure is either about that against which we are passive or about ourselves as an active *principle* of good and evil through freedom. The latter is the moral feeling. Past physical evil gladdens us, but moral evil saddens us. The joy about the good which befalls us is of an entirely different kind than the joy that we do.⁴⁶ (BGSE: 108)

As we can gather from these passages, Kant's view of the relation between moral feeling and pleasure is quite similar to the view at work in the 1780s ethics, where the former is taken to be a "subjective effect exercised on the will by the moral law", an effect which presupposes that reason has a "power [*Vermögen*] of infusing the feeling of pleasure or liking [*Wohlgefallen*] in the fulfillment of duty" (GMS 4:460.9–11).⁴⁷ But let us also bear in mind the latently egoistic thrust of the account of moral feeling in the 1760s *Remarks*, where Kant has

---

45 "Die Fähigkeit etwas als Vollkommenheit an andern zu erkennen bringt noch gar nicht die Folge hervor daß wir selbst daran Vergnügen fühlen. Wenn wir aber ein Gefühl haben daran Vergnügen zu finden so werden wir auch bewogen es zu begehren und unsre Kräfte dazu anzuwenden. Es frägt sich also ob wir unmittelbar an andrer Wohl Vergnügen fühlen oder ob eigentlich die unmittelbare Lust in der möglichen Anwendung unsrer Kraft liegt es zu befördern. Es ist beydes möglich welches aber ist wirklich. Die Erfahrung lehrt daß beym einfältigen Zustande ein Mensch andrer Glük mit Gleichgültigkeit ansieht hat er es aber befördert so gefällt es ihm unendlich mehr. Andrer Übel is gemeiniglich eben so gleichgültig habe ich es aber verursacht so kränk es imgleichen wenn es ein andrer gethan hat. Und was die theilnehmende Instinkte des Mitleidens und der Wohlgewogenheit anlangt so haben wir Ursach zu glauben es seyen blos große Bestrebungen andrer Übel zu lindern aus der Selbstbilligung der Seele hergenommen welche diese Empfindungen hervorbringen.

Wir haben Vergnügen an gewissen von unseren Vollkommenheiten aber weit mehr wenn wir selbst die Ursache seyn. Am allermeisten wenn wir die frey wirkende Ursache seyn. Der freyen Willkühr alles zu *suordiniren* ist die größeste Vollkommenheit. Und die Vollkommenheit der freyen Willkühr also einer Ursache der Möglichkeit ist weit größer als alle andere Ursachen des Guten wenn sie gleich die Wirklichkeit hervorbrächten".

46 "Das Gefühl der Lust und Unlust ist entweder über das wogenen wir leidend seyn oder über uns selbst als ein thätig *principium* durch Freyheit von dem Guten und Bösen. Das letztere is das moralische Gefühl. Das vergangene physische Böse [kränkt] erfreuet uns aber das moralische betrübt uns und es ist eine gantz andre Art Freude über das Gute was uns zufällt und da s was wir thun".

47 See also KpV 5:74.1–76.23, 5:116.21–117.24; MS 6:399.19–400.4.

not yet clarified the distinction between the properly practical and the pathological causation of feeling that is crucial to the later account.[48] The basis of the interest that we take in the well-being of others is evidently assumed to lie in the free power of choice as a cause of possibility. But in the absence of any sharp line separating the two types of causation of feeling, Kant is here, in the *Remarks*, faced with a problem that closely parallels the fundamental difficulty that he would later, by 1788, think Hutcheson must face in attempting to determine the moral law by appealing to the faculty of a moral sense: The pleasure and displeasure involved in the perfection of the will at stake in the *Remarks* can just as plausibly be "ceded to the hankering after one's own happiness" (see chapter 8, p. 177) as the corresponding sensations associated with Hutcheson's sensuous faculty of approving and disapproving actions.[49]

As was indicated in chapter 8, Hutcheson's use of the distinction between desire and its accompanying sensations would put him in a position to counter Kant's charge that the sentimentalist conception of moral motivation reduces to a matter of refined self-interest. But how could Kant respond to the parallel charge once he has made freedom of the will the highest principle of all virtue? In the mid-1760s, he might have attempted to combine the theory of universal moral feeling adumbrated in the *Observations* with the rudiments of the theory of autonomy contained in the *Remarks*.[50] Presumably, that would have meant linking the portrayal of the conditions of actions' categorical necessity to the aforementioned considerations on practical love and the sense-based conditions of human actions (see pp. 185–187). We will inquire into why Kant did not take up this option in the next section. At this juncture it suffices to say that there is no evidence of Kant's willingness seriously to entertain it on his way toward the mature autonomous ethics.[51] In the course of his foundational work on the doctrine of morals after the *Remarks*, he carefully separates his account of the causal basis of moral feeling from the empirical description of sensible motivational conditions, thereby excluding the option offered in principle by the *Observations*.

---

48 For this distinction, see GMS 4:460.27–37; KpV 5:74.8–75.34, 5:116.21–33, 15:17.15–21; MS 6:399.19–27.
49 For Hutcheson's basic conception of the relationship between the moral sense, pleasure or displeasure, and moral approval or disapproval, see IBV 89–92.
50 See the sources cited in notes 43 and 44 of this chapter.
51 See the reference to *Praktische Philosophie Herder* in note 15 of chapter 8.

We can already recognize the direction that would Kant's thought would take if we consider Part I, Chapter 2 of the *Dreams of a Spirit-Seer* (1766).[52] Although in a context of metaphysical speculation plainly unacceptable from the standpoint of the mature critical theory of knowledge,[53] it is with implicit reference to Rousseau's opposition between *volonté du tous* and *volonté générale* that Kant offers there a dualistic account of the "forces that move the human heart" (TG 2:334.3).[54] The self-interested and the benevolent "tendencies of our impulses [*Regungen*]" give rise to a "conflict between the force of self-centeredness [*Eigenheit*] [...] and the force of public utility [*Gemeinnützigkeit*] by which the heart is driven or attracted out of itself toward others" (TG 2:334.7–11). Moral feeling is linked to the latter, but it cannot be thought of as deriving simply from the affective aspect of human nature. For it is now defined as the "sensed dependency of the private will on the universal will" (TG 2:335.27–28), and the universal will is conceived as so to speak an *alien* will that establishes the purely spiritual laws of moral unity among rational beings:

> When we relate external things to our need, we cannot do this without at the same time feeling ourselves bound and restricted by a certain sensation that lets us notice that an alien will, as it were, is operative within us and that our own choosing [*Belieben*] requires external assent as its condition. A secret power compels us to direct our aim at the same time toward the well-being of others or according to the power of choice of another, although this often happens reluctantly and in strong opposition to selfish inclination [...]. From this spring forth the moral impulses that often sweep us along contrary to the call of self-interest, and that relate to the strong law of indebtedness and the weaker law of kindliness, each of which wrings from us many a sacrifice. Although both of these laws are from time to time outweighed by self-interested inclinations, they still never fail to assert their reality in human nature. We thereby see ourselves in our most secret motives dependent upon the *rule of the universal will*; and from this there originates in the world of all thinking beings a *moral unity* and systematic constitution according to purely spiritual laws. If one wants to call this internally sensed necessitation of the will to agree with the universal will the *moral feeling*, then one speaks of this only as an appearance of that which really takes place within us, without establishing its causes.[55] (TG 2:334.27–335.16)

---

52 The manuscript for this work was written in 1765, and the work itself was published by the end of January 1766. In accordance with Rischmüller's dating criteria (see BGSE: xvi-xvii), I thus put the composition period of the *Dreams of a Spirit-Seer* after that of the *Remarks*.
53 The pneumatological speculations of TG are treated systematically in Schmucker 1961, pp. 54–165. Schmucker maintains (p. 165) that Kant's pneumatological constructions do not impinge upon his considerations on the *foundations* of moral philosophy. I fully concur with this assessment.
54 On the relation to Rousseau, see above all Rischmüller's commentary in BGSE: 209. See also Forschner 1974, pp. 104–109 and Schmucker 1961, pp. 171–172.
55 "Wenn wir äußere Dinge auf unser Bedürfniß beziehen, so können wir dieses nicht thun, ohne uns zugleich durch eine gewisse Empfindung gebunden und eingeschränkt zu fühlen,

The conception of moral unity and systematic constitution according to purely spiritual laws points toward the *Groundwork* and its idea of the realm of ends. Also, in mentioning the stronger law of indebtedness and the weaker law of kindliness, Kant indicates a distinction that will be central to the systematic divisions in his later accounts of different types of duties.[56] But he obviously still has to make the decisive step toward the theory of the autonomy of reason: He does not explain how the universal will's lawgiving role could be the internal source of the individual moral agent's *own* lawgiving. Nonetheless, we can see how the merely conjectural and heuristic appeal to the concept of an alien universal will permits him to sever the connection between the ground of moral feeling and the affective conditions of human action that, in the *Remarks*, had exposed him to the kind of objection he would raise against Hutcheson at the end of the 1780s. By 1766, then, the way is open to cleanly separate the exposition of the motivating force of self-legislative practical reason from the explication of sense-based desire and inclination.

§ 3 The Idea of Universal Lawgiving and Rousseau's Anthropology

As noted in the previous section, we witness a fundamental change in the orientation of Kant's moral philosophy in the writings and reflections composed in

---

die uns merken läßt, daß in uns gleichsam ein fremder Wille wirksam sei, und unser eigen Belieben die Bedingung von äußerer Beistimmung nöthig habe. Eine geheime Macht nöthigt uns unsere Absicht zugleich auf anderer Wohl oder nach fremder Willkür zu richten, ob dieses gleich öfters ungern geschieht und der eigennützigen Neigung stark widerstreitet [...]. Daher entspringen die sittlichen Antriebe, die uns oft wider den Dank des Eigennutzes fortreißen, das starke Gesetz der Schuldigkeit und das schwächere der Gütigkeit, deren jedes uns manche Aufopferung abdringt, und obgleich beide dann und wann durch eigennützige Neigungen überwogen werden, doch nirgend in der menschlichen Natur ermangeln, ihre Wirklichkeit zu äußern. Dadurch sehen wir uns in den geheimsten Beweggründen abhängig von der *Regel des allgemeinen Willens*, und es entspringt daraus in der Welt aller denkenden Naturen eine *moralische Einheit* und systematische Verfassung nach bloß geistigen Gesetzen. Will man diese in uns empfundene Nöthigung unseres Willens zur Einstimmung mit dem allgemeinen Willen das *sittliche Gefühl* nennen, so redet man davon nur als von einer Erscheinung dessen, was in uns wirklich vorgeht, ohne die Ursachen desselben auszumachen".

[56] For discussion of the historical background of the distinction between perfect and imperfect duties as well as the implications of this distinction for Kant's systematic treatment of juridical duties and duties of virtue in the *Metaphysics of Morals*, see Kersting 1982. See also, Schneiders 1971, pp. 79–83, 86–96, 113–116, 315–337.

the immediate wake of the 1764 *Inquiry*.[57] The most obvious aspect of this change in orientation has long been subject to extensive source documentation: Kant appropriates for his ethics the account of the self-legislative function of a unitary will that underlies Rousseau's employment of the concept of *volonté générale* in his juridical theory of right. For Kant, the idea of such a lawgiving function —i.e., the rational concept of the autonomy of the will—is what provides for a strictly formal principle of universal lawgiving that is also the *sole* principle of all laws and of all duties that supply the matter of all obligation (both juridical and ethical). The second feature of Kant's change in orientation is rather less obvious, however, and it arguably deserves a great deal more attention than it has standardly received to date. It can be discerned in an aspect of the moral anthropology that supplies the empirical part of Kant's ethics.

The development of Kant's moral anthropology during the 1760s and in the decades thereafter is substantially informed by the study of Rousseau's second *Discours*, *Émile*, and the philosophic novel *Julie*.[58] Yet it is a striking feature of this developmental history that Kant shows little interest in exploiting a key conceptual distinction that lies at the very core of Rousseau's anthropological project. In the *Discourse on the Origins of Inequality* it is apparent that Rousseau's concern to rethink the whole relationship between nature-determined sentiment and law-determined action—between *la morale sensitive* and the morality of duty, if you will[59]—depends on the distinction drawn between *amour de soi* and *amour-propre* as originally and fundamentally different forms of self-love.[60] Rousseau requires this essential distinction in order to dismantle all historically available portrayals of the relationship between action motivated by self-love and the natural sociability of human beings—including the generically Stoic portrayals that signally influenced modern (Grotian) theories of natural law. I will discuss this aspect of Rousseau's moral anthropology in greater detail below. At this juncture I wish merely to underscore the following claim regarding Kant's relation to Rousseau: Although Kant employs, as the supreme principle of his foundational theory of ethics, a principle of autonomy that accords with the interpretation of the form of lawgiving at issue Rousseau's idea of *volonté génér*-

---

[57] For discussion, see Edwards 2000a, pp. 420–432.
[58] For details, see the annotations pertaining to Rousseau in BGSE, as already cited in notes 39 and 41.
[59] Cf. Rousseau OC 1:1052–1053/CW 8:51–52.
[60] On *amour de soi* and *amour-propre*, see Neuhouser 2008, pp. 29–53, 90–116, 142–151, 218–264; O'Hagan 1999, pp. 162–179; Masters 1968, pp. 37–53; Melzer 1990, pp. 6–46.

ale,⁶¹ he does not undertake anything like the radical reassessment of the relationship between affective motivational conditions and prescriptive natural law that seems to underlie Rousseau's thinking in the *Discourse on the Origins of Inequality*. As the overall development of the empirical part of his ethics shows, Kant is evidently satisfied with a largely traditional account of the natural conditions of sense-based desire and the sensible grounds of natural human sociability. It is an account that, as Kant himself suggests, traces its primary origin to the historical figure of Epicurus—a figure whose theory of the human good has always been acknowledged to involve a hedonistic and egoistic account of the affective conditions of human motivation.⁶²

If the last chapter's treatment of Kant's historiographic scheme of 1788 is acceptable, however, there is reason to think that Kant ought not to have been so complacent in his willingness to make sweeping assimilative use of such an account in his classification of material practical principles and material determining grounds of the will. Moreover, given the questions raised by Kant's Epicurean assimilation of the Stoic principle of internal perfection, we may well wonder why Kant did not think that his principle of the autonomy of the will required a rethinking of the sensible conditions of human agency that was as radical as the account that Rousseau seems to give in his *Discourse*. Why didn't Kant embark on this sort of theoretical enterprise?

§ 4 Rousseau, Self-Love, and the "One-Source View" of Stoic Oikeiôsis

A philologically well-founded answer to this last question would require treatment of the full array of source materials relevant to Kant's early reception of Rousseau, and this is a task that goes well beyond the scope of this book. Nonetheless, there is also good reason to think that the most important part of the answer is provided by Rousseau himself. Let me shed light what I mean by concen-

---

61 See, e.g., Rousseau, OC 3:377–380/ CW 4:152–154. Cf. also the view of 'maxim' as a subjective principle of volition that Rousseau, in his *Discourse on Political Economy*, links to the concepts of the will of all and practical law *qua* law of freedom: OC 3:146/CW 3:248 (compare Kant, GMS 4:400.34–37, 4:434.1–10).
62 See (jointly) RGV 6:26–27; V-MS/Vigil 27:483.29–484.4, 27: 646.12–650.8; cf. also Refl 19:198.17–22; KpV 5:23.39–24.25, 5:64.6–34, 6:88.21–37, 5:115.18–116.20; TL 6:484.30–486.31).

trating on several aspects of Rousseau's thought in the *Discourse* on inequality and in *Émile*.[63]

In the *Discourse* at issue, Rousseau takes up the question of human nature in connection with the problem of the "real foundations of human society" and the "true definition of natural Right" (OC 3:124/CW 3:13). Regarding this problem, he takes ancient philosophers to task for having "tried their best to contradict each other on the most fundamental principles" (OC 3:124/CW 3:13), and he holds that the Roman jurists fared little better on account of their conflation of the specifically prescriptive and the broader normative meanings of natural law. Modern thinkers thus have a distinct advantage in this respect:

> The Moderns, recognizing under the name Law only a rule prescribed to a moral being, that is to say, intelligent, free, and considered in his relations with other beings, consequently limited the competence of natural law to the sole animal endowed with reason, namely, man.[64] (OC 3:124–125/CW 3:14)

Still, all of the available theories of natural law or natural right, both ancient and modern, share a common defect. They assume that

> it is impossible to understand the Law of nature and consequently to obey it without being a great reasoner and a profound Metaphysician: which means precisely that men must have used, for the establishment of society, enlightenment which only develops with great difficulty and in very few people in the midst of society itself. (OC III 125/CW III 14).[65]

To remedy this defect, then, we must leave aside "all scientific books which teach us to see men as they have made themselves" and meditate on "the first and simplest operations of the human soul" (OC 3:125/CW 3:14). Thus, considered in connection with the definition of natural right and the specifically prescriptive character of natural law, the crucial initial task of philosophical anthropology is to focus on "two principles anterior to reason, of which one interests us ardently

---

[63] For general treatments of these texts as well as the basic principles of Rousseau's anthropology, see J. Cohen 2010, pp. 97–130; Nguyen 1991, pp. 1–127; Gauthier 2006, pp. 1–51; Neuhouser 2014, pp. 16–212; O'Hagan 1999, pp. 33–86. See also James 2015, pp. 18–51.

[64] "Les Modernes ne reconnoissant, sous le nom de Loy, qu'une regle prescrite à un être moral, c'est-à-dire intelligent, libre, et considéré dans ses rapports avec d'autres êtres, bornent conséquemment au seul animal doué de raison, c'est-à-dire à l'homme, la compétence de la Loy naturelle".

[65] "qu'il est impossible d'entendre la Loy de Nature, & par conséquent d'y obéir, sans être un très grand raisonneur et un profond Métaphisicien. Ce qui signifie précisément que les hommes ont dû employer pour l'établissement de la société, des lumiéres qui ne se développent qu'avec beaucoup de peine, et pour fort peu de gens, dans le sein de la société même".

in our well-being and our self-preservation, and the other inspires in us a natural repugnance to see any sensitive being perish or suffer, principally those like ourselves" (OC 3:125–126/CW 3:14–15). For it is

> from the conjunction and the combination that our mind is able to make of these two principles, without the necessity of introducing sociability that all the rules of natural right appear [...] to flow: rules which reason is later forced to reestablish upon other foundations when, by its successive developments, it has succeeded in stifling nature.[66] (OC 3:126/CW 3:15)

Rousseau goes on to maintain that the conjunction and combination of the non-rational motivating principles of self-love and pity takes place in connection with two morally salient features of the human make, namely, the consciousness of freedom that goes hand in hand with the use of power of choice (*la puissance de vouloir, ou plutôt de choisir*) and the faculty of self-perfection (*la faculté de se perfectioner*) (OC 3:142/CW 3:26).

It is on account of these latter features of the human constitution that the progress of reason in the human species (not to mention the stifling of nature) is possible. Still, no theoretically viable portrayal of species development from a moral point of view may lose sight of the underlying effect of the two original, non-rational springs of action. For pity is what moderates the love of self that inclines each individual to seek self-preservation; and self-love "is a natural sentiment [...] which, directed in man by reason and modified by pity, produces humanity and virtue" (OC 3:219/CW 3:91).[67] It is in this sense, then, that pity, conjoined and combined with self-love, must be understood as the source of the maxim of natural goodness, i.e., the maxim to "[d]o what is good for you with the least possible harm to others" (OC 3:156/CW 3:38).

---

66 'Laissant donc tous les livres scientifiques, qui ne nous apprennent qu'à voir les hommes tels qu'ils se sont faits, et méditant sur les premieres et plus simples opérations de l'Ame humaine, j'y crois appercevoir deux principes antérieure à la raison, dont l'un nous intéresse ardemment à notre bien-être et à la conservation de nous-mêmes, et l'autre nous inspire une répugnance naturelle à voir périr ou souffrir tout être sensible, et principalement nos semblables. C'est du concours et de la combinaison que notre esprit est en état de faire de ces deux Principes, sans qu'il soit nécessaire d'y faire entrer celui de la sociabilité, que me paroissent découler toutes les régles du droit naturel; regles que la raison est ensuite forcée de rétablir sur d'autres fondemens, quand, par me développemens successifs, elle est venue à bout d'étouffer la Nature" (OC 3:126/CW 3:15).
67 "L'Amour de soi-même est un sentiment naturel qui port tout animal à veiller à sa propre conservation et qui, dirigé dan l'homme par la raison et modifié par la pitié, produit l'humanité et la vertu" (OC 3:219/CW 3:91).

The love of self that combines with pity to furnish the basis in natural sentiment of this fundamental maxim of the power of choice is, of course, distinct from *amour-propre* taken in its narrower signification. This latter type of self-love is "only a relative sentiment, artificial and born in society, which, inclining each individual to have a greater esteem from himself than for anyone else, inspires in men all the harm they do to one another, and is the true source of honor" (OC 3:219/CW 3:91).[68] We have here the description of *amour-propre* that is of primary significance for Rousseau's account of humankind's progression through the emergence of sociability towards the condition of despotism in which "the sole Law of the stronger" (OC 3:191/CW 3:65) holds sway—that is, towards "a new State of Nature" that is "the fruit of an excess of corruption" (OC 3:191/CW 3:65) and in which reason is later forced to reestablish the rules of natural right upon other foundations" (OC 3:126/CW 3:15).[69]

This is not the place to go into the particulars of Rousseau's account of *amour-propre* as a relative and artificial sentiment.[70] Instead, bearing in mind the distinction between the two forms of self-love as it relates to the development of benevolent concern for others, and thus to the origin of sociability, let us maintain our focus on the form immediately connected with self-preservation. To do this, I would like to turn without further ado to two passages in *Émile* where self-love—or *amour-propre* in its extended sense—is treated both as a motivational condition for self-preservation and as the basis in natural sentiment for the emergence of the love of others that is essential to human sociability.

The first passage pertains to the transition from conduct in accordance with the maxim of natural goodness to conduct governed by the "sublime maxim of reasoned justice [*(la) maxime sublime de justice raisonée*]", i.e., by the Golden-Rule principle "to do unto others as you would have them do unto you" (OC 3:156/CW 3:37). In the fourth book of *Émile*, in the context of his characterization of this transition as "the point at which love of self turns into amour-propre" (OC 4:523/CW 13:389), Rousseau writes:

> Even the precept of doing unto others as we would have them do unto us has no true foundation other than conscience and sentiment; for where is the precise reason for me, being myself, to act as if I were another, especially when I am morally certain of never finding

---

[68] "L'Amour propre n'est qu'un sentiment rélatif, factice, et né dans la société, qui porte chaque individu à faire plus de cas de soi que de toute autre, qui inspire aux hommes tous les maux qu'ils se font mutuellement , et qui est la véritable source de l'honneur".
[69] In reestablishing these rules, reason requires conformity with the laws of the general will by which human beings can be forced to be free in keeping with the rules of natural right (i.e., the laws of natural right like those treated in the first book of Rousseau's *On the Social Contract*).
[70] See, however, the sources cited in note 60 of this chapter.

myself in the same situation? And who will guarantee me that in very faithfully following this maxim I will get others to follow it similarly with me? [...] But when the strength of an expansive soul makes me identify myself with my fellow, and I feel that I am, so to speak, in him, *it is in order not to suffer that I do not want him to suffer. I am interested in him for love of myself, and the reason for the precept is Nature, itself, which inspires in me the desire of my well-being in whatever place I feel my existence.* From this I conclude that it is not true that the precepts of natural law are founded on reason alone. They have a base more solid and sure. *Love of men derived from love of self is the principle of human justice.* The summation of all morality is given by the Gospel in its summation of the law.[71] (OC 4:523/CW 13:389 —italics mine [J. E.])

The second (closely related) passage is also found in *Émile* IV. Given the strength that an expansive soul derives from the self-love that is combined with pity, the following demand for universal beneficence can be made as an extension of the requirement contained in the maxim of reasoned justice:

Let us extend amour-propre to other beings. We shall transform it into a virtue, and there is no man's heart in which this virtue does not have its root. The less the object of our care is immediately involved with us, the less the illusion of particular interest is to be feared. The more one generalizes this interest, the more it becomes equitable, and *the love of mankind is nothing other than the love of justice.* [... ¶] To prevent pity from generating into weakness, it must, therefore, be generalized and extended to the whole of mankind. Then one yields to it only insofar as it accords with justice, because of all the virtues justice is the one that contributes most to the common good of men. For the sake of reason, *for the sake of love of ourselves*, we must have pity for our species still more than for our neighbor, and pity for the wicked is a very great cruelty to men.[72] (OC 4:547–548/CW 13:409–410—italics mine [J. E.])

---

[71] "Le précepte même d'agir avec autrui comme nous voulons qu'on agisse avec nous, n'a de vrai fondement que la conscience et le sentiment; car où est la raison précise d'agir étant moi comme si j'étois un autre, sur-tout quand je suis moralement sûr de ne jamais me trouver dans le même cas; et qui me répondra qu'en suivant bien fidèlement cette maxime j'obtiendrai qu'on la suive de même avec moi? Le méchant tire avantage de la probité du juste et de sa propre injustice; il est bien aise que tout le monde soit juste excepté lui. Cet accord-là, quoi qu'on en dise, n'est pas fort avantageux aux gens de bien. Mais quand la force d'une âme expansive m'identifie avec mon semblable et que je me sens pour ainsi dire en lui, c'est pour ne pas souffrir que je ne veux pas qu'il souffre; je m'intéresse à lui pour l'amour de moi, et la raison du précepte est dans la nature elle-même, qui m'inspire le désir de mon bien-être en quelque lieu que je me sente exister. D'où je conclus qu'il n'est pas vrai que les préceptes de la loi naturelle soient fondés sur la raison seule; ils ont une base plus solide et plus sûre. L'amour des hommes dérivé de l'amour de soi est le principe de la justice humaine. Le sommaire de toute la morale est donné dans l'Evangile par celui de la loi" (OC 4:523/CW 13:389).
[72] "Étendons l'amour-propre sur les autres êtres, nous le transformerons en vertu, et il n'y a point de cœur d'homme dans lequel cette vertu n'ait sa racine. Moins l'objet de nos soins tient immédiatement à nous-mêmes, moins l'illusion de l'intérêt particulier est à craindre;

Let us consider the following positional claims involved in the passages just quoted: (1) We can act from sentiment-based concern for the well-being or interests of others. (2) Such other-directed concern, or care, derives from the extension of self-love to others, i.e., from the extension of the type of self-love that by nature is combined with pity. (3) Such an extension of self-love leads to the practical love of humanity as a whole. (4) As a principle of reason-determined action, the maxim of justice is a principle of practical love enjoining the impartial love of justice that is the same as the practical love of humankind. (5) Despite the universal scope of its extension with respect to all members of the human species, this kind of practical love has its *source* in the love of self that moves every human being to desire her well-being in whatever place she senses her own existence.

From our interpretive perspective, the key thing to emphasize regarding these claims is this: For Rousseau, even the practical love that that perfectly fulfills the universality requirement of impartial justice has its *sole* source in *self-love*. To be sure, this is the kind of self-love that by nature is conjoined and combined with pity as a second original, non-rational feature of the human affective constitution. Yet the role of pity, as understood in relation to reasoned justice, is merely to *modify* self-love in its increasingly general self-identifying extension to include other beings. Thus, while it is for the sake of reason that we must have pity for the whole of humankind even more than for our immediate neighbor, it is still *for the sake of love of ourselves* that we are enjoined to act in accordance with this deontic requirement of universal justice.

Obviously, the position just characterized raises the question of how Rousseau's treatment of the transformation of expansive *amour-propre* into virtue fits the account of individual moral development provided in the rest of *Émile*. Given this chapter's thematic focus, however, I propose to let this question slide past us at the same time as it is noted in passing. I will concentrate instead on the much broader historical question of how Rousseau's position relates to the Stoic notion of *oikeiôsis* with which it so clearly has direct affinity.

Modern English does not seem to provide a single word that we can use to do proper semantic justice to the Stoic term of art, *oikeiôsis*. We do, however,

---

plus on généralise cet intérêt, plus il devient equitable, et l'amour du genre humain n'est autre chose en nous que l'amour de la justice. [...]

Pour empêcher la pitié de dégénérer en faiblesse il faut donc la généraliser, et l'étendre sur tout le genre humain. Alors on ne s'y livre qu'autant qu'elle est d'accord avec la justice, parce que, de toutes les vertus la justice est celle qui concourt le plus au bien commun des hommes. Il faut par raison, par amour pour nous, avoir pitié de notre espèce encore plus que de notre prochain, et c'est une très grande cruauté envers les hommes que la pitié pour les méchants".

have a rather effective and useful word for rendering what is opposed to *oikeiôsis*, namely, 'alienation'; and we can use this terminological opposition to get clear about the basic meaning of the notion that we are interested in. When I make another *oikeion* to me, thereby making myself *oikeion* to another, then I make that other non-alien to me just as I make myself non-alien to what is other than me. In other words, I 'appropriate' another being—especially another rational being—to myself insofar as I make that other a being non-alien to me as someone who makes myself non-alien to others. How, then, does this process of other-directed self-appropriation actually work out for any given human being?

According to the Stoic theory of moral development—the available textual sources go back at least to Chrysippus—the human process of *oikeiôsis* begins with the infant's impulse toward self-love and comes to *include* the tendency to develop a concern for others that is increasingly extended in its scope. In the wise person of perfected virtue, the latter tendency culminates in the recognition of the kinship of all rational beings. The sage is characterized as the agent who has cultivated the rationally informed affective disposition to show impartial concern for all others, and thus to be sensitive to ethical demands posed by even the most remotely placed of human beings.

Now in view of what Rousseau maintains in a very similar developmental frame of reference, the crucial thing for us to bear in mind is this: In the original versions of Stoic *oikeiôsis* doctrine, the source of the naturally anchored human tendency toward other-regarding concern is *not* self-love. The emergence of this second natural tendency results from a determination of the human affective constitution that is distinct from self-love and its concomitant natural impulse to self-preservation. Julia Annas, on whose study of ancient *oikeiôsis* I here largely rely,[73] makes this point by way of contrast with the Aristotelian conception of the development of other-regarding concern:

> [T]he Stoics differ strikingly from Aristotle [...] in having a theory in which self-concern and other-concern are two distinct sources of human behaviour, neither developing from the other. Oikeiôsis is a disjunctive notion: it covers the rational development of both self- and other-concern. What these have in common is simply that they are both cases of rational development of the agent's initially narrow, instinctive attitude to a wider rationally based concern.[74]

---

[73] See Annas 1993, pp. 159–179, 248–290. See also Algra 2003, pp. 265–296; Brennan 207, pp. 154–168; Cooper 2008, pp. 20–24; Inwood 2002, pp. 190–201; Long 1996, 124–130; Miller 2015, pp. 167–175, 189, 250–263; Striker 1996, pp. 281–297; Vogt 2008, 99–110.
[74] See Annas 1993, p. 275.

Thus, the disjunctive 'two-source' view is what characterizes the genuinely Stoic doctrinal article in question. In fact, as Annas argues, the 'one-source' interpretation of *oikeiôsis* emerges from the eclectic appropriation of this Stoic term on the part of Hellenistic thinkers whose accounts of the development of other-regarding concern derive, directly or indirectly, from the conception of the relation between self-love and friendship discussed in Aristotle's *Nicomachean Ethics*.[75]

Annas has traced the single-source interpretation of *oikeiôsis* from an anonymous commentary on Plato's *Timaeus* to Arius Didymus as well as to Antiochus, whose views lie at the basis of the criticism of Stoic ethics that Cicero presents in the fourth book of his *De finibus*. Against the background of Annas's investigations, it would probably be a fairly straightforward project to follow the further history of the single-source interpretation from Cicero's *De finibus* to major modern theories of natural law—especially up to Pufendorf's theory of natural sociability and to the textual commentaries on Grotius and Pufendorf that were written by Jean Barbeyrac and used by Rousseau.[76] But treating the historiographic and philological *minutiae* of the single-source interpretation would take us too far afield for our particular purposes in this chapter. The only points that I wish to underscore regarding the entire history of interpretation under consideration are these: First, Rousseau's developmental portrayal of the relationship between non-rational human motivational conditions and the universal principle of impartial justice is entirely in keeping with the single-source view that underlies the eclectic reception of Stoic *oikeiôsis* doctrine. Second, this interpretive view is fully consistent with a key theorematic claim of Kant's account of empirically conditioned practical reason, notably, the claim that all material practical principles belong under the general principle of self-love or one's own happiness (see chapter 3, pp. 55–58). Even Rousseau's fundamental maxim of reasoned justice is a principle that has its ultimate ground in self-love. It is a practical principle that derives its prescriptive force, for any given human agent, from *self-regarding* concern.

The discussion of Rousseau has been guided by the question posed at the end of this chapter's third section: Why did Kant not hold that adopting a foundational principle of the will's autonomy merited a rethinking of the sensible (i.e., the affective) conditions of human agency that was at least as radical as Rousseau's. The answer, I trust, should by now be plain enough: Rousseau's rethinking of these conditions ends up being not nearly as radical as it may seem

---

[75] See Annas 1993, pp. 276–290.
[76] See note 24 in this chapter. See also Long 2003, pp. 7–29; Miller 2015, pp. 105–107, 126–130, 137; Stauman 2003/2004.

to be if one judges his anthropological project simply from the account of the "principles anterior to reason" provided in the *Discourse on the Origins of Inequality*. In any event, we can see that Rousseau's moral anthropology does not necessarily involve any claim concerning the nature of non-rational motivational conditions that would be inconsistent with the historical view of material practical principles required by Kant's self-love theorem, i.e., the view articulated by the *Critique of Practical Reason's* classification of practical material determining grounds in the principle of morality (see chapter 8, pp. 172–176).

Not only is Rousseau's juridico-philosphic concept of a general will essential to understanding the emergence of Kant's idea of reason's autonomy. It has also become apparent that Rousseau's moral anthropology, at least as it was developed after the *Discourse* on inequality, poses no challenges to the historiographic classificatory strategy entailed by Kant's self-love theorem. Indeed, Rousseau's single-source portrayal of the transformation of *amour-propre* into virtue through its extension to others objectively provides support for the application of that strategy to the idea of the human being's internal perfection that underlies the historically prevalent interpretation of Stoic *oikeiôsis* doctrine. For even the Stoic principle of internal perfection is exposed to Epicurean assimilation as long as all material practical principles are thought to belong under the general principle of self-love or one's own happiness.

If this is the case, however, there is a further question that has yet to be answered: What happens to Kant's classificatory strategy if there is a sentimentalist approach to the foundations of morals that radically undermines the possibility of that sort of interpretation? This is where Hutcheson himself again steps onto the stage.

Chapter 10 Sentimentalist Ethics and Natural Law

The first section of this long chapter treats the account of the relation between benevolence and obligation that Francis Hutcheson gives in his *Inquiry Concerning Moral Good and Evil*. My main focus there is Hutcheson's aim to provide a clear alternative to the theories of obligation prevalent in the Grotian natural-law tradition by insisting on the morally foundational role of benevolent inclination. In view of this aim, I discuss Hutcheson's position that Richard Cumberland and Samuel Pufendorf sought to establish the necessary connection between prescriptive natural law and obligation on the basis of self-love. The second section evaluates this interpretive position by considering the doctrines of natural obligation at issue in Cumberland's *De legibus naturae* and in Pufendorf's *De jure naturae et gentium*. I argue that while Hutcheson's assessment of the egoistic import of Cumberland's law-based theory of natural obligation is clearly on the mark, it is far more difficult to show that the same kind of assessment applies to Pufendorf. Yet I show in this chapter's third and fourth sections that the broader significance of Hutcheson's interpretive position becomes evident if we investigate Pufendorf's criticism of a key argument on the nature of obligation that Thomas Hobbes had presented in *De cive*. Drawing together the threads of investigation stemming from Hutcheson's sentimentalist approach to obligation and criticism of modern natural law theories, I discuss why Kant would find it reasonable in effect to reverse the Hutchesonian view of the relationship between the affective aspect of human motivation and law-determined action when he came to recognize the far-reaching systematic significance of Rousseau's conception of the will's lawgiving function.

§ 1 Benevolent Inclination and Law in Hutcheson's Account of the Origin of Obligation

Hutcheson's *Inquiry Concerning Moral Good and Evil*, first published in 1725, has two closely linked programmatic objectives. The first of these goals has two parts: (a) to establish that by a moral sense we take pleasure in contemplating actions that have "an immediate goodness" (IBV 88); and (b) to show that in perceiving the pleasure taken in contemplating these actions, we are "determined to love the Agent [...] without any View of further natural Advantage from them" (IBV 88). The *Inquiry's* second main objective is determined in connection with the notion of moral pleasure just addressed. It is to demonstrate that what moves us to perform the actions that we perceive to be immediately good is not "the future Rewards from the Sanctions of Law, or any other natural Good, which may be the Consequence of virtuous Action" (IBV 88). Nor is it even the prospect of obtaining the sensible pleasure that we take in contemplating such an action. The second objective is thus to prove that the entire basis of moral motivation must derive from "an entirely different Principle of Action [...] from Interest or Self-Love" (IBV 88).

Given the tasks just described, Hutcheson's central aim in the 1725 *Inquiry* is to show that benevolence, understood as the practical love of others stemming from an instinctually rooted "determination" (IBV 147) of the human mind and affective constitution, constitutes the "one general Foundation of our Sense of Virtue" (IBV 116); "the Foundation of all apparent moral Excellence" (IBV 118); "the Foundation of all apprehended Excellence in social Virtues" (IBV 118); "the universal Foundation of our sense of moral Good, or Evil" (IBV120); and the foundation of all mankind's "Approbation of moral Actions" (IBV 135).[77] According to Hutcheson, all of the actions that we count as morally good or virtuous are those that "always appear as benevolent or flowing from the love of others and a Study of their Happiness" (IBV116). Moreover, he holds that in our assessment of the moral qualities of actions as well as the dispositions and capacities of the agents who perform them, it is always "some apparent Species of Benevolence, which commands our Approbation" (IBV 136).

For Hutcheson, then, the source of other-directed benevolence is something *completely independent* of self-love and the natural inclination to promote one's own good or advantage. Benevolence springs from an original and non-rational feature of the mind by which the human agent can be inclined to promote the good or happiness of others without direct regard to her own good. It is this conception of an affectively rooted inclination to perform other-regarding beneficent actions that Hutcheson has in mind when he underscores the foundational role of benevolence in his theory of morals. Thus, insisting that benevolent inclination is an original feature of the human make that cannot derive from any modality of self-love, Hutcheson holds that his conception of benevolence provides the key to explaining both moral motivation and the basis of our moral assessment of action and character.

The explanatory role of benevolence, however, is not limited to these general foundational aspects of the theory of morals. Hutcheson also regards benevolent inclination as the lynchpin of his account of obligation.

---

[77] For further discussion of this aim, see Edwards 2006; Paletta 2011; Radcliffe 2004, pp. 635–639. See also McGregor 2015, pp. 745–752.

In the final section of the 1725 *Inquiry*, Hutcheson is concerned to establish that the theoretical role of benevolence extends to the treatment of the idea of obligation as well as to ideas of various kinds of rights that figure prominently in modern theories of natural jurisprudence, especially in treatments of the normative underpinnings of human government. His general concern there is to show how his account of benevolence as a subjective attribute offers the best way of showing how we are able to acquire such deontic ideas, even "abstracting from any Law, Human or Divine" (IBV 176). Thus, he takes up the question of obligation by asking if we can "have any Sense of Obligation, abstracting from the Laws of a Superior" (IBV 176).

Hutcheson distinguishes between the different interpretations of obligation that frame what he takes to be the three at least initially plausible approaches to this question. One approach assumes that our selfish passions are so strong that our capacity for benevolent action is insufficient to overcome them. Given this assumption, the external sanctions of law and the power of a superior agent that is sufficient to enforce these sanctions is necessary in order to "induce a steady Sense of an Obligation to act for the public Good" (IBV 177). This type of approach, which implicitly makes self-love the chief motivating factor in an agent's obedience to law when faced with the coercive power of a superior, obviously does not allow for an affirmative response to the question of obligation at issue since it does not involve abstraction from the laws of a superior. But there is still the option of interpreting obligation as a relation based on self-love without linking the egoistic account of human motivation to the external sanctions of law and their enforcement by a superior. Accordingly, a second approach to that question is to regard obligation simply as "a Motive from Self-Interest, sufficient to determine all those who duly consider it, and pursue their own Advantage wisely, to a certain Course of Action" (IBV 177). Hutcheson discusses two directions taken in this prudential approach, which grounds obligation in self-interest. Prudentially grounded obligation can be interpreted in terms of action undertaken for the sake of the pleasure or happiness that ensues when we reflect on having acted virtuously. Or it can be interpreted in terms of the motives that we have when we consider the "Reasons which prove a constant Course of benevolent and social Actions, to be the most probable means of promoting the Good of every Individual" (IBV 177).[78]

---

[78] Turco (1999) and Tilley (2015) treat the advocates of the first variant of the prudential approach (namely, Archibald Campbell and John Clarke of Hull). Hutcheson links the second variant to Cumberland and Pufendorf (of which more presently).

§ 1 Benevolent Inclination, Law, and Obligation in Hutcheson — 209

The third approach to understanding the nature of obligation is furnished by Hutcheson's own account of other-directed benevolence. This approach eschews the attempt to ground moral obligation by linking self-love to the external sanctions of law and the power of a superior. It also repudiates the attempt to use the tenets of rational egoism in order to account for our sense of obligation without relying on the notions of law and external sanctions:

> If by Obligation we understand a Determination, without regard to our own Interest, to approve Actions, and to perform them; which Determination shall also make us displeas'd with our selves, and uneasy upon having acted contrary to it; in this meaning of the word Obligation, there is naturally an Obligation upon all Men to Benevolence; and they are still under its Influence, even when by false, or partial Opinions of the natural Tendency of their Actions, this moral Sense leads them to Evil; unless by long inveterate Habits it be exceedingly weaken'd. For it scarce seems possible wholly to extinguish it. Or, which is to the same purpose, this internal Sense, and Instinct toward Benevolence, will either influence our Actions, or else make us very uneasy and dissatisfy'd; and we shall be conscious that we are in a base unhappy State, even without considering any Law whatsoever, or any external Advantages lost, or Disadvantages impending from its Sanctions. (IBV 176–177)

In this passage, Hutcheson is by no means especially scrupulous about sorting through the range of distinctions that we might care to see drawn between (i) obligation as such, (ii) the obligation to benevolence *qua* universal natural obligation, (iii) the moral sense that can lead us to evil on account of false or partial opinions of the tendencies of our actions, and (iv) the internal sense and—or— instinct toward benevolence that either influences our actions or else makes us uneasy or dissatisfied with ourselves. Nor does he explain precisely how the moral sense is related to the instinct toward benevolence when that sense is understood as the determination of the mind by which we approve and perform actions. Yet one thing is quite clear from these considerations on the connection between obligation and benevolence: If our basic conception of what binds us to act is couched in terms of an affective determination to perform the actions that our moral sense leads us to approve, then we must understand the obligation to act benevolently as the deontic determination of the human affective constitution by which we can be naturally inclined to act without regard to our own interest or to agent-external factors that constrain us to act in obedience to practical laws. In other words, as Hutcheson puts them, the "Obligation upon all Men *to* Benevolence" must be thought of as the ground of action supplied by, and originating in, the "Instinct *toward* Benevolence" (italics mine [J. E.]), i.e., the affective determination of the human soul (or mind) that can move us to act for the good of others independently of every consideration of self-interest, law, sanction, and external advantage.

The two key points to emphasize thus far, then, are the following. First, insofar as benevolence (on Hutcheson's account) is an original component of our affective constitution, it is also a primitive deontic feature of our motivational make-up that cannot be explained reductively as a kind of self-love, nor even as an effect or function of self-love. Second, both the nature of this original feature and the moral qualities of the actions that spring from it are fully intelligible apart from any notion of prescriptive law and its external sanctions.

Up to this point, we have seen that Hutcheson sets his portrayal of the origin of our consciousness of obligation in opposition to two theoretical views, each of which involves the assumption that obligation cannot be understood without reference to rational self-interest or to practical law and its interest-imposing sanctions. The question that arises at this juncture, then, is why Hutcheson should consider his portrayal to be superior to these competing general views.

Hutcheson takes the following position when addressing this issue. Although only one of the two competing views relies on the idea of practical law and its external sanctions, both views presuppose the same basic definition of obligation. That is because the proponents of each competing view assume that the decisive motivating factor by which any given agent is bound to the performance of certain types of action must be *some* advantage that he can obtain through that performance. As Hutcheson puts it, "Obligation, with them, is only such a Constitution, either of Nature, or of some governing Power, as makes it advantageous for the Agent to act in a certain Manner" (IBV 180).

Thus, the fundamental difficulties to which the competing views at issue are exposed must derive from this shared assumption, i.e., the assumption which inseparably links the idea of obligation to something that a self-interested agent can regard as his *own* advantage. One such difficulty, Hutcheson emphasizes, stems from the fact that this assumption is simply not in keeping with our use of moral words—that it cannot be made consistent with our morally prescriptive employment of words like 'ought', 'should', and 'must'. The chief difficulty, however, lies in this: If obligation has to be understood only in connection with the advantage of the self-interested agent, then there is no basis for drawing a distinction between the meaning of constraint and the morally relevant meaning of obligation.

The problem of distinguishing between mere constraint and obligation is an obvious one for the law-and-sanction view, which directly links the advantage and disadvantage of the obligated agent to a law-enforcing superior's power to reward and punish. The problem may seem to be less pressing when we consider the other competing view. For the proponents of this second general view seek to determine the nature of obligation by abstracting from the idea of law, even when they insist on understanding it in terms of "a Constitution which makes an Action eligible from Self-Interest" (IBV 180). Still, not even this second type of prudential account can surmount the principal difficulty at issue since there seems to be "a universally acknowledg'd Difference between even this sort of Constraint, and Obligation" (IBV 180). In other words, not even the consideration of the internal constraint involved in the egoistically refined pursuit of pleasure and the avoidance of uneasiness[79] offers a way to do justice to the semantic distinction in question, i.e., the distinction between mere constraint and obligation that we are able to make on the basis of our natural capacity to approve and perform actions *without regard* to our own interest.[80]

Hutcheson concludes his treatment of his theoretically pivotal distinction between constraint and obligation by relating it to the idea of a divine lawgiver and the sanctions of divine law:

> We never say we are oblig'd to do an Action which we count base, but we may be constrain'd to it; we never say that the divine Laws, by their Sanctions, constrain us, but oblige us; nor do we call Obedience to the Deity Constraint, unless by a Metaphor, tho many own they are influenc'd by fear of Punishments. And yet supposing an almighty evil Being should require, under grievous Penaltys, Treachery, Cruelty, Ingratitude, we would call this Constraint. The difference is plainly this. When any Sanctions co-operate with our moral Sense, in exciting us to Actions which we count morally good, we say we are oblig'd; but when Sanctions of Rewards or Punishments oppose our moral Sense, then we say we are brib'd or constrain'd. In the former Case we call the Lawgiver good, as designing the publick Happiness; in the latter we call him evil, or unjust, for the suppos'd contrary Intention. But were all our Ideas of moral Good or Evil, deriv'd solely from opinions of private Advantage or Loss in Actions, I see no possible difference which could be made in the meaning of these words. (IBV 181–182)

Here, too, even when treating the idea of the lawgiving will of a divine superior, Hutcheson implicitly insists on upholding the connection between obligation and benevolence as the ground of morally good action.[81] To be sure, we can

---

79 That is, the pursuit of pleasure taken in reflection on the performance of virtuous action and the avoidance of the uneasiness caused by reflection on having acted basely.

80 Though not contrary to our own good. Like practically all other moralists, Hutcheson insists that everyone may be, and ought to be, "innocently solicitous about himself" (IBV123).

81 In this case, the connection is between obligation and the benevolent intention of a powerful superior being whose objective *must* be the public happiness of human beings if its actions are to be consistent with the evaluative deliverances and the motivational impulses of our moral sense. Hutcheson repudiates the voluntarist conception of the prescriptive force of law, especially as this applies to the will of God: "[T]o call the Laws of the Supreme Deity good, or holy, or just, if all Goodness, Holiness, and Justice be constituted by Laws, or the Will of a Superior any way reveal'd, must be an insignificant Tautology, amounting to no more than this, 'That God wills what he wills'" (IBV 180–181).

be constrained to act in conformity with the requirements set by a lawgiver, even if benevolence is nowhere in play. Moreover, we can be aware that our relation to these requirements is one of constraint insofar as we are able discern the causal link between the lawgiver's power and our private advantage or loss. But all this is quite different from having a sense of *obligation* with respect to the requirements of law. It is fundamentally different from being conscious that we are morally bound to conformity with these requirements *because* this conformity is what tends to realize the benevolent aim of the lawgiver. According to Hutcheson, this sense of obligation is simply not intelligible except in connection with the "universal determination to Benevolence in Mankind" (IBV 147).

For Hutcheson, then, no approach to the foundations of moral philosophy that attempts to derive our sense of obligation from any form of private advantage can account for our ability to draw a distinction between constraint and obligation. Moreover, holding that no coherent account of obligation is possible unless this distinction is clearly drawn, Hutcheson insists that the external constraint imposed by the sanctioning power of a lawgiving superior cannot furnish a constitutive component of the idea of obligation. Nor can such a component be supplied by the internal constraint linked to the egoistically refined pleasure involved in virtuous actions and to the uneasiness resulting from base actions.

We are now in a position to turn to Hutcheson's treatment of modern natural-law theories of obligation. As we do this, however, let us bear in mind the following general considerations on the relationship between Hutcheson's foundational account of obligation and theories that give pride of place to the notion of prescriptive law. For Hutcheson, as we have seen, instinctually anchored benevolent inclination is an original deontic feature of the human make and frame. As such, it is the morally salient characteristic of our affective constitution that lies at the basis of our sense of obligation. Taken by itself, however, it is not a law-*receptive* characteristic by which we are made subject to the external sanctions of superior authority. Nor is it a law*giving* (i.e., a nomo*thetic*) determination of the human mind. According to Hutcheson, the source of obligation is not only independent of our receptivity to the demands of external legislation. That source is also entirely distinct from any nomothetic operation of the mind that might be thought to issue from a faculty superior to the affective capacity of the soul that gives rise to benevolence as its morally salient motivating feature. It is significant in this latter regard that Hutcheson gives no indication that an agent could be considered her *own law* (cf. Paul, *Romans* 2:14), simply on account of the structure of human moral sensibility, *even if* she is fully aware of being able to act in keeping with the obligation to other-directed benevolence. In brief, his strikingly radical sentimentalist theory of obligation is at least as far removed from the idea of the autonomy of the will *qua* practical reason as it is from every other law-based approach, including every approach that builds on assumption that the notions of obligation, law, and *external* constraint (or compulsion) cannot be pulled apart.[82]

I will return to the relationship between Hutcheson's account of obligation and Kant's theory of autonomy in the final section of this chapter. In the two following sections I will investigate whether Hutcheson's sentimentalist criticism of all law-based approaches can effectively target the particular natural law theories of obligation that he has in mind.

§ 2 Cumberland and Pufendorf in Light of Hutcheson's Criticism

Hutcheson singles out for explicit refutation the doctrines of obligation put forward by Samuel Pufendorf and Richard Cumberland. He proceeds against Pufendorf and Cumberland by addressing the connection that these two representative natural lawyers sought to establish between benevolence and the natural good of rational beings. He is willing to grant that both Pufendorf and Cumberland succeeded in proving that consistently performing benevolent actions is likely to be to be the most fitting means of promoting the good of each individual agent, and he states that they accomplished this "without relation to a Law" (IBV 177). Consequently, Hutcheson acknowledges that Pufendorf and Cumberland can be said to have established that human agents are obligated to pursue their advantage wisely; and he concedes that these two natural lawyers accomplished this without appealing to the legislative and sanctioning power of a superior. But he also holds that they did not account for obligation in its properly moral sense because the prudential line of argument that they pursued could not extend beyond the characterization of obligation in terms of self-interested motivation rooted in self-love. Thus, although Pufendorf and Cumberland did succeed in providing one kind of account of obligation without appealing to the concept of law, this

---

[82] In a comment on VII § 56 of *The Meditations of the Emperor Marcus Aurelius Antoninus*, Hutchson makes it clear that he accepts the Pauline notion of "conforming our selves to the law of God written in the heart" (MMA: 91). On Hutcheson's account of the sense of obligation, however, the human capacity for such a law to be so inscribed is not *itself* an originally law-receptive capacity. Much less is it a faculty by which we self-reflectively give to ourselves the law already written in our hearts. Instead, it is simply the (God-given) capacity to be moved to act by benevolent inclination and to approve of benevolently motivated actions.

cannot be the foundational theory that grounds principles of duty which are distinguishable from mere maxims of (enlightened) self-interest.

How plausible is Hutcheson's interpretation of Cumberland and Pufendorf as paradigmatic representatives of modern natural-law theories of obligation? Does Hutcheson actually succeed in establishing that the modern conception of prescriptive natural law is inseparably linked to self-interest, advantage and self-love?

To answer these queries I will discuss Cumberland and Pufendorf in relation to the question of natural obligation in modern natural law theories. Thus, the considerations on Cumberland and Pufendorf offered in the rest of this section concern the problem of determining how a prescriptive natural law can intelligibly be said to be normatively binding simply insofar as it is regarded as a law of *nature*. More particularly, I will address the way in which these thinkers could regard a law of nature as having obligatory force for human agents even when considered in abstraction from the conditions of civil union or the coercive power of a state.

To avoid misunderstanding, I want to emphasize one point before proceeding further. Of the two thinkers treated, only Cumberland can really be said to offer a fully articulated *doctrine* of natural obligation. It would therefore be an exaggeration to contend that Pufendorf provides a developed doctrine of this type when he addresses the question of the obligation of natural law. Nevertheless, the following considerations will show various ways in which the *concept* of natural obligation plays an essential and pivotal role in both Cumberland's and Pufendorf's portrayals of the nature of obligation in connection with the deontic requirements of right reason.

Cumberland's *De legibus naturae* (1672) contains a running criticism of the central tenets of Thomas Hobbes's natural law theory. The arguments that Cumberland directs against Hobbes in this work's chapter on natural obligation furnish pivotal elements of his overall criticism of Hobbes' moral philosophy. I refer above all to Cumberland's arguments against Hobbes's position that a prescriptive law of nature is binding only *in foro interno* except when it can be kept without prejudice to the internally obligated agent's self-preservation. Cumberland interprets Hobbes as implying that laws of nature assert *no* obligation to external actions for those existing in a state of nature.[83]

---

[83] See DLN V.50–57/TLN 620–642. (Citation of Cumberland is explained on p. X of this book.)

Let us not be stopped in our tracks at this point by questions concerning the plausibility (not to mention the textual accuracy) of this sort of interpretation.[84] Instead, let us just concentrate on the position on natural obligation that Cumberland wants to take against Hobbes. In order to counter the (purportedly) Hobbesian implication just mentioned, Cumberland approaches the question of the natural obligation to external action by considering the standpoint of the divine lawgiver who establishes the causal connection between the achievement of happiness as one's own natural good and the promotion of the good of the whole system of rational beings—the *bonum rationalium commune*. Accordingly, he seeks to ground the moral necessity of acting in obedience to the precepts of natural law by demonstrating the divinely established connection between the happiness of the particular human agent and the happiness of rational beings in general.

---

[84] Neither one of the most obviously relevant passages from *De cive* and *Leviathan* provides support for Cumberland's line of interpretation:

Non est igitur existimandum, natura, hoc est, ratione obligari homines ad exercitium earum omnium, in eo statu hominum in quo non exercentur ab aliis. Interea tamen obligamur ad animum eas obseruandi, quandocunque ad finem ad quem ordinantur earum obseruatio conducere videbitur. Ideoque concludendum est, legem natuae semper & vbique obligare in *Foro interno*, siue *conscientia*, non semper *in foro externo:* sed tum solum modo cum secure id fieri possit. (*De cive* III.27)

The Lawes of nature oblige *in foro interno*; that is to say, they bind to a desire they should take place: but *in foro externo*; that is, to the putting them in act, not always. [...]

The same Lawes, because they oblige only to a desire, and endeavour, I mean an unfeigned and constant endeavour. For in that they require nothing but endeavour; he that endeavoureth in their performance, fulfilleth them; and he that fulfilleth the Law,is just. (*Levathan* XV.36 – 38; cf. *De cive* III.30).

To assert that a law of nature is not *always* binding *in foro externo*, but only when it can be kept with safety, is not to claim that it is *never* binding *in foro externo* in a state of nature. For it may just happen, on occasion, that it *can* be kept with safety in such a state, although no one is obligated to keep *all* laws in a state of nature in which not everyone is constrained to keep every law. Moreover, and more importantly, even if the laws of nature always and everywhere obligate us only to an unfeigned and constant endeavor to put them into effect whenever and wherever they cannot be kept with safety, it is still true that they obligate us to endeavor in their *performance*. Apart from this latter condition of obligation, it would be difficult to make sense of Hobbes's *exeundum* requirement, i.e., right reason's commandment to emerge from the state of nature by establishing the conditions under which everyone is bound *in foro externo* to perform actions in keeping with all laws of nature (regarding which, see notes 130 and 131 in this chapter). For the *exeunudum* requirement presupposes that each of us is obligated *in foro interno* to the performance of *external* actions prescribed by the laws of nature. This presupposition holds, although not one of these laws is *always* binding *in foro externo*. Not even internally binding laws of conscience necessarily obligate only to internal actions when reason's demand to exit the state of nature is in play.

The causal linkage here at issue is made fully evident in the first (and best known) version of Cumberland's general formulation of the law of nature: [85]

> The law of nature is a proposition, presented to or impressed upon the mind clearly enough from the nature of things from the will of the first cause, which indicates the possible action of a rational being that best [*maxime*] promotes the common good, and by which alone the happiness of individuals can be obtained.[86] (DLN V.1/TLN 495–496 [Maxwell translation modified])

The reference to the promotion of the common good as the means by which *alone* the integral happiness of any particular agent can be obtained is crucial for Cumberland's understanding of natural obligation. On Cumberland's view, no precept of natural law that presents a requirement for human action can be said to *obligate* unless it enables that same agent to know some means of promoting its own happiness. It is this enabling effect of natural law that furnishes the essential condition for any particular agent's being obligated to promote the common good. But how exactly does natural law have this effect?

While Cumberland holds that all obligation proceeds wholly from the law and the lawgiver,[87] he also maintains that the "whole force of obligation [*summa vis obligandi*]" (DLN V.11/TLN 543) derives from the sanctions (i.e., the rewards and punishments) that a lawgiver annexes to the performance or non-performance of actions in conformity with its laws.[88] In keeping with this understanding of obligation in general, he maintains, in the course of the fifth chapter of *De legibus naturae*, that the following tenets apply to the source of obligation and the nature of human moral agency: (1) Moral obligation must be understood as the immediate effect of nature's laws. (2) The source of such an effect—i.e., the source of all natural obligation—is the will and counsel of God, who enacts as laws of nature the practical propositions by which all rational agents are directed to promote the common good (i.e., the happiness of all rational beings,

---

[85] Cumberland provides a second version of his fundamental law of nature ("Lex Nature est propositio natura rerum ex voluntate primae causae menti satis aperte oblata vel impressa actionem indicans Bono Rationalium communi observientem, quam si praestetur praemia, sin negligatur poenae sufficientes ex Natura Rationalium sequunter" [DLN V.1]). We need not be concerned here with the relationship between the two versions, but see Kirk 1987, p. 79; Haakonssen 2001, pp. 35–41; Parkin 199, p. 108. For a concise explanation of the issues involved, see Parkins' note on pp. 495–496 of TLN.

[86] "Lex Nature est propositio natura rerum ex voluntate primae causae menti satis aperte oblata vel impressa, quae actionem agentis rationalis possibilem communi bono maxime deservientem indicat, & integram singulorum foelicitatem exinde solum obtineri posse".

[87] See DLN V.22/TLN 543.

[88] See DLN V.11/TLN 519–520.

conjoined with the honor of God). (3) We human beings are so constituted that we can *discover* the obligation of law only on the strength of law's sanctions. (4) Consequently, the particular precepts of natural law are practical propositions that furnish dictates of reason (*dictamina rationis*), i.e., universal practical propositions, expressible in the form of commands, by which we can know that that good and evil follow upon our actions.

Given the tenets just listed, Cumberland holds that "we are determined by a kind of natural necessity to purse good [...] and to avoid evil" (DLN V.27/TLN 554).[89] Moreover, he maintains that we can know that the attainment of good and the avoidance of evil are necessarily connected with every rational being's pursuit of its own happiness. Accordingly, he also maintains that the necessity of performing actions commanded by the law of nature and its derivative precepts can qualify as necessity *to* a (finite) rational agent only when such an agent understands a commanded action to be the cause of its own happiness.[90] Thus, although the law of nature enjoins each one of us to promote the happiness of all rational beings, the finite agent who understands the lawful necessity of so acting will be someone who is moved to act in conformity with law only if he understands his commanded action to be a cause of the happiness that he necessarily pursues as his own:

> Obligation is the act of a legislator by which he indicates that actions conforming to his law are necessary to those for whom the law is made. An action is then understood to be necessary when it is certainly included in the causes necessarily required for that happiness which he [i.e., an agent for whom the law is made] naturally, and consequently necessarily, aims at.[91] (DLN V.27/TLN 554)

According to Cumberland, then, no precept of natural law that asserts a universality requirement of practical reason can obligate *me*, as a particular human agent, unless it makes known to me some means of promoting my *own* happiness (or at least a way of avoiding my own misery). Cumberland takes this posi-

---

89 "naturali quadam necessitate ad bona [...] quaerenda, ad mala fugienda determinemur".
90 See DLN V.27/TLN 554.
91 "Obligatio est actus Legislatoris quo actionis Legi suae conformes eis quibus lex fertur necessaries esse indicat. Actio autem tum necessaria esse intelligitur, cum certum est eam contineri in causis necessario requisitis ad foelicitatem illam quam naturaliter adeoque necessario expetit". Given the context in which this passage is presented, it would make no sense to refer the subject of the second sentence's *expetit* to the *legislator* of the first sentence. That is why Maxwell translated the second sentence as follows: "An *Action* is then understood to be *necessary to a rational Agent when it is certainly one of the Causes necessarily requir'd to that Happiness which he naturally, and consequently necessarily, desires*" (TLN 554).

tion despite the fact that he also maintains that the obligation made known by the precepts of natural law is one that proceeds wholly from the will and counsel of God. What connects these two positions on natural obligation is the following assumption: God has so determined the nature of things that every finite rational agent has the capacity to discover that she can promote her own happiness only by acting in conformity with the universal law of nature that enjoins the promotion of the common good of rational beings to the honor of God.

Cumberland is greatly concerned to clarify the issues involved in, and generated by, this connecting assumption. He has good reason to be concerned. For it is hardly obvious to begin with why I should *not* know myself to be morally bound to promote the common good whenever I apprehend (in virtue of my understanding of what the law of nature requires) that God wills that every agent ought to promote the happiness of all rational beings.

Perhaps the most remarkable response to this type of consideration can be found in DLN V.35/TLN 570–575. The relevant line of argument runs as follows: The universal law concerning the promotion of the common good is a practical proposition that commands the pursuit of this most general good as the highest and greatest "effect" (i.e., end) that is achievable by means of human action. But if the promotion of this end is held to be a necessary means to one and the same end's achievement, then the practical proposition in question will be identical (i.e., will have the form "A is A"). Thus, since no identical proposition can contain (or generate) an incentive to action, our promotion of the common good as the highest and greatest good that we are capable of promoting must be regarded as the necessary means of promoting a dependent but lesser good, namely, the own-happiness that each of us is rightly supposed to desire.

One may wish to ask how such an argument responds to the problematizing consideration mentioned above since it is not clear why even an identical proposition should not contain an incentive to action as long as (i) it *is a practical* proposition (i.e., a prescription for action) and (ii) the type of action that it enjoins derives its necessity from a volitional act of the lawgiver (i.e., God). Be that as it may, we can grasp the position that Cumberland is attempting to establish if we take into account what he says elsewhere about the relationship between practical propositions, laws, commands, and prudential reasoning.[92] As I understand it, the position is as follows.

A principle of universal benevolence, which is contained in the law of nature, furnishes the general precept that indicates the kind of action by which a rational agent will best promote the common good. Because that principle de-

---

[92] See, e.g., DLN IV.1–4/TLN 480–486.

§ 2 Cumberland and Pufendorf in Light of Hutcheson's Criticism — 219

rives from and expresses the will of God, it categorically commands each of us to promote the common good as best we can, thereby promoting the happiness of all human beings and, consequently, our own happiness as a constitutive component of the happiness of all rational beings. But when taken in abstraction from the notion of sanction, which is also contained (at least implicitly[93]) in the general formula of the law of nature, no such precept can express the necessity of beneficent action *to* a particular human being (*qua* rational agent). That is because only sanctions can motivate us to act beneficently by causally linking other-directed benevolence to the own-happiness of each one of us. Thus, no precept (or principle) of universal benevolence can properly be said to obligate a human agent unless it allows for the specification of some sanction in connection with its demand for conformity with law. In other words, if the law of nature is to obligate *us*—i.e., if it is to contain a principle that can qualify as both a practical law *and* a moral imperative that actually binds each one of us to action—then the laws of duty that it grounds must be knowable (to us) as hypothetical imperatives of prudence.

Whatever we may think of this position, we can well understand how Cumberland's natural-law theory would present a prime critical target for Hutcheson's sentimentalist foundational deontology.[94] In particular, we can see how Cumberland's account of the law of nature and its obligation falls under the blanket criticism that Hutcheson levels against law-based doctrines of obligation. That is, we can grasp how Cumberland's account is exposed to the broadside critical charge that such doctrines must miss the point of a theory of *moral* obligation because they cannot cleanly sever the connection between practical law, on the one hand, and private advantage and self-love, on the other. Let us turn to Pufendorf bearing these points in mind.

In the first book of his *De jure naturae et gentium* (1672), Pufendorf defines obligation as a morally operative quality by which a subject is required to perform or suffer something.[95] In keeping with this general understanding of obligation, he defines law as a decree by which a superior being binds a subject to the performance of actions in accordance with that superior's command (*praescriptum*).[96] In view of our discussion of Cumberland, it may be noted that Pufen-

---

[93] See note 85 in this chapter.
[94] On the notion of foundational deontology and its application to Hutcheson, see Edwards 2006, pp. 20–24.
[95] "Obligationem [...] definivimus, per qualitatem moralem operativam, qua quis praestare aut pati quid tenetur" (DJN I.6.5/GW 4.1: 72; cf. DJN I.1.21/GW 4.1: 25).
[96] "In genere [...] commodissime videtur definiri per decretum, quo superior sibi subjectum obligat, ut ad istius praescriptum actiones suas componat" (DJN I.6.4/GW 4.1: 71).

dorf's ground-level determination of the relation between obligation and law involves no connection between the commanding will of a lawgiving agent and the good of the subject who is bound in obedience to law. According to its basic Pufendorfian account, then, the relation of obligation as such must be understood in terms of straightforward subjection to the command of a superior. The treatment of natural obligation in the second book of *De jure naturae* is fully consistent with this basic definitional account. Unlike Cumberland, Pufendorf does not hold that our obligation to obey the fundamental law of nature, or the particular action-guiding precepts that it contains, is something that *depends* on the divinely established causal connection between law-determined action, the own-happiness of the particular agent, and the common good of rational beings.

Pufendorf's version of the fundamental law of nature presents what I will henceforth refer to as the *socialitas* requirement of reason. The law itself runs as follows:

> A human being ought, as far as in him lies, to cultivate and preserve a peaceful sociability with others, agreeable to the end and natural disposition of humankind.[97] (DJN II.3.15/GW 4.1: 148 [Kennett and Seidler translations modified])

Pufendorf derives his *socialitas* requirement by considering what he takes to be the fundamental normatively salient features of human nature, above all the individual human being's instinctually anchored desire for self-preservation in the face of his observable weakness and lack of self-sufficiency.[98] Pufendorf thus emphasizes that there is an empirically knowable connection between, on the one hand, securing one's individual self-preservation and well-being and, on the other hand, acting in accordance with the particular precepts of natural law that set out different ways of being bound to promote human sociability. Nevertheless, the obligations to different types of action that are imposed by these universal prescriptions of reason do not depend on the sort of causal linkage that Cumberland, as we have seen, wants to establish between (i) the divinely instituted order of nature, (ii) the natural good—that is, the well-being and happiness—of particular human subjects, and (iii) the common good of rational beings. The theoretical relevance of this sort of nexus should in fact by ruled out by Pufendorf's appeal to the commanding power of God in his account of the ultimate ground of our obligation to obey the fundamental law of nature by promoting and preserving peaceful sociability. Indeed, one might say that the whole

---

[97] "cuilibet homini, quantum in se, colendum & conservandum esse pacificam adversus alios socialitatem, indoli & scopo generis humani in universum congruentem".
[98] See DJN II.3.15/GW 4.1: 148.

point of this appeal is to show that such a causal nexus, which is essential to the *type* of approach to obligation taken by Cumberland, is not directly relevant to the explanation of the ultimate source of our natural obligation to further the sociable disposition of human beings:

> *Even if* the creator [...] by virtue of his commanding power [*pro imperio*] might have required obedience from us without our deriving any advantage from this, it has *nonetheless* pleased his goodness so to dispose the nature of things and of human beings that by a certain natural connection some goods should follow the observance, and some evils the transgression of the laws of nature.[99] (DJN II.3.21/ GW 4.1: 158 [italics mine (J. E.)]

Happily for us, it has as a matter of fact pleased God to order creation in such a way that our lawful actions have beneficial consequences and actions contrary to what God commands will have correspondingly bad outcomes. Nevertheless, each of us would always be subject to the obligation imposed by God, even in the event that none of us derived any benefit whatsoever from acting in accordance with the *socialitas* requirement which the fundamental law of nature asserts and the derivative precepts of natural law specify.[100] According to Pufendorf's account of this deontic requirement, then, we are bound to promote human sociability independently of any assumed causal connection between one's *own* good and the common good of rational beings. Thus, we would be bound to foster this condition of peaceful human agency *whether or not* anyone obtained any good of any kind by acting in conformity with the natural laws that God has providentially linked to the production of good and bad consequences.

The various precepts of reason that the fundamental law of nature grounds are principles of duty that set out the ways in which we are to cultivate and preserve the peaceful sociability that, as the fundamental law itself declares, is congruent with the constitution and end of the human species in general. Moreover, the sociability that is congruent with this generic constitution and its corresponding end must itself be understood in terms of the kind of disposition by

---

[99] "Etsi Creator [...] obsequium a nobis pro imperio potuisset exigere, fructu aliquo in nos redundante plane sterile; placuisse tamen ipsius bonitati naturam rerum & hominum ita disponere, ut observantium legum naturalium bona quadeam, violationem mala naturali quadam connexione sequerentur".

[100] What Pufendorf says about rules of justice that conform to God's *perfections* and about God *necessarily* "not willing otherwise" (see DJN II.1.3/ GW 4.1: 108, DJN II.3.5/GW 4.1: 133–135, DJN II.3.20/GW 4.1: 154–157) does not run counter to this point, which is that each of us *would* still be subject to the obligation of natural law *even if* no one derived any benefit or advantage from actions consistent with the *socialitas* requirement.

which each member of the human species is joined to any (and every) other member by benevolence, by peace and charity, and so by mutual obligation.[101] Thus, in prescribing the promotion of sociability as the disposition to act benevolently, peaceably and charitably, the precepts of natural law bind us to furthering a relation of mutual obligation that accords with human nature. For Pufendorf, however, the prescriptive character of these laws cannot depend on there being a causal connection between the source of all obligation—namely, the commanding will of God—and some end achievable *through* the promotion of sociability, *even if* the condition of peaceful sociability is itself an end that is fully congruent with the human constitution. It cannot, for example, depend on the promotion of the common good of rational beings as a means of furthering the own-happiness of particular human agents who are by nature obligated to make it their end to promote the common good. On Pufendorf's account, then, the precepts of natural law prescribe actions only in virtue of their origination as laws in the will of God; and the obligatory character of the actions prescribed depends on a formal property that they share: their consistency with the fundamental law of nature and its derivative precepts.[102]

If we are to know what we are under a natural obligation to do *in order* to promote sociability, of course, then we must consider the good and bad consequences of our actions in connection with the features of the human constitution that determine the particular character of our sociability. For example, we must take account of the relative weakness of the individual human being that gives rise to the universal human need for relations of reciprocal benevolence. But the natural obligation itself must be understood according to a merely formal condition: the *conformity* of human actions with the law-imposing volitional act(s) by which God creates human beings with the particular nature that they in fact have (i.e., the nature by which they can be, and indeed *need* to be, joined together in a relation of mutual obligation). To be sure, Pufendorf considers it to be empirically evident that God has so ordered the natural world that we all stand in need of this relation and draw advantages from bringing it about. Nevertheless, Pufendorf's conformity condition is such that the lawgiving efficacy of God is the only *causal* factor relevant to the account of the basis of natural obligation. For the will of God is by itself fully sufficient to bind us to actions that conform to the universal prescriptions of natural law. And without reference to the nomothetic function of God's will, there is simply no way to account for how such

---

[101] "per socialitatem innuimus ejusmodi dispositionem hominis erga quemvis hominem, per quam ipsi benevolentia, pace & caritate, mutuaque adeo obligatione conjunctus intelligitur" (DJN II.3.15/GW 4.1:148).
[102] See DJN I.2.6/GW 4.1: 31.

prescriptions of reason could enjoin us to promote our natural sociability as a relation of mutual *obligation* among all those who are conjoined by affective ties of benevolence, peace, and charity.[103]

If this is the case, however, we must ask whether the position that Hutcheson takes on modern natural-law theories of obligation is supportable. As indicated above, Hutcheson claims that such law-based approaches ground obligation in self-interest and private advantage (and thus in self-love). Given the conception of natural obligation just considered, however, is it not obvious that this claim is quite simply false when applied to someone like Pufendorf? On the face of things, it may well seem so. But this should not lead us to ignore the broader significance of Hutcheson's interpretive claim. That significance will come to light if we dig just a bit deeper into the Pufendorfian subsoil, thereby ferreting Hobbes out of his hole and bringing him into the running.

---

103 Consider this last point in connection with the two renderings that Jean Barbeyrac provides for Pufendorf's definitional account of sociability in *De jure naturae:*
   [La Sociabilité] consist dans ces sentimens d'un Homme envers toute autre, qui font qu'il le regarde comme uni avec lui par la paix, la bienveillance, l'affection, & meme par des obligations réciproques. (Pufendorf/Barbeyrac 1732)
   [La Sociabilité] consist dans une disposition générale d'un Homme envers tout autre, en consequence de laquelle on les regarde comme unis ensemble par les liens de la paix, de la bienveillance, de l'affection, d'ou il résulte un obligation réciproque. (Pufendorf/Barbeyrac 1740)
   The later rendering is closer to the actual formulation that Pufendorf gives of his definition of sociability in DJN II.3.15/GW 4.1: 148. Yet it encourages the type of reading according to which the relation of mutual obligation in which human beings are conjoined is one that *results* from benevolence and charity as affective determinations of the human constitution. Moreover, it *allows* the general disposition in consequence of which human beings can establish ties of peace to be interpreted as a disposition based on the instinctually rooted concern for individual self-preservation and natural reason's prudential concern with self-advantage. It may be noted that neither of these interpretive options sits easily with the understanding of natural obligation that Barbeyrac requires, in his *Jugement d'un anonyme*, for the defense of Pufendorf against Leibniz's anti-voluntarist onslaught (see Barbeyrac 1718, pp. 413–417). For discussion of Pufendorf's voluntarism, Leibniz's criticism, and Pufendorf's defense of Leibniz, see Korkmann 2002 and Saatsmanen 1995. See also Hartung 1999, pp. 77–125; Schneewind 1987; Schneewind 1998, pp. 134–140.

§ 3 "Kick Not Against the Pricks": Pufendorf and Hobbes on Natural Obligation

As we have just seen, Pufendorf builds a crucial element of formalistic voluntarism into his explanation of the source of the obligation to obey the law of nature and its derivative precepts. He thus offers—or at least seems to offer—a clear alternative to the doctrine of natural obligation that Cumberland put forward in response to what he took to be Hobbes's position on the relationship between natural law and the obligation to external action. Yet if we consider Hobbes's own position on natural obligation, we find that Pufendorf is confronted by a key problem to which the egoistic features of Cumberland's doctrine provide a ready (if not ultimately viable) response by linking the external sanctions of God-commanded law to the human being's pursuit of his own happiness. The problem that Pufendorf must deal with, of course, is one shared by every consistently voluntaristic account of obligation: the problem of distinguishing conceptually between being obligated to the performance of actions and being externally compelled to act.[104] Pufendorf squarely faces the difficulties inherent in drawing this distinction in connection with the general explanation of obligation that he gives in the first book of *De jure naturae*. The key difficulties that Pufendorf must successfully address there are presented by the conception of natural obligation that informs an argument on the origin and grounds of obligation that Hobbes presents in the fifteenth chapter of *De cive*, i.e., the chapter which bears the title "Of the Kingdom of God by Nature [*De Regno Dei per naturam*]". Pufendorf provides detailed criticism intended to refute this argument; but before assessing the criticism, a brief summary of Hobbes's argument itself is here in order.

Like all of Hobbes's pivotal arguments, the deductive argument running through §§ 1–7 of *De cive* XV is so tightly wound that the attempt to summarize it inevitably distorts its logical progression and fails to do justice to its rhetorical balance (not to mention its sheer eloquential force). So let me focus here merely on the preliminary assumptions and the clusters of inference steps that are directly relevant to Pufendorf's refuting argument:

(1) In accordance with what is established in the preceding chapters of *De cive*, we must recognize that the rational precepts by which the condition of ab-

---

[104] On the problem of obligation in modern natural-law theories, see the sources cited in note 103 as well as Gregor 1993, pp. 52–60. More generally, for discussion of issues concerning the normative authority of natural law (especially in relation to the reception of Hobbes), see Dreitzel 2003; Hartung 1999; Hüning 2002; Hüning 2007b; Lloyd 2001; Palladini 1990; Palladini 2007; Zurbuchen 2004.

solute liberty and universal enmity is avoided are precepts that qualify as laws of nature. In keeping with this recognition, we must also acknowledge that we must obey those who hold sovereign power insofar as our obedience is compatible with the commandments of God.[105]

(2) One is said to reign (*regnare*) if one rules (*regere*) by precepts and threats; but one can be said to rule by precepts only if one somehow openly declares these precepts to those who are to be ruled. One of ways in which God's laws are declared is by the silent dictates of right reason (*per tacita rectae rationis dictamina*), and these dictates furnish laws of the natural domain that God rules by precepts.[106]

(3) The natural domain subject to these laws, i.e., the kingdom (*regnum*) in which God rules through dictates of right reason, is one that excludes non-rational beings as well as human beings who fail or refuse to recognize God's rule. It is therefore a universal kingdom with respect to all those who acknowledge the divine power on account of the rational nature that is common to everyone.[107] Within this universal kingdom, the right to reign (*ius regnandi*) can arise from the agreement (*pactum*) to abolish each rational being's natural right to all things, i.e., the agreement based on the idea that the universal exercise of this *ius in omnia* is inconsistent with the dictation of right reason. Yet the right to reign can also derive directly from nature itself by the very fact that nature has not taken it away.[108] Thus, if there were (or ever had been) a human being whose power could not be resisted even by the united strength of all others combined, his right of dominion (*jus dominij*) would obtain without restriction precisely because of his pre-eminent power. For there would have been no reason whatsoever for him to give up the right granted to him by nature.[109]

(4) The conclusion just drawn applies *a fortiori* to God's right to rule in the kingdom of nature, and consequently to his right to rule over all *members* of this universal natural domain. In the kingdom of nature, then, God's *ius dominandi* with respect to all rational beings is simply a function of divine omnipotence, as is clear from the consideration of the right to punish that is conjoined with such a right to rule by precepts:

---

[105] *De cive* XV.1.
[106] *De cive* XV.3
[107] "quodque uniuersale est in omnes qui diuinam agnoscunt potentiam, propter naturam rationalem omnibus commune" (*De cive* XV.4).
[108] "A Natura idem ius deriuatur, eo ipso quod a natura non sit sublatum" (*De cive* XV.5).
[109] "ratio quare de iure sibi a natura concesso decederet nulla omnino fuisset" (*De cive* XV.5).

> For those whose power cannot be resisted, and thus for God *omnipotent*, the right of dominion is derived from the *power* itself. And however often God punishes, or even kills, a sinner, it is not to be said that He could not justly have afflicted him, or even killed him, even if he had not sinned.[110] (*De cive* XV.5 [Silverthorne/Tuck translation slightly modified])

(5) Since God's right to reign is based on nothing apart from the irresistible power that we must attribute to God as an omnipotent being, it is evident that human beings, *qua* rational agents, incur the obligation to obey God solely on account of their weakness relative to God's power. For the kind of obligation that can arise from agreement has no possible application when the right to command (*ius imperandi*) arises from the nature of irresistible power itself. Our obligation to obey God must therefore be understood as a form of obligation that we incur in virtue of our capacity for reason-determined action in the face of God's irresistible power. This is the type of obligation that we must think of as a relation born of fear, or the consciousness of one's own weakness in the face of divine power (*a metu, siue imbecillitatis propriae (respectu diuinae potentiae) conscientia*).[111] It is the natural bond in the face of which of which reason dictates, and our savior counsels (*admonere*), that no one with insufficient power to resist ought to "kick against the pricks" (*non esse calcitrandum contra stimulum*).[112]

What we have here, then, is an uncompromisingly voluntarist account of the role of God's power in relation to the basis of natural obligation.[113] Hobbes's ar-

---

110 "Iis igitur quorum potentiae resisti non potest, & per consequens Deo *omnipotenti*, ius dominandi ab ipsa *potentia* deriuatur. Et quotiescunque Deus peccatorem punit, vel etiam interficit, etsi ideo puniat quia peccauerat, non tamen dicendum est non potuisse eum eundem iuste affligere, vel etiam occidere, etsi non peccasset".

111 *De cive* XV.7.

112 *De cive* XV.7. The New Testament text of reference is *Actus apostolorum* 26:14: "omnesque nos cum decidissemus in terram audivi vocem loquentem mihi hebraica lingua Saule Saule quid me persequeris durum est tibi contra stimulum calcitrare". The King James version translates: "And when we were all fallen to the earth, I heard a voice speaking unto me, and saying in the Hebrew tongue, 'Saul, Saul, why persecutest thou me? it is hard for thee to kick against the pricks'".

113 The account is in fact so uncompromising that it may well be, strictly speaking, a misnomer to call it 'voluntarist' at all. It should be noted in this connection that Hobbes's account does not explicitly employ any concept of will. Moreover, it is apparent that the argument of *De cive* XV.1–7 involves, in effect, the reduction of divine *voluntas* to the exercise of God's omnipotent power to command. But this is not the place to go into detail concerning Hobbes' concepts of the will. At least for the purposes of this chapter, it seems advisable to stay close to conventional terminology when referring to Hobbes' omnipotentialist reduction of the voluntarist position. Hobbes's 'reductive voluntarism' or 'hypervolunterism' should work well enough.

gument on natural obligation is constructed with (literally!) sovereign disregard for any normatively relevant factor apart from what he takes to be the conceptual link between the supreme being's coercive power and the deontic requirements of right reason: the *dictamina rationis rectae*. It is, of course, true that the voice of "our savior" (i.e., Jesus) does not *threaten* even when he admonishes the recalcitrant but insufficiently powerful man (namely Paul, as described in *Acts* 26:12–20) not to act contrary to right reason's dictation by freely disobeying the commanding power of God. Yet that is merely because threats made by even the holiest of (previously) human agents are quite beside the point where liberty is excluded by weakness and fear, and where God's omnipotence necessarily excludes all human hope of being able to resist what God wills.[114] To the question why one *ought* to render obedience to irresistible power, Hobbes's response is in effect the following. It is contrary to the most basic principles of reason-determined action—that is to say: it is contrary to the fundamental requirements of natural law—to think that one can do otherwise than one can do, and necessarily will do. Thus, what one may desire to do is simply irrelevant to what one ought to do when there is no possibility of doing otherwise than one can and will do.

Hobbes's *De cive* argument on the ground of obligation in the kingdom of God by nature thus addresses the conceptual difficulty of drawing the distinction between bare external compulsion and obligation by portraying the conditions under which such a distinction is necessarily irrelevant to any human being who has the capacity to know the fundamental requirements of reason-determined action. Pufendorf, who of course recognizes full well that his own theory of obligation is beset by same sort of difficulty, tries to work out an alternative solution by subjecting Hobbes's reductive argument to systematic criticism and refutation in *De jure naturae*. I will discuss this criticism and attempted refutation in some detail before turning to Pufendorf's alternative solution.

Pufendorf's criticism of Hobbes in DJN I.6.10 (GW 4.1: 76) has four main components. The first component—let us call it the 'non-equivalence' objection—focuses on two pivotal assertions involved in Hobbes' attempt to show that the right to command (*ius imperandi*) is attributable to some agents simply by virtue of their irresistible strength (*vires*). The assertions are these: (a) this right can be something granted (*concessum*) by nature; and (b) it can derive from nature by the very fact that it is not taken away (*non sublatum*) by nature. Pufendorf points

---

[114] Needless to say, this is hardly the point of the biblical story about what happened to Paul on the road to Damascus. Yet it is a Hobbesian point *entailed* by the *De cive* argument that makes use of this story.

out that Hobbes's demonstration of the right to command in the kingdom of nature hinges on the substitutional equivalence of *non sublatum* and *concessum esse*. But he also contends that the assumption of such equivalence is illicit because the expressions do not mean the same thing. Thus, according to Pufendorf, it is possible for the *ius imperandi* at issue to be granted by something *other* than nature itself, even if it is not taken away by nature.

A second target of Pufendorf's criticism is Hobbes's purported employment of the principle "nature has given the right to all things [*Natura dedit ius in Omnia*]" in his characterization of the relationship between God and nature. Pufendorf holds that this principle can have no intelligible application to God's relation to nature. For whether we interpret nature as God itself or else as the product of the transcendent God's creative activity, nature cannot *give* anything to God as the being that necessarily lacks nothing.[115] Call this the '*natura non dedit*' objection.

A third objection considers the relation between weakness and power. Pufendorf holds that Hobbes is just wrong to conclude that human beings are obligated to obey God because of their weakness. Taken by itself, the fact of weakness can provide nothing more than a ground for judging that it is stupid (*stultus*) not to avoid evil by obeying God when evil (*qua* human prick-kicking ill-being) is the unavoidable consequence of disobedience to God. It does not take away a human agent's *right* to desire escape from subjection to God's power or, for that matter, the right to desire escape from subjection to any other agent with superior power. Nor does it take away the right to use all possible means to escape such subjection. Call this the 'stupidity of resistance' objection.

A fourth objection focuses on what Pufendorf takes to be Hobbes's basic understanding of the relationship between obligation, power, and right: Even if we accept that each human being is permitted, by right of nature, to use his natural powers against whomever his reason dictates their use, this does not entail that anyone else is thereby obligated to anything at all. For 'to obligate' (*obligare*) is conceptually distinct from 'to compel' (*cogere*); and while an act of compelling someone can achieve its end (i.e., constraining someone to do what one wills) simply through the exercise of natural powers, no act of obligating can be so performed. As Hobbes himself recognizes, everyone existing in the state of nature

---

[115] This argument rests on the assumption that any coherent account of God, including the Spinozistic account, must involve the understanding of God as *ens perfectissimum*, and thus as the one possible being that necessarily lacks nothing. Pufendorf evidently regards this assumption as something too obvious to require explicit mention—as indeed it is.

§ 3 "Kick Not Against the Pricks": Pufendorf and Hobbes on Natural Obligation — 229

has the right to compel anyone else, just as anyone (or everyone) resists by right those who desire to compel them.[116] But wherever (and whenever) there is a *right* to resist, there can be no obligation not to do so. Thus, even granting (for the sake of argument) Hobbes' conceptual specification of *ius in omnia* as well as the description of the state of nature that this specification generates, Hobbes' argument on natural obligation lacks the logical wherewithal needed for drawing the conclusion that obligation can arise as a normatively grounded relation simply from the irresistible power of a being superior in strength. Call this the 'conceptual misunderstanding' objection.

How telling are these objections to Hobbes' position on natural obligation?

Non-equivalence: Consider the semantic distinction that Pufendorf draws between *non sublatum* and *concessum* (*esse*) in order to show that the right of command at issue in Hobbes's account of *ius regendi* does not necessarily depend on nature. The distinction itself, of course, is quite apt. Yet it is not at all clear how the conclusion of Pufendorf's initial line of attack—i.e., the assertion that it is possible for the *ius imperandi* at issue to be granted by something other than nature itself, even if it is not taken away by nature—could do damage to Hobbes's argument in *De cive* XV. That is because Hobbes by no means denies that this right to command can arise from a principle other than that of nature. Indeed, he explicitly underscores how such a right can arise from agreement (*ex pacto*).[117] Thus, it seems that Hobbes could very handily agree with Pufendorf's distinction between 'not taking away' and 'granting' a right while still maintaining that the *ius imperandi* in question can be a right that depends on nature. For any right that depends on nature, and not on human agreement, may be considered a right granted by nature. And even if it is taken away, either by nature or by human agreement, it can still be considered a right that originally was granted by nature, and not by human agreement.

Natura non dedit: This second objection may seem oddly misplaced in view of the fact that Hobbes' argument in *De cive* XV does not explicitly employ the principle that nature originally has given the right to all things. Nevertheless, Pufendorf is arguably on target, at least in the sense that the concept of the right to all things (*ius in omnia*) does figure in the sections of *De cive* XV under consideration. Moreover, the principle that nature bestows right is obviously a key feature of Hobbes' thinking in this same chapter. This being the case, however, the notion that nature has given a right to God must involve the same basic under-

---

116 "Nam ex mente Hobbesii in statu naturali uti jus est alios cogendi; ita alii cogentibus jure resistant" (DJN I.6.10/ GW 4.1: 76).

117 Establishing that, and showing how, such a right arises *ex pacto*, after all, is the whole point of the theory of *imperium* presented in the second part of *De cive*.

standing of 'giving' that we encounter in the notion of nature's giving of right to human beings. Hobbes already clarifies what the latter notion involves when, in the first chapter of *De cive*, he indicates the way in which we must understand the juridical, biblical, and popular commonplace "nature has given everything to everyone [*natura dedit omia omnibus*]"—notably, as a way of expressing the *permissibility* of having all things and doing all things without being subject to deontic constraint.[118] Thus, as far as the argument of *De cive* XV is concerned, nature's giving of *ius* to God has to be interpreted with reference to the different degrees of power attributable to human beings and to God. Because of their limited powers, human beings are *by nature* subject to a fundamental constraint insofar as they are rational agents. Specifically, they are subject to the requirement not to perform actions that are inconsistent with self-preservation.[119] This requirement, however, pertains to the most basic necessary condition of continuing finite agency. It has no application to God. God cannot be *subject* to such a requirement precisely because its power is incomparably greater than the powers of anything and everything apart from God that could limit the conservation of its existence, thereby principally restricting its power to act. As long as God's omnipotence is granted, then, there is no possible external constraint on divine power. And such power is always exercised as God wills,[120] without reference to possible constraint or limitation. Even if God wills to restrict its own power to act, this self-constraining limitation on the exercise of divine power will still be placed *only* as God wills, and only so long as God actually *wills* to restrict its power through self-constraint.[121] Thus, since not even self-constraint furnishes a possible limitation on God's *power* to act, it makes perfectly good sense to characterize nature as giving (or having given) a right to God whenever God is thought of as exercising power over all members of its kingdom *by* nature.

Stupidity of resistance: I take it that a Hobbesian response to this sort of objection must run roughly as follows. As is clear from the counsel that Jesus gives

---

[118] See *De cive* I.10.
[119] See *De cive* I.9–10 and 15 in conjunction with *De cive* II.1–2.
[120] That is to say: is always exercised simply *as* the exercise of God's infinite and irresistible commanding power. On this point, see note 113 in this chapter.
[121] In other words: the self-constraining limitation imposed on the exercise of God's power will be a limitation imposed only *as* the exercise of God's infinite and irresistible power; and it must therefore be a limitation imposed *only insofar* as God continues to exercise such unrestricted power of self-constraint. Obviously, there is not much normative content of the will left for God (or anyone else) to work with here. Yet *that*, arguably (cf. note 113), is exactly Hobbes's implicitly reductive point with regard to the will of God.

§ 3 "Kick Not Against the Pricks": Pufendorf and Hobbes on Natural Obligation — 231

to Paul concerning the futility of kicking against pricks,[122] it is unquestionably stupid to disobey the commanding power of an irresistibly powerful being. We can therefore perfectly well agree with Pufendorf's acknowledgment of this practical truth. We can also agree with Pufendorf's point that accepting this same truth is by no means inconsistent with attributing to a human being the right to desire escape from subjection to another rational being with superior power. Yet having a right to desire escape from subjection to another does not imply that one also has the right to use all possible means to escape it. For it does not follow that one may *do* everything possible to escape the subjecting power of another rational being if it *is* impossible to escape that power on account of the omnipotence of the other agent. There can be no right to do what is impossible to do, and there can be no right to use the means to an impossible end. Nor can there be a right to act contrary to the dictates of right reason as long as these deontic requirements pertain to the fundamental laws of human action, i.e., the laws by which "a man is forbidden to do, that, which is destructive of his life, or taketh away the means of preserving the same; and to omit, that, by which he thinketh it may be *best* preserved" (*Leviathan* XIV.3).[123] There is no right of stupidity—no *ius stultitiae*—that that is compatible with the universal *dictation* of right reason, which is what grounds our natural obligation to obey these laws of self-preservation.

Conceptual misunderstanding: Consider the charge that Hobbes has no theoretical purchase on the nature of the relationship between the concepts of obligation, power, and right, which is arguably the most substantial objection that Pufendorf brings against Hobbes. Presumably, Hobbes's response would be that this objection fundamentally misconstrues the role played by the concept of *ius in omnia* in the description of the kingdom of nature, and that it consequently misinterprets the whole account of the basis of natural obligation in this domain. That concept is indeed employed in order to establish the logical connection between *ius imperandi* and irresistible power. But establishing this connection serves only to clarify the necessary condition for there being a natural obligation to obey the commands of a superior being. Grounding the obligation itself requires, in addition, reason's prescription that all those who acknowledge the power and providence of God are "not to kick against the pricks". Thus, evidently contrary to what Pufendorf supposes, it is the universally prescriptive role of right reason, and not the concept of irresistible power *as such*, that supplies the

---

[122] Why anyone would wish to renounce the glories of Jacobean English in favor of a more modern rendering of *Acts* 26:14 (see note 112) is quite beyond me.
[123] *Lev.* XIV.3—italics mine. See also the *De cive* passages cited in note 119 of this chapter.

logical lynchpin of Hobbes's view of natural obligation in *De cive* XV. This should be obvious from the fact that, according to Hobbes, no one who refuses to accept God's precepts or threats can be counted as members of the kingdom of God by nature.[124] For however weak or strong—or however stupid or intelligent—such a rational being may be, it will not be conscious of its *own* weakness with respect to the divine power that it thinks itself strong enough to resist, or simply disregard. And where there is no such consciousness of weakness in relation to God's power—thus, where there is no fear of God—there can be no natural *obligation* to obey God. Even if all natural beings are necessarily ruled by the power of God, and even if God's right to reign and punish derives from irresistible power alone, reason does not dictate to *me* that I *ought* not to kick against the pricks, unless I acknowledge that such a restriction placed upon my power of acting is a constraint set by God. If it exists, this sort of constraint unquestionably presents an irresistible obstacle to the exercise of my power, whether I know this or not. But nothing binds me to *non-resistance* unless I acknowledge the constraint-imposing power of God for what it is. Although I may be stupid and a fool if I do not acknowledge this power, I am still not subject to any *natural* obligation as a *member* of God's kingdom by nature in the event that I reject, or simply fail to recognize, the fundamental condition of membership in that natural domain. Yet if I do recognize such constraint-imposing power for what it is— namely, as recognizably irresistible power—then it is a deontic requirement of reason itself that I must also acknowledge the impossibility of my doing otherwise than I am bound to do, and necessarily will do, when I am bound to act in virtue of irresistible power. Such is the character and the basis of natural obligation in God's kingdom by nature as long as stupidity in acting is incompatible with laws of nature as dictates of right reason. And it is undeniably stupid

---

[124] Cf. Zagorin 2000, p. 28. Hobbes' stipulation of the conditions for membership in God's kingdom by nature is quite stringent: "Soli [...] in Regno Dei censendi sunt, qui ipsum & rectorum omnium rerum esse, & *praecepta* hominibus *dedisse*, & *poenas* in transgressores *statuisse* agnoscunt. Caeteros non subditos, sed hostes Dei appellare debemus [The only ones to be numbered in the kingdom of God are those who acknowledge him as the ruler of all things, that He has *given precepts* to human beings and *set penalties* for transgressors. The rest we should not call subjects, but enemies of God]" (*De cive* XV.2 [Silverthorne/Tuck translation slightly modified]; cf. *De cive* XIV.19).

In view of these conditions, one may well find the possibility of relations of mutual obligation between all non-members of God's natural domain to be hope-inspiring—especially if one believes (as I am inclined to believe) that Hobbes provides a conceptually adequate account of the connection between natural obligation and the power of God.

§ 3 "Kick Not Against the Pricks": Pufendorf and Hobbes on Natural Obligation — 233

for me to think that I can do otherwise than I am bound to do when irresistible power is what constrains me to act as I must.

It seems clear that the overall result of Pufendorf's frontal assault against Hobbes' hypervoluntarist portrayal of obligation in God's kingdom by nature is a good deal less than conclusive. Even if we accept this, however, it still does not follow that Pufendorf's general theory of obligation lacks the resources needed to provide a coherent alternative to the opposing doctrines of natural obligation offered by Cumberland and Hobbes. To determine whether these resources are in fact available, let us consider more closely the constructive account of obligation that Pufendorf gives in DJN I.6.12 (GW 4.1: 79) shortly after his criticism of Hobbes.

According to Pufendorf, powers do not suffice to generate obligation since they simply are not enough to bind any agent to the *will* of another.[125] Thus, if obligation is to take place, it is further requisite that one should have received some signal benefits (*insignia quaedam bona*) on account of another agent's volition, or at least that one should give one's consent to another agent's guidance (*directio*). For inasmuch as we naturally yield ourselves to someone from whom we have received many benefits, there is no reason to question a benefactor's commanding governance (*imperium*) if it appears that he both wills our good and can consult it better than we ourselves can do. This is true especially if the benefactor is the being to whom we are beholden for our very existence. Thus, we can see that the force of all obligations flows from the sources just mentioned (i.e., from our consent to being guided by another as well as from another being's benevolence in general and the existence-bestowing beneficence of God in particular). It is this force that forges the inner bond (*intrinsecum vinculum*) on the liberty of our wills; and this *inner* bond is what allows us to distinguish between obligation and compulsion. While obligations derive their final *strength and stability* from the fear of some agent who has the power to inflict ill or evil upon on those who would act in violation of what they are bound to do, obligation as such cannot be understood in abstraction from the intrinsic moral bond that is founded on the benefit-bestowing quality of the volitional acts by which a superior has just cause to limit our liberty of will.[126]

Given Pufendorf's theory of the binding character of natural law, of course, we can see that there are two key difficulties that emerge from the general explanation of the origin of obligation just summarized. First, it is not apparent

---

125 "non solas vires sufficere, ut mihi ex alterius voluntate obligatio nascatur" (DJN I.6.12/GW 4.1: 79). This assertion implicitly opposes Hobbes' 'omnipotentialist' reduction of the voluntarist position: see again note 113.
126 Cf. DJN I.6.9/GW 4.1: 75.

how this explanation could satisfactorily come to grips with the question of whether the laws of nature can in any sense bind us to the performance of *external* actions independently of the power of a superior. Thus, Pufendorf's general explanation might offer a promising way to demonstrate that precepts of natural law have binding force *in foro interno* without (like Cumberland) linking them to the promotion of the obligated agent's own happiness—or even (like Hobbes) tying them to self-preservation in the face of irresistible power. Yet it is not clear how that explanation could provide an adequate basis for establishing that those precepts bind us to the performance of external actions without some essential grounding reference to a superior's power to compel obedience to law.[127]

Second, Pufendorf's insistence that the origin of obligation must be understood in terms of the connection between beneficence and fitting responsiveness to the benevolent aims of a benefactor seems just inconsistent with the element of formalistic voluntarism on which he bases his conception of the fundamental law of nature's prescriptive import. According to this conception, as we have seen, both this law and the particular precepts of duty that it grounds must be considered morally binding, even in the event that no *good* to anyone could result from any action performed in accordance with the *socialitas* requirement of practical reason. Yet if all obligation is thought to depend on a benefactor's will, then it seems that the volitional acts of nature's lawgiver should have benevolence as their ultimate normative ground. Thus, as far as the fundamental law of nature and its derivative precepts of duty are concerned, it looks as though God's lawgiving acts ought to take place in conformity with a practical law of beneficence that determines or expresses the *necessarily* good-promoting character of the divine will. In that case, however, we are back on the road that led Cumberland to insist, against Hobbes, that we must make sense of the law of nature and its obligation to external actions by understanding moral necessity in terms of the causal efficacy through which the divine lawgiver coordinates the own-happiness of the particular human agent with the happiness of all finite rational beings.[128]

As long as obligation hangs on the will of God, it is hard to have it both ways without blinking at least once. How, then, does one circumvent the egoistic (and

---

[127] That is to say: while Pufendorf's general explanation of the origin of obligation might suffice for the sort of moral theology that focuses on the demands of individual conscience (see Pufendorf's introductory salutation to the reader in *De officio hominiis& civis* [GW 2: 6]), it is not clear how it can apply to the theory of natural law that Pufendorf in fact constructs.

[128] We are of course also on the road to the general repudiation of voluntarism as it applies to the theory of obligation.

proto-utilitarian) pathways of Cumberland's natural-law theory while avoiding the unflinchingly reductive voluntarist conception of natural obligation that Hobbes advocates in *De cive* XV? Arguably, one can't.[129] And Hobbes, arguably, is quite right to admonish us not to kick against the pricks so long as we take lawgiving reason to be something other than our own.[130]

§ 4 Benevolent Inclination and Reason's Lawgiving Function: Kant and Hutcheson as Mirror-Image Counterparts

I have discussed how Cumberland's treatment of the law of nature and natural obligation is exposed to Hutcheson's charge that law-based accounts of obligation fail to break the link between practical law and self-love. While it is not evident that this same charge can be made to apply directly to Pufendorf's theory of the obligation of natural law, I also claimed that the broader significance of Hutcheson's interpretive position can be clarified by examining Pufendorf's attempt to provide an alternative to the conception of natural obligation advocated by Hobbes. So just what is that significance?

As was suggested in the last section's final paragraph, one cannot have it both ways at once. That is, one cannot ground the obligation to obey the law of nature in God's lawgiving efficacy while also insisting that *all* obligation depends on the benefit-bestowing will of a superior. If this is the case, however, then the theoretically coherent alternative to the type of approach to natural obligation taken by Cumberland cannot be the one offered by Pufendorf. Instead, it turns out to be the approach epitomized by Hobbes in his portrayal of the kingdom of God by nature. According to Hobbes's portrayal, the ground of natural obligation in this domain lies in the connection that right reason forges between, on the one hand, its universally prescriptive role in human action and, on the

---

[129] Cf. Palladini 1990, p. 79; Schneewind 1998, pp. 137–137. For a different view, see Korkmann 2003; Saatsmoinen 1995. Cf. also Ludwig 2000, pp. 13–14.

[130] Please note well in this connection that Hobbes's admonition applies specifically to the relation of natural obligation treated in the third part of *De cive* (*Religio*). In this chapter I have not directly addressed the concept of natural obligation at issue in the book's first part (*Libertas*), where Hobbes argues that the essential natural equality of human beings precludes that the right of ruling and commanding can be given by sure and irresistible *power* (see *De cive* I.14–15). Thus, I have not discussed the question of obligation as it applies to Hobbes's portrayal of the condition of natural freedom. According to this portrayal, the laws that we are "by nature"—i.e., (equivalently) "by reason"—bound to keep are laws requiring the act of reciprocal agreement by which each "obligates *himself* [italics mine (J. E.)]" not to resist the "*single will* of all" that makes peace possible (see *De cive* III.27 and *De cive* V.6–7).

other hand, the constraint-imposing and irresistible power of an omnipotent being. For it is through the dictation of right reason that non-resistance to divine power is tied to the fundamental requirement of self-preservation that features in Hobbes's concept of natural law.[131] Thus, to spell out the wider ramifications of the critical broadside charge that Hutcheson levels against law-based theories, let us attempt to answer the following question in view of this deontic requirement of reason. Assuming that Hobbes provides a coherent account of natural obligation in God's kingdom by nature, how would Hutcheson's sentimentalist charge have to be loaded if it is to hit the target provided by that Hobbesian account?

Let me approach this question by emphasizing a point implicit in this chapter's preceding considerations on Hutcheson and Cumberland: That Hutchesonian charge *could* hit its Hobbesian target quite precisely if Hobbes's conception of natural obligation required the coupling of the human agent's rationally anchored capacity for self-preservation with the love of self, thus linking the motivation for law-determined action to the pursuit of one's own happiness. But is this actually the case? In other words, does Hobbes have to combine self-preservation, as a prescribed end of action, with self-love in order to offer a coherent account of natural obligation? The answer, as far as I can see, must be negative. To be sure, the combination of self-love with the creaturely impulse to self-preservation may be unproblematic as far as the tenets of Hobbes's anthropology are concerned. Be that as it may, however, his conception of the prescriptive force of natural law—i.e., the conception that Pufendorf targets when disputing

---

131 I have already called attention to this requirement when quoting Hobbes's *Leviathan* definition of the law of nature (see p. 231). The corresponding requirement in *De cive* is formulated in the definition of natural law that furnishes the conclusion of the following deduction: "[...] cum concedant omnes *iure* fieri, quod non fit contra rectam Rationem, *iniuria* factum censere debemus, quod rectae rationi repugnant, (hoc est, quod contradicit alicui veritati a veris principiis reccte ratiocinando collectae.) Quod autem *iniuria* factum est, contra *legem* aliquam fieri dicimus. Est igitur *lex* auaedam *recta Ratio*, quae (cum non minus sit pars naturae humanae, quam quaelibet alia facultas verl affectus animi) naturalis quoque dicitur. Est igitur *lex naturalis*, vt eam definiam, Dictamen rectae rationis circa ea, quae agenda vel omittenda sunt ad vitae membrorumque conseruationem, quantum fieri potest, diuturnam [(A)ll men allow that what is not done contrary to right reason is done *by right* , and therefore we must hold that what is repugnant to right reason (i.e., what contradicts some truth reached by correct reasoning from true principles) is *wrong*. But we speak of *wrong* that is done because it is done contrary to some law. Thus, *law* is a certain *right reason*, which (since it is no less a part of human nature than any other faculty or passion of the mind) is also said to be natural. The *natural law* therefore (to define it) is the Dictate of right reason about those things which are to be done or omitted for the longest possible preservation of life and limb. (Silverthorne/Tuck translation modified)]" (De cive II.1).

the Hobbesian account of natural obligation—does not logically depend on it.[132] And the reason for this independence seems straightforward enough: Instead of regarding self-preservation simply as a hormetic impulse or as an end of inclination, Hobbes implicitly treats it as an obligatory end of right reason in the definitional portrayals of natural law that his conception of natural obligation presupposes.[133]

Thus, our detour through Pufendorf's criticism of Hobbes puts us in a position to see why Hutcheson's broadside charge against law-based approaches to obligation must fall short. Its plausibility extends well enough to the type of approach taken by Cumberland; and it may well do some damage to Pufendorf as well, at least to the extent that he appeals to the benevolence of nature's lawgiver in order to alleviate the impact of his voluntarist view. But Hutcheson's charge cannot reach the self-consistently voluntarist positon taken by Hobbes for the simple reason that self-love does not feature in the concept of natural law upon which Hobbes's approach to natural obligation is based. While this approach requires that self-preservation be linked to the lawgiving function of an irresistibly powerful being, self-love plays no role in guaranteeing the connection between this function and the preservation of life and limb as right reason's obligatory end.

---

[132] Hobbes might be thought to link self-love inseparably to self-preservation in the following passage from the *Elements of Law:* "And forasmuch as necessity of nature maketh men to will and desire *bonum sibi*, which is good for themselves, and to avoid that which is hurtful; but most of all that terrible enemy of nature, death, from whom we expect both the loss of all power, and also the greatest of bodily pains in the losing; it is not against reason that a man doth all he can to preserve his own body and limbs, both from death and pain. And that which is not against reason, men call RIGHT, or *jus*, or blameless liberty of using our own natural power and ability. It is therefore a *right of nature:* that every man may preserve his own life and limbs, with all the power he hath" (Elements XIV.6). But the *bonum sibi* specifically relevant to the derivation of natural right is here self-preservation as the *primum bonorum* (De homine XI.6; cf. De homine XI.15), i.e., the primary good among all other goods that one may desire for oneself. Besides, a *right* of nature, according to Hobbes, is what grounds moral permissibility. It is not a *law*, which specifies a deontic requirement of reason.

[133] See note 131 in this chapter, especially the final sentence of the passage quoted. The defined natural law, which in *De cive* is the dictate of right reason pertaining to the means of the maximal conservation of life and limb, tacitly makes self-preservation the *originally* obligatory end of our actions. Similarly (see again *Leviathan* XIV.3), a law that prohibits a human being from (i) performing life-destructive actions and (ii) omitting actions that best preserve life is a law of nature that makes self-preservation an obligatory end by direct implication. (If it is impermissible for me *not* to act in keeping with the conditions of self-preservation just mentioned, then I am obligated to satisfy those conditions. That is, I am bound to promote, as best I can, self-preservation as an end that is also a duty.)

Now if Hutcheson's sentimentalist criticism of law-based theories cannot stretch even to Hobbes's conception of natural obligation, much less will it be to do damage to the approach to obligation involved in a theory of reason's autonomy that explicitly eschews the connection between the prescriptive force of practical law and the principle of self-love or one's own happiness. But before turning once again to Kant's relation to Hutcheson, there is one further point to underscore concerning Hutcheson's approach to obligation and law. We can bring out this point against the broader backdrop of the modern reception of Stoic *oikeiôsis* doctrine discussed in chapter 9.

As was explained in the first section of this current chapter (see pp. 206–219), Hutcheson insists that the subjective source of benevolence is completely independent of self-love. His refutations of motivational egoism are intended to clarify and uphold the metaphysical distinction between, on the one hand, the original determination of the human soul that gives rise to other-directed benevolent inclination and, on the other hand, the source of the human agent's inclination to pursue her own good or advantage. The crucial point for us to note at this juncture is therefore the following one. To the extent that those refutations are successful, Hutcheson implicitly undercuts the venerable single-source interpretation of individual and social *oikeiôsis* that was discussed in the final section of chapter 9 in connection with Rousseau's project of rethinking of the non-rational conditions of human agency.[134]

That discussion of Rousseau was guided by this question: Why did Kant not hold that his principle of the will's autonomy merited a rethinking of the affective or sense-based conditions of human agency that was at least as radical as Rousseau's? And the answer turned out to be this: From Kant's perspective, from the mid-1760s onwards, Rousseau's moral anthropology does not ultimately involve any basic tenet that is clearly inconsistent with the view of empirically conditioned practical reason that Kant would go on to develop in his major works on the foundations of the doctrine of morals. In particular, Rousseau's theory of human nature turns out to be broadly consistent with Kant's critical view that all material practical principles belong under the general principle of self-love or one's own happiness. It is precisely this *kind* of view, however, that is called into question when Hutcheson tacitly repudiates the single-source interpretation on his way toward rejecting all law-based theories of obligation.

---

[134] See again the textual passages already cited when discussing Hutcheson in second section of chapter 8 (pp. 177–178). For closely related passages in which the single-source interpretation is explicitly or implicitly targeted, see Butler 2006 [1726], pp. 39, 42–44, 111, 113–116, 120. Regarding Butler's relation to Stoic ethical thought, see Brook 2012, pp. 165–167; Irwin 2003, pp. 274–300.

I will be concerned with this implication of Hutcheson's theory of morals in the next chapter, where I treat the role played by the Stoic idea of the *honestum* in various eighteenth-century debates concerning moral worth. As we move toward the consideration of that idea, the main thing for us to bear in mind is this: Given his explicitly stated concern to isolate the explanatory basis of obligation from all concepts of law and lawgiving, Hutcheson is perhaps further removed from the foundations of Kant's theory of the autonomy of reason than any other major figure in modern moral philosophy's history—at least any figure with whose writings Kant was acquainted. The key structural elements of Hutcheson's portrayal of the relationship between the sensible nature of human beings and practical law are diametrically opposed to the corresponding elements of the portrayal that Kant would come to endorse during the 1760s, and thereafter, in wake of his study of Rousseau. Hutcheson's and Kant's foundational accounts of obligation and law are in fact mirror-image counterparts.

Given the nature of the opposition just described, we can well understand why Kant would come to take a position diametrically opposed to Hutcheson's stance on the affective conditions of human moral motivation and obligation. In particular, we can discern why it would be (and indeed was) reasonable for Kant in effect to reverse the Hutchesonian sentimentalist view of the proper relationship between the sensible nature of human beings and law-determined action when he came to recognize the far-reaching systematic significance of Rousseau's juridico-philosophic idea of the self-legislative function of a unitary will. Yet we can also grasp how that straightforward reversal of theoretical orientation with respect to the sentimentalist view leaves Kant with an interpretation of material practical principles and empirically conditioned practical reason that is both highly questionable on its own terms, given the egoistic assumptions that underlie it, and not required by the strictly formalistic understanding of the autonomy of the will that grounds his theory of morally practical reason. Rousseau still has a great deal to teach us about why this is so. But it is Hutcheson's de facto, if implicit, repudiation of the venerable single-source interpretation of Stoic *oikeiôsis* doctrine that points the way toward a non-reductive theory of affective motivational conditions which is consistent with the idea of reason's autonomy.

Chapter 11 Kant and the Role of the *Honestum* in Sentimentalist and Rationalist Ethics

§ 1 Retrospectus and Hume's Puzzling Letter to Hutcheson

This is the last main chapter devoted to treating the foundational elements of Kant's ethics against its historical backdrop. (Chapter 12 examines the historical significance of Kant's juridical theory of original acquisition, and the concluding chapter takes its cues from post-Kantian developments that concern contemporary ethical theory and the theory of distributive justice.) It will therefore be useful to begin by repainting in very broad strokes the main strands and stages of the overall argument that has brought us to this point.

Chapter 1 brought out the pivotal significance of Kant's metaphysical exposition of the a priori concept of obligatory end that underlies his doctrine of virtue: It is only on the basis of the concept of an end that is also a duty that others' happiness and one's own perfection can be coherently thought of as a priori given ends that we are bound to promote; and without building such promotable ends into the foundations of his metaphysical theory of morals by introducing that a priori concept, Kant's crucial architectonic division of labor between the juridical theory of right and ethics as a doctrine of virtue cannot be grounded by analysis of the distinctive roles that juridical and ethical lawgiving must play with respect to the different kinds of duties presented by the laws of morally practical reason.

The investigations concerning Kant's ethics that have been pursued since chapter 2 stem from a fundamental problem that is inherent in that metaphysical exposition: If the ends that are also duties are also ends that supply *material* determining grounds of the power of choice, then why is it that no *empirically* grounded maxim can furnish a practical law? In other words, why can no such maxim furnish a practical law, even though (given Kant's basic definitional considerations on maxims and laws as propositions) it seems that some empirically grounded maxims of ends ought to qualify for a universal lawgiving without further ado?

I argued that one essential condition must be satisfied if this question is to be answered in the way that Kant evidently thinks it should be: No a priori given end of pure practical reason, i.e., no end that is also a duty, can *also* be an end of inclination if it is to be "set up against the end arising from sensible impulses" (TL 6:381.13–14). I also argued that Kant can regard the latter type of end, i.e., the end arising from sensible impulses, as the self-seeking end that figures in maxims of self-love: one's own happiness. Thus, since own-happiness regarded as a (or, indeed, as *the*) self-seeking end of inclination is one that can readily serve for the empirical grounding of maxims, it seemed that the solution to our problem concerning material determining grounds, empirically grounded maxims, and practical laws ought to lie in the following supposition: All empirically grounded maxims are in, some sense, maxims of self-love.

While we found significant support for this initially promising solution in the theorematic assumptions of Kant's account of empirically conditioned practical reason in the *Critique of Practical Reason*, we also saw that the proposed solution collapses when it is even-handedly applied to both facets of the dualistic theory of obligatory ends that generates the problem to begin with. It was precisely this collapse, however, that allowed us to exploit a key aspect of asymmetry exhibited by Kant's two obligatory ends, thereby extending the scope of our investigations to include his doctrine of the moral worth. This opportunity for extension is what led to the assessment of Kant's *Groundwork* account of actions' moral worth in view of the sentimentalist alternative account proved by Hume. The outcome of this assessment, explained at the end of chapter 5, was to put in place a provisional platform for delivering an effective Kantian response to the kind of sentimentalist position on the moral worth of actions that is implicit in the 'undoubted maxim' of Hume's *Treatise*.

The investigations on Kant's ethics (as distinguished from his juridical theory of right) carried out since chapter 5 have aimed to ascertain whether this platform can bear the weight of the theory of reason's obligatory ends that Kant first presents in finished form in the 1797 Introduction to Doctrine of Virtue. Those investigations have been shaped primarily by issues pertaining to Kant's early (1760s) relation to Hutcheson and Rousseau. But I advanced these issues by focusing on several problematic features of the 1788 classification of "all previous *material* principles of morality" (KpV 39.6–7) that Kant offers in the *Critique of Practical Reason* on the basis of his view of the relationship between material practical principles and self-love. Thus, the discussion of the parallels between Rousseau's portrayal of individual moral development and the historically prevalent single-source interpretation of Stoic *oikeiôsis* doctrine put us in a position to understand how Kant—despite his early attempt to combine a perfectionist version of the supreme principle of obligation with material principles of obligation and moral cognition—would ultimately (by 1788) come to regard even the Stoic principle of internal perfection as assimilable to Epicurean eudaimonism. Moreover, it was in view of those same parallels that I went on to consider Hutcheson's approach to the source of obligation. I asked what happens if this sentimentalist and non-reductive approach to the subjective source of obligation undercuts the type of portrayal of affective motivational conditions that Kant (by the second half of the 1760s decade) shares with Rousseau as well as with the venerable single-source interpretation of Stoic *oikeiôsis*. It was in response to this question that I examined Hutcheson's criticism of law-based conceptions of obligation.

I discussed this criticism's applicability to Cumberland's and Pufendorf's respective conceptions of natural obligation. And by paying close attention to Hobbes's conception of reason's originally obligatory end, I also I also brought out its essential limitation with respect to law-based theories of obligation in general. But our response is still far from being finished. For we still have to understand exactly what follows if Hutcheson's foundational account of obligation is thought to provide for a sentimentalist doctrine of action's moral worth that could compete with the corresponding doctrine that is implicit in Kant's theory of morally practical reason's obligatory ends.

In this eleventh chapter, then, I will continue our line of response by extending once again the scope of the historical investigations pursued thus far—this time by including in it another element of Stoic moral philosophy that had a decisive impact on modern doctrines of moral worth. Specifically, I will consider certain parts played by the Stoic idea of the *honestum* in eighteenth-century sentimentalist and rationalist ethics.

Needless to say, discussing this idea's multifaceted impact makes for an exceedingly broad field of inquiry. So I will have to narrow the field to the point that it can be sensibly cultivated in the space of a single chapter. I will thus endeavor to clarify the significance of the *honestum* for certain dimensions of eighteenth-century sentimentalist ethics by building upon the considerations on Hume and Hutcheson already presented in chapters 4 and 10. As for the rationalist side of the theoretical divide in question, I will pay special attention to the role played by the *honestum* in Thomas Reid's criticism of Hume's account of actions' moral worth. In effect, then, I will examine various parts assigned to the idea of the *honestum* in the views of moral worth held by three major figures of Scottish Enlightenment philosophy. I do this, however, with the aim of coming to grips with the theory of moral worth at issue in Kant's account of morally practical reason's obligatory ends.

To begin our advance toward achieving the aim just mentioned, let me quote one of the more intriguing passages in the history of modern ethics, which is found in a well-known letter of Hume to Hutcheson dated September 17, 1739:[135]

> You are a great admirer of *Cicero*, as well as I am. Please to review the 4th book, *de finibus bonorum & malorum*; where you find him prove against the *Stoics*, that if there be no other

---

[135] For discussion concerning the background of this letter as well as its ramifications for Hume's professional relationship with Hutcheson, see Moore 2002, pp. 376–379.

Goods but Virtue, tis impossible there can be any Virtue; because the Mind would then want all Motives to begin its Actions upon: And tis on the Goodness or Badness of the Motives that the Virtue of the Action depends. This proves, that to every virtuous Action there must be a Motive or impelling Passion distinct from the Virtue, & that Virtue can never be the sole Motive to any Action. You do not assent to this; tho' I think there is no Proposition more certain or important. I must own my Proofs were not distinct enough, & must be altered. (*Letters* [Grieg] 1:35)

A rather puzzling interpretive issue immediately arises in view of the lines just quoted: Why is Hutcheson, whose approach to the foundations of morals is in many respects similar to Hume's, unwilling to assent to what Hume wants to establish by appealing to what Cicero proves?[136]

In order to respond effectively to this query, we will have to determine what Hutcheson does not assent to. There is of course no question here that Hume wants Hutcheson to assent to the proposition at issue, i.e., to the proposition that Hume wants to prove when he calls attention to his view of the dependency relation between "the Virtue of the Action" and "the Goodness or Badness of the Motives".[137] Yet acknowledging what Hume would like Hutcheson to do *regarding* this proposition does not suffice to determine precisely what it is that Hutcheson does not assent to when *Cicero's* argument against the Stoics is brought into play. For Hume's appeal to this argument leaves open three distinct ways of understanding the point of contention between Hutcheson and Hume. First, Hutcheson could reject the proposition itself that Hume wants to prove as certain by appealing to Cicero's anti-Stoic argument. Second, Hutcheson could hold that what Cicero proves against the Stoics does not in fact establish the proposition that Hume wants to prove as certain.[138] Third, it may be that Hutcheson rejects both Hume's proposition itself and Hume's claim that Cicero's proof against the Stoics can serve to establish that proposition's certainty.

---

136 See note 179 in this chapter.
137 In the passage quoted, Hume is evidently not claiming that the assumption stated after the colon ("And tis on the Goodness [...] the Virtue of the Action depends") is part of *Cicero's* proof against the Stoics. In the preceding paragraph of the 1739 letter Hume writes: "I cannot forbear recommending another thing to your Consideration. Actions are not virtuous nor vicious; but only so far as they are proofs of certain Qualitys or durable principles in the mind. This is a Point I shou'd have establish'd more expressly than I have done" (*Letters* [Grieg] 1:34; cf. THN 3.2.1.2–4).
138 We may accept that the proofs to which Hume refers in the final sentence of the passage quoted are linked to the "Point" already mentioned in note 137—that is, the point that Hume thinks he should have "establish'd more expressly" because it concerns the dependency of the moral qualities of actions on certain qualities or principles in the mind (*Letters* [Grieg] 1:34).

Taken jointly, these interpretive options pertaining to Hutcheson's evident disagreement with Hume drive this chapter's overall argument in sections two through six. The first three of these sections (i.e., §§ 2–4) are devoted to constructing a historical and conceptual framework in which they can be properly addressed. The second section treats the "Proofs" that Hume mentions in his letter to Hutcheson as well as some basic assumptions of the type of approach to the foundations of morals—specifically, the eighteenth-century 'rationalist' approach—that Hume was opposing when calling upon Cicero's proof for support. The third section provides analysis of this proof in relation to Hume's key claims in the passage quoted above. The fourth section discusses a Ciceronian and Stoic dimension of Reid's criticism of Hume—a dimension that sheds light on the historical opposition between sentimentalist and rationalist accounts of the basis of moral motivation and the grounds of obligation. Against the background terrain cultivated in sections two through four, the fifth section of this chapter comes to grips with the three interpretive options mentioned by examining how Hutcheson's sentimentalist portrayal of the origin of our sense of obligation or duty is linked, by way of Cicero, to the Stoic conception of the *honestum*. I argue there (in § 5) that the connection between Hutcheson's theory of obligation and this Stoic conception indicates an essential aspect of compatibility between Hutcheson's approach to the foundations of morals and the rationalist approach taken by Reid. I argue further, in this chapter's final section (§ 6), that this aspect of compatibility points to a way out of the impasse concerning the nature of moral motivation that has often characterized discussions of moral worth and the sources of obligation since Hume's time—*provided*, that is, that Kant's theory of morally practical reason's obligatory ends can support a doctrine of moral worth according to which it is *always* possible to act from respect for law as one's incentive.

§ 2 Cicero's "Proof against the Stoics" and Hume's Undoubted Maxim

Let us focus, then, on the proposition that Hume proposes, in the September 1739 letter, appealing to Cicero's anti-Stoic proof, i.e., the twofold proposition that (a) for every virtuous action there must be a motive or impelling passion distinct from the virtue attributable to the action, and (b) virtue (in the sense of moral goodness) can never be the sole motive for any action. This compound proposition requires understanding of the proofs that Hume thinks must be altered on account of their insufficient distinctness, namely, the proofs which he presents in the third book of *A Treatise of Human Nature* (THN).[139] For these proofs are meant to establish, as we will see, the basic principle of the moral value of actions for which the 1739 compound proposition serves as a specifying interpretation.

The features of these proofs that are specifically relevant to Hume's appeal to Cicero have already been covered by the discussion of Hume's 'undoubted maxim' and the sentimentalist conception of moral worth in chapter 4 (see pp. 91–96). I therefore limit my comments here to restating the main points of that discussion.

First, Hume insists that that "the first virtuous motive" (THN 3.2.1.4) which bestows merit on our actions can never be a regard paid to their virtue (i.e., their moral goodness) or to their morally obligatory character. Nor can that first motive consist in, or be supplied by, the sense of morality or duty that would incite us to perform morally good actions "without any other motive" (THN 3.2.1.8). Instead, it must be some "natural motive or principle" (THN 3.2.1.4) that lies in the human being's affective constitution. Second, Hume takes this position regarding the merit-bestowing character of natural motives to be necessary since the contrary supposition unavoidably leads to a circular explanation of the relationship between the motivational basis for morally good action and the moral goodness of the actions that we are motivated to perform. Third, having exposed the explanatory circle generated by the supposition that the mere regard to an action's virtue could furnish the primary motive that "excites" its performance and makes it virtuous, Hume goes on to formulate the principle which provides the grounding tenet of the sentimentalist doctrine of actions' moral worth to which his thinking in THN 3.2.1 leads. This is the "undoubted maxim" which asserts that "*no action can be virtuous, or morally good, unless there be in human nature some motive to produce it, distinct from the sense of its morality*" (THN 3.2.1.7). Fourth, the obvious objection that can be raised against this (purportedly) undoubted principle—i.e., the objection that "the sense of morality or duty" (THN 3.2.1.8) can produce an action without any other motive being in play—is in truth no objection at all. For the possibility of acting from duty in this sense presupposes the efficacy of certain affective

---

[139] The following discussion of Hume as well as the corresponding considerations on Reid presented in the fourth section of this chapter draw directly from an article that has recently appeared in the *Journal of Scottish Philosophy*. As Hume's and Hutcheson's relation to Cicero's account of Stoic ethics forms the centerpiece of the investigation at hand, I have here reduced my treatments of Hume and Reid to the bare essentials. This procedure, of course, raises various interpretive issues that are addressed in the far more detailed treatments found in the JSP article (see Edwards 2014, pp. 120–135).

conditions that are distinct from the regard paid to the morally obligatory character of actions.

Hume's undoubted maxim implies, then, that an agent's capacity to act from the sense of duty (or sense of morality; or regard to moral obligation; or regard to virtue, etc.) depends on her being subject to an affective motivational condition that makes it possible for her to have such a sense. This implication is what provides the key tenet that is expressed in the first part of the September 1739 letter's "certain" proposition when Hume asserts that for every virtuous action—that is, for every morally good action whose performance is meritorious—there must be a motive or impelling passion distinct from the virtue attributable to such an action. Moreover, it is in view of this tenet that we can understand why Hume would consider the two parts of his 1739 proposition to be the components of a single principle of morally good action. For it is clear from the foregoing considerations on Hume's *Treatise* account of the basis of actions' moral worth why he would think that these two parts of his compound proposition entail one another. We can discern the character of this entailment if we consider the notion of acting from the sense of duty in conjunction with Hume's argument that the regard to the virtue (or moral goodness) of an action cannot be the primary motive for its performance. Let us therefore endorse (for the sake of clarification) the circularity charge that Hume levels against the opposing approach to the explanation of moral motivation.[140] Let us also spell out the contents of the two components of Hume's 1739 proposition in connection with Hume's response to the sense-of-duty objection that, as we have seen, can be raised against his undoubted maxim. If we do this, we can see that the following relations obtain between those propositional components: (1) If there must be a motive for action distinct from the virtue that one pays heed to when acting from the sense of duty or a regard to moral obligation, then it is not possible to perform an action from the *sole* motive of virtue. (2) Conversely, if it is not possible to act from the sole motive of virtue (even when paying heed to the sense of duty or a regard to moral obligation), then there must be a motive for action distinct from the virtue that one pays heed to when acting from that sense or regard. Thus, given the material equivalence of these claims, it is apparent how the twofold proposition at issue in Hume's 1739 letter to Hutcheson can be considered a

---

140 Thus, we may accept (again, for the sake of clarification) the crucial Humean supposition on which that argument depends—namely, the supposition that one falls prey to circular reasoning if one assumes that "the mere regard to the virtue of the action, may be the first motive, which produc'd the action, and render'd it virtuous" (THN 3.2.1.4).

§ 2 Cicero's "Proof against the Stoics" and Hume's Undoubted Maxim — 247

specifying interpretation of the undoubted maxim of the third book of Hume's *Treatise*.[141]

Even after clarifying the connection between this maxim and the 1739 letter's twofold proposition, of course, it is not yet apparent why Hume was dissatisfied with the arguments that he had previously provided in order to establish his undoubted maxim and, implicitly, this proposition. This is, I believe, an interesting question for the overall interpretation of Hume's theory of morals in the *Treatise of Human Nature*.[142] Nevertheless, for the purposes of this chapter's argument, I will take Hume's expression of dissatisfaction at face value and concentrate on the following question: Can Hume legitimately appeal to Cicero in order to support the position that he takes on the moral worth of actions in both the *Treatise* and his letter to Hutcheson?

Before turning to Cicero's *De finibus*, let me make several very general points regarding the type of philosophical approach against which Hume's maxim and proposition were directed.

I have in mind here the approach to the closely linked issues of the basis (i.e., the origin or source and grounds) of obligation and actions' moral worth that was taken by eighteenth-century intellectualist or rationalist thinkers when they presented their theories of the foundational principles of morals.[143] I will consider various aspects of this sort of approach in my later (§ 4) discussion of Reid's criticism of Hume. But it will be important to bear in mind the following positional claims, typically at work in rationalist ethics, as we go on in the next section to assess Hume's use of Cicero's *De finibus* argument against the Stoics:[144]

---

[141] This would be the kind of interpretation that Hume could use in order to try to make 'distinct enough' his proofs pertaining to this maxim.
[142] See especially THN 2.3.3.3–5, 6, 8; THN 3.1.1.4, 6, 9–10, 16, 22, 25; THN 3.1.2.1–3; THN 3.2.1.2–4.
[143] When discussing 'rationalism' in ethics, I have mind mainly the eighteenth-century thinkers mentioned in notes 145–149 of this chapter. My considerations on "sentimentalism" are directed primarily to Hutcheson and Hume, although Shaftesbury (in his own way), Adam Smith, and Rousseau (of *Émile*) figure in the background as well. Thus, I would like to underscore the limited use to which I am putting these epithets. While there are plenty of other modern thinkers who can be classified as moral rationalists and as moral sentimentalists, I do not hold that the rationalism vs. sentimentalism opposition can deliver a viable scheme for understanding the history of moral philosophy since the eighteenth century—or even during the eighteenth century for that matter. My reasons for taking this position will be apparent from notes 165 and 171.
[144] In setting forth these claims I am not attempting to give a definitional account of rationalism in ethics, nor even to furnish a laundry list of assumptions shared by *all* eighteenth-century moral philosophers who can plausibly be classified as rationalists. My aim here is simply to provide a useful sketch of some key theoretical tenets that were *typically* involved in, or presup-

(1) Morality is based on principles apprehended by the rational faculty.[145]

(2) Our moral cognition is itself prescriptive for action insofar as it involves the apprehension of rational principles that are principles of obligation.[146]

(3) The contents of such principles can furnish motives in the sense that any rational agent can be moved to act simply in virtue of its capacity to apprehend the fundamental deontic requirements of the faculty of reason that those principles express.[147]

(4) It is on account of *this* capacity, and not on account of any non-rational feature of our affective constitution, that the human agent is able to act from a sense of duty or a regard to obligation when paying heed to the moral qualities of her actions.[148]

(5) Insofar as we are motivated to act in paying heed to the deontic requirements of our rational faculty, the sense of duty, or regard to obligation, is fully sufficient to lend an action moral worth.[149]

---

posed by, an approach to the basis of obligation and actions' moral worth that requires the repudiation of Hume's 'undoubted maxim' and its specifying proposition of 1739.

145 See Clarke, 1708 [1705], pp. 67–70; Balguy 1728 [1727], pp. 31–32, 47–48, 56–57; Balguy 1729 [1728], pp. 15–16; Price 1787 [1758], pp. 41–42, 61–62, 108, 184; Reid 2010 [1788], pp. 176–180, 270–271, 275, 276–278, 309, 311, 352–356, 360–362. See also Wolff 1976 [1720], §§ 12, 29, 90, 137; Crusius 1969 [1744], § 81.

146 See Clarke 1708 [1705], pp. 45–46, 62, 67, 67–71, 81, 141–142, 155; Balguy 1728 [1727], pp. 31–32; Balguy 1729 [1728], pp. 7–11; Price 1787 [1758], pp. 104–105, 108–111; Reid 2010 [1788], pp. 179–180. See also Wolff 1976 [1720], §§ 29, 45, 90, 137; Crusius,1969 [1744], §§ 133, 137, 160, 162, 181, 372.

147 See Clarke 1708 [1705], pp. 69, 70–71; Balguy 1728 [1727], pp. 47–48; 56–57; Balguy 1729 [1728], pp. 15–16; Price 1787 [1758], pp. 105–106, 186–187; Reid,2010 1788], p. 170. See also Wolff 1976 [1720], §§ 38, 78, 81, 244; Crusius 1969 [1744], §§ 137, 166, 194. In saying that such principles *can* furnish motives, and that a rational agent *can* be moved to act simply in virtue of its capacity to apprehend reason's deontic requirements, I mean to signal that one *may* qualify as a rationalist in ethics whether or not one endorses motivational internalism. Viewed from the perspective of contemporary ethical theory, of course, the very act of signaling these possibilities amounts to a testy issue; but nothing in this chapter depends on trying to make this less contestable.

148 See Clarke 1708 [1705], p. 69; Balguy 1728 [1727], pp. 31–32; Price [1758], pp. 108, 187–191; Reid 2010 [1788], pp. 299–301, 305, 339. See also Wolff 1976 [1720], §§ 90; Crusius 1969 [1744], §§ 162, 166, 173, 177.

149 See Balguy 1728 [1728], pp. 11–14; 47–48; Balguy 1729 [1728], pp. 15–16; Reid 2010 [1788], pp. 296–299, 337. Cf. Price 1787 [1758], pp. 199, 188–199; Crusius 1969 [1744], §§ 173, 177.

§ 3 The Idea of the Honestum and Cicero's "Proof against the Stoics" in De finibus IV

The previous section was mainly concerned to determine the connection between the two elements of the proposition at issue in Hume's 1739 letter to Hutcheson. Having clarified this connection, let us now consider the (purportedly) Ciceronian core of what Hume takes to be the basis for adequately proving his proposition pertaining to the moral worth of actions. This core argument (see lines 2–4 of the passage from the 1739 letter quoted on p. 242–243) can be explicated as follows: (1) Assume that virtue is the sole good. (2) On this assumption, the mind must lack any motive that could incite to action, from which it in turn follows that (3) there could be no virtue (hence no good *qua* virtue) with respect to actions. Did Cicero actually achieve what Hume says he did with regard to this sort of logical *reductio* move, which Hume takes to be essential to the anti-Stoic proof that is supposed to support his certain proposition? We turn directly to the fourth book of Cicero's *De finibus* with this question in mind.

There would be a great deal to say about Cicero's *De finibus* in view of its signal influence on the history of modern ethics as a crucial source for the transmission of Epicurean and Stoic treatments of good and evil. But I will limit the scope of my comments to *De finibus* 4:14–48[150] since these segments of the fourth book contain the key arguments for Cicero's assessment of Stoic ethics with respect to the concepts of virtue and moral good or moral worth (*honestum*). My particular focus will be the passage in *De finibus* that Hume had in view when emphasizing the Ciceronian origin of the argument just discussed.

When examining the principles of Stoic eudaimonism, Cicero wants to understand Stoic thinkers' special contributions to the account of the supreme good (*summum bonum*). He therefore focuses especially on the role played by the prescription to live in accordance with nature (*secundum naturam vivere*). He demands of his Stoic interlocutor (Cato the Younger) an explanation of why even the earliest Stoic theories of value interpret the *secundum naturam* prescription in ways that imply a radical break with all hitherto available theories of the good—that is, with theories which standardly sought to combine their accounts of particular natural goods (for example, health, freedom from pain, wealth, and power) with a single, integrated conception of the supreme good

---

[150] Citation of Cicero's *De finibus* and *De officiis* in this chapter accords with the book and marginal numbering conventions followd in the respective Oxford Classical Texts editions of these works.

for human beings.[151] Cicero's objective in putting forward his demand is to show that the Stoic view of the *honestum* as the sole good (*solum bonum*) is insupportable. Specifically, Cicero wants to demonstrate why, even if we accept that the good for human beings must be understood in terms of the eudaimonic state that constitutes the perfection of the human being as a rational agent, it is implausible for the Stoics to maintain that the *honestum* furnishes the only possible component of the supreme good. According to Cicero, the implausibility of the Stoic view stems from the fact that Stoic thinkers, starting with Zeno of Citium, provide inadmissibly restrictive interpretations of the necessary connection between living in accordance with nature (*secundum naturam vivere*) and living virtuously (*honeste vivere*).[152]

Cicero's attack against Stoic ethics proceeds along three intersecting pathways in *De finibus* 4:14–48. First, he targets the Stoic doctrine of choice with respect to morally indifferent things (αδιάφορα). He does this by arguing that the distinction which Stoic thinkers draw between "preferred" and "good" things amounts to a distinction between things lacking distinguishing features as far as the notion of good is concerned.[153] Second, in keeping with his rejection of the Stoic axiological distinction between 'preferred' and 'good', Cicero maintains that the Stoics have no viable way of coming to grips with the affective components of the human constitution—the *prima naturae*—that nature itself provides as starting points for the self-perfecting agent's development of virtue.[154] Third, given the theoretical deficiencies just mentioned, Cicero contends that Stoic ethics creaks under the weight of a fundamental systemic flaw. On the one hand, the proponent of Stoic ethical theory must maintain that natural desire and impulse (*naturalis appetitio*, 'ὁρμή'[155]) are non-rational motivating factors that have positive normative significance because of the indispensable roles that they play in the emergence of virtue. On the other hand, the Stoic theory of the supreme good is such that these nature-given hormetic factors cannot be integrated with the account of a single end of action that is also an all-embracing good: the *ultimum*

---

[151] For immensely useful, historically contextualized discussion of Cicero's work on ethics as well as his particular aims in *De finibus* as a whole, see Julia Annas's introduction to Cicero 2001, pp. vii-xxvii. See also Patzig 1996, pp. 251–272.
[152] See *De finibus* 4:14, 20–29, 43–44.
[153] See *De finibus* 4:20–23, 27, 30–31, 39.
[154] See *De finibus* 4:24, 32–36, 39–47. Keeping an eye on key concerns of eighteenth-century moral philosophers, it is worth noting that William Guthrie renders Cicero's *prima naturae* as primary or first "affections" in his 1744 translation of *De finibus* (see, e.g., pp. 141, 199, 235).
[155] *De finibus* 4:39; cf. *De finibus* 3:23.

bonorum—literally, the ultimation of goods.¹⁵⁶ Stoic ethics is unable to provide a coherent account of a unified supreme good, which according to Cicero is what any viable form of philosophical ethics must be able to provide.¹⁵⁷

The pathways of criticism just mapped bring us to the *De finibus* passage that Hume had primarily in mind in his 1739 communication with Hutcheson.¹⁵⁸ I quote this passage as it is rendered in the recent Cambridge translation of *De finibus:*¹⁵⁹

> Here is [...] a point to which I take great exception. You show, at least to your own satisfaction that what is moral [*quod honestum sit*] is the only good [*solum bonum*]. You then claim, however, that there are starting-points laid before us which are adapted and suited to our nature, and that it is in selecting from among these that virtue [*virtus*] may arise. It was wrong of you to have located virtue in an act of selection, since it means that the ultimate good [*bonorum ultimum*] will itself be in pursuit of some further thing. The sum total of goods must include everything worth adopting, choosing or wishing for, or else the ones who possess it will still want something more. [...] But you Stoics propose as your good nothing other than rightness and morality [*rectum atque honestum*]. All of you who are looking for such a principle will return to nature, [...]. To you all, nature will make the following just riposte: it is wrong to seek the standard for a happy life [*finem beate vivendi*] elsewhere, while seeking the principles of conduct from nature herself; there is a single unified system [*unam rationem*] encompassing both principles of conduct and ultimate goods [*principia rerum agendarum et ultima bonorum*] [...]. In just the same way Zeno was wrong was wrong to claim that nothing other than virtue carries any weight in the attainment of the supreme good [*summum bonum*]. It is completely inconsistent of the Stoics to say that one returns to nature to seek out a principle of appropriate action and duty [*agendi principium, id est offici*]. Considerations of action and duty do not motivate us to desire the things that are in accordance with nature. Rather, the latter are what motivate our desires and our actions.¹⁶⁰ (*De finibus* 4:46–48)

---

156 See *De finibus* 4:39–41, 46 (cf. Cicero, *Tusculanae Disputationes* 5:18–19). I gratefully adopt 'ultimation of goods' from Guthrie's 1744 translation, where *ultimum bonorum* is rendered as "Ultimation of Good Things". Raphael Woolf translates the same term as "ultimate good", but this conceals the distinction between good and goods that is specifically relevant to Cicero's criticism of the Stoic doctrine of the *adiaphora*.

157 For discussion pertinent to this last point, see Annas 1993, pp. 3–10, 47–66, 120–141, 214–220, 439–455.

158 Norton and Norton helpfully focus on exactly this passage in their annotation to THN 3.2.1.4 (see THN p. 540).

159 Cicero 2001, p. 105. I have inserted the square-bracketed Latin terms and phrases into Woolf's translation in order to facilitate comparison with Cicero's text. I should point out here that Woolf's work embodies the best contemporary English translation of *De finibus* that I know of.

160 "Minime vero illud probo quod, cum docuistis ut vobis videmini solum bonum esse quod honestum sit, tum rursum dicitis initia proponi necesse esse apta et accommodata naturae quorum ex selectione virtus possit existere. Non enim in selectione virtus ponenda erat, ut id ipsum

The final sentence of the Latin text—which for stylistic reasons is broken up into two sentences in most English translations—displays the key move in the anti-Stoic proof that Hume emphasizes when in his letter to Hutcheson he writes: "if there be no other Goods but virtue, tis impossible there can be any Virtue; because the Mind would then want all Motives to begin its Action upon" (*Letters* [Grieg] 1:35). The question that we must deal with, again, is whether Cicero actually does what Hume thinks he does when making this move. To decide this, let me first provide a (somewhat charitable) gloss for the argument that runs through the passage as a whole:

> (1) The basic Stoic position is this: The *honestum* (understood as living virtuously, in accordance with nature) constitutes the sole good. But the Stoics also propose that we are subject to natural motivating factors that have essential normative import for our living in conformity with what the *honestum* requires. For, while the Stoics hold that these factors do not supply constitutive features of the sole good as such, they recognize that our developed capacity to live in conformity with the *honestum* (in the sense of *honeste vivere*) depends on the appropriateness of our selective activity with respect to the things that furnish the natural starting points for the development of virtue. Thus, given the normative salience of these starting points with respect to the end of living happily, the Stoics implicitly acknowledge that the sum total of goods (*summum bonorum*) must include everything that is to be adopted, chosen, or wished for even when they insist that the *honestum* is the sole good.
>
> (2) Hence the monumental inconsistency that underlies and drives Stoic ethics: The Stoics appeal to nature in order to have a single rational ground that would contain both the principles of action and the principle of ultimations of goods (*una ratio qua et principia rerum agendarum et ultima bonorum continerentur*). At the same time, however, their understanding of the *honestum* as the sole good requires them to hold that nothing other than virtue or vice affects the attainment of the supreme good.
>
> (3) One cannot, then, self-consistently hold *both* that the supreme good must be understood as the *honestum* alone *and* that one returns to nature in order to seek out a principle of ac-

---

quod erat bonorum ultimum aliud aliquid acquireret. Nam omnia quae sumenda quaeque legenda aut optanda sunt inesse debent in summa bonorum, ut is qui eam adeptus sit nihil praeterea desideret. [...] Vobis autem, quibus nihil est aliud propositum nisi rectum atque honestum, unde offici, unde agendi principium nascatur non reperietis. Hoc igitur quaerentes omnes [...] ad naturam revertemini. Quibus natura iure responderit non esse verum aliunde finem beate vivendi, a se principia rei gerendae peti; esse enim unam rationem qua et principia reurm agendarum et ultima bonorum continerentur, [...] sic errare Zenonem , qui nulla in re nisi in virtute aut vitio propensionem ne minimi quidem momenti ad summum bonum adipiscendum esse diceret et, cum ad beatam vitam nullum momentum certera habarent, ad appetitionem tamen rerum esse in iis momenta diceret; quasi vero haec appetitio non ad summi boni adeptionem pertineret! Quid autem minus consentaneum est quam quod aiunt cognito summo bono reverti se ad naturam ut ex ea petant agendi principium, id est offici? Non enim actionis aut offici ratio impellit ad ea quae secundum naturam sunt appetenda, sed ab iis et eppetio et action commovetur".

§ 3 The Idea of the Honestum and Cicero's Proof — 253

tion that is also a principle of duty (*agendi principium, id est offici*)—namely, the rational ground of action and duty which contains the prescription that we are to desire the things that are in accordance with nature, even when these things are what supplies the impulse for our desire.[161]

So much for Cicero's capstone argument against the Stoics in *De finibus* 4:46–48. How exactly does Hume's basic understanding of this argument, as discussed in the first paragraph of this section (see p. 244–245), stack up against what Cicero in fact maintains?

In coming to grips with this question, the first thing to notice is a point concerning the semantic content of the final sentence of the Latin text. I refer here to the phrase *ad ea quae secundum naturam sunt appetenda*. In rendering this phrase as "to desire the things that are in accordance with nature", the English translation that I have quoted above does not capture the prescriptive import of Cicero's use of the gerundive (*sunt appetenda*) in order to express, periphrastically, necessity in respect of action—that is, in order to indicate practical necessity. Here, then, is an alternative translation of the last compound sentence of the Latin passage, a translation that is meant to capture not only the prescriptive force of the gerundive but also to do proper justice to the technical philosophic import of the expression *ratio actionis aut offici*:

> For the rational ground of action or duty does not impel [us] toward those things which in accordance with nature are to be desired. Instead, both desire and action are motivated by these things.

What are the "these things" by which desire and action *are* motivated? They are the things that in accordance with nature *are to be* desired. More precisely, they are the things which, in accordance with nature, we ought to desire even if they are what supplies the hormetic impulse to act in conformity with the rational ground contained in the principle of acting that is also the principle of duty which prescribes that things in accordance with nature are to be desired.

That's it. That is all that Cicero's argument purports to establish. It is supposed to establish that the Stoics cannot self-consistently maintain that the *honestum* is the sole good while also adhering to a *principium offici* that prescribes the attainment of certain natural goods as conditions for the realization of virtue. It is not meant to establish, and it does not establish, that there could be *no* motive to action—and consequently no virtue with respect to actions—if virtue (in

---

[161] Note well the correlation between Cicero's *impellit* [...] *appetenda* at *De finibus* 4:48 and Hume's use of "impelling passion" in his 1739 letter to Hutcheson (see p. 243).

the sense of *honeste vivere* that features in the idea of the *honestum*) were the sole good. Nor does Cicero's argument support either one of the mutually implicative parts of Hume's certain proposition. It does not prove, nor was it meant to prove, that for every action there must be in the agent "an impelling Passion"—that is, a hormetic impulse[162]—distinct from virtue or the regard to virtue. Nor does Cicero's argument serve to prove that virtue or the regard to virtue cannot be the sole motive to any action.

We may grant, then, that Cicero successfully proves that Hume's "Virtue" (on its interpretation as *honestum* and in terms of the corresponding *honeste vivere* requirement) *cannot* be the sole good if there is a principle of duty or appropriate action[163] that calls for the attainment of certain natural goods. Yet it does not follow that this Ciceronian disproof is what furnishes the theoretical stage from which to prove that for every virtuous action there must be a motive distinct from virtue or the regard paid to it. Nor does it follow that one may use the disproof that Cicero directs against the Stoics as a way to establish that neither virtue nor the mere regard to virtue can furnish the sole motive for any action. Thus, Hume's justificatory appeal to Cicero's capstone argument against the Stoics in the fourth book of *De finibus* is off its proper mark.

Moreover, the appeal to Cicero's capstone argument seems to be straightforwardly counterproductive as far as Hume's own purpose is concerned. We should note well the contra-Humean circle implicit in the final sentence of that argument, which is in fact the sentence that furnishes the focal point of Hume's call for support from Cicero. According to Cicero, the things by which virtue-promoting desire and action *are* motivated are the very things which, in accordance

---

[162] See (again) *De finibus* 4:39; cf. *De officiis* 1:101.

[163] Recent translation practice has been to render Stoic *kathêkon*, hence Cicero's *officium*, as 'appropriate action', 'appropriate act' or 'appropriate function' in order to dampen down the full-bore deontological connotations of its traditional English rendering as 'duty'. Given the highly differentiated ways of asserting obligation in classical Greek, I am not entirely confident that this is always good practice, even with respect to the relevant Greek texts and fragments themselves. (Woolf, it may be noted, seems to be sensitive to this kind of background issue when he translates *agendi principium, id est offici* as "a principle of appropriate action *and* duty" [italics mine (J. E.)].) But more importantly for the purposes of this chapter: the difficulties that we have always had in finding adequate and uniform ways of expressing the *range* of deontic distinctions at issue in the ancient Stoics' use of *kathêkon* should not lead us to ignore the historical circumstance that Cicero's *officium* was subject to quite robustly duty-orientated interpretation by seventeenth and eighteenth-century philosophers—from the Grotian natural lawyers to Christian Garve and Immanuel Kant (and well beyond these). One normally does well enough to think of a *principium offici* as a principle of duty when dealing with a Scottish Enlightenment philosopher's interpretation of a Ciceronian text.

§ 3 The Idea of the Honestum and Cicero's Proof — 255

with nature, we *ought* to desire precisely *insofar as* they impel us to act in conformity with the *rational* ground contained in the principle of acting that is also the principle of duty which prescribes that things in accordance with nature are to be desired. Whatever we—historically freighted as we are with all manner of naturalistic fallacy detection equipment[164]—may wish to say about this final step in Cicero's argument, the least we can say is that it does not offer an obvious way to establish that the regard to virtue, or to duty, presupposes a virtuous motive that is *necessarily antecedent* to that regard. There is, then, apparently some historical irony in Hume's justificatory appeal to Cicero. For it may even initially look like the conclusion of Cicero's argument against the Stoics should lend greater support for an anti-Humean rationalist theory of actions' moral worth than it does for the theory implicit in Hume's *Treatise*. And indeed, it would do this if the following tenet were essential to the approach to the nature of moral obligation taken by eighteenth-century rationalists—namely, the tenet that actions motivated solely by the regard to duty are actions motivated on account of a rational ground which prescribes, in accordance with nature, that some things are to be desired insofar as they impel us to act on non-rational grounds.

To my knowledge, though, no eighteenth-century rationalist would be intent on establishing *this* as an essential tenet of the theory of morals,[165] any more than Hume would try to show that the mere regard to duty can suffice to ensure that an action's positive moral value derives from its being motivated by such a regard antecedently to every affective motivational condition. Let us recall that the rationalist approach to the foundations of morals may involve the supposition that the sense of duty, or the regard to obligation, is sufficient to lend an action moral worth. It should be noted here that this supposition entails that the regard which one pays to duty and moral obligation can suffice for an action

---

164 Cf. Long 1996, pp. 134–141,
165 One might propose that Joseph Butler was (or at any rate ought to have been) prepared to endorse such a tenet on account of his stated indifference about calling the moral faculty "conscience, moral reason, moral sense, or divine reason; whether considered a sentiment of the understanding or a perception of the heart; or which seems the truth, as including both" (Butler 2006 [1736], p. 309; cf. Schneewind 1998, p. 348). If such a proposal could be supported, however, it would only go to show that a moral philosopher like Butler defies classification as either a rationalist or a sentimentalist. I am quite content to accommodate this sort of defiance, especially since nothing in this chapter's argument hinges on overcoming (let alone suppressing) it. I am therefore also equally content to consider sweeping claims like the following one to be historiographically implausible even when restricted to the eighteenth century context: "Modern [moral] thought is *divided between* moral rationalists and moral sentimentalists […]" (Slote 2010, p. 41).

to have a positive moral value independently not only of all opposing or concurrent motives, but also of any motive that might be thought to furnish a condition of our coming to have that kind of regard. When considered using the deontic vocabulary that Hume and his contemporaries link to their characterizations of virtuous action, however, the whole point of Cicero's capstone argument against the Stoics is to show that conditions of our regard to duty or obligation can perfectly well be furnished by motives for action that cannot be supplied by that regard alone. Thus, while Cicero's argument does not serve to bolster Hume's position that the mere regard to duty or obligation cannot supply a motive for any action that has genuine moral worth, neither does it lend support to the rationalist supposition that this sort of regard alone can be sufficient to give an action such worth. This is quite apart from every motive that opposes, concurs with or furnishes a condition of our having and exercising that exclusive regard.

§ 4 The Value of the Honestum in Reid's Repudiation of Hume's Undoubted Maxim

The appeal to Cicero contained in the 1739 letter to Hutcheson does not indicate a way of justifying Hume's undoubted maxim that no action can be virtuous, or morally good, unless there is in human nature some motive to produce it distinct from the sense of its morality or the regard to its moral obligation. Moreover, it is Hume himself who, in connection with this appeal to Cicero for justificatory support, admits the dubious character of his own arguments in favor of that maxim. Yet the failure of Hume's appeal, even when combined with his admission of the inadequacy of these arguments as they are presented in *Treatise*, does not provide fodder for the argument that an advocate of the rationalist approach to the source and grounds of moral obligation has to muster if he is successfully to counter the charge of explanatory circularity that Hume levels against non-sentimentalist theories of moral worth in order to establish the purported certainty of his maxim. Thus, given that it is Hume himself who leads us to the *Ciceronian* path of doubt regarding the truth of this maxim (and, by implication, regarding the certainty of the twofold proposition endorsed in the letter of 1739), we appear to be at an impasse as far as *both* the Humean sentimentalist approach and its rationalist alternative are concerned.

To shed further light on the character of this impasse, I would like to direct our attention to the criticism of Hume's conception of the moral worth of actions that Thomas Reid presents in chapters 4–6 of Essay 5 in the *Essays on the Active Powers of Man* (AP). It is in the context of this criticism—specifically, in the sixth chapter of AP Essay 5—that Reid explicitly targets the undoubted maxim of THN

3.2.1. When attacking this Humean maxim, he takes the position that the *sole consideration of*—the *mere* regard to—duty can furnish a motive that is fully sufficient to render an action morally meritorious:

> Virtuous actions are so far from needing other motives, besides their being virtuous, to give them their merit, that their merit is then greatest and most conspicuous, when every motive that can be put in the opposite scale is outweighed by the sole consideration of these being our duty. (AP 337).

Reid's opposition to Hume's undoubted maxim thus involves the supposition that the consideration of duty suffices for an action to have its moral merit independently of all motives distinct from this consideration itself. And this supposition entails that the regard to duty can suffice for an action to have positive moral value independently of any other motive that might be thought to oppose, concur with or *furnish a condition of* our coming to have that kind of regard.[166]

How, then, does Reid justify the position that he takes against Hume? Consider the following passage from the fifth chapter of AP Essay 5:

> [I]f it be true, and I think it is evident to every man of common understanding, that a judge or arbiter acts the most virtuous part when his sentence is produced by no other motive but a regard to justice and a good conscience—nay, when all other motives distinct from this are on the other side: if this, I say, be true, then that undoubted maxim of Mr. Hume must be false, and all the considerations built upon it must fall to the ground. (AP 229)

Reid here uses as an example the juridical duty of impartial justice—or more precisely: a duty of judicial impartiality—to illustrate how Hume's undoubted maxim runs counter to evidence available to everyone of common understanding. The reference to such universally available evidence leads us directly into Reid's intuitional theory of the foundations of moral cognition and deliberation.

It is a fundamental tenet of this theory that our sense of duty and knowledge of moral obligation must be deduced from "first principles of moral reasoning" whose truth is "immediately testified by our moral faculty" (AP 176–177). These principles of moral reasoning are thus self-evident principles that must be apprehended as "dictates of the moral faculty" or, in other words, as "dictates of conscience" (AP 179, 180, 271, 276). As such, they are prescriptive—and indeed, universally prescriptive—principles that furnish the first principles of morals, i.e., the principles for all action-guiding conclusions to be drawn on the basis of our moral faculty's immediate testimony, but also in view of the contingent empirical conditions of human conduct. Given his understanding of the relationship

---

[166] For detailed analysis of the entailment in question, see Edwards 2014, pp. 27–29.

between the sense of duty, knowledge of moral obligation, self-evident first principles, and rational prescriptions for action, Reid holds that "no action may be called morally good, in which a regard to what is right has not some influence" (AP 193). Moreover, he argues that in some cases of action a regard to what is right—i.e., a regard to duty—"may be the sole motive, without the consequence or opposition of any other principle of action" (AP 193).

If we accept the theoretical tenets just presented, it may initially seem that Reid's anti-Humean position can be justified merely by pointing a finger at the relevant first principle of moral reasoning that grounds the deontic regard that can be the sole motive to morally meritorious action.[167] There is, however, a significant difficulty involved in taking such an approach: Its outcome is unlikely to move anyone (not least Hume) who endorses Hume's undoubted maxim to doubt its truth. As we have seen, Hume's purpose in putting forward and seeking to establish his undoubted maxim is to show the inadequacy of appealing to anything other than affective—i.e., non-rational (or at least not necessarily rational)—motivational conditions as the basis for explaining the moral goodness or merit of actions. Thus, whatever Reid has to do in order to demonstrate the falsity of Hume's maxim, it certainly cannot consist in pointing to evidence for common *understanding* as long as such evidence is supposed to be supplied by appealing to intuitively self-evident first principles of moral *reasoning*. What Reid needs for his refutation of Hume on this point, then, is an *argument* that can effectively block the anti-rationalist undermining strategy that is implicit in the fundamental maxim of Hume's sentimentalist account of actions' moral goodness or merit.

Does Reid seek to offer such an argument in the *Essays on the Active Powers*? He does indeed; and the clue to understanding how it is supposed to work is provided by his concern to link Hume to Epicurean ethics by opposing the conception of moral worth at issue in Hume's maxim to the Stoic idea of the *honestum*.

When insisting, in the sixth chapter of AP Essay 5, that the consideration of duty suffices to render an action morally meritorious or virtuous, Reid quite

---

[167] If we are philosophically energetic, it seems that we could even quote this principle full-blast against Hume in the expectation that the sheer weight of its self-evidence will knock him flat: "It ought to be our most serious concern to do our duty as far as we know it, and to fortify our minds against every temptation to deviate from it; by maintaining a lively sense of the beauty of right conduct, and of its present and future reward, of the turpitude of vice, and of its bad consequences here and hereafter; by having always in our eye the noblest examples; by the habit of subjecting our passions to the government of reason; by firm purposes and resolutions with regard to our conduct; by avoiding occasions of temptation when we can; and by imploring the aid of him who made us, in every hour of temptation" (AP 271).

forcefully calls attention to the agreement between Hume's undoubted maxim and principles that underlie the Epicurean account of the relationship between virtue and pleasure as one's own good:

> This maxim, therefore, of Mr. Hume [...] was never, so far as I know, maintained by any moralist, but by the Epicureans; and it savours of the very dregs of that sect. It agrees well with the principles of those who maintained, that virtue is an empty name, and that it is entitled to no regard but in as far as it to pleasure and profit. (AP 337).

Polemical flourishes aside, Reid intends here to make fully clear the essentially Epicurean character of Hume's account of the moral goodness of actions. Reid thereby means to build on the account of the relationship between Hume's theory of morals and Epicurean eudaimonism already presented in the preceding chapter of Essay 5.

In this fifth chapter of AP Essay 5, Reid focuses on what he takes to be Hume's inadmissible account of moral approbation. Reid holds that this account requires that Hume should be able to prove that personal merit, virtue, and indeed everything that is the object of moral approbation "consists in the qualities of mind which are *agreeable* or *useful* to the person who possesses them, or to others" (AP 302). Reid therefore maintains that Hume's treatment of moral approbation implicitly makes the agreeable and the useful "the whole sum of merit in every character, in every quality of mind, and in every action of life" (AP 302)—which of course precludes that the view of moral good at issue in Hume's account of moral approbation could be compatible with the view of the *honestum* as something intrinsically good. As Reid puts this point, with explicit reference to what Cicero (in *De finibus* II) considers a defensible feature of the Stoic idea of the *honestum:*

> There is no room left for that *honestum* which Cicero thus defines: *Honestum igitur id intelligimus, quod tale est, ut detracta omni utilitate, sine ullis premiis fructibusve, per seipsum jure possit laudari* (AP 302).[168]

Having thus exposed what he takes to be the source of Hume's exclusion of the *honestum* as an intrinsic good, Reid goes on to pursue a dual strategy against the account of moral worth that is implicit in Hume's undoubted maxim. First, Reid seeks to establish the essential agreement between the crucial assumptions of

---

[168] The Cicero quote is taken from *De finibus* 2.45: "The *honestum*, therefore, we understand to be that which, taking away all utility, and without any reward or advantage, is such that it may rightly be praised for its very self".

Hume's system of morals and the key hedonistic tenet of the Epicurean account of moral worth:

> Among the ancient moralists, the Epicureans were the only sect who denied that there is any such thing as *honestum*, or moral worth, distinct from pleasure. In this, Mr. Hume's system agrees with theirs. For the addition of utility to pleasure, as a foundation of morals, makes only a verbal, but no real difference. What is useful has no value in itself, but derives all its merit from the end for which it is useful. That end, in this system, is agreeableness or pleasure. So that, in both systems, pleasure is the only end, the only thing that is good in itself, and desirable for its own sake; and virtue derives all its merit from its tendency to produce pleasure. (AP 302)

Second, even when indicating the shared tenets of Hume's ethics and Epicurean eudaimonism with respect to the question of moral worth, Reid pays close attention to the ways in which the two systems of moral philosophy diverge from one another. He thus acknowledges that Hume is in a position to reject the (purportedly) *egoistic* Epicurean principle that "virtue is whatever is agreeable to ourselves" (AP 303). Still, Reid insists that Hume can deflect the force of this principle only at an unjustifiably high cost. For Hume's opposition to egoistic hedonism, Reid argues, requires that *every* quality of mind that is useful and agreeable *either* to each one of us (taken singly on our own) *or* to others must somehow be accommodated by giving it a place in the catalogue of virtues that structures the Humean system of morals. The result, according to Reid, can only be an absurdly inflated account of the virtues—an account in which even useful and agreeable qualities of body and fortune must end up having their place in the list of the moral virtues:

> This theory of the nature of virtue, it must be acknowledged, enlarges greatly the catalogue of moral virtues, by bringing into that catalogue every quality of mind that is useful or agreeable. Nor does there appear any good reason why the useful and agreeable qualities of body and of fortune, as well as those of the mind, should not have a place among moral virtues in the system. They have the essence of virtue; that is agreeableness and utility, why then should they not have the name? [169] (AP 303)

---

[169] Hume, of course, would be sovereignly untroubled by what Reid asserts in the first sentence of this passage (see EPM Appendix 4; cf. Sidgwick 1981, pp. 423–424). Thus, if blood is to be drawn by the hyperinflationist arrows shot in the remaining sentences, Reid has to be able to establish that the way in which Hume accounts for useful and agreeable qualities does not allow for essential distinctions to be drawn between, on the one hand, qualities of the mind and, on the other hand, qualities of the body and external goods of fortune. That is a tall order.

The strategy of Reid's argument is strikingly elegant. Reid's overarching plan is, so to speak, to stretch Hume out by the arms and hang him between the horns of a slippery dilemma. If Hume were to attempt an escape from his theoretical predicament by grasping the Epicurean egoistic horn with both hands, he would slide downward on his own hedonic lard and end up flopping face-first into the muck of the proverbial philosophy-of-swine sty. Yet by swinging himself over to the other horn—the one greased by qualities both agreeable and useful to ourselves *or* to *others*—Hume has no choice but to inflate his bag-of-virtues balloon, which in turn inexorably pulls him up and away toward deontological Never Never Land as far as the *honestum* concerned.

It remains unclear, though, how Reid's strategy of combining his Epicurean reduction of Hume's theory of moral worth with the charge of aretaic inflationism could block the sentimentalist undermining strategy by which Hume purports to establish that our regard to the morally obligatory character of actions must have its ground in a feature of our non-rational, affective constitution. For even if he is left dangling from the horn of general agreeableness and utility, happily pumping away at the bellows for his aretaic balloon, it is still far from clear that Hume should not be well warranted in upholding his sentimentalist principle that no action can be morally good unless there is some affect-based motive to produce it that is distinct from (and antecedent to) the sense of its morality, i.e., the sense of duty or regard to its moral obligation.[170] Or more specifically, if less graphically: even if Hume can be compelled to concede that upholding his sentimentalist principle depends on the supposition that "agreeableness or pleasure" (AP 302) provides for the only possible motive to perform a morally good action, it still seems that he could self-consistently maintain that the regard to that action's obligatory character, and thus the regard paid to the sense that it is one's duty to perform it, must be distinct from the motive upon which its moral goodness and merit depends.

So does Reid's critical onslaught against Hume, taken by itself, provide no decisive reason to reject Hume's undoubted maxim? Evidently not—at least not in the way that Reid thinks it should when he attempts to link Hume to Epicurean ethics by opposing the Humean conception of moral worth to the Stoic idea of the *honestum*. Indeed, in following Reid's connecting strategy we seem to have arrived at a classic expression of the 'standoff' relation that has so often characterized the discussion of moral sentimentalism and rationalist ethics

---

170 At least as long as one of his feet remains tied to the pleasures of self-approbation that derive from the cultivation of qualities of mind that have agreeableness and utility.

down to the present day.[171] The further question, then, is whether the eighteenth-century century discussion itself provides clues that show the way out of the impasse. It is in connection with this philosophical task of historical inquiry that the Hutcheson question posed at the beginning of this chapter's first section (see p. 243) can now most fruitfully be brought to bear.[172]

§ 5 The Form of the Honestum and Hutcheson's Account of Obligation

That question, once again, is this: Why is Hutcheson (whose approach to the foundations of ethics is many respects similar to Hume's) unwilling to assent to what Hume wants to establish by appealing to what Cicero proves against the Stoics? As I pointed out before, we need to know exactly what it is that Hutcheson does not assent to if we are to respond confidently to this general query. Is it (1) the *proposition* whose certainty Hume wants to establish by appealing to Cicero's proof against the Stoics? Or is it (2) that what *Cicero* is supposed to demonstrate by means of this proof does not establish the certainty of the proposition that Hume wants to prove? Or is it (3) both Hume's proposition and Cicero's proof taken together? To be sure, dealing in a philologically respon-

---

171 This is not to suggest that this discussion has taken place in unbroken continuity down to the present day. As J. B. Schneewind has pointed out: "In the nineteenth century sentimentalism dropped out of sight. Interest in it was revived only in the twentieth century, first by positivists and then by philosophers concerned with explaining the connections between moral conviction and moral motivation" (Schneewind 1998, p. 403). Bearing these points in mind, see for example Mandeville 1988 [1714], vol. 1 pp. 76, 405 (cf. Edwards 2014, pp. 136–137); Balguy 1728 [1727], pp. 3–14 (especially p. 9), 22–25; Price 1787 [1758], pp. 190–193; Sidgwick 1981, pp. 103–104; Mill 1969, pp. 207–208, 228–223, 240, 248–250; Ross 2002, pp. 131–132, 164–165, 170–173; Blackburn 1998, pp. 32–33, 201–212; Blackburn 2006, pp. 153–158; Slote 2001, pp. vii-ix, 19–28, 42–43, 82–87; Slote 2010, pp. 42–46, 88–89, 99–100. See also Stratton-Lake 2000, pp. 60–110; Darwall 2002, pp. 248–270; Audi 2004, pp. 248–270.

172 In view of the aporetic situation just described, it may be tempting to turn away from the historical terrain that we have been moving across. We might, for example, wish to look for clarification in contemporary discussions of motivational internalism vs. externalism with respect to moral judgment and reasons for action. Moreover, in doing this we might also be prepared to expand the scope of our clarifying endeavors to include the consideration of topics such as anti-sentimentalist realism vs. anti-realist constructivism. Yet I am unable to see the point of moving off in directions like these unless the issues addressed in the final section of this chapter—above all, those adumbrated in its final paragraph—are first sorted. That is why I propose to conclude this chapter by concentrating exclusively on the ramifications of the Hutcheson question that I posed at the beginning.

§ 5 The Form of the Honestum and Hutcheson's Account of Obligation — 263

sible manner with all three of these sub-queries would demand a far more nuanced treatment of Hutcheson's relation to Stoic thought than can be undertaken here.[173] Still, given the results of our analysis of Cicero's capstone argument against the Stoics, I think that we can state at least the following with quite considerable confidence: Hutcheson has in any event very good reason not to assent to the claim that what Cicero proves against the Stoics establishes the certainty of the proposition that "to every virtuous Action there must be a Motive or impelling Passion distinct from the Virtue, & that Virtue can never be the sole Motive to any Action" (*Letters* [Grieg] 1:35). For Hutcheson has every reason to reject Hume's supposition about what Cicero proves—namely, the supposition "that if there be no other Goods but Virtue, tis impossible there can be any Virtue; because the mind would then want all Motives to begin its Actions upon" (*Letters* [Grieg] 1:35).

Thus, by having shown (in this chapter's second section) that this supposition is in fact misplaced—that it is not an assumption shared by Cicero in his *De finibus* argument against the Stoics—we are able to provide a tenable response to query (2). That is, as long as we can accept that Hutcheson was acquainted with this argument, we can also plausibly conclude that Hutcheson rejects the claim that what Cicero proves establishes the certainty of the proposition that Hume wants to prove.

Now what about the first and third queries? Clearly, our conclusion concerning query (2) brings us to the point of departure for a partial response to query (3) as well. For as long as Hutcheson is willing to hold that there *are* goods apart from 'Virtue' (or the *honestum*), he can have no reason to repudiate Cicero's argument against the Stoics—not the argument in its entirety, at any rate—unless he is prepared to endorse what he has every reason to regard as a misplaced supposition about what Cicero proves.[174] Yet this addresses only the second part of the third query. It still leaves wide open the answer to its first part, i.e., the part that is one and the same as the question posed by query (1). Perhaps, though, our investigations thus far furnish us with everything that we need in order to take on even this single remaining question. To see how this can work, let us pro-

---

[173] Ahnert (2010) and Maurer (2010) have recently surveyed important features of the landscape. In view of the particular issues raised in the final section of this chapter, my own inclination would be to start with careful analysis of Hutcheson's translating work and annotations in Books I-VIII of *The Meditations of the Emperor Marcus Aurelius Antoninus* (2008 [1742]). In view of this task, see James Moore's and Michael Silverthorne's superb introduction to this edition of *The Meditations*.

[174] Hutcheson, of course, does hold that there are goods apart from virtue or moral good. See, e.g., IBV 85–88.

ceed by spelling out what follows from the rejection of Hume's misplaced supposition when our analysis of Cicero's capstone argument is taken in conjunction with the considerations that have already been presented on the sentimentalist and rationalist approaches to the moral worth of actions.

As we have seen, the response to our second specifying query is based on the analytic result that Cicero's capstone argument proves neither that there must be in the agent a hormetic impulse distinct from *honestum*-determined virtue nor that such virtue cannot be the sole motive to any action. Consequently, given this negative result, we may sensibly ask whether Hutcheson's understanding of what Cicero does *not* prove *against* the Stoics furnishes him (namely, Hutcheson) with good reason to hold that the regard to virtue—and consequently the sense of duty or the regard to moral obligation—*can* be the sufficient (and even the sole) motive to action. If it does, then there will be decisive reason to think that Hutcheson's sentimentalist approach to ethics involves the acceptance of a doctrine of moral worth that is foundationally compatible with the corresponding doctrine that underlies much of eighteenth-century rationalist ethics, and thus involves the repudiation of Hume's 'certain' proposition concerning the basis of actions' moral worth.

The last question posed is also one that takes us well beyond what can be effectively established in the space of a single chapter. But it is still feasible to set the stage for a reply that can be supported by full-fledged investigation. Consider, then, the following lines from Cicero's *De officiis*, which are translated from the epigraph inscribed on the title page of Hutcheson's *Inquiry into the Original of Our Ideas of Beauty and Virtue* (IBV):

> [N]ature and reason [...] hold that beauty, abiding consistency, and order in deliberation and deed are to be preserved. From these elements is forged and fashioned that *honestum* which is the subject our inquiry—something that, even though it be not [generally] esteemed as noble, is still the *honestum*; and that by [its] nature is praiseworthy even if it be praised by no one. You see here the very form and, as it were, the face of the *honestum* which, if it could be discerned by the eye, would call forth a wonderful love of wisdom.[175]

Let us suppose here that, for a thinker of Hutcheson's caliber, epigrammatic inscriptions on title pages are there for the sake of something more than ornamentation. On this supposition, there are two salient points to underscore when the

---

[175] [N]atura ratioque [...] pulchritudinem, constantiam, ordinem in consiliis, factisque conservandum putat. Quibus ex rebus conflatur & eficitur id quod quaerimus honestum: Quod etiamsi nobiliatiatum non sit, tamen honestum sit; quodque etiamsi a nullo laudetur, natura est ladabile. Formam quidem ipsam & tanquam faciem honesti vides, quae si oculis ceneretur, mirabiles amores excitaret sapientiae.—Cic. *de Off.* lib.I.c.4. (IBV 3; cf. *De Officiis* I:14–15)

§ 5 The Form of the Honestum and Hutcheson's Account of Obligation — 265

lines just quoted are viewed against the backdrop of our analysis of Cicero's capstone argument against the Stoics. First, Hutcheson clearly acknowledges that Cicero leaves plenty of 'room for the *honestum*', as Reid would no doubt put it. Second, even though he had to be well aware that Cicero repudiates the idea of the *honestum* as the one and only good, Hutcheson seems to be suggesting that the investigation of the *honestum*'s constitutive elements as well as the *forma honesti* itself can still provide the subject matter for inquiry into the *original* of our ideas of virtue.

The relevant investigation in this regard is furnished by the second treatise in Hutcheson's aesthetic and moral *Inquiry*, namely, his "Inquiry Concerning the Original of Our Ideas of Virtue or Moral Good". As it happens, the underlying centrality of the idea of the *honestum* for Hutcheson's foundational theory of morality in this second treatise is well known from recent scholarship, especially from James Moore's examination of the relationship between Cicero-inspired modern uses of that idea and Hutcheson's conception of benevolence as the "Universal Foundation of our Sense of Moral Good"[176] Thus, presupposing this centrality as already established (at least in principle), I will proceed here by focusing on the general account of obligation that Hutcheson provides in the context of his *honestum*-imbued theory of morals, i.e., the account found in the final chapter of Treatise II.

The first section of chapter 10 (see especially pp. 208–212) contains detailed discussion of this general account. Consequently, I will again limit my comments to calling attention to several salient points of an analysis already provided: (1) Hutcheson endeavors to show how instinctually anchored benevolence furnishes the only proper basis for understanding the origin of our idea of obligation as well as the nature of obligation itself. (2) Accordingly, he holds that the "Obligation upon all men to Benevolence" (IBV 177) must be understood as the deontic ground of action supplied by other-directed benevolence itself as an affective determination of the human frame. (3) It is in virtue of this affective determination that we can be moved to act independently of every consideration of law and whatever sanctions of law that may be linked to advantage or self-interest.

From the perspective of this chapter's argument, the crucial implication of Hutcheson's considerations on the natural basis of obligation is therefore this: No *motivational* condition antecedent to the sense of obligation is required in order to explain how acting from the sense of duty, or from a regard to moral

---

[176] See Moore 2002, pp. 365–386 (particularly pp. 372–374). For a brief discussion of further literature and debate in this area of research, see Harris 2009, pp. 161–164 (see also pp. 169–174, 176–177).

obligation, is possible. For no Humean charge of explanatory circularity (see p. 245) can reasonably be leveled if no such condition can be prior to the *obligation* that moves us to act. In other words, there can be no plausible circularity charge if there is no motivational condition in play that is distinct from, and hence possibly antecedent to, the determination of our affective frame that moves us to act in the manner that it is our duty to act. And as long as we act in this manner—that is, as long as we are actually moved to act from benevolence as an affective determination—we will necessarily be acting from a sense of duty or a regard to moral obligation insofar as we are aware of what we are doing. Thus, on Hutcheson's account of the subjective source of obligation, there is simply nothing that could ever keep that kind of sense or regard from being *able* to be the motive—and indeed, the *sole* motive—to morally good action, as long as benevolence is understood to be the original determination of the human affective constitution that is itself also a *deontic* determination.

From Hutcheson's perspective, then, it seems that this last point ought to provide the crucial component of a general theory of obligation grounded in a consistently sentimentalist account of the origin of our sense of obligation or duty, an account that in turn has its place in a foundational ethical theory that treats of the elements and the form of the *honestum*.[177] It is also the point that, as I indicated above, allows for the aforementioned compatibility between Hutcheson's sentimentalist approach to the foundations of morals and the approach taken by Reid as well as by other rationalists.[178] Moreover, judging from what Hume writes in September 1739 about his disagreement with Hutcheson, it would also seem to be the essential *Hutchesonian* point that Hume implicitly rejects when he appeals to what Cicero is supposed to prove against the Stoics' conception of the *honestum* as the sole good. Thus, as long as we can be confident that Hutcheson rejects the supposition that what Cicero proves against the Stoics supports the position that Hume takes regarding the basis of moral motivation, we also have good reason to think that Hutcheson rejects the proposition concerning the moral worth of actions that Hume wants to prove.[179]

---

[177] From Hutcheson's perspective, Hume's treatment of his undoubted maxim fails to exploit the position on the basis of obligation implicit in the following lines quoted in chapter 4 (see p. 94): "We blame a father for neglecting his child. Why? Because it shows a want of natural affection, which *is* the duty of every parent" (THN 3.2.1.5—italics mine).

[178] See notes 145–149 and 171 in this chapter.

[179] In a recent discussion of Reid's and Hume's accounts of justice, James Harris has focused on the crucial 1739 passage (see, again, pp. 242–243 this chapter). Regarding this passage's penultimate sentence, Harris writes: "Hume goes on to intimate that Hutcheson might disagree with him here. This is puzzling since there is nothing in Hutcheson's moral philosophy to sug-

If this last consideration is acceptable, however, I suggest that we may unavoidably be confronted with a further problem of some interest. I have in mind here the problem presented by the following question: What exactly have we been disputing *about* for more than two and a half centuries when we have endorsed opposing positions taken in eighteenth-century rationalist and sentimentalist ethics, thereby intervening in a debate on moral worth that goes back to the Hellenistic school disputes pertaining to the nature of the *honestum*. We may have been brought to an impasse concerning the nature of moral motivation and the sources of obligation that—given our historically conditioned disposition to follow in Hume's footsteps while leaving a rather less canonical figure like Hutcheson to trot along half a step behind—is purely of our own making. Finding ourselves back at square one, then, might not be such a bad place to set out from again if there should never have been an impasse to begin with.

§ 6 Kant's Theory of Reason's Autonomy and the Historic Impasse that Need Never Have Been

Achieving clarity about what Cicero, in *De finibus* IV, was actually arguing against the Stoics is in any case a good way to get back to the starting square just mentioned, if we are dealing with a historic impasse that need never have been. But what could Kant have to say about such an impasse if it is in truth merely of our own making? [180]

---

gest that in this respect, at least, he and Hume are at odds with one another" (Harris 2010, p. 208). If the argument of this paper is sound, though, it goes to show that Hume and Hutcheson are in fact fundamentally at odds with one another in precisely the respect signaled by Hume himself.

180 What is of our own making is of course not necessarily of our more recent making: "Hutcheson, in his essay upon beauty and virtue, founds the morality of actions on a certain quality of actions, that procures approbation and love to the agent. But this account of morality is also imperfect, as it makes no distinction between duty and simple benevolence. [...] But it is chiefly to be observed, that in this account of morality, the terms *obligation, duty, ought* and *should*, have no distinct meaning; which shows, that the entire foundation of morality is not taken in by this author" (Home [Lord Kames] 2005 [1751], p. 51). It is worth emphasizing here that Kant, during the 1760s (see UG 2:300.19–25; NEV 2:311.24–29), did not at all share the type of assessment of Hutcheson advocated by Home (see chapter 9, pp. 185–188). And while Kant would come to repudiate Hutcheson's whole approach to the basis of moral obligation and motivation, he never maintained that Hutcheson failed to take in the entire foundation of morality when seeking to provide a coherently sentimentalist account of that basis.

Let us again turn to the staging platform that I mentioned in the first section of this chapter. This platform, provisionally set up at the end of chapter 5, is intended to provide for an effective Kantian response to the sentimentalist approach to actions' moral worth that is implicit in the undoubted maxim of Hume's *Treatise*, i.e., the kind of sentimentalist approach which excludes that an action performed from the sense of duty or regard to obligation *alone* can have genuine moral worth. As the argument of chapter 5 has shown, the crucial plank in the proposed platform is furnished by the supposition that an action can have genuine moral worth *only if* one can will that its maxim should become a universal law, and *even if* acting on its maxim infringes upon all of one's inclinations. For this supposition is what would enable Kant to counter Hume's exclusionary approach by establishing that it is always possible to act from respect for law as one's incentive *whenever* one's maxim is apt for a universal lawgiving, whether or not one is inclined to act on such a maxim. Thus, it was in view of that same supposition that I posed two questions about our Kantian staging platform's capacity. First, can it bear the weight of Kant's theory of obligatory ends as material determining grounds of the power of choice? Second, can a theory of moral worth that incorporates grounds like these accommodate an empirically grounded maxim of self-perfection?

The response to the first of these queries is a straightforward matter, especially since it is already implicit in the considerations on one's own perfection as a promotable end that were presented prior to chapter 5, i.e., the considerations pertaining to own-perfection as an end that "I" ought to have as a material determining ground of my power of choice insofar as "I am bound to make my end something that lies in concepts of practical reason" (TL 6:381.9–10). As we determined when taking account of the aspect of asymmetry exhibited by Kant's dual concepts of obligatory end, the concept of own-perfection can ground a law requiring the promotion of the greatest perfection of which a human being is capable, i.e., the cultivated disposition "to do his duty *from duty* (for the law to be not only the rule but also the incentive for his actions)" (TL 6:392.21–23). Clearly, then, the theoretical platform whose central plank supports the possibility of always being able to act from respect for law as one's incentive is one that can easily bear the weight of a theory of reason's obligatory ends.

But what about our proposed platforms's capacity to accommodate a maxim of self-perfection that is supposed to have its ground in an empirically cognizable feature of the human affective constitution? Given the outcome of the investigations undertaken in §§ 2–5 of this chapter, I will take up this question in view of the role played by benevolence in Hutcheson's foundational account of obligation. Before delving into this, though, let me once again draw our attention to the venerable single-source interpretation of Stoic *oikeiôsis* doctrine that I first discussed in chapter 9, when examining the relationship between Rousseau's moral anthropology and the development of Kant's ethics during the 1760s.

At this juncture there are two primary points to underscore regarding this historically prevalent interpretive view of *oikeiôsis*, i.e., the view according to which the development of the human being's increasingly expansive concern for the well-being of others has its ultimate source solely in the love of self that goes hand in hand with the individual's striving for self-preservation. First, the single-source view is consistent with a key theorematic claim that underlies Kant's attempted Epicurean assimilation of the generically Stoic principle of internal perfection (see chapter 8, pp. 174–175, 180–183), notably, the claim that all material practical principles belong under the general principle of self-love or one's own happiness. Second, Hutcheson's account of benevolence as an original and irreducible determination of the human affective frame undercuts the kind of explanation of non-rational conditions of action that is implicit in the single-source view. In particular, his account of benevolence as an original *deontic* determination undercuts the type of explanation of affective motivational conditions on which Kant's assimilative interpretation of the Stoic principle of perfection depends.

So let us address the problem of our Kantian platform's accommodation capacity by first posing this query about Hutcheson's theory of the foundations of morals: Can this theory accommodate a principle of internal perfection that is grounded in the (deontically salient) human affective capacity to act for the good of others?

It can indeed. For Hutcheson explicitly emphasizes, in the context of his considerations on the origin of our ideas of obligation and law, that the human agent's "Natural Propensity to Benevolence" can be shaped by empirical inquiry into "what course of Action does most effectively promote the universal Good, what universal Rules or Maxims are to be observ'd" so that "our good inclinations may be directed by Reason, and a just Knowledge of the Interests of Mankind" (IBV 177). Moreover, in keeping with this emphasis on the possibility of reason-directed action according to universal rules or maxims, Hutcheson also maintains that the human being can cultivate the disposition to perform actions that are "the most perfectly virtuous; viz., such as appear to have the most universal Tendency to the greatest and most extensive Happiness of all rational agents, to whom our influence can reach" (IBV 126; cf. IBV 148, 150). Thus, while the Hutchesonian *source* of our obligation to promote the happiness of others cannot (contrary to Kant) lie in any lawgiving function of the human frame's rational aspect, Hutcheson's action-guiding universal maxims as well as his greatest-happiness version of the principle of universal benevolence leave plenty of room (as Reid might say) for a principle of greatest human perfection.

But this is exactly the *type* of principle that Kant requires in order to ground a theory of moral worth in his account of practical reason's obligatory ends. Although Kant's principle of greatest human perfection certainly does not prescribe acting to promote the greatest and most extensive happiness of all rational agents, it can nonetheless *accommodate* an empirically grounded principle of internal perfection that prescribes cultivating the disposition to perform actions that are the most perfectly virtuous. At least Kant's principle can do this as long as it can make room for the thought that it is always possible to act from respect for law as one's incentive.

Thus, provided that there is in fact room for this thought, there is just one further requirement to fulfill in order to shore up our Kantian platform's carrying capacity: We must be prepared to jettison the implicitly single-source based self-love theorem that underlies Kant's Epicurean assimilation strategy. And that, in the greater scheme of things, is a theoretical price to pay that more than pays for itself.

To wrap up this chapter, let us take a moment to revisit the two stock characters mentioned in connection with the belletristic folly that tempted us, as long ago as chapter 5 (see pp. 102–103), to plunge off the deep end of philological disreputability. Our sympathetically attuned, amiably sentimental Squire Allworthy was even then lured away from the pleasures of country life in Fielding's Somersetshire and unceremoniously transported to fields ruled by reason's autonomy. Yet in making this move we also left Rousseau's estimable Monsieur de Wolmar behind to bide his time, sitting in Julie's garden. So let us now drag this insensitive wretch as well off his comfortable bench and make him even more unsympathetically rule and law-worshipping by depositing him on some wind-blown shore in Kant's domain of promotable ends that are also duties.[181]

In view of this (rather dubious, to say the least) relocation scenario, the concluding question that I would like to pose is the following one. In the event that our two worthy gentlemen should encounter one another on one of their joy-spreading (Allworthy) or beneficence-imposing (Wolmar) walks, what exactly would they have to dispute *about* as far the moral worth of their benevolent actions is concerned?

Evidently not much to begin with. Nor, more importantly, could either one of them have anything decisive to say against Kant's account of reason's autonomy

---

[181] Note well that this is not the same as anybody's *kingdom* of ends.

as long as they are willing to warm up to each other by agreeing to the following condition: It is always possible to act from respect to law as one's incentive whenever one's maxim is apt for a possible universal lawgiving, whether or not one is inclined to act on such a maxim.

To be sure, it is unrealistic to expect that our two disputants will be able to achieve even provisional agreement about the meaning of this condition without first sorting through nearly two millennia worth of historical baggage. So let us leave them talking past one another as we move on to some unfinished business regarding Kant's juridical theory of right and its account of original acquisition. It seems only right to leave *both* of our sentimentalist and rationalist disputants behind when taking this step. For autonomous ethics had no good reason to accept the terms of their dispute to begin with. Nor has it ever had such a reason.

Chapter 12
Natural Right, Material Equality, and the Normative Basis of Acquisition

Part III was centrally concerned with two pivotal concepts in Kant's account of the normative basis of external acquisition: the idea of appropriation through first seizure, or *prima occupatio*, and the idea of an a priori united will of all. As we have seen, Kant's joint employment of these concepts leads to a fundamental problem for his theory of property: Why should first seizure, which is necessarily a unilaterally possession-taking act, receive the favor (*Gunst*) of any universal law of juridico-practical reason? More particularly, why should such a unilateral act be permissible to begin with when, as Kant himself admits, its performance on the part of all appropriating agents must be thought of as containing the seeds of universal conflict?

Dealing with this question led us to investigate the historical backdrop to Kant's treatment of original acquisition. We considered Grotius's attempt to ground ownership using the concept of a dominative natural right in conjunction with a contractualist principle of agreement. We also examined the line of argument by which Selden drew out a key consequence of Grotius's theory of acquisition—i.e. the implication that the natural right which warrants the unilateral first seizure of things from the common *dominium* of humankind is in effect a right to all things as far as the doctrine of original acquisition is concerned.

After clarifying Selden's proximity to Kant with respect to the role of first seizure and the idea of universal agreement, I pointed out that the solution to Kant's problem of original acquisition has to be consistent with the conception of innate freedom and the innate equality of human beings that underlies his basic view of rights as moral "capacities [*Vermögen*] for putting others under obligation" (RL 6:237.18). Accordingly, I argued that the principle of distribution at issue in Kant's conceptual determination of original acquisition ought to one of equality.

To be sure, as already indicated at the end of chapter 7, making this argument gives rise to a significant difficulty. It demands that we forge a link between the Kantian accounts of the innate right of freedom and the principle of external acquisition that Kant simply does not explicitly acknowledge in the systematic context of his doctrine of original acquisition. Specifically, it requires us to focus on the concept of innate equality involved in the principle of innate freedom (see RL 6:237.32–238.11) in order to show that Kant's doctrine can provide a sound normative basis for property law only if in incorporates a formal principle of *material* equality. Thus, one may reasonably ask why my proposed solution to Kant's problem of original acquisition should be judged compelling if it is one that Kant does not expressly acknowledge because it is based on a link-forging interpretive inference that he himself does not draw.

I will address this issue in the final section of this chapter. To set the stage for doing so, I will first shed some light on several further patches of the historical tapestry into which Kant's account of the foundations of property law is woven. The first patch has to do with some pre-modern background to Grotius's theory of property. The second concerns Hobbes's repudiation of the type of doctrine of original acquisition that we encountered in Part III when considering Kant's relation to Grotius and Selden.

§ 1 Ius Utendi, Ius Appropriandi, and the Emergence of the Modern Conception of Natural Right: Grotius and Ockham on Original Acquisition

As explained in chapter 7 (see pp. 150 – 152), Grotius holds that human beings in the state of nature have common *dominium* in all things to which they are originally related through a use-warranting power: the *facultas non iniusta utendi*. Unsurprisingly, Grotius recognizes that a conceptual distinction must be drawn between seizing something in order to use it and seizing something to use in order to make it one's own. Yet he also maintains that such a distinction is not specifically relevant to the grounding of original acquisition. For in the state of nature, the initial step in a human subject's appropriative activity— i.e., the use of something consumable to satisfy a basic natural need—unavoidably amounts to a unilateral act of first seizure or occupation that can be extended to things in addition those consumed through use. As Grotius writes in *Mare liberum:*

> It is apparent that the present-day distinction of ownerships [*dominia*] did not come about all of a sudden, but gradually and with nature [itself] showing the initial step. For there are some things whose use consists in using them up, either because having been converted into the substance of the user they afterward admit of no further use,[182] or because by use they become less fit for further use. Thus it very soon became apparent, with respect to things of the first sort, such as food and drink, that a certain kind of ownership [*proprie-*

---

[182] Grotius places a reference to "*Extrav., VIV 3 et 5*" after this clause. Regarding the significance of this reference, see note 185 of this chapter.

tas quaedam] was inseparable from use.¹⁸³ For to be one's own is to belong to someone in such a way that it may not also belong to another. By a certain reasoning [*ratione quadam*] this [relation of ownership] was then extended to things of the latter sort.¹⁸⁴ (ML 24/DJP 215–216)

I have already discussed (see pp. 152–155) how Grotius accounts for the extension of ownership in accordance with the rational ground mentioned in the final sentence of this passage by eventually introducing (in *De jure belli ac pacis*) a principle of universal agreement into his theory of original acquisition. What is of primary interest to us at this juncture is Grotius's claim that there are certain things for which ownership is initially inseparable from use.

On the face of things, this pivotal Grotian claim about the initial inseparability of ownership and use in the state of nature may seem unassailable as far as the idea of original acquisition is concerned. Yet it was the decisive bone of contention in one of the greatest debates pertaining to the normative foundations of property law in the history of western thought. I refer here to the dispute concerning poverty and property which took place between representatives of the Franciscan Order and the advocates of papal authority during the late thirteenth and early fourteenth centuries. Grotius's familiarity with the substance of this dispute is indicated by the fact that he cites the major titular advocate of the papal position—Pope John XXII—in support of his pivotal claim.¹⁸⁵ Implicitly, then, what Grotius does in the preceding passage translated from *Mare liberum* is this: In order to ground the initial step that "nature shows" on the way to the emergence of distinct human *dominia*, he rejects a key position concerning use and ownership that was taken by Pope John's most prominent Franciscan opponent, namely, William of Ockham. Let us take a closer look at the terms of the opposition in question.

---

183 On the issues raised by the translation of *proprietas* as 'property' and *dominium* as 'ownership', see Robinson 2013, pp. 24–27.
184 "Ad eam vero quae nunc est dominiorum distinctionem non impetus quodam, sed paulatim ventum vedetur, initium ejus monstrante natura. Cum enim res sint nonnullae, quarum usus in abusu consistit, aut quia conversae in substantiam utentis nullum postea usum admittunt, aut qui utendo fiunt ad usum deteriores, in rebus prioris generis, ut cibo et potu, proprietas statim quaedam ab usu non sejuncta emicuit. Hoc enim est proprium esse, ita esse cujusquam ut et alterius esse non possit; quod deinde ad res posterioris, [...], ratione quadam productum est".
185 Tierney (1997, pp. 330–331) calls attention to the direct link to the papal position indicated by Grotius's reference to "*Extra[vagantes]*" in the passage from *Mare liberum* quoted above (see note 182 in this chapter). Feenstra (1978) provides a general account of the sources of Grotius's knowledge concerning the Franciscan debate on property.

The dispute concerning Franciscan poverty is generally recognized for its direct or indirect impact on all subsequent medieval and early modern developments in the theory of property.[186] It arguably represents the most significant debate concerning the question of property to have occurred prior to the seventeenth century.[187] Central to this long-term debate were the different attempts made on both sides to clarify the grounds of property ownership or *dominium* in external things. A characteristic component of the Franciscans' attempts was the thesis that a clear distinction must *always* be drawn between use and ownership since the use of things is analytically separable from *dominium* even when things are consumed through their very use and are therefore no longer available for acquisition by anyone. As already noted, the counterpart to this 'separability thesis' was endorsed by the Franciscans' key opponents—most notably by Pope John XXII, to whom Grotius refers when in effect rejecting the relevance of separability thesis for his doctrine of original acquisition.

In keeping with the separability thesis, the Franciscan disputants were able to maintain that they could rightfully renounce *every* claim to property, even with regard to things consumed through use (e.g., food). Insisting that this stance on ownership was unacceptable,[188] Pope John presented the following views about the nature and origin of property: As the result of God's magnanimity in His original act of donation, the first human being—Adam—received *dominium* over all temporal things before the creation and the ensuing procreation of everyone else. Thus, it must be the case that this *dominium* belonging to a single finite being served as the basis for the emergence of all further property relations. Accordingly, it is excluded that the original property relation, i.e., the God-granted relation of *dominium* which grounded all subsequent property relations between human beings, can be thought of in terms of common ownership extending to humanity as a whole. For it is nonsensical to speak of common ownership with reference to the time when only one human being existed. And it is incomprehensible how anyone (including of course the Franciscan mendicants) could renounce every possible claim to property ownership if humanity, in the person of a single human being, was originally granted *dominium* in all things on earth.

---

186 In this section, I have made extensive use of Brian Tierney's and Jonathan Robinson's magisterial treatments of the dispute (see Tierney 1997, pp. 93–203; Robinson 2013, especially pp. 44–63; 107–111, 114–124, 161–174, 209–225, 246–254). For two other excellent treatments of the dispute and its background, see Brett 1997, pp. 10–22, 49–68 and Coleman 1988, pp. 607–648. For a survey of the broader background terrain, see P. Garnsey 2007, pp. 59–135.
187 Or including the seventeenth century and thereafter, for that matter.
188 Cf. Tierney 1997, p. 131.

William of Ockham's *Work of Ninety Days* (*Opus nonaginta dierum* [OND]),[189] offers a running account of the origins of property that is opposed to the papal views just summarized. Ockham's argument concerning these origins is as notoriously convoluted as it is superbly polemical. It stretches over many pages and is not obviously free of inconsistencies. But its import can be fairly summarized as follows.

Both in their original condition of innocence and immediately after their fall from divine grace, Adam and Eve had no property at all. That is, they possessed property neither individually nor in common. To understand how this could be, one has merely to distinguish properly between the two quite separate meanings of *dominium* that Pope John failed to take into account. According to both meanings, *dominium* has to be understood as an authorizing power (*potestas*) attributable to human agents. Yet it is essential to distinguish between, on the one hand, the characterization of *dominium* as a power of appropriating and acquiring what is one's own and, on the other hand, its more general interpretation as a power of ruling over worldly things.[190] On the basis of this distinction, one can clearly see that the original *dominium* granted to Adam, and consequently to Eve, did not pertain to property as such. Instead, it must be understood more broadly as *potestas rationaliter regendi et gubernandi temporalia* (OND 14.74–76)—a power of rationally ruling and directing temporal things. Thus, instead of endowing Adam and Eve with property, either individually or in common, God gave them merely a *potestas utendi*—a power of using that could be exercised on external things. Although having this originally granted power is not the same as having *dominium* in these things, the power itself is one that permits the use of things over which humanity was originally granted *dominium* in the broader sense just noted. It is thus a use-warranting power that must be understood as a right (*ius*) attributable to human subjects. Moreover, this *ius utendi* is also inalienable since no human being can possibly renounce it. As such, it has been in effect throughout the course of humanity's historical existence. But it is not a right that, taken by itself, allows for any act that could establish particularized *dominium* in external things. There are two reasons for this circumstance. First, the originally granted *dominium* over worldly things—the *potestas regendi et gubernandi*—was lost to human beings very early on in the order of time as the result of original sin. Second, the inalienable right or power of using is in any case distinguishable from the power of acquiring or ap-

---

[189] My references to *Opus nonaginta dierum* are to the text edited by H. S. Offler and published in volumes 1 and 2 of Ockham's *Opera politica* (Manchester 1974). Passages are cited according to chapter and line numbers of this edition (e.g., OND 2.270–470).
[190] OND 2.270–420.

propriating things for oneself. That is to say: *postestas utendi* must always be treated as separable from *potestas appropriandi*, even in circumstances in which things are consumed through the very act of using them. Consequently, that use-warranting power or right cannot suffice to ground the permissibility of an appropriative act that would initially establish property ownership.

According to Ockham, then, the power of appropriating cannot be ascribed to human beings in their original natural condition; and there is in any event no way to establish directly a necessary link between the exercise of that power and this condition. But if that is so, then how does one explain how appropriation licitly occurs in the first place? What are the grounds for attributing to human beings the power to appropriate things as a *right?* Consistently with the Franciscan position Ockham was defending, the argument of OND denies that the power of appropriating derives directly from God, and it emphasizes that the normative basis of this power lies in natural human reason. Specifically, Ockham's argument relies on the connection between the prescriptive requirements of natural reason and the determination of utility in humanity's fallen condition resulting from original sin. As Ockham puts this point: "It is demonstrated from the dictate of natural reason that it is useful to those able to sin that they also have the power of appropriating". [191] (OND 14.203–205).

For the purposes of this chapter's argument, there are three key points to underscore concerning doctrine of property acquisition that Ockham anchors in the utility-directed character of natural reason's dictation. First, Ockham holds that the initial expression of the *postestas appropriandi* in keeping with natural reason's dictate is the act which *founded* a relation of *dominium* that was shared by the original human appropriators. Second, this act of original acquisition obviously could not apply to what was already *owned* by everyone in common, or indeed by anyone at all.[192] The appropriation-warranting *potestas* is therefore intelligible as a subjective power exercised upon a common world of external things. But this is nonetheless a world of things belonging to no one, i.e., a shared world in which each and every acquirable thing qualifies as *res nullius*.[193]

---

191 "[E]x dictamine rationis naturalis convincitur quod expedit posse peccantibus quod etiam habebant potestatem appropriandi sibi". This connection between utility and natural reason's prescription regarding the possibility of appropriation, however, is subject to an essential restriction on Ockham's account: Appropriation must be in keeping with the natural equity that obtains among human beings, even in their fallen condition. See, e.g., OND 3.395–442, 61.123–144, 65.197–217.
192 See OND 14.178–215, 28.37–67.
193 Ockham thus employs the Roman-law concept of *res nullius* in order to clarify this line of argument. Even immediately after the Fall, Adam and Eve *owned* nothing. Nevertheless, they did

Such a world furnished the collective object of all possible acquisition on the part of the originally available appropriators (namely, Adam and Eve). Yet precisely because it furnished this kind of object, i.e., the object constituted by all acquirable external things belonging to no one, it cannot be said ever to have *belonged* originally to any appropriator or appropriators. This is true even if the appropriating subjects involved in the act of original acquisition made up the collective whole of humanity at the time when that act was performed.[194]

The third point, which is closely wedded to the two just mentioned, can end up being obscured if one is overly ambitious in attempting to link Ockham to modern accounts of the origins of private property by way of Grotius's implicit denial of the separability thesis discussed above. According to Ockham, the *postestas appropriandi* (or, equivalently, the *potestas acquirendi*) is indeed grounded in human reason in the sense that it follows from a requirement of natural reason (*ex dictamine rationis naturalis*). Moreover, at various junctures in OND, Ockham's argument quite clearly furnishes definitional accounts of natural right (and rights) in the subjective sense.[195] Yet this argument does not entail that the subjective power of appropriating can *itself* be understood as a natural right of distributive acquisition. Although Ockham holds that externally acquirable objects are originally subject to appropriation by humankind in accordance with the requirements of natural reason, his doctrine of the origin of property does not contain the concept of a dominative *natural* right that applies directly to the acquisition of *dominia distincta*.[196]

Clearly, Ockham could not have employed such a concept as long as he wished to pursue a coherent line of argument against the papal position on apos-

---

retain the power of appropriating things so as to acquire common *dominium* since things that are among no one's good are conceded to whomever seizes them ("habebant potestatem appropriandi sibi et acquirendi commune dominium; quia quae in nullius boni sunt, occupanti conceduntur" [OND 14.190–2]).

[194] Thus, if it is proper to speak of a community of things with respect to what is *in bonis nullius*, then this community can only be conceived negatively. In effect, Ockham's doctrine of original acquisition builds on the conceptual construct of a *communio negativa* even when he insists that what was originally acquired was determined positively as the common *dominium* of all available human appropriators. Cf. Pufendorf, DJN IV.2.2–5/GW 4.1:354–358. (Brian Tierney calls attention to the similarities between Ockham and Pufendorf in this connection: see Tierney 1997, p. 163.)

[195] See OND 3.395–416, 49.104–122, 61.12–144, 62.58–95, 65.76–89, 65.197–260, 83.80–107. See also Mäkinnen 2012, pp. 512–522.

[196] See OND 14.340–367.By 'dominative' right I mean simply a right (in the subjective sense) that grounds *dominium*, especially with respect to externally acquirable things. As indicated in note 62 of chapter 7, I take the term from Francisco Suarez, who uses it in exactly this sense.

tolic poverty and property. In order to offer support for the Franciscan opposition, Ockham had to uphold the full-bore theoretical relevance of the sharpest possible conceptual distinction between, on the one hand, a voluntarily relinquishable *potestas appropriandi* (with reference to which the origin of *dominium* could be understood as deriving from the prescriptive requirements of human rational agency) and, on the other hand, the inalienable *ius utendi* that qualifies as a natural right in the subjective sense. Designating the first of these subjective attributes as a natural right would have resulted not merely in terminological confusion that would have weakened the polemical force of Ockham's argument against Pope John. It would also have undermined the very position that Ockham was trying to support.[197] Only by cleanly separating the notion of a subject's power or right of using from that of an appropriating power could Ockham attempt to establish that the normative basis of ownership does not lie in the original relation of human beings to a world of usable things given by God for their use, but is instead dependent on the prescription of natural reason that authorizes the establishment of *dominium* in external things on account of its demonstrated utility to those who are able to sin (i.e., every one of us).

§ 2 The Right to All Things and Communitas Rerum: Hobbes on the Conceptual Incoherence of Natural Right-Based Acquisition

If we combine the previous section's considerations on Grotius and Ockham with those on Grotius and Selden presented in Part III, we can discern that we have been dealing with historically influential accounts of original acquisition based on three quite different conceptions of the proper relationship between natural right and the appropriation of external things. We have encountered in Ockham a natural *ius* (i.e., *potestas*) *utendi* that must be kept strictly separate from the dominative right of appropriation that follows from the dictation of natural reason. In addition, we have encountered in Grotius a natural *ius* (i.e., *facultas*) *utendi* that is also a dominative right which grounds the permissibility of extended appropriation on the basis of first seizure. Finally, we have encountered in Selden a nature-given dominative right that grounds the permissibility

---

[197] Tierney (1997, pp. 164–165) comes uncomfortably close to maintaining that it was for essentially rhetorical purposes that Ockham avoided using the terminology of natural rights in his account of the origins of property. I believe that this reflects a fundamental misreading of this account's central philosophical point, not to mention its social and political import.

of unrestricted appropriation through first seizure independently of any limiting conditions of use or usefulness.

As we found in chapter 7 (pp. 155–160), Selden's conception of the relationship between his dominative right and the originally unrestricted scope of appropriation derives from the anti-Grotian consequences that he draws from Grotius's own application of the contractualist principle of universal agreement to the conditions of permissible appropriation from humanity's originally common *dominium*. According to Selden, the principle of universal agreement cannot limit the scope of anyone's unilateral act of appropriation through first seizure as long as it presupposes that what everyone *had* occupied should be possessed as one's own. In effect, then, Selden works with a natural right of appropriation that amounts to *ius in omnia*—a (or the) right to any and all things not already subject to distributive appropriation.

This reference to a right to all things obviously raises the question of how Hobbes fits into the line of investigation that we have just been tracing from Ockham through Grotius and Selden on our way back to Kant. In this section, I will take up this question by starting with a passage in Hobbes's *De cive*. The passage that I have in mind is of fundamental importance for assessing the theories of original acquisition with which we have been concerned in this book thus far. It allows us to locate and track a crucial implication of Hobbes's description of the natural condition of humankind, i.e., the implication that the very project of basing a theory of property law on the idea of original acquisition is tantamount to an incoherent exercise in juridico-philosophic thinking. Let us begin our tracking efforts by examining the Latin version of the *De cive* passage in question in conjunction with its historically most influential English rendering.

The 1651 translation of Thomas Hobbes's *De cive* has by and large been held in high regard over the past three and a half centuries. Indeed, until quite recently it could plausibly be maintained that Hobbes himself translated his Latin text of 1642, or at least that he was sufficiently well acquainted with the actual translator's work as to have been in a position to approve it. For some years now, however, this interpretive stance has been decisively undermined by historical scholarship; and I work here on the assumption that the 1651 translation cannot lay claim being authored or authorized by Hobbes.[198] Still, given its centuries-long influence on the interpretation of Hobbes's juridical and political thought, it is worth pausing to see what lessons might be learned from the old translation be-

---

198 See above Malcolm 2002, pp. 234–258.

fore too much dust settles upon it.¹⁹⁹ The most important lesson, for our purposes, can be gleaned from the explanation of the background of his concern with natural law theory that Hobbes gives in *De cive's* dedicatory letter to William Cavendish. I quote here from the 1651 translation as well as from Hobbes's own text:

> There is a certain Clue of Reason, whose beginning is in the dark, but by the benefit of whose Conduct, wee are led as 'twere by the hand into the clearest light [...] As often therefore as any writer, doth either weakly forsake that Clue, or wilfully cut it asunder, he describes the Footsteps, not of his progresse in *Science*, but of his wandrings from it. And upon this it was, that when I applyed my Thoughts to the Investigation of Naturall Justice, I was presently advertised from the very word *Justice*, (wich signifies a steady Will of giving every one his *Owne*) that my first enquiry was to be, from whence it proceeded, that any man should call any thing rather is *Owne* then *another mans*. And when I found that this proceeded not from Nature, but Consent, (for what nature at first laid forth in common, men did afterwards distribute into severall *Impropriations*, I was conducted from thence to another Inquiry, namely to what end, and upon what Impulsives, when all was equally every mans in common, men did rather think it fitting, that every man should have his Inclosure; And I found the reason was, that from a Community of Goods, there must needs arise Contention whose enjoyment should be greatest, and from that Contention all kind of Calamities must unavoydably ensue, which by the instinct of Nature, every man is taught to shun. Having therefore thus arrived at two maximes of humane Nature, the one arising from the *concupiscible* part, which desires to appropriate to it selfe the use of those things in which all others have a joynt interest, the other proceeding from the *rationall*, which teaches every man to fly a contre-naturall Dissolution, as the greatest mischiefe that can arrive to Nature; which Principles being laid down, I seem from them to have demonstrated by a most evident connexion [...] first the absolute necessity of Leagues and Contracts, and thence the rudiments both of morall and of civill Prudence.²⁰⁰

> (Incipit in ipsis dubitandi tenebris filum quodam rationis, cuius ductu euaditur in lucem clarissimam [...] Quoties ergo scriptor filum illud, vel inscitia deserit, vel cupiditatibus abrumpit, non scientiae, sed errationum suarum vestigia literis describit. Quapropter, cùm cogitationes meas ad inquisititionem iustitiae naturalis conuertissem, admonitus sum ab ipsa iustitiae appellatione, qua constans voluntas unicuique *Ius suum* tribuendi significatur, quaerendum prius esse, unde esset quod quis rem aliquam *suam* potius quam *alienam* esse diceret; quod cum non à natura, sed à consensu hominum profectum constaret (Nam quae natura in medium protulit, homines postea distribuerunt) ducebar inde ad quaestionem aliam, nimirum cui bono, & qua necessitati coacti, cùm omnia essent omnium, voluerint potius sua cuique esse propria. Videbam autem ex communitate rerum bellum, atque inde omne genus calamitatis, hominibus de earum usu per vim certantibus, necessario sequuturum esse; id quod omnes natura fugiunt. Nactus ergo duo certissima na-

---

199 The recent English translation by Tuck and Silverthorne (1998) generally provides a more accurate rendering of the Latin text than is found in the 1651 version.
200 Hobbes 1983 [1651], p. 27.

> turae humanae postulata, unum cupiditatis naturalis, qua quisque rerum communium usum postulat sibi proprium; alterum rationis naturalis, qua quisque mortem violentam tanquam summum naturae malum studet euitare. Ab his principiis pactorum & fidei conseruandae necessitatem, atque inde virtutis moralis officiorumque ciulium Elementa [...] euidentissima connexione videor mihi demonstrasse.[201])

A number of interesting differences emerge from these two versions of Hobbes's "thread of reason" (*filum rationis*) considerations. The first striking item, of course, is the apparent discrepancy between the nominal definition of justice that Hobbes accepts—i.e., the determination of justice as the constant will to give everyone their *right*[202]—and the translator's "steady Will of giving every one his *Owne*". I will say something more about this presently. But let us focus on the main item of interest—notably, the fact that the translation fails to capture adequately the import of Hobbes's conception of the original community of things (*communitas rerum*) that is characteristic of humanity's natural condition.

Compare the first of Hobbes's most certain *postulata* of human nature—i.e., the postulate of natural cupidity by which any user of common things claims the use of such things as his own (*qua quisque rerum communium usum postulat sibi proprium*)—with the translators's maxim "arising from the concupiscible part [of human nature], which desires to appropriate to itself the use of those things in which all others have a joint interest". Quite apart from the syntactical liberties taken in this rendering, it joins the *filum rationis* line of inquiry that Hobbes portrays to a conception of original community that he does not clearly endorse. For the injection of "joynt interest" into this portrayal suggests that Hobbes regards the things laid forth by nature for all in common are already in some sense *owned* prior to every unilateral act of use on the part of any given appropriator. In other words, the translator evidently supposes that Hobbes works with the idea of an originally common *dominium* when he lays out the salient characteristics of humankind's natural condition as the calamitous state of war that follows *ex communitate rerum*.

While this supposition goes together quite nicely with the interpretation of Hobbes's nominal definition of justice in terms of giving to everyone his *own*,

---

201 Hobbes 1982 [1642], pp. 75–76. The page numbers here cited are those of the Warrender edition (Thomas Hobbes, *De cive: The Latin Version*). In subsequent references to Hobbes's Latin text, I cite from this same edition, but in accordance with chapter and paragraph numbers.
202 That is to say, the nominal definition that largely coincides with the standard definition of justice that informs the corpus of juridical thought anchored in the source texts of Roman Law: "Iustitia est constans et perpetua voluntas ius suum cuique tribuere" (*Inst. Iustin.* I.I; see also, e. g., *Digesta*, I.1.10 pr. [Ulpianus]). For pertinent discussion, see Dieter Hüning 1998, pp. 53–70.

it can hardly be entailed by Hobbes's own basic account of justice as the constant will to give to each his *"own Right [Ius suum]"*.²⁰³ For the whole point of following the thread of reason that starts from this definitional account is to inquire into how everyone can be given their right, even if no one could originally claim the use of anything as one's own when nature preferred things in common (*in medium protulit*) for later distribution by human beings. Thus, it would make little sense for Hobbes to pursue such a line of inquiry if this presupposed that claiming the use of something as one's own was tantamount to laying claim to something in which everyone *already* had a joint ownership interest in virtue of what the postulate of natural cupidity asserts about the use of common things.

It is implausible, then, to construe Hobbes's overall project of inquiry into natural justice as involving a concept of common *dominium* that in turn can be explicated in terms of some form of joint ownership.²⁰⁴ But if the translator's suggestive employment of "joynt interest" leads in this direction, thus serving to misconstrue the key component of Hobbes's portrayal of humankind's natural state in the passage under consideration, then we must ask exactly what Hobbes does have in mind when he refers to the community of things, i.e., the type of community that *necessarily* gives rise to the natural condition of conflict, as long as men do not act fully in accordance with the postulate of natural reason by which each strives to avoid the supreme evil in nature (i.e., violent death).

---

203 Hobbes himself makes essentially this same point in *A Dialogue between a Philosopher and a Student* when he asks the expert on Common Law: "When you say that justice gives to every man his own, what mean you by his own? How can that be given to me, which is my own already? Or, if it not be my own, how can justice make it mine?" (*English Works* VI, p. 9). It may be noted here that all of Hobbes considerations on natural right, justice, and injustice in *De cive* are consistent with the nominal definition of justice presented in the dedicatory letter (see *De cive* I.7, I.10 nota, III.4 nota, III.5–6, III.27 nota, III.30, XII.1). In *Leviathan*, of course, Hobbes does employ the definition of justice as "the constant Will of giving to every man his own" (*Leviathan* XV.3; see also *Leviathan* XV.14–15, XXIV.5, XXVI.8, XXX.12). Yet the two most important *Leviathan* passages involving this "ordinary definition" also make it plain that Hobbes considers himself to be conforming to demands of custom going back not only to "the Schooles" (XV.4), but also to those "who called that Νόμος (that is to say, *Distribution,*) which we call Law" (XXIV.5).

204 Hobbes's *communitas rerum* may not plausibly be understood as, for example, an expanded and unrestricted version of the type of property relation that as a matter of historical fact undergirded the use of the English village common lands in the days before enclosure (cf. Tuck 1999, p. 117), which is exactly sort of view of original community that seems to be reflected in the 1651 translation's rendering of "cur bono, & qua necessitates coacti, cum omnia essent omnium, volerint potius sua cuique esse propria" as "to what end, and upon what impulsives, when all was equally every mans in common, men did rather think it fitting that every man should have his Inclosure".

One version of original community that Hobbes cannot have in mind, of course, is the positive view of common *dominium* that correlates with Selden's natural right of unrestricted first seizure, i.e., the view on which everyone is a joint owner of everything originally given to all in common. But to explain why this is so, let consider one more time the negative view of original community that Grotius, as we have seen, endorses—that is, the view that abstracts from all positive features of ownership in order to show how property is distributively grounded in the real identity of (i) the originally restricted use of consumable things (as warranted by the subject's natural *facultas utendi*) and (ii) the act of appropriation that permits extended acquisition of the means of production for such things. Hobbes cannot endorse even this Grotian minimalist conception of the identity of originally restricted use and appropriation. That is because, according to Hobbes, no one can claim even the *use* of something as one's own (*postulat* [...] *usum sibi proprium*) as long as everything is commonly available for the use-making seizure of each—which is to say: as long as humanity's natural condition must be characterized as one of conflict (*bellum*) just because conflict is unavoidably the essential characteristic of the community of things in which nothing can properly belong to anyone as one's own.

To be sure, as far as the form of such universal community is concerned, Hobbes's implicitly anti-Grotian portrayal of this natural condition places him in the immediate vicinity of Selden's conception of the relationship between original community and *ius commune* as a right to all things. Contrary to what is suggested by the seventeenth-century translator, however, there is a crucial difference between Hobbes and Selden in this frame of reference.[205] Selden's conception, as we have seen, requires the interpretation of *ius commune* as a *dominative* natural right. Yet precisely this kind of interpretation is ruled out by the connection that Hobbes makes between his *communitas rerum* and the natural condition of war. Given this connection, Hobbes does not, and cannot, maintain that each human being's unilateral act(s) of use-making seizure can be linked to the idea of an original and universally shared proprietary relation that permits the use of anything whatsoever as one's own.

To see why this is so, we have merely to consider how the implications of the connection just mentioned are spelled out in the main body of *De cive*, where Hobbes demonstrates that the very notion of a dominative right must prove to

---

[205] Marchamont Nedham uses "common interest" when rendering Selden's phrase "ut a communione seu a pristino jure eorum[, ... ,] plane discederetur" in his 1652 translation of *Mare clausum* (compare Selden 1726, p. 1197 [2nd column] with Selden 1652, p. 21.) This might be an indication that the seventeenth-century translator of *De cive* (i.e., Charles Cotton) was well aware of how Selden's idea of originally common *dominium* was being interpreted at the time.

be incoherent if it is understood as a *natural* right that everywhere permits acts of unrestricted appropriative use. According to Hobbes, the right that grounds such use is one that has the least possible utility to human beings. And since the very measure of such a right of use can logically be nothing apart from its utility, the determination of the necessary consequences of that right's universal exercise shows it to be of as much use as no right at all. For as *ius commune in omnia*, it permits actions on the part of all agents which exclude that anyone can have a right to anything in particular.[206] Moreover, if actions performed in conformity with this right of nature are permitted without restriction, then no one can as much as *claim*, except on pain of self-contradiction, that any given thing is one's own and only one's own. It therefore follows that no such common right could qualify as the normative ground for any type of *dominium* with respect to usable things.[207]

In sum, Hobbes's understanding of *communitas rerum* in *De cive* excludes that the idea of original community could be linked to a common right of use that can serve for the establishment of property. It makes no difference whether original community is interpreted merely negatively, i.e., as abstracting from all positive features of the juridical concept of *dominium*, or positively as a kind of joint ownership first constituted independently of human volition and agreement. For according to Hobbes, the permissible exercise of *everybody's* right of use in relation to the common possession of humankind is exactly what must perpetuate the state of affairs in which having something as one's own is impossible.

Thus far in this section, I have concentrated on Hobbes's references to the community of things in *De cive*. I have thereby endeavored to clarify the connection between the idea of original community, as it figures in Hobbes's initial considerations on natural justice, and the concept of a common right to all things. Since Hobbes portrays the natural condition of humankind in terms of the necessary consequences of this right's universally permissible exercise, it is apparent that the idea of original community should play only a negative systematic role in the constructive part Hobbes's natural-law theory, above all in its general account of the prescriptive laws of nature. And indeed, Hobbes's conceptual determination of the right of nature in *De cive* confirms this view of that idea's systematic standing. Proceeding from the account of liberty of action in conformity with the requirements of right reason, Hobbes derives his formula of the right to

---

[206] See *De cive* I.10–11.
[207] See *De cive* VI.15 and *De cive* XIV.9.

all things from the concept of unconditional freedom.[208] The right itself is specified in terms of the license that each agent has to possess and to *do* all things that he judges to be conducive to the protection of life and limb. The idea of original community is introduced and explicated in this connection as a common-parlance way of characterizing what is entailed by the philosophically precise specification of *ius in omnia:*

> Nature has given *to each a right to all things*. That is, in the bare state of nature, or before men bound themselves by any agreement with each other, it was permitted to each to do anything to anyone, and to possess, use, and enjoy everything that he wanted to or could get. Since, then, [...] things are done, and had, *by right of nature* that necessarily lead to the protection of life and limbs, it follows that, in the state of nature, all are permitted to have and to do all things. And this is what is meant by the common saying, *nature has given all things to all*. [209] (*De cive* I.10 [Silverthorne/Tuck translation modified])

Now given this explication of the underlying meaning of original community, it seems that the deduction of the basic laws of nature as well as their corresponding derivative laws should in principle be possible without reference to the notion of *communitas rerum* that Hobbes, in the dedicatory letter considered above, links to the origin of his investigation of natural justice. Clearly, though, Hobbes does not take advantage of this theoretical opportunity in the context of his *De cive* treatment of the laws of nature, as can be gathered from his interpretation of the law demanding the non-retention of the right to all things.[210] When establishing the equivalence of his prescriptive natural laws with the precepts of divine law in the fourth chapter of *De cive*, Hobbes explicitly characterizes this first de-

---

208 See *De cive* I.7–10.

209 "Natura dedit *unicuique ius in omnia*. Hoc est, in statu mere naturali, siue antequam homines vllis pactis sese inuicem osbstrinxissent, vnicuique licebat facere quaecunque & in quoscunque libebat, & possidere, vti, frui omnibus quae volebat & poterat. Quoniam enim [...] *iure naturae* fiunt, & habentur, quae necessario conducunt ad tuitionem propriae vitae & membroum, sequitur, omnia habere & facere in statu naturae omnibus licere. Et hoc est quod vulgo dicitur, *natura dedit omnia omnibus*."

Hobbes's argument in this passage presupposes, of course, the *ipse iudex* principle established in De cive I.9: "By natural law *one is oneself the judge* whether the means one is about to use and the action one is about to perform are necessary to the preservation of life and limbs" ["Vtrum autem media quibus usurus quispiam est, & actio quam acturus est, ad conseruationem vitae vel membrorum suorum necessaria sint necne, *ipse iure naturali iudex est*]" .

210 This law, i.e., the natural law representing the first specification of the fundamental law to seek peace, commands the following: "[T]he right of all to all things must not be retained, but certain rights must be either transferred or relinquished [ius omnium in omnia retinendum non esse, sed iura quaedam transferenda, vel relinguenda esse]" (De cive II.3).

rivative law of nature as one that pertains to the abolition of the community of things, and thus to the introduction of property.[211] According to this characterization, the law not to retain the right to all things is none other than the law to lay down the right that underlies the form of the universal community whose abolition is dictated by right reason.[212] It is in keeping with this understanding that Hobbes employs the idea of original community in subsequent chapters when describing the civil condition and the natural condition of humankind.[213]

Thus, while it is apparently correct to maintain that *De cive* does not in principle *require* the idea of original community for its deduction of the laws of nature, Hobbes' still acknowledges that this idea can be employed as the logical correlate to the concept of the common right to all things. Arguably, it is this conception of the connection between *ius commune in omnia* and *communitas rerum* that changes in *Leviathan*. The change is subtle, but its implications seem to be significant. Hobbes does not characterize the natural right of every man to every given thing by making use of the standardly employed notion that nature gave all things to all men in common. He does not explicitly refer to the community of things in his formulation of the fundamental law of nature and his derivation of the second law. Nor does he at any point in his overall account of the laws of nature treat the law demanding the non-retention of *ius in omnia* (which in *Leviathan* furnishes the second law of nature[214]) as a prescription to abolish the universal natural community of things. In *Leviathan*, then, the connection between the right to all things and the idea of original community is no longer addressed even as a peripheral theme in the systematic derivation of these laws.

It is sometimes claimed that Hobbes's arguments in *De cive* are often tighter and conceptually more rigorous than the corresponding arguments found in *Leviathan*. So one way of regarding the absence of any explicit reference to the connection between the right to all things and original community might be to take it as an indication of nothing more than Hobbes's desire to provide a more easily accessible (English) version of his principles of natural law and politics. Yet

---

211 "*lex de communitate omnium rerum abolenda, siue de introductione Mei & Tui*" (*De cive* IV.4)
212 See *De cive* I.15 and II.1–2.
213 See *De cive* XII.7 and *De cive* XIV.7.
214 "[I]t is a precept, or generall rule of Reason, *That every man, ought to endeavour Peace, as farre as he has hope of obtaining it;* [...] From this Fundamentall Law of Nature, why which men are commanded to endeavour Peace, is derived this second Law; *That a man be willing, when others are so too, as farre-forth, as for Peace, and defence of himselfe he shall think it necessary, to lay down this right to all things; and to be contented with so much liberty against other men, as he would allow other men against himselfe*. For so long as every man holdeth this Right, of doing any thing he liketh; so long are all men in the condition of Warre" (*Leviathan* XIV.4).

whatever merit this kind of reading might have in general, there is also reason to think that it would miss the deeper import of the circumstance that the idea of *communitas rerum* does no systematic work in *Leviathan's* 1651 account of the laws of nature. For it may well be that Hobbes comes to take a more radical position with regard to this idea of original community than he had taken in *De cive*.

Evidence for such a position is found in chapter XXIV of *Leviathan* ("Of the Nutrition and Procreation of a Common-wealth"):

> The distribution of the Materials of this Nourishment, is the constitution of *Mine*, and *Thine*, and *His*; that is to say, in one word, *Propriety*; and belongeth in all kinds of Common-wealth to the Sovereign Power. For where there is no Common-wealth, there is [...] a perpetuall warre of every man against his neighbour; And therefore every thing is his that getteth it, and keepeth it by force; which is neither *Propriety*, nor *Community*; but *Uncertainty*. (*Leviathan* XXIV.6)

Seen against the historical background discussed in this book, the threefold classification set forth in the final line of this passage can plausibly be interpreted as follows. Not only is it the case that property ownership is conceivable solely in connection with the *status civilis*. It is also true that the very meaning of "Community" is unintelligible apart from its analytic link to sovereign power. Apart from this connection, all is "Uncertainty"—not only existentially, but also conceptually.[215]

If this reading is acceptable, then we are in a position to see why the idea of original community does not, and *cannot*, play a role in *Leviathan's* deduction of the prescriptive laws of nature as precepts of practical reason. It is because the very thought of *original* community can have no coherent meaning when the juridico-philosophic implications of the right of nature are spelled out. This in turn allows us to recognize how Hobbes's *Leviathan* breaks decisively with one of the key tenets of traditional natural-law theories of property—namely, the standardly employed tenet concerning an original community of things. In view of this break, it may well be permissible to see Hobbes as an aberrant figure in the history of natural law thought, especially if we bear in mind the uses to which the

---

[215] In *De cive* VI.I Hobbes gives two distinct characterizations of what men may be said to have independently of the sovereign person's constitution: (1) Each has his own right and property (*Ius & Proprietatem*) through particular contracts. (2) No one has what is his own (*meum & tuum*), because in the state of nature all things belong to all men (*omni omnium sunt*). Apart from the instance cited below, in note 217, nothing that Hobbes says in Leviathan about property gives rise to the kind of problem of consistency that is raised by these contrasting characterizations.

idea of original community was put in late seventeenth and eighteenth century theories of property.[216] But if Hobbes's thought does represent an aberration in this regard, it is evidently because he insists on drawing a crucial lesson from an assumption that has in so many ways shaped the theoretical terrain for modern philosophical treatments of property since Grotius's repudiation of the separability thesis (i.e., the thesis discussed in this chapter's first section in connection with the dispute between Pope John XXII and William of Ockham). That assumption is that any viable account of original acquisition must presuppose the notion of a dominative right that *by nature* permits appropriation through first seizure or *prima occupatio*. And the lesson that Hobbes draws from it is simply this: It is not possible to provide a conceptually viable account of the normative basis of property—not to mention civil society in general—once such an assumption is made.

Ironically, perhaps, the text of *Leviathan* itself is what tends to make this lesson all but unrecognizable. For Hobbes, by 1651, does not find it necessary there to clarify his view of the connection between the concept of the right of nature and the idea of an original community of things.[217] After more than three and a half centuries of *Leviathan's* continuing impact, however, we might do well to bear this point in mind.

§ 3 Original Acquisition and the Formal Principle of Material Equality in Distribution: Kant's Surprising Affinity with Both Ockham and Hobbes

At the outset of this chapter I called attention to my proposal (first presented at the end of chapter 7) that Kant requires a formal principle of material equality if there is to be a viable solution to the problem of original acquisition that ensues from his joint employment of the concept of *prima occupatio* and the idea of an a

---

216 See, e.g., Tierney 1997, pp. 339–342. (I criticize Tierney's view of Hobbes in Edwards 2000.) For related discussion, see Lloyd 2001 and Olsthoorn 2015.

217 Apart from the textual factor just mentioned, it must also be said here that Hobbes himself seems to obscure this lesson when he treats his thirteenth derivative law of nature as containing a clause that authorizes *prima occupatio* (see *Leviathan* XV.27; *De cive* III.18;). It is true, of course, that this clause applies only to things that cannot be divided or else positively possessed in common in the form of joint ownership secured by the commonwealth's sovereign authority. But in view of the concept of natural right that underlies both *Leviathan* and *De cive*, it is far from clear that *any* law pertaining to first seizure ought to qualify as a natural law instead of belonging (at best) to the body of positive law.

priori united will of all. As I also pointed out there, the obvious difficulty with my proposal is that it requires us to ascertain a connection between the Kantian principles of innate freedom and external acquisition that Kant himself does not expressly acknowledge. Thus, the issue that we must now address is whether the line of historical inquiry followed in the last two sections leads us to the point where a stronger case can be made for establishing that connection.

Marked by its essential signposts, the path of interpretation that I have followed between Ockham and Hobbes runs as follows:

> (1) Upholding the thesis that a distinction must always be drawn between use and ownership, Ockham excludes that the human being's inalienable *ius utendi* can suffice to ground the permissibility of originally distributive acquisition. Ockham thus works from the thesis that this use-warranting natural right must be kept strictly separate from the dominative right of appropriation that follows from the dictation of natural reason.

> (2) Rejecting the germaneness of this separability thesis for his doctrine of original acquisition, Grotius maintains that the naturally restricted use of things unilaterally seized from humankind's common *dominium* establishes a relation of ownership that is capable of indefinite extension. Grotius thus works with a natural right of using that also serves as a dominative right which grounds the permissibility of extended appropriation on the basis of first seizure (i.e., *prima occupatio*).

> (3) Spelling out the implications of Grotius's doctrine of original acquisition, Selden works with the concept of a dominative right of appropriation that in principle permits unrestricted acquisition through first seizure. Selden's nature-given dominative right of first seizure thus grounds the permissibility of unrestricted appropriation independently of any limiting conditions of use or usefulness.

> (4) Hobbes's works with a concept of natural right that that can neither furnish nor ground a dominative right to appropriate anything at all as one's own precisely because it permits the unrestricted unilaterally use-making seizure of everything by everyone. He thereby seeks, in effect, to pull out the rug from under all theories of original acquisition that employ the idea of a community of things.

How, then, should we understand Kant's account of original acquisition in relation to these views on natural right and the normative basis of appropriation and ownership?

As was amply discussed in Part II, Kant's account of what it is to possess something does not entail that I can have something as my own independently of the permissive law of practical reason which authorizes me to put others under an obligation to refrain from using it *because* I was the *first* to take possession of it (cf. RL 6:247.1–6). Thus, in view of Ockham, we may note first of all that Kant should easily be able to accommodate the thesis according to which a use-warranting natural right must be kept separate from the right of appropriation in which the permissibility of distributive acquisition is anchored.

§ 3 Original Acquisition and Material Equality — 291

Not to put too crude a historical gloss on it, but there is no reason why Kant should be bothered by the existence of beggarly friars who wish to claim nothing as their own—*provided*, of course, that their chief defender should be willing to concede that "a maxim by which, if it were to become a LAW, an object of the power of choice would *in itself* (objectively) have to BECOME *something belonging to no one* (res nullius) is contrary to right" (RL 6:246.6–8 [capitalizing emphasis mine (J. E.)]). And indeed, Ockham, would have to be willing to grant this immediate implication of Kant's juridical postulate of practical reason, i.e., the postulate which is supposed to ground the possibility of all external acquisition by excluding that "*usable* objects" may rightfully be put "beyond all possibility of *use*" (RL 6:246.15–16).[218] That is because Ockham in fact acknowledges a dominative right of appropriation as a requirement of natural reason that applies to the common world of things which *originally* belonged to no one.

Thus, there is a clear affinity between Kant and Ockham as far as the separability thesis itself is concerned, especially if (as Kant insists) the warranting basis of appropriation is not tied to temporal conditions.[219] But the similarity of their starting positions in this regard also serves to underscore the difficulty that Kant faces when he attempts to show that an obligation-founding act of first seizure can be consistent with his Doctrine of Right's fundamental universality requirement, i.e., the prescription (contained in Kant's overarching principle and law of right) to "act externally in such a way that the free use of your power of choice can coexist with the freedom of everyone in accordance with a universal law" (RL 6:231.10–12). For the separability thesis suffices merely to determine the essential distinction between the use of things and their appropriation. It does not suffice to establish that the distributive acquisition of things through an external act of seizure *can* be in accordance with a universal law, which is precisely the fundamental Kantian problem that emerges when we consider the remaining stretches of the path leading to Hobbes.

Let us recall here the upshot of the discussion of Kant's relation to Grotius and Selden in chapter 7: Given Kant's proximity to Selden with respect to first seizure and original community, the opposite of the condition of right—i.e., the condition of universal conflict in the use of things—is unavoidably built into Kant's doctrine of original acquisition, unless it can incorporate a principle that grounds equality in distribution. Moreover, as we have seen in the course of this twelfth chapter, such a condition of conflict is implied in the Hobbesian tenet that natural right permits the unilateral use-making seizure of things

---

218 Cf. Tierney 1997, p. 165.
219 On this, see chapter 7, pp. 161–162.

held in common. Thus, if my proposed solution to Kant's problem is to be viable, it has to be able to withstand the criticism that Hobbes's directs against accounts of original acquisition that rely on the idea of a community of things. Specifically, that solution must be able to counter the rug-pulling criticism that would eliminate Kant's problem by demonstrating the underlying conceptual incoherence of his entire project of original acquisition.

In defending Kant against this line of attack, let us first take note of some ground that is shared by Hobbes and Ockham. According to both of these thinkers, there is no use-warranting right which could *suffice* to establish that anything whatsoever can be appropriated as one's own. To be sure, they find themselves sharing this ground for radically different reasons. While Hobbes holds that the right which permits everyone's unrestricted use of all things is an effectively useless right that makes it impossible for anyone to appropriate anything at all, Ockham insists that the inalienable *ius utendi* that originally authorizes things' restricted use is compatible with a right of appropriation that reason prescribes on account of its usefulness. Nonetheless, the ground they share must be common even if their reasons for sharing it cannot be common to both of them. Is there, then, some feature of this common terrain that can offer Kant a foothold for withstanding Hobbes's eliminative solution to the problem of original acquisition?

On the one hand, it is clear that such a foothold cannot lie simply in the separability thesis itself since Hobbes, as just indicated, can accommodate this Ockhamite thesis as readily as Kant. Indeed, Hobbes's de facto acceptance of the separability thesis is exactly what enables him to set about eliminating original acquisition as a problem that has to be addressed in the context of a theory of right reason's fundamental prescriptive laws. On the other hand, though, there is no foothold to be had without paying such a thesis its proper due when accounting for the rational ground of permissible acquisition. For Kant must be able to distinguish between use-making seizure, by which one comes to possess something empirically, and the type of action by which one can obligate others to refrain from using something because of being the first to take possession of it. Moreover, he also has to be able to do this in the face of Hobbes's denial that such a distinction can apply to things insofar as they are thought of as originally possessed by all in common. What, then, is the foothold condition that would enable Kant to do accomplish both of these tasks in one fell swoop while adhering to the universality requirement asserted by his fundamental law of right?

Once again, we come back to the principle of innate freedom that Kant must be well positioned to bring to bear, even if he does not explicitly employ it within the framework of his doctrine of original acquisition. More particularly, we return to the idea of innate equality that this principle of freedom involves, i.e., "independence from being bound by others to *more* than one can reciprocally bind them" (RL 6:237.35 – 36 [italics mine (J. E.)]. As argued above (see chapter 7, pp. 166 – 168), this interpretation of innate equality, when applied to the problem of original acquisition, can serve to limit the permissible scope of external acquisition on the part of everyone who can be reciprocally bound to one another in virtue of the relation of each to the originally common possession of humankind. Thus, if Kant's principle of innate freedom can be employed in this way to substantiate the deontic demand for material equality in the distribution of usable things, it is by insisting on this strictly formal categorical requirement of practical reason that Kant can counter the eliminative solution that Hobbes in effect proposes. For it is in keeping with the formal principle of material equality entailed by that principle of freedom that a maxim to put usable objects *within* the reach of everyone's possible use can become a law without also being the maxim responsible for humanity's inability to get *beyond* the reach of its own cannons.

That said, of course, this non-eliminative solution to Kant's problem of original acquisition gives rise to a further question of considerable interest: How do we determine what qualifies as material equality for the purposes of the theory public right, i.e., for the account the civil condition that deals with laws of right applying to "a society subject to distributive justice" (RL 6:21 – 22)? While a comprehensive response to this question lies beyond the scope of this book, I will address it in the concluding chapter in connection with a principle of distribution endorsed by Karl Marx.

Conclusion

Kantian Consequentialism, Equal Right, and a Marxian Principle of Distributive Justice

The following considerations point well beyond the central topics covered in Parts I-IV. This concluding chapter's first section relates the Doctrine of Virtue's theory of obligatory ends to a field of discussion in contemporary ethical theory that goes under the heading of 'Kantian consequentialism'. I argue that there is a clear, though restricted, sense in which Kant's account of ends that are also duties allows for and, moreover, grounds a consequentialist interpretation of a practical law that presents a duty of virtue. I then return, in the second section, to the solution that I have put forward for Kant's problem of original acquisition. As we have seen, Kant's theory of the normative basis of property must incorporate a formal principle of material equality that applies to the acquisition of usable things if it is to be consistent with his account of freedom as the innate right of human beings.[1] To spell out the ramifications of this proposed solution, I relate our Kantian principle of material (i.e., contentful) equality to a principle requiring unequal distribution that, on the face of things, seems incompatible with the fundamental assumptions of Kant's juridical theory of right. This is a principle distributive justice which, when considered in conjunction with the purely formal principle of equal right that it presupposes, brings Kant's principle of material equality face to face with the political thought of a figure well known for his opposition to the formalism of modern theories of right: Karl Marx.

§ 1 Consequentialism in Ethics and Kant's Obligatory Ends

The notion of Kantian consequentialism has gained traction in recent years in discussions that have revolved around the customary classificatory distinction between consequentialist and deontological theories.[2] While a concluding chapter is not the place to become involved in the details of this area of inquiry in contemporary ethical theory, it is still feasible to contribute something to shifting the predominant focus of discussion away from the *Groundwork for the*

---

[1] See pp. 165–169 of chapter 7 and pp. 192–193 of chapter 12.
[2] See Cummiskey 2006; Cummiskey 2011; Hare 1997, pp. 147–165; Herman 2011c; Kagan 2002; Morgan 2009; Parfit 2011–2017, vol. 1 pp. 371–419; Parfit 2011–2017, vol. 3 pp. 433–437; Otsuka 2009; Ridge 2009; Ross 2009; Weinstock 2009; Wolf 2011.

Metaphysics of Morals to the theory of intrinsically obligatory ends that underlies the *Metaphysics of Morals* itself. To undertake this task, however, it will be necessary to venture into some thematic territory that I have not set foot upon thus far—notably, the systematic portrayal of duties of virtue that Kant provides in the main body of the Doctrine of Virtue. In particular, I will concentrate on the duty of mutual benevolence that features prominently in Kant's portrayal of duties of virtue to others. It is by relating the practical law which presents this duty of active benevolence to Kant's foundational account of own-perfection and others' happiness as obligatory ends that we will be able to understand how at least one key component of Kant's ethics is consistent with a straightforward and, indeed, robust version of consequentialism.

Let me begin the venture by setting forth what I take to be the crucial presuppositions of such a version. First of all, I take it that a consequentialist ethical theory should be based upon, or should at least be able to accommodate, the following principle of moral permissibility:

> An act (or action) is morally permissible if and only if it has the best consequences, results or outcomes with reference to the good (whatever the account of the good may be).[3]

In keeping with this principle of permissibility, I take it that a proponent of consequentialism in ethics should be able to accept this general principle of obligation:

> It is morally obligatory always to promote the good by performing actions that have the best consequences, results or outcomes.[4]

---

[3] For the purposes of this section's argument, it makes no difference whether 'the good' is understood in terms of hedonic welfare, or else in terms of preference satisfaction or desire fulfillment, etc. I have also formulated what I take to be the strongest feasible version of the consequentialist account of the moral permissibility of actions. I do not attempt to qualify or restrict the consequentialist position on moral permissibility in light of the epistemic limitations to which human agents may be (and in fact normally are) subject when considering the consequences of their actions. Thus, for example, I do not refer to the best *expectable* consequences of actions. Moreover, I take it that every theory which builds on that principle of permissibility must be one of a straightforwardly maximizing and optimizing type. I am therefore not interested, here, in the possibility of 'satisficing' forms of consequentialist ethical theory (see Slote 1989 and, for critical assessment, Bradley 2006).

[4] This is in keeping with standard deontic logic, which allows for the derivation of the principle of obligation just stated from the immediately preceding principle of permissibility. (If it is not permissible not to perform act (or action) *p* on condition *c*, then it is obligatory to perform *p* on condition *c*.)

Given the principles of permissibility and obligation just formulated, I will also suppose that a consequentialist theory in ethics should be able to endorse two further general tenets: (1) There is no morally permissible *option* not always to promote the good as best one can. (2) No *constraint* can be placed on the requirement to promote the good as best one can.[5]

Accordingly, I will hold that deontological theories in ethics involve the rejection of these consequentialist tenets pertaining to options and constraints.[6] Specifically, I will maintain that a proponent of deontology in ethics must accept the notion that that there are normative barriers that restrict the range of morally permissible choice with respect to the good and its promotion. I take it, then, that the acceptance of such barriers, or deontic constraints, is the basic defining characteristic of a deontological theory. But the proponent of this type of theory can also accept that there are options *not* to promote the good as best one can. Unlike deontic constraints, such options increase the range of morally permissible choice by limiting whatever requirement there may be to promote the good.

The preceding considerations on moral permissibility, obligation, deontic constraints, and options furnish the framework for my treatment of consequentialism in connection with the Doctrine of Virtue's theory of obligatory ends. Just one further preliminary clarification is needed before we turn to Kant and the question of Kantian consequentialism: I will suppose that any *universalistic* version of consequentialism will link the aforementioned principles of moral permissibility and the obligatory character of actions to some interpretation of the 'overall good'—i.e., to an interpretation of the good that is couched in terms of the well-being of everyone, and that considers the well-being of each

---

[5] I assume here that one promotes the good as best one can by performing actions that have the best outcomes for the purpose of bringing about the good. Needless to say, to hold that one is always obligated to promote the good as *best* one *can* is not to suppose that one always ought to promote the good through each action that one performs. This is true even if an action is held to be morally permissible only if it promotes the good in virtue of its tendency to produce the best consequences, outcomes, or results with respect to the good. For always acting on the principle that one always ought to promote the good through every one of one's actions may well have as a consequence that one performs actions that are not conducive to bringing about any good at all. (Experience confirms the point, particularly when one considers the roads to hell that have been paved with do-gooders' good intentions.) For related considerations, see John Stuart Mill's classic criticism of the overdemandingness objection standardly leveled against utilitarian moral thinking: Mill 1969, pp. 219–220. See also Broadie 1991, pp. 8–17, 24–50.

[6] My conception of the relationship between consequentialist and deontological theories is much indebted to Shelly Kagan's work. Regarding my use of the notions of deontic constraints and options, see Kagan 1998, pp. 63, 94, 215 and Kagan 2002, pp. 111–156. More generally, see Kagan 1989 and Kagan 2012 (especially pp. 627–635).

from an impartial point of view.[7] Thus, I will assume that a proponent of universalistic consequentialism in ethics—a 'classic' utilitarian, for example, who understands the overall good in terms of everyone's happiness—must be able to employ *some* specification of the concept of overall good as the basis for her description of the state of affairs that ought to be brought about by means of our good-promoting actions.

We have seen that Kant's metaphysical theory of morals demands the portrayal of own-perfection and others' happiness as intrinsically obligatory ends of action. This is a portrayal based on the notion that there must be certain material determining grounds of the power of choice which, when represented as the matter of maxims of ends, furnish laws for maxims of actions. As was explained at the end of chapter 1, such laws for maxims—i.e., the laws which present us with duties of virtue—are grounded in the representation of one's own perfection and the happiness of others as mutually supportive ends. Moreover, we saw that neither one of these obligatory ends, given their mutual dependency, can be assigned theoretical priority over the other as a single ultimate end whose promotion is prescribed by morally practical reason's laws for maxims. Thus, Kant's conceptual portrayal of own-perfection and others' happiness as ends that are also duties amounts to an irreducibly dualistic account of the rational ultimate ends that our actions ought to promote.

But what about the principles supported by this foundational portrayal? What are the implications of Kant's dualistic theory of ends that are also duties for our assessment of the action-guiding principles that Kant systematically treats, in the main body of the 1797 Doctrine of Virtue, as laws for maxims that present duties of virtue? In particular, how should we understand the character of the practical laws furnished by these principles in view of the classificatory framework constructed above? In what follows, I will address this issue by focusing on the concept of overall good as it features in Kant's treatment of one of these laws.

I refer here to a duty of benevolence that Kant treats in §§ 25–30 of the Doctrine of Virtue in connection with the idea of practical love for all human beings (*allgemeine Menschenliebe*).[8] In the context of his treatment of this duty, Kant understands practical love in general as *active* benevolence, and active benevolence (i.e. beneficence) as promoting the happiness of others by making others'

---

[7] Cf. Kagan 1998, pp. 63, 194, 215. I leave it open whether well-being (hence happiness) is best specified in terms of hedonic welfare or preference satisfaction.
[8] Dieter Schönecker (2013) provides systematic commentary covering the sections here mentioned. See also Schönecker 2010 as well as Esser 2004, pp. 370–380; Gregor 1963, pp. 181–189; Johnson 2010.

happiness one's end. He also understands the promotion of this happiness as the furthering of others' well-being. Finally, he holds that there is a universal law which makes the happiness of *all* human beings, including oneself, an end to be promoted by everyone's beneficent actions.[9] Kant's considerations on the concept of practical love and its corresponding duties thus show that his account of intrinsically obligatory ends grounds a duty of mutual and universal benevolence as a duty of virtue. Moreover, those same considerations show that the end that is to be promoted through such active benevolence is one that satisfies the interpretation of 'overall good' presented above, i.e., interpretation of the good for human beings in terms of the well-being of everyone, as considered from an impartial point of view. It is important to note here that the concept of happiness at issue in Kant's references to human well-being in the sections under consideration is the concept of a *natural* good of each human being, i.e., contentment with one's state as far as one is assured of its lasting. Broadly speaking, then, we can say that the interpretation of overall good that is implicit in the Doctrine of Virtue involves a naturalistic account of a good for human beings.[10]

Having shed light on this interpretation, we are in a position to bear down on the notion of Kantian consequentialism by asking a second question: Does the account of overall good that underlies Kant's treatment of universal benevolence support the notion that Kant's ethics, as a moral doctrine founded on the theory of intrinsically obligatory ends, involves options in the sense indicated above?

As we had occasion to observe in chapter 1, when discussing the properties of duties of virtue as duties of wide obligation, the law of duty that demands active concern for the happiness of others in general by no means cancels the pull

---

[9] See TL 6:450.16–19, 450.31–451.19, 452.26–30, 453.2–4.
[10] As was explained in chapter 1 (p. 27), contentment with one's state or condition (*Zustand*) as far as one is assured of its lasting is Kant's basic definition of happiness in the Doctrine of Virtue is (see again TL 6: 387.26–27). Although this definition leaves open-ended the construal of contentment (*Zufriedenheit*), the concept of overall good at issue in TL §§ 25–30 fully intelligible without reference to the idea of the highest good (*das höchste Gut*) linked to morally practical reason's a priori postulates, especially the postulates concerning immortality and God. On Kant's view, the first component of the highest good—morality—represents something that can be fully accomplished only in an eternity (see KpV 5:124.11), which is why the idea of morality leads to the postulate of personal immortality. The second component—an agent's happiness proportioned to morality—requires that the existence of God be postulated as the intelligibility condition for our pursuit of the highest good as a task of pure practical reason (see KpV 5:124.29–125.7; cf. KU 5:448.17–450.25). *Taken by itself*, Kant's foundational theory of obligatory ends does not generate the kind of account of good just described.

of the various forms of 'special obligation' to which each of us is subject.[11] Still, on Kant's account of duties of wide obligation, I am bound to make it my maxim to promote the happiness of *all* human beings (including myself). We cannot, of course, be *equally* benevolent to everyone since each of us is under obligation to greater benevolence to those closer to us. Nonetheless, we are all equally *obligated* to be benevolent toward everyone just because mutual active benevolence is a duty of all human beings toward one another.[12] To be sure, the consideration of such duties opens up a range of options for the practice of moral judgment. That is because wide obligation not only extends to the whole of humanity, but also encompasses special relations to others as well as the self-relation that underlies the practical reason's demand to further one's own perfection as an ultimate end.[13] Nevertheless, the options for judgment that Kant's portrayal allows do *not* increase the range of morally permissible choice by limiting the scope of the requirement to promote the overall good. To the contrary, it is by opening up the range of options for moral judgment that the overall good can coherently be thought of as an end that all human agents are obligated to promote, i.e., to strive to bring about as *best* we can, given the circumstances in which we find ourselves and the means at our disposal. Duties of wide obligation involve options for the exercise of moral judgment. But options for moral judgment by no means restrict the obligation to promote, impartially, the overall good of everyone.

So much for options that apply to promoting the overall good. What about deontic constraints? Do the laws and duties that are grounded in Kant's analysis

---

11 See pp. 31–34.
12 "[§ 27] Die Maxime des Wohlwollens (die praktische Menschenliebe) ist aller Menschen Pflicht gegen einander, man mag diese nun liebenswürdig finden oder nicht, nach dem ethischen Gesetz der Vollkommenheit: Liebe deinen Nebenmenschen als dich selbst [...] [§ 28] Aber Einer ist mir doch näher als der Andere, und ich bin im Wohlwollen mir selbst der Nächste. Wie stimmt das nun mit der Formel: Liebe deinen Nächsten (deinen Mitmenschen) als dich selbst? Wenn einer mir näher ist (in der Pflicht des Wohlwollens) als der Andere, ich also zum größeren Wohlwollen gegen Einen als gegen den Anderen verbunden, mir selber aber geständlich näher (selbst der Pflicht nach) bin, als jeder Andere, so kann ich, wie es scheint, ohne mir selbst zu widersprechen, nicht sagen: ich soll jeden Menschen lieben wie mich selbst; denn der Maßstab der Selbstliebe würde keinen Unterschied in Graden zulassen.—Man sieht bald: daß hier nicht blos das Wohlwollen des *Wunsches*, [...] sondern ein thätiges, praktisches Wohlwollen, sich das Wohl und Heil des Anderen zum Zweck zu machen, (das Wohlthun) gemeint sei. Denn im Wünschen kann ich allen gleich wohlwollen, aber im Thun kann der Grad nach Verschiedenheit der Geliebten (deren Einer mich näher angeht als der Andere), ohne die Allgemeinheit der Maxime zu verletzen, doch sehr verschieden sein" (TL 6:451.29–452.9—see also TL 6:450.31–34, 6:451.12–16).
13 See note 12 and TL 6:417.5–418.23, 444.9–447.17.

of obligatory ends erect barriers to the promotion of the overall good? Since the acceptance of constraints is (I take it) basic to the deontological rejection of the consequentialist approach, the response to this question calls for discussion more extensive than what I have provided for the notion of options. I will therefore consider the different relations of obligation involved in Kant's general views on the happiness and perfectibility of human moral agents.

Let us proceed by asking whether the consideration of one's own happiness, as a permissible end of action, can ground a constraint on the promotion of the overall good. From the arguments presented in §§ 26–30 of the Doctrine of Virtue, it is clear that own-happiness is necessarily covered by the duty of universal benevolence at issue in Kant's discussion of the practical love of all human beings. That is because there can be no promoting the happiness of all (as distinguished from the happiness of all *others*) unless one is permitted to promote one's own happiness as an end.[14] For it is analytically true that one's own happiness and the happiness of (all) others are the components of everyone's happiness. To the extent, then, that own-happiness is represented as an end of action that is also a component of the overall good, the permissibility of promoting one's own happiness clearly does not erect any barrier to the promotion of that universal good. To be sure, since furthering one's own happiness must be compatible with the promotion of others' happiness as an intrinsically obligatory end, there must obviously be some restriction placed on the extent to which one is permitted to promote one's own happiness; and this will be true even if that restriction cannot be precisely fixed by applying the laws that prescribe duties of wide obligation. Yet it by no means follows from *this* that

---

14 "alles moralisch-praktische Verhältniß gegen Menschen ist ein Verhältniß derselben in der Vorstellung der reinen Vernunft, d. i. der freien Handlungen nach Maximen, welche sich zur allgemeinen Gesetzgebung qualificiren, die also nicht selbstsüchtig (*ex solipsismo prodeuntes*) sein können. Ich will jedes Anderen Wohlwollen (*benevolentiam*) gegen mich; ich soll also auch gegen jeden Anderen wohlwollend sein. Da aber alle *Anderen* außer mir nicht *Alle* sein, mithin die Maxime nicht die Allgemeinheit eines Gesetzes an sich haben würde, welche doch zur Verpflichtung nothwendig ist: so wird das Pflichtgesetz des Wohlwollens mich als Object desselben im Gebot der praktischen Vernunft mit begreifen: nicht als ob ich dadurch verbunden würde, mich selbst zu lieben (denn das geschieht ohne das unvermeidlich, und dazu giebts also keine Verpflichtung), sondern die gesetzgebende Vernunft, welche in ihrer Idee der Menschheit überhaupt die ganze Gattung (mich also mit) einschließt, nicht der Mensch, schließt als allgemeingesetzgebend mich in der Pflicht des wechselseitigen Wohlwollens nach dem Princip der Gleichheit wie alle Andere neben mir mit ein und *erlaubt* es dir dir selbst wohlzuwollen, unter der Bedingung, daß du auch jedem Anderen wohl willst: weil so allein deine Maxime (des Wohlthuns) sich zu einer allgemeinen Gesetzgebung qualificirt, als worauf alles Pflichtgesetz gegründet ist" (TL 6:450.34–451.19—see also TL 6:452.27–28).

there is any constraint placed on the promotion of the overall good. To the contrary, the obligation to promote the overall good would not be possible as a categorical requirement of morally practical reason if the pursuit of one's own happiness were not necessarily a permissible end of action.

Recall, however, that Kant's treatment of intrinsically obligatory ends establishes that own-perfection is an end that grounds the obligation of every agent to promote her own happiness as a permitted means of furthering the form of perfection that qualifies as an end that is also a duty (see chapter 1, p. 29). Does this *indirect* relation of ethical obligation erect a barrier to the promotion of the overall good? Clearly, the fact that own-happiness is indirectly a duty (though not an intrinsically obligatory end) will place a constraint on the promotion of others' happiness, at least to the extent that the promotion of one's own happiness is a means of perfecting oneself that cannot be pursued by promoting the happiness of others. But here again, it does not follow from *this* that there is any constraint on promoting the overall good. Even if every agent is obligated to promote her own happiness as a permitted means of furthering her own perfection, all agents can still be obligated—and, according to Kant, necessarily are obligated—to promote the overall good.

Thus far, I have taken happiness—own-happiness, others' happiness, and the happiness of everyone—as the main platform for the potential derivation of constraints on the promotion of the overall good. But what happens when we approach this issue specifically in view of the perfectibility of human beings? Let us take up this question by tracing out the relations of ethical obligation that obtain when own-happiness is considered in connection with own-perfection and the perfection of others. We have just seen that I am obligated, not merely permitted, to promote my own happiness since this happiness is a means to an end that, for me, is an intrinsically obligatory end: my own perfection as a moral agent. I cannot, however, hold myself bound to promote the perfection of others by making either my own perfection or, even more indirectly, my own happiness the means to this end. For the obligation that I am under to further my own perfection (and thus, indirectly, my own happiness) binds me to an end that is in itself a duty, while the perfection of others cannot be such an end for me, or for anyone else. That is why only the happiness of everyone, and not the universal perfection of human beings, can fulfill the definitional requirements of the overall good. To the extent, then, that any human agent can make the perfection of all human beings some kind of end of action, she can do this only by promoting the happiness of others, which is an intrinsically obligatory end, and by promoting her own happiness as a means to furthering her own perfection. That is *all* that anyone can do with respect to the perfectibility of human beings. This limitation, however, does not restrict the scope of the obligation to promote the overall good. To the contrary, every one of us is bound to promote the happiness of everyone, including oneself, since others' happiness and one's own happiness are (on Kant's interpretation) the components of the overall good. The obligation to promote the happiness of others is indeed limited by the requirement to further one's own perfection *to the extent* that (i) own-happiness represents a means to this obligatory end and (ii) the obligation to perfect oneself by pursuing this means is limited by the requirement to promote the happiness of others. But these limitations can place no constraint on the promotion of the overall good. Instead, they are conditions that make possible the promotion of this universal natural good of human beings.

Consider, however, the components of own-perfection itself. Is the requirement to promote the overall good not limited by the obligation to cultivate one's physical capacities for achieving rationally grounded ends as well as one's moral cast of mind, i.e., "the morality in us"?[15] No—not if the concept of own-perfection is what grounds the obligation to pursue one's own happiness as a means of cultivating those capacities; and not if the cultivation of morality in us requires each of us to promote the happiness of others as we strive to achieve the greatest perfection of which we are capable in this natural world: the disposition to do our duty *from* duty.[16] Since the law that defines this degree of perfection is one that requires every agent to strive, one way or another, to bring about everyone's happiness, the obligation to develop one's end-achieving capacities as well as to cultivate one's moral cast of mind can place no constraint on the promotion of the overall good. To the contrary, the development of these characteristics is precisely what enables each agent to strive to bring about this universal natural good as *best* she can.

Kant's moral doctrine of ends thus excludes both deontic constraints and options with reference to the obligation to promote the overall good. The laws that prescribe duties of virtue cannot erect barriers to the promotion of the overall good of everyone insofar as these laws for maxims are grounded in Kant's theory of obligatory ends. Nor can such laws, thus grounded, increase the range of morally permissible choice by limiting the requirement to promote the overall good. If this is the case, then the following general conclusion seems inescapable: Kant's foundational account of morally practical reason's obligatory ends is consistent with a consequentialist understanding of the practical law of benevolence that requires the promotion of the happiness of all

---

15 For details, see pp. 26–27 in chapter 1 and pp. 87–91 in chapter 4.
16 "Die größte moralische Vollkommenheit des Menschen ist: seine Pflicht zu thun und zwar aus Pflicht (daß das Gesetz nicht blos die Regel, sondern auch die Triebfeder der Handlungen sei)" (TL 6:392.20–21; see also TL 6:391.3–7).

human beings. Indeed, precisely this dualistic account *grounds* such an understanding.

Given the long history of construing Kant's ethics as a paradigm instance of the deontological approach to moral philosophy, of course, this conclusion is apt to appear more than a little remarkable—if not downright perverse. But perhaps the most striking thing about it is how unremarkable it *ought* to appear, at least once we are clear about the systematic and historical import of Kant's theory of intrinsically obligatory ends. In fact, I think that this conclusion will be found remarkable or perverse only if we neglect to take into proper account the following three factors, each of which pertains to the systematic foundations of Kant's metaphysics of morals.

First—very briefly at this juncture—the conclusion in question applies only to a law of Kant's ethics as a doctrine of virtue. It does not apply to any of the juridical laws that Kant presents in his doctrine of right. The argument which supports that conclusion neither presupposes nor implies that any Kantian law of right is necessarily linked to some concept of promotable good. I will return to this factor at the beginning of the next section.

Second, the consequentialist interpretation that I have offered is possible because of the features of mutual reference involved in the two concepts of obligatory end that lie at the foundation of Kant's ethics as a doctrine of virtue.[17] It is by paying close attention to these features of the jointly employed concepts of others' happiness and one's own perfection that I have been able to offer a consequentialist interpretation of morally practical reason's categorical requirement to promote the overall good of everyone. Moreover, the joint employment of these concepts presupposes that the two ends that are also duties cannot be absorbed, as it were, into a more comprehensive or inclusive end that could be brought about by our actions. According to Kant's dualistic theory of practical reason's objectively necessary ends, there is no *one* end of action—no *solum bonum*, and no single *summum bonum*—whose concept could be employed to ground the laws that present duties of virtue.[18] At the same time, however, the laws grounded by Kant's two jointly employed concepts of obligatory end necessarily include the law that makes a single universal end of action—namely, the happiness of all human beings—an end that we are all obligated to promote as best we can.

Third, although I have offered a consequentialist interpretation of the particular law of virtue that makes universal benevolence a duty, my argument does

---

17 For details on these features, see the final section of chapter 1.
18 On this, see the third section of chapter 11.

not entail that this law for maxims is *based* on an appeal to the intrinsic moral significance of any promotable good. While happiness, *qua* contentment with one's state or condition, may well be thought of as a potentially achievable good for the human subject, it figures as a ground of the law of active benevolence in question only insofar as its representation furnishes a constitutive feature of a deontic concept, i.e., a concept of an end that is also a *duty*. Thus, my interpretation of the law that prescribes the promotion of everyone's happiness is by no means inconsistent with the claim that Kant's ethics is *foundationally* non-consequentialist, at least in the sense that it does not purport to ground that law of benevolence in any concept of good which could be employed to exclude the possibility of deontic constraints and options pertaining to the overall good as a promotable end.

One might, of course, mount an objection to this claim by asking why even this foundational aspect of Kant's ethics should be characterized as non-consequentialist (and, accordingly, as deontological) in the sense just indicated. For it is far from obvious that either one of the two mutually supporting ends that are also duties can be adequately specified without substantive reference to promotable happiness as a natural good for human beings.[19] This point is, I think, of considerable interest. But it concerns a question that is not directly relevant to the consistency claim that I am making. Specifically, it concerns the question whether standard ways of drawing the distinction between deontological and consequentialist theories are ultimately of much use in making sense of the metaphysical assumptions that underlie Kant's dualistic account of intrinsically obligatory ends.

Whatever answer may be given to this last question, it will not alter the fact that each of the concepts of end at issue in this dualistic account is a deontic concept. Neither one of these concepts is the concept of *the* good. Nor is either one of them the concept of *a* good. In point of fact, neither one of them is a concept of good at all. To the extent that it figures in Kant's account of *obligatory* ends, not even the concept of others' happiness is a concept of good, even if the end that it picks out is one that qualifies as a natural good for human beings. While it is the concept by which we think of others' happiness as a natural good that is also an objectively necessary end of our actions, it is not itself a concept of happiness *qua* natural good. It is a concept of duty *qua* matter of obligation.

So what is the upshot of this last line of commentary? The main upshot, I take it, is this: While the appropriately restricted notion of Kantian consequentialism ought to be considered unremarkable, the significance of Kant's dualistic

---

19 See note 10 of this concluding chapter.

foundational doctrine of obligatory ends is anything but uninteresting. For it is by examining the key tenets of this theory of ends, in view of the factors just considered, that we can see how the historically predominant way of classifying Kant's moral philosophy may well be both systematically untenable and philosophically beside the point. The consideration of these factors shows that ethics can perfectly well do two things that are not in keeping with the constraints imposed by the still prevalent classificatory scheme for understanding how ethical theories are supposed to work with respect to concepts of good and concepts of ends of action. Specifically, that consideration shows how ethics, as a doctrine of virtue, can ground a principle of universal benevolence using a concept of end that is not a concept of good, *although* a natural good for human beings furnishes the constitutive feature that makes it the concept of a promotable end that is also a duty. That consideration also shows how ethics can accomplish this theoretical task by conjoining this concept of end with a concept of perfection in such a way that (i) no barrier is erected to the promotion of the overall good of everyone and (ii) the range of morally permissible choice is not increased by limiting the requirement to promote the good.

In this section I have attempted to lay bare what I take to be several interesting implications of Kant's moral doctrine of ends by focusing on a concept of good as it is currently employed in one strand of contemporary discussion in ethics. In choosing to concentrate on the implications of this doctrine for contemporary views of consequentialist ethics, I have in effect linked Kant's treatment of benevolence in the universal love of human beings (*das Wohlwollen in der allgemeinen Menschenliebe* [TL 6:451.21.]) to a strain of modern moral philosophy that stretches from seventeenth and eighteenth-century portrayals of universal benevolence through the universalistic hedonism of classic modern utilitarianism, and to various contemporary utilitarian approaches which reject the assumption that the explanation of obligation requires grounding by means of a substantial account of happiness.[20] Casting the net more broadly, however, it would be possible to call attention to similarly interesting implications that Kant's moral doctrine of ends holds for other theoretical approaches standardly taken in contemporary normative ethics.[21] Indeed, I would be hard pressed to name any contemporary approach that would not yield surprising results

---

20 For relevant discussion, see Part IV of this book and the secondary sources cited therein.
21 For instance, it would be fruitful to examine Kant's arguments on imperfect duties of self-perfection (see §§ 19 – 22 of the Doctrine of Virtue) in connection with contemporary forms of perfectionist ethics and virtue ethics that rely on historically available interpretations of *eudaimonia*. See, for example, Hurka 1993, especially pp. 53 – 68); Hurka, 2003, pp. 219 – 256; Hursthouse, 1998, pp. 25 – 42. 91 – 238.

when investigated using the conceptual tool chest offered by Kant's 1797 doctrine of ends.

But doesn't our very propensity to find such results surprising raise the question of the extent to which contemporary classifications of ethical theories neglect the novel significance Kant's foundational theory of intrinsically obligatory ends? At any rate, looking at the history of Western philosophical ethics, it seems that only Immanuel Kant has grounded a moral doctrine ends by employing the concepts of two mutually supporting ends that are *both* duties and material determining grounds of the power of choice.

§ 2 Equal Right, Material Equality, and Marx's Twofold Principle

As indicated above, my reflections on the notion of Kantian consequentialism are limited to Kant's ethics as a doctrine of virtue. The line of argument followed in the preceding section does not apply to any law of duty that Kant seeks to establish within the systematic framework of his juridical theory of right. To emphasize once again what was repeatedly stated in Parts III and IV of this book, Kant's theory of the a priori foundations of right treats only the formal conditions under which different subjects whose powers of choice are reciprocally related can make free use of these choice-determining powers in accordance with practical reason's fundamental juridical prescription, "so act externally that the free use of your power of choice can coexist with the freedom of everyone in accordance with a universal law" (MS 6:231.10 – 12). The various laws of right that are grounded in this fundamental law take no account of any particular end that a person may have in mind, or any object of the power of choice that she may wish to have or want to bring about. Thus, whatever good a person may want to achieve or promote by acting in accordance with a maxim of ends is not strictly relevant to the validity of the practical laws that present us with duties of right.[22] Furthermore, the laws that prescribe duties of this type are precisely those which do place deontic constraints on the use of the power of choice; and given the analytic connection between strict right and the possible use of external coercion, the choice-limiting constraints that they impose have no direct bearing on any concept of promotable end that could ground a law for maxims of actions.[23] The arguments presented in the preceding section therefore do not

---

22 See RL 6:231.9 – 11.
23 See jointly RL 6:231.2 – 29; TL 6:383.18 – 20, 6:388.32 – 389.15.

support a consequentialist interpretation of any aspect of Kant's metaphysical theory of the foundations of right.

The boundary marker just set in place to show the limit of Kantian consequentialism applies to the formal principle of material equality that we have obtained by forging a link between Kant's portrayal of the innate right of freedom and his theory of original acquisition.[24] It is important to bear this consideration in mind as we go on to investigate the distributive side of a conception of original acquisition that would incorporate this principle of equality as the basis for a theory of distributive justice that is consistent with the deontological character of Kant's juridical theory of right.

As was mentioned at the outset of this chapter, my aim in this final section is to clarify the significance of the Kantian principle of material equality in original acquisition by treating it in view of a principle of unequal distribution that, at least to begin with, seems incompatible with Kant's juridical theory of right. To achieve this aim, I will examine the relationship between this Kantian principle and a principle of justice which requires that the distribution of usable things take place according to the unequal needs of unequal human individuals. I will therefore undertake to shed light on several key implications that our Kantian principle of equality holds for a theory of distributive justice which focuses on the Marxian distinction between the means of consumption and the means of production by which distributable means of consumption are made available for individual acquisition.

To arrive at this point, however, we will first need to clarify the conceptions of equal right and just distribution that Marx addresses in the *Critique of the Gotha Program*.[25] It will therefore be useful to begin with the assumptions that underlie Marx's discussion of those two closely related conceptions in this text. The major assumptions are as follows:

(1) Nature, regarded as the source of all means and all objects of labor, is just as much the source of use values (hence material wealth [*sachliches Reichtum*]) as labor itself, which in turn is the expression of one of nature's own powers: human labor power. Labor becomes the source of use values, and therefore *a* source of material wealth, only insofar as the human being (generically speaking) is related to nature as its *owner*.[26]

---

24 See chapters 7 and 12.
25 For extended textual explanations pertaining to Marx's critical commentary as well as details on the historical context of the *Gotha Program* and its role as a workers' party platform, see the editors' introduction on volume 25 of the *Marx-Engels Gesamtausgabe* (MEGA 25:515– 559).
26 See MEGA 25:9.11– 20.

(2) Given the natural determinacy of human labor, the following principle applies to all conditions of society and culture: The human being who possesses no other property than his own labor power must be *unfree* with respect to (literally: must be "the slave of") those who have made themselves the owners of labor's objective conditions (*gegenständliche Arbeitsbedingungen*).[27]

(3) For any given mode of production, the distribution of the means of consumption (*Consumtionsbedingungen*) is only a consequence of the distribution of the conditions of production. Thus, if the objective conditions of production (*sachliche Productionsbedingungen*)— i.e., the conditions of production other than the personal condition supplied by the labor power of individual workers—are the cooperative common property (*genossenschaftliches Eigenthum*) of the workers themselves, then there results of its own accord a distribution of the means of consumption that differs from the various forms of distribution that prevail when those objective or non-personal conditions are assigned to non-workers.[28]

In keeping with the theoretical tenets just summarized, Marx's treatment of equal right and just distribution targets two programmatic statements, which are found in the first part of the draft of the workers' party platform document at his disposal:

[*Paragraph 1:*] Labor is the source of all wealth and all culture, *and because* useful labor is possible only in society and through society, the output of labor belongs undiminished, by equal right, to all members of society.[29] (MEGA 25:9.4–7)

[*Paragraph 3:*] The emancipation of labor requires the promotion of the means of labor to the common property [*Gemeingut*] of society and the cooperative regulation of total labor with a just distribution of the output of labor.[30] (MEGA 25:11.39–41)

Marx rejects the Gotha Program draft's mutually supporting declarations that only labor is the source of material wealth and that useful labor is possible only in and through society. Consequently, after disposing of these positional claims, the thrust of his critical analysis shifts in the direction of the questions posed by the platform document's characterizations of equal right and just distribution in connection with the notion of labor output.

---

27 See MEGA 25:9.17–27.
28 See MEGA 25:15.33–16.2.
29 "Die Arbeit ist die Quelle alles Reichthums und aller Kultur, *und da* nutzbringende Arbeit nur in der Gesellschaft und durch die Gesellschaft möglich ist, gehört der Ertrag der Arbeti unverkürzt, nach gleichem Rechte, allen Gesellschaftsgliedern".
30 "Die Befreiung der Arbeti erfordert die Erhebung der Arbeitsmittel zu Gemeingut der Gesellschaft und die genossenschaftliche Regelung der Gesammtarbeti mit gerechter Vertheilung des Arbeitsertrags".

According to Marx, the following queries concerning individual distribution of the products of labor arise, and have to be dealt with, when the first paragraph's notion of undiminished labor output (i.e., the output that belongs by equal right to all members of society) is linked to the third paragraph's dual emancipatory requirement (i.e., the requirement that the means of labor must be common property and that society's total labor must be cooperatively regulated):

> "[Distribution to] all members of society?" To those not working as well? Where is then the "undiminished labor output"? Only to the working members of society? Then where is "the equal right" of all members of society?[31] (MEGA 25:12.23–25)

Marx's response to these queries begins by relating the first paragraphs's implicit programmatic demand that every worker is entitled to his undiminished labor output to the third paragraph's view of cooperatively regulated labor power. Thus, replacing the (inadmissibly imprecise) notions of labor output and total labor with the concepts of product of labor and total social product (*gesellschaftliches Gesammtproduct*), Marx holds that we must take the following approach to the question of distribution when we assume that the means of production are (or ought to be) owned in common. We first take account of the deductions from the total social product of labor that must be made prior to individual distribution. This is the part of the social product which "the producer does not get in his capacity as a private individual, but which benefits him directly or indirectly as a member of society" (MEGA 25:13.21–23). The deductions pertaining to this part include those that are necessary for maintaining and expanding the means of production as well as a substantial portion of the means of consumption themselves.[32] Thus, it is only after determining the extent of these deductions that we can arrive at the portion of the total social product available for distribution as individually assignable means of consumption. In what follows, I will refer to this portion as the 'available means of consumption' or, more simply, as 'distributable means'.

How, then, do the notions of equal right and just distribution relate to the specified concept of distributable means here at issue? According to Marx, this

---

31 "'Allen Gesellschaftsgliedern?' Auch den nicht Arbeitenden? Wo bleibt da 'der unverkürzte Arbeitsertrag'? Nur den arbeitenden Geselschaftsgliedern? Wo bleibt da 'das gleiche Recht' aller Gesellschaftsglieder?"
32 The latter include administrative costs not directly related to the process of production and resources to be devoted to communally satisfiable needs (e.g., the resources necessary for education, health services, etc.). See MEGA 25:13.1–15)

question has to be addressed in two distinct ways in view of two distinguishable developmental phases of post-capitalistic society. The first avenue of approach involves the assertion that the individual worker receives back, after the required deductions, exactly what he contributes to the total social product. Thus, since any given worker's contribution consists in the *quantum* of given labor, the individual worker takes from the available means of consumption in equal exchange for a given amount of labor. We have here, then, a reciprocal exchange relation between society and the worker in her capacity as a private individual. While this relation excludes individual distribution of the means of production, since "nothing can pass into the property of individuals except individual means of consumption" (MEGA 25:16.12–13), Marx insists that the same principle of right applies to the acquisition of individual property under post-capitalistic conditions as is supposed to apply to the exchange of commodity equivalents in a society that permits private ownership of those productive means. As he puts this thought, "just as much labor in one form is exchanged for just as much labor in another form" (MEGA 25:14.15–17). Accordingly, "*equal right* is here still in principle—*bourgeois right*", although "principle and practice are no longer at loggerheads" (MEGA 25:14.18–20).

In putting forward this last claim about equal right, Marx has in mind the principle of equal exchange that is *supposed* to apply to value-equivalent commodities in capitalistic society, but which—despite appearances—cannot apply to the exchange relation between labor power and labor's wages when the means of production are subject to individual acquisition and private ownership.[33] This is not the place, however, to become involved in Marx's accounts of the source of surplus value, let alone his theory of capitalist exploitation. At least for the purpose of my argument in the final section of this book, it suffices for us to pay careful attention to just one implication of his claim about what equal right is *in principle:* It is that the same principle of *right* will apply to the distribution of the available means of consumption when the means of production are owned in common as is supposed to apply when these means are subject to private ownership.

Marx of course holds that the restriction of individual property to the available means of consumption represents a signal advance over all hitherto existing social and economic formations. In particular, he maintains that the relations of production which this restriction makes possible are those of a higher form of society than one in which the capitalist mode of production prevails. That is primarily because common ownership of the means of production is what furnishes

---

33 On this, see, e.g., MEGA 25:19.9–23.

the necessary foundation for overcoming the condition of human servitude or unfreedom that is an essential and unavoidable feature of capitalism (see above, p. 307–308). Nonetheless, despite the historical advancement of freedom made possible by the restriction imposed upon the private appropriation of productive means, Marx insists that *equal* right is here "still subject to its bourgeois limitation" (MEGA 25:14.22–23), even though it is now a right of the producers that pertains only to individual ownership of the available means of consumption. For it remains a right that is itself subject to two essential restrictions that obtain *whether or not* the means of production are available for individual acquisition and private ownership. First, it is a right by which the distributable means that producers receive must be "*proportional* to their contributions of labor" (MEGA 25:14.23–24). Second, it a right according to which rightful equality consists in nothing more than the circumstance that individual labor contributions are "measured with an *equal standard*" (MEGA 25:14.24–25).

So much for the first way of approaching the issue of how 'equal right' (and, by implication, the 'just distribution' that accords with equal right) relates to the concept of distributable means. We now turn to the second avenue of approach, i.e., the way that takes proper account of the crucial anthropological factor that has to be brought to bear if the restrictions that subject equal right to its bourgeois limitation are to be overcome. The passage that introduces this factor merits quotation in full:

> But one [producer] is physically or mentally superior to another, and thus delivers more labor in more time, or can labor for a longer period of time; and labor, in order to serve as a measure, must be determined according to duration or intensity; otherwise it ceases to be an equal measuring standard. This *equal* right is an unequal right for unequal labor. It acknowledges no class differences, because everyone is now a worker like everyone else; yet it tacitly recognizes unequal natural endowment, and thus workers' unequal performance ability, as natural privileges. *It is therefore a right of inequality, in terms of its content [dem Inhalt nach], like every right.* Right, by its very nature, can consist only in the application of an equal standard; but unequal individuals (and they would not be different individuals if they were not unequal) are measured by an equal standard only insofar as one brings them under an equal point of view, [that is,] apprehends them from a *determinate* side—for example, in the present case, one considers them *only as workers* and sees nothing more in them, disregarding everything else.
>
> Further: One worker is married, another is not; one has more children than another, etc., etc. Thus, with equal performance of labor and therefore equal share in the social consumption fund, one will in fact receive more than another, one will be richer than another, etc. In order to avoid these defects [*Missstände*] right would have to be unequal instead of being equal.[34] (MEGA 25:14.25–15.5).

---

34 "Der eine ist aber physisch oder geistig dem andern überlegen, liefert also in derselben Zeit

Given our focus on the relationship between equal right and just distribution, five facets of Marx's reasoning in this passage are of particular interest: First, inequality is *constitutive* for human individuality. Second, human beings are *naturally* unequal in their respective capacities for productive labor. Third, given this natural inequality, *any* right is a right of inequality in terms of its *content*. Fourth, with respect to distribution of the means of consumption, the equal right that is proportional to labor contributions amounts to a right of unequal acquisition when the individual human being is regarded as something more than as a contributor of labor *quanta*. Fifth, to avoid the contentful inequalities that always occur when right conforms to the proportionality condition just indicated, right would have to be unequal instead of being equal.

According to Marx, then, contentful inequalities will unavoidably occur *whenever* distribution takes place in accordance with equal right, but under the conditions imposed by naturally determined human inequality and differences in workers' socially contingent domestic arrangements. *These* distributive inequalities are, however, defects. Thus, even if they are in fact unavoidable in the first stage of non-capitalistic society, they represent normatively unacceptable shortcomings which, as such, ought to be overcome.

To overcome these defects, the elimination of natural inequality among human beings is not an option that Marx entertains.[35] Nor does he advocate, in the text at issue, fundamental alterations of historically contingent domestic arrangements that are typical of (economically) non-productive relations be-

---

mehr Arbeit oder kann während mehr Zeit arbeiten; und die Arbeit, um als Maas zu dienen, muss der Ausdehnung oder der Intensivität nach bestimmt warden; sonst hörte sie auf Maasstab zu sein. Diess *gleiche* Recht ist ungleiches Recht für ungleiche Arbeit. Es erkennt keine Klassenschiede an, weil jeder nun Arbeiter ist wie der andre, aber es erkennt stillschweigend die ungleiche individuelle Begabung und daher Leistungsfähigkeit der Arbeiter als natürliche Privilegien an. *Es ist daher ein Recht der Ungleichheit, seinem Inhalt nach, wie alles Recht.* Das Recht kann seiner Natur nach nur in Anwendung von gleichem Maasstab bestehn; aber die ungleichen Individuen (und sie wären nicht verschiedne Individuen, wenn sie nicht Ungleiche wären) sich nur an gleichem Massstab messbar, so weit man sie unter einen gleichen Gesichtspunkt bringt, sie nur von einer *bestimmten* Seit fast, z. B. im gegebnen Fall sie *nur als Arbeiter* betrachtet, und weiter nichts in ihnen sieht, von allem andern absieht.

Ferner: Ein Arbeiter is verheirathet, der andre nicht; einer hat mehr Kinder als der andre, etc. etc. Bei gleicher Arbeitsleistung und daher gleichem Antheil an dem gesellschaftlichen Consumtionsfonds erhält also der eine faktisch mehr als der andre, ist der eine reicher als der andre, et. Um all diese Missstände zu vermeiden müsste das Recht, statt gleich, vielmehr ungleich sein".

35 While Marx lived long before the wonders of genetic engineering, there is no indication that he would have been willing to countenance the destruction of what he took to be the very foundation of human individuality.

tween human beings.³⁶ Instead, maintaining the restriction on the distributive availability of the means of production, Marx proposes that we move beyond the proportionality principle that limits equal right in its application to the available means of consumption. The classic lines are well known; and they, too, bear quotation in full:

> In a higher phase of communistic society, after the enslaving subordination of individuals to the division of labor, and therewith also the opposition between mental and physical labor has vanished; after labor has become not only the means of life but life's primary need; after the forces of production have increased with the all-round development of individuals and the wellsprings of cooperative wealth flow more freely—only then can the narrow horizon of bourgeois right be fully crossed and society inscribe on its banner: from each according to his abilities , to each according to his needs!'³⁷ (MEGA 25:15.11–20)

At this juncture, we must take special note of the following ramifications of Marx's banner-inscribed principle. The first part of this twofold principle (from each according to one's abilities) is, of course, contrary to any proportionality principle that would require distribution in accordance with equal contribution. The second part of Marx's principle (to each according to one's needs) is inconsistent with the proportionality principle by which equal right is subject to the 'bourgeois limitation' mentioned above. Both parts of Marx's principle are necessarily distinct from any principle of right that abstracts from the needs of individual human beings, or that disregards what the individual human agent may be inclined to contribute according to the abilities that she possesses. Neither part of Marx's twofold principle, however, would necessarily be inconsistent with every principle of right if it can be established that there is a formal principle of equal right that allows for unequal distributions to individuals whose abilities to contribute are unequal.

This latter possibility is of course the major item of interest to us, given our underlying concern with the relationship between a Kantian formal principle of

---

36 The point here is not that domestic arrangements will remain unaltered when the means of production are owned in common, but that Marx's *argument* does not rely on the assumption that they will change (or remain the same) in certain ways.

37 "In einer höheren Phase der kommunistischen Gesellschaft, nachdem die knechtende Unterordnung der Individuen unter die Theilung der Arbeit, damit auch der Gegensatz geistiger und körperlicher Arbeit, verschwunden ist; nachdem die Arbeit nicht nur Mittel zum Leben, sondern selbst das erste Lebensbedürfniss geworden; nachdem mit der allseitigen Entwicklung der Individuen auch ihre Productivkräfte gewachsen und alle Springquellen des genossenschaftlichen Reichthums voller fliessen—erst dann kann der enge bürgerliche Rechtshorizont ganz überschritten werden und die Gesellschaft auf ihre Fahne schreiben: Jeder nach seinen Fähigkeiten, Jedem nach seinen Bedürfnissen!"

distributive equality in acquisition and Marx's banner-inscribed principle. But let us continue to keep this concern well in the background for the time being and concentrate, first of all, on a purely formal point that pertains to the content of the Marxian principle at issue, i.e., the twofold principle that prescribes contributions and distributions proportionally to abilities and needs. The point is this: To the extent that Marx's twofold principle can be considered a principle of *right* at all, it must be one that is in fully in keeping with his claim that every right is a right of inequality in terms of its *content*. Indeed, if there can be such a thing as a principle of right that is also a principle of contentful inequality, then exactly this kind of principle is codified in Marx's proposed banner inscription. The only question is whether there can be such a principle if (as Marx insists) right can consist only in the application of an equal standard, i.e., the standard by which distributions of the means of consumption must be proportional to labor contributions.

Before coming to grips with this last question, we need to be clear about a distinction that has to be drawn between what Marx intends to accomplish politically, in the text here at issue, and what his argument actually establishes with respect to the juridical conceptions of right, equality, and equal right. It is of course evident that whole line of argument pursued in the in the first part of the *Critique of the Gotha Program* is intended to demonstrate the normative inadequacy of 'equal right' when equality of right is combined with a principle of distributive proportionality that requires the exchange of (quantitatively determined) equivalents. Yet it is essential to take note of the fact that the text under consideration does not provide an argument against equal right *as such*, i.e., an argument against equal right *sans phrase*, as it were. Even when Marx explicitly characterizes equal right as being "in principle bourgeois right", his substantive reference to the concept of right is limited to right as it is subject to the particular proportionality principle that makes it not only unequal in terms of its content, but *also* the ground of distributive inequalities that are defects. Moreover, when he maintains that "right *would* [italics mine (J. E.)] have to be unequal instead of being unequal" in order to provide a basis for overcoming distributive inequalities, his point of reference remains the equal right that conforms to the proportionality principle which *limits* right in general. Thus, whatever Marx's broader intentions may have been in these two respects, his considerations do not entail that equal right, even as a right of contentful inequality, must amount to a ground of *defective* distributive inequalities when it is not subject to the restrictions imposed by the proportionality principle that limits right.[38]

To be sure, immediately after formulating his banner-inscribed principle Marx goes on to explain that his aim in dealing with equal right and just distribution is to show the highly disadvantageous political consequences of "trying to foist upon our party again, as dogmas, ideas which at a certain time had a meaning but have now become obsolete verbiage [*Phrasenkram*]" (MEGA 25:15.23–25). More generally, he insists that the programmatic platform under scrutiny is mistaken in the emphasis it places on the question of distribution when "in every case distribution of the means of consumption is always only a consequence of the distribution of the conditions of production themselves" (MEGA 25:15.23–25). But to maintain that several planks of a political party platform amount to verbal rubbish from the standpoint of the critique of political economy is something quite different from disposing of the philosophical problem of just distribution that is linked to the concept of equal right—especially if one endorses a principle of individual distribution which prescribes that each should receive according to need while contributing according to ability.

It may be noted in this connection that Marx's description of a form of society in which the wellsprings of cooperative wealth flow more freely does not eliminate the problem of just distribution, no matter how wide a society's horizon of right may be.[39] Even if we assume that society's wealth-generating wellsprings can, in principle, provide for unlimited need-satisfying means of consumption, cooperative wealth would presumably not be something that just spreads itself over ever everyone in common. It would still have to be something made available for *distribution* by those who contribute to the satisfaction of needs.

To illustrate this point, let us entertain a scenario tailor-made for consumption by science fiction fans, video-game addicts, post-humanists, and right-wing

---

[38] That is, the proportionality principle that (a) is supposed to govern the distribution of both the means of production and the means of consumption in capitalistic society, and that (b) actually *can* govern the distribution of the available means of consumption alone when human society is no longer constrained by the capitalist mode of production.

[39] Jerry (G. A.) Cohen has maintained that Marx attempts to circumvent the question of distributive justice by assuming that practically *unlimited* material abundance can be provided by socialistically furthered increases in the forces of production (see Cohen [1995] 10–11, 16, 125–127.) While I fully agree that Marx cannot get around that question, I am unable to discern this assumption in the *Critique of the Gotha Program*. Marx holds only that the wellsprings of wealth will flow "*more* freely" (italics mine [J. E.]) when the forces of production are no longer subject to the limitations imposed by the capitalist mode of production and residually present in emerging non-capitalistic society. I discern nothing inherently unrealistic in taking this position.

paranoiacs: Imagine a communistic society in which, for the purpose of satisfying human needs, the means and conditions of production have been developed as the means of producing virtual realities, i.e., 'not really real' realities, whatever that means. (I ignore here all metaphysical complications that would detract from the force of the example.) Imagine, too, that everyone has agreed to develop the means of production in this way in order to ensure that all distribution of the means of consumption is fully in keeping with Marx's twofold banner inscription. Finally, imagine that every member of society now has the means to satisfy every imaginable need just by wishfully thinking of the means of satisfying it.[40] Even leaving aside the problem of how need satisfaction in these circumstances could amount to anything more than the merely virtual satisfaction of real or imaginary needs, it is entirely unclear how our depicted scenario could eliminate the "need" (as it were) for distributive justice as long as the means of virtual need satisfaction are in fact *distributed* to individual virtual-reality communists—or at least to imaginary communists whose (imagined) real needs are virtually satisfiable.

Needless to say, thankfully, this kind of imaginary (if not delusional) scenario does not fall within the horizon of Marx's thinking.[41] Yet the same presupposition of just distribution can be seen to apply to our virtual-reality communism as applies to a 'really existing' communistic society in which the means of consumption would be distributable without individual limitations because of the (practically) unlimited availability of need-satisfying means. In both cases, I (like anyone else) would have sufficient reason to complain, in keeping with the prescription "to each according to one's needs", that I am not treated *justly* if I am not able to acquire all of the available means necessary to satisfy my needs; and my reason would suffice simply because I would not treated *equally* to every other individual, no matter what means I may require to satisfy whatever needs I may have. For my *freedom* to acquire such means would be subject to a restriction that does not apply to everyone in common, taken individually, whenever the means of consumption are subject to individual distribution. In other words, the restriction of my freedom to acquire *whatever* I need from these dis-

---

40 Assuming a highly developed state of our virtual-reality generating means of production, we can imagine that all wishful thinking brings about its own wish fulfillment. The roads to hell paved by such thinking need not be especially worrisome, at least as long as they remain only virtually real.

41 Thus, especially now that America is being made great again, we can safely return to the imaginary communists lurking under our historically existing beds. (One can only hope that the political import of this remark will be initially unintelligible to anyone who might happen to read this note a hundred years hence.)

tributable means would be inconsistent with a principle of equality in acquisition that must obtain if there is to be the distribution of need-satisfying means in accordance with the Marx's "to each" prescription.

What is this principle of equality? It is the principle of right by which I, like anyone else, am free to acquire the means that I need in order to satisfy my needs, whatever the *content* of need may be. As such, it is a formal principle of right. Moreover, it is the formal principle of equality *qua* right that Marx's "to each" prescription *presupposes*. For this prescription could not permit contentful *inequality* in the distribution (and thus the individual acquisition) of the means of need satisfaction unless it applied equally to the needs of each and every member of society who is to contribute according to her abilities. We have here, then, a formal principle of equality that serves as a principle of equal right. But it is the formal principle that permits inequality in the distributive acquisition of the means of need satisfaction proportionally to the unequal needs of those who are not naturally of equal ability.

Obviously, from the point of view of this book's argument, the burning question is how the formal principle presupposed by Marx's banner inscription relates to the Kantian principle of material equality in acquisition that we arrive at when we stretch Kant's theory of original acquisition to its proper limits. Before coming to grips with this question, however, we need to clarify how the second part of Marx's twofold principle fits into the picture just outlined. I have in mind here the problem of obligation at issue in Marx's "from each" prescription.

It must be emphasized that this problem is not eliminated by the supposition that human agents will be *inclined* to perform productive labor because they live in circumstances in which labor itself has become life's prime need. For it always remains possible, even in the best of need-fulfilling circumstances, that some human beings will not be so inclined. Thus, even if we assume that society's wealth-generating wellsprings can always produce at least as many distributable means of consumption as can always satisfy everyone's needs, the mere possibility that someone may be disinclined to contribute proportionally to ability presents the issue of obligation.[42] And this remains an issue, although

---

42 Even under optimal conditions of unlimited need-satisfying material wealth, there could very well be many people who just get bored with perfecting themselves through self-realizing social labor. Moreover, given circumstances of relative scarcity, we can quite plausibly expect that there are always likely to be many more people who, from sheer bloody-mindedness, will refuse to provide their ability-proportional contributions—especially when they get tired of listening to moralistic, politically correct pieties distributed by those whose own substantive contributions are inversely proportional to *quanta* of air passing across their vocal cords. (One can sympathize with the sentiment even when agreeing that everyone ought to contribute according

it may not present a central practical concern for those interested in ensuring distributive justice as long as they can reasonably expect that everyone's needs will be readily satisfiable.[43]

In brief, the theoretical problem with which we are concerned is that of the *kind* of obligation raised by Marx's "from each" prescription. Moreover, if the obligation involved in this prescription is to be compatible with the concept of right presupposed by the other part of Marx's twofold principle, then it must be of the kind that involves the *possible* use of external coercion to ensure compliance with a duty linked to a formal principle of equal right. For it must take account of at least the possibility (if not the probability) that the greater or lesser needs of all unequal individuals can be *equally*, hence justly, satisfied only if everyone contributes in proportion to their abilities.[44] It is thus in view of a duty of right linked to a principle of equality that we return to the consideration of Kant.

There can be no doubt that both parts of Marx's banner-inscribed principle can qualify as maxims that are apt for ethical lawgiving, or that each one of these parts fits together quite handily with Kant's theory of morally practical reason's obligatory ends: I can further my own perfection by developing the talents needed for improving my abilities to contribute to the satisfaction of everyone's needs, which promotes the happiness of others. And everyone else can do the same for me by contributing to the satisfaction of my needs, which in turn enables me to contribute to the happiness-promoting satisfaction of others' needs. These forms of ability-furthering and need-satisfying action are not only fully in keeping with what is required by the supreme principle of Kant's

---

to the abilities of each so that everyone's needs—at any rate, everyone's basic material needs—can be satisfied.)

43 One may agree with Hume (see EPM 3.2–5) that material superabundance would make justice unnecessary as a *virtue*. But this cannot do away with the *obligation* of justice that applies to the distribution of need-satisfying means.

44 Even with practically limitless abundance, internal self-constraint cannot *suffice* to ensure ability-proportional contribution as long as one can act from an inclination to contribute less than one can and (according to Marx's "from each" prescription) should. Furthermore, given the ecological devastations stemming from overpopulation as well as from the effects of the capitalist mode of production's global reach, one hardly needs to emphasize the low probability that material abundance will ever be sufficient to make distributive justice a merely theoretical concern. While the "from each" prescription does not entail that everybody must always contribute *as much* as they possibly can (cf. note 5 of this chapter), it does preclude that anyone may contribute proportionally less than others of lesser ability—*especially* if the wellsprings of cooperative wealth are such that the needs of unequal individuals can be equally satisfied only by the ability-proportional contributions of everyone.

doctrine of virtue.[45] They also highlight the mutually supporting relationship between own-perfection and others' happiness as ends that are also duties. Yet none of this is directly relevant to two crucial questions that emerge when we consider the juridico-philosophic import of Marx's twofold principle in connection with Kant's theory of original acquisition. The relevant questions are these:

> How does (i) the formal principle of equal right that Marx's twofold principle *presupposes* in its application to (naturally) unequal human individuals relate to (ii) our Kantian principle of material equality, i.e., the principle that we arrive at when we combine Kant's idea of original acquisition with the idea of innate equality involved in his account of freedom *qua* innate right?

> Does the kind of obligation at issue in the juridico-philosophic interpretation of Marx's twofold principle allow for the distinction between juridical and ethical lawgiving that Kant requires in order to keep all laws of right separate from the application of morally practical reason's laws to virtue and its duties?

Providing a coherent, not to mention plausible, response to either one of these queries goes far beyond the narrow horizon of this book. But several brief parting comments may suffice to set the stage for further inquiry.

Let us ask what happens if we combine (a) our Kantian principle of material equality in original acquisition with (b) the formal principle of equal right that Marx's twofold principle presupposes, while assuming (c) that the means of production ought to belong to everyone in common for the sake of human freedom? In other words, let us consider the theoretical issues that immediately arise if we attempt to ground the permissibility of individual acquisition in a (Kantian) formal principle of contentful equality while restricting the scope of permissible acquisition in view of the necessary condition of freedom that Marx's twofold principle assumes, even when it also presupposes a purely formal principle of equality *qua* right.[46] As we have seen, this merely formal principle of equality allows for the unequal distribution of need-satisfying means insofar as it pertains to Marx's "to each" prescription.[47] But if this is the case, then how could our Kantian principle of original acquisition, which is a principle of material or contentful *equality*, allow for (let alone ground) this kind of distribution?

---

45 See TL 6:395.15–21.
46 For the sake of provisional clarification, I disregard here the highly significant complication that this restriction makes the Kantian principle apply to a common possession which includes means of production that are themselves the products of human labor.
47 If you happen to be looking a good target for leveling a charge of empty formalism, then you are here face to face with a really good one. It is, however, the strictly formal principle without which Marx's "to each" prescription cannot possibly furnish a prescription of *right*.

If a Kantian theory of (restricted) original acquisition is to have any normative import at all when it is brought into alignment with Marx's "to each" prescription, it must be able to offer a coherent response to the question just posed. One way of dealing with this question, of course, would be to maintain that the Kantian principle just cannot provide any warrant for unequal distribution. One could therefore oppose the Marxian distributive prescription to our Kantian principle of material equality. We could attempt to do this by completely severing whatever connections there may be between this principle and the concept of equal right as such (i.e., the concept of equal right *sans phrase* that, in Marx's case, allows for unequal distribution of the available means of consumption). Yet this, I submit, is an exceedingly tall order for a theory of original acquisition that must be compatible with the innate equality that features in Kant's concept of freedom as the innate right of human beings.[48]

In any event, it seems to me that there is a rather more intriguing line of approach, i.e., the alternative approach that would require the integration of our Kantian principle of material equality with a theory of the forms of distribution by which access to equality-*establishing* means can be ensured for those whose needs are, in fact, proportionally greater than those whose abilities are proportional to their needs.[49] If we take this second line of approach, however, then

---

[48] If (see TL 6:237.29 – 238.11) (a) freedom, i.e., independence from being constrained by another's power of choice, is the only innate or original right belonging to every human being in virtue of his humanity; and if (b) this principle of freedom involves innate equality, i.e., independence from being bound by others to more than one could in turn be bound by them—then how could there be a theory of original acquisition that has no connection to the formal principle by which everyone has the right *equally* to acquire need-satisfying means? The elimination of such a connection does not seem possible as long as it is assumed that everyone has the *original* (i.e., non-acquired) right to acquire objects of the power of choice consistently with the innate equality of everyone else. At any rate, the principle of equal right that distribution according to unequal needs presupposes is at least necessarily consistent with the principle of material equality that the a priori concept of original acquisition requires if is to be compatible with Kant's definition of innate equality. This is true even if that presupposed principle of equal right (*sans phrase*) permits contentful inequality in the acquisition of the means of need satisfaction when the empirically specifiable needs of human beings are brought into play.

[49] By equality-establishing means I have in mind distributable means of consumption that can be individually acquired in order to eliminate (or at least compensate for) involuntary disadvantages due to brute luck or the vicissitudes of fortune. I take it that access to such means is equivalent to what Jerry Cohen called "equal access to advantage" (see Cohen 2011, pp. 13 – 14, 18, 69, 220 – 221; cf. Cohen 2008, 181 – 183). While Cohen insisted that "advantage", as he employed the term, should not be understood as denoting "advantage *over* somebody" (Cohen 2011, p. 14 [note]), the view of justice that it involves bears certain similarities to "the advantage of the weaker": τo τoυ ἥττoνoς συμφέρον (Plato *Rep.* 340b; contrast Aristotle *Pol.* 1282b18 – 30). But

how exactly should we understand the obligation to ensure this sort of access from the standpoint of a theory of right that would link equal right to material equality in the account of acquisition which is supposed to furnish the normative basis of individual property? And what, according to principles of strictly juridical lawgiving, would be the limits (if any) of equality-establishing distribution if this is unavoidably the type of distribution that obliges those whose abilities are greater to contribute *more* than those of lesser ability?

In view of the questions just posed, my final comment has to do with a figure who plays a significant, even if not easily discernible, background role in Marx's *Critique of the Gotha Program*. When repudiating the thesis that useful labor is possible only in and through society, Marx delivers an apparently dismissive remark about the thinker who, historically, has perhaps had the most of abiding interest to offer concerning the natural equality as well as the inequality of human beings.[50] The remark, which on first reading seems to be one of unqualified extravagance, runs as follows:

> One could just as well have said that only in society can useless and generally harmful labor become a branch of gainful employment, that only in society can one live by idleness, etc., etc.—in short, one could just as well have copied the whole of Rousseau.[51] (MEGA 25:10.16 – 19)

The exaggerated quality of the suggestion about copying Rousseau is, of course, part and parcel of this remark's polemical aim. Yet it is precisely the exaggeration that makes the challenge presented by the suggestion impossible to dismiss. Why, indeed, shouldn't we bring the whole of Rousseau to bear when the stakes are nothing less than the conditions of human equality and freedom?

---

this, obviously, opens up an entirely different line of inquiry than the one suggested in this paragraph.
50 In his treatment of the relationship between Rousseau and Marx, Robert Wokler (2012, p. 128) takes note of the remark. But he does not consider its implications for Marx's and Rousseau's divergent views on the nature of human equality and inequality. See, however, Neuhouser 2014, pp. 214 – 247 for considerations relevant to this task.
51 "Man hätte ebenso gut sagen können, dass nur in der Gesellschaft nutzlose und selbst gemeinschädliche Arbeit ein Erwerbszwieg werden kann, dass man nur in der Gesellschaft vom Müssiggang leben kann, etc. etc., kurz den genzen Rousseau abschreiben können".

Bibliography

Primary Sources

(Years given in brackets indicate years of original publication, if different from the editions cited.)

Abegg, Johan Friedrich (1976): *Reisetagebuch von 1798.* Walter Abegg/Jolanda Abegg (Eds.). Frankfurt am Main: Insel Verlag.

Aristotle (1957). *Aristotelis politica.* Sir David Ross (Ed.). Oxford: Oxford University Press.

Balguy, John (1728): *The Foundations of Moral Goodness; Or a Further Inquiry into the Original of Our Idea of Virtue.* London: J. Pemberton.

Balguy, John (1729): *The Second Part of the Foundations of Moral Goodness; Illustrating and Enforcing the Principles of Reasoning Contained in the Former.* London: J. Pemberton.

Barbeyrac, Jean (1749): "An Historical and Critical Account of the Science of Morality". In: Pufendorf, Samuel. *Of the Law of Nature and Nations* [5th edition]. Kennett, B. (Trans.). London: L. Lichfield.

Barbeyrac, Jean (1992 [1718]): "Jugement d'un anonyme, sur l'original de cet abbregé avec des réfléxions du traducteur". In: Pufendorf, Samuel: *Les devoirs de l'homme et du citoyen tels qu'ils lui sont préscrits par la loi naturelle.* Jean Barbeyrac (Trans.). Hildesheim: Georg Olms; reprint of Amsterdam, Coup & Kuyper (1734–1735).

Baumgarten, Alexander Gottlieb, (1760): *Initia philosophiae practicae prima acromatice.* Halle: Hemmerde.

Butler, J. (2006a): "The Analogy of Religion, Natural and Revealed, to the Constitution and Course of Nature". In: White, David E. (Ed.): *The Works of Bishop Butler.* Rochester: University of Rochester Press, pp. (147–314).

Butler, J. (2006b): "Fifteen Sermons Preached at the Rolls Chapel". In: White, David E. (ed.): *The Works of Bishop Butler.* Rochester: University of Rochester Press, pp. 33–146.

Carmichael, Gershom (2002 [1724]): "Supplements and Observations upon Samuel Pufendorf's *On the Duty of Man and Citizen according to the Law of Nature,* composed for the Use of Students in the Universities". In: Moore, James/Silverthorne, Michael (Eds.), Silverthorne, Michael (Trans.): *Natural Rights on the Threshold of the Scottish Enlightenment: The Writings of Gershom Carmichael.* Indianapolis: Liberty Fund, pp. 7–211.

Cicero, Marcus Tullius. (1744): *Morals, containing the Conferences on Good and Evil, and the Academical Treatises.* William Guthrie, (Trans.). London: T. Waller.

Cicero, Marcus Tullius (1945): *Tusculan Disputations / Tusculanae Disputationes.* Cambridge, MA: Harvard University Press (Loeb Classical Library).

Cicero, Marcus Tullius (1994): *De officiis.* Michael Winterbottom (Ed.). Oxford: Clarendon Press.

Cicero, Marcus Tullius (1998): *De finibus bonorum et malorum.* L. D. Reynolds (Ed.). Oxford: Clarendon Press.

Cicero, Marcus Tullius (2001): *On Moral Ends,* Julia Annas (Ed.)/Raphael Woolf (Trans.). Cambridge: Cambridge University Press.

Clarke, Samuel (1708): *A Discourse Concerning the Unchangeable Obligations of Natural Religion, and the Truth and Certainty of the Christian Revelation.* London: J. Knapton.

Crusius, Christian August (1969 [1744]): *Anweisung vernünftig zu leben, Darinnen nach Erklärung der Nature des menschlichen Willens die natürlichen Pflichten und allgemeine Klugheitslehren im richtigen Zusammenhange vorgetragen werden*. Hildesheim: Georg Olms.

Cumberland, Richard (1672) *De legibus disquisitio philosophica*, London.

Cumberland, Richard (2005 [1727]): *A Treatise of the Laws of Nature*. Jon Parkin (Ed.)/John Maxwell (Trans.). Indianapolis: Liberty Fund.

Diogenes Laertius. (1991): *Lives of the Eminent Philosophers*. Greek text with English translation by Robert Drew Hicks, 2 vols. Cambridge MA: Harvard University Press.

Garve, Chrisitan (1792a [4th edition]): *Abhandlung über die menschlichen Pflichten in drei Büchern aus dem Lateinischen des Marcus Tullius Cicero, übersetzt von Christian Garve*. Breslau: Wilhelm Gottlieb Korn.

Garve, Christian (1792b): *Philosophische Anmerkungen und Abhandlungen zu Ciceros Büchern von den Pflichten, Anmerkungen zu dem ersten Buche*. Breslau: Wilhelm Gottlieb Korn.

Grotius, Hugo (1868): *De jure praedae commentarius*. H. G. Hamaker (Ed.). The Hague: Matinus Nijhoff.

Grotius, Hugo (1913 [1625 (2nd ed. 1631)]): *De jure belli ac pacis, libri tres*. Scott, James Brown (Ed.)/Francis W. Kelsey (Trans.). Washington DC: Carnegie Endownment for International Peace. (Photomechanical reproduction of 1746 Latin text.)

Grotius, Hugo (1916 [1608]): *The Freedom of the Seas*. Ralf van Deman Magofin (Trans.). Oxford: Oxford University Press. (References are to the Latin text of Grotius's *Mare liberum*, which is published in conjunction with the Magofin translation.)

Hobbes, Thomas (1840 [1662]): "A Dialogue Between a Philosopher and a Student of the Common Laws of England". In: Molesworth, William (Ed.): *The English Works of Thomas Hobbes*, vol. 6. London: John Bohn, pp. 1–160.

Hobbes, Thomas (1990 [1640]): *The Elements of Law, Natural and Politic*. J. C. A. Gaskin (Ed.). Oxford: Oxford University Press.

Hobbes, Thomas (1982 [1651]): *De cive: The English Version*. Howard Warrender (Ed.). Oxford: Clarendon Press.

Hobbes, T (1983 [1642]): *De cive: The Latin Version*. Howard Warrender (Ed.). Oxford: Clarendon Press.

Hobbes, Thomas (1839 ff. [1658]): *De homine*. In: Thomas Hobbes: *Opera philosophica quae scripsit omnia*. Sir William Molesworth (Ed.). Vol. 2. London: John Bohn, pp. 1–54.

Hobbes, Thomas (1996 [1651]): *Leviathan*. Richard Tuck (Ed.). Cambridge: Cambridge University Press.

Home, Henry [Lord Kames] (2005 [1751]): *Essays on the Principles of Morality and Natural Religion*. Mary Catherine Moran (Ed.). Indianapolis: Liberty Fund.

Hume, David (1932): *The Letters of David Hume*. G. Y. T. Grieg (Ed.). Vol. 1. Oxford: Oxford University Press.

Hume, David (1998 [1751]): *An Enquiry Concerning the Principles of Morals*. Tom L. Beauchamp (Ed.). Oxford: Oxford University Press.

Hume, David (2000 [1738–1740]): *A Treatise of Human Nature*. David Fate Norton/Mary J. Norton (Eds.). Oxford: Oxford University Press.

Hutcheson, Francis (2004 [1725]): *An Inquiry into the Original of Our Ideas of Beauty and Virtue*. Wolfgang Leidhold (Ed.). Indianapolis: Liberty Fund.

Hutcheson, Francis (2002 [1728]): *An Essay on the Nature and Conduct of the Passions and Affections, with Illustrations on the Moral Sense*. Aaron Garrett (Ed.). Indianapolis: Liberty Fund.

Hutcheson, Francis (1969 [1742]): *Philosophiae moralis institutio compendiaria, with A Short Introduction to Moral Philosophy*. Luigi Turco (Ed.). Indianapolis: Liberty Fund.

Hutcheson, Francis (2000 [1755]): *A System of Moral Philosophy*, vol. 1. Bristol: Thoemmes Press.

Hutcheson, Francis (2006 [1730]): *Logic, Metaphysics, and the Natural Sociability of Mankind*. James Moore /Michael Silverthorne (Eds.). Indianapolis: Liberty Fund.

Hutcheson, Francis/James Moor (2008 [1742]): *The Meditations of the Emperor Marcus Aurelius Antoninus*. James Moore/M. Silverthorne (Eds.). Indianapolis: Liberty Fund.

Jacobi, Friedrich Heinrich (1776): "Eduard Allwills Papiere". In: *Der Teutsche Merkur*. No. 14.2, pp. 14–75; No. 15.3: pp. 57–71; No. 16.4: pp. 229–262.

Jacobi, Friedrich Heinrich (1779): *Woldemar: Eine Seltenheit aus der Naturgeschichte, Erster Band*. Flensburg, Leipzig: Kortensche Buchhandlung.

Kant, Immanuel (1902ff.): *Kants gesammelte Schriften*. Berlin: Walter De Gruyter.

Kant, Immanuel (1991): *Bemerkungen in den "Beobachtungen über das Gefühl des Schönen und Erhabenen*. Rischmüller, Marie Rischmüller (Ed.). Hamburg: Meiner.

Kant, Immanuel (1990): *Metaphysische Anfangsgründe der Tugendlehre*. Bernd Ludwig (Ed.). Hamburg: Meiner.

Kant, Immanuel (1998): *Metaphysische Anfangsgründe der Rechtslehre*. Bernd Ludwig (Ed.). Hamburg: Meiner.

Locke, John (1975 [1689]): *An Essay concerning Human Understanding*. Nidditch, P. (Ed.). Oxford: Clarendon Press.

Mandeville, Bernard (1988 [1732]): *The Fable of the Bees, Or Private Vices, Public Benefits*. F. B. Kaye (Ed.), 2 vols. Indianapolis: Liberty Classics.

Marx, Karl/Engels, Friedrich (1961ff.): *Werke*. 43 vols. Berlin: Dietz Verlag.

Marx, Karl/Engels, Friedrich (1975ff.): *Marx/Engels Gesamtausgabe (MEGA), Erste Abteilung*. Berlin: Dietz Verlag.

Mill, John Stuart (1969). *Utilitarianism*. In: *Collected Works of John Stuart Mill*. John M. Robson, (Ed.). Vol. 10. Toronto: University of Toronto Press, pp. 203–259.

Ockham, William (1974): *Opera nonaginta dierum*. In: *Opera politica*. Hilary S. Offler/Jeffrey J. Sikes (Eds.), Vol. 4. Manchester: Manchester University Press.

Plato (2003): *Platonis rempublicam*. S. L. Slings (Ed.). Oxford: Oxford University Press.

Price, Richard (1974 [1758]): *A Review of the Principal Questions of Morals*. D. D. Raphael (Ed.). Oxford: Oxford University Press.

Pufendorf, Samuel (1932 [1672]): *De jure naturae et gentium libri octo*. Oxford: Claredon Press. (Latin text of 1688 published in conjunction with English translation by C. H. Oldfather and W. A. Oldfather.)

Pufendorf, Samuel (1998 [1672]): *De Jure naturae et gentium*. Frank Böhling (Ed.). In: Pufendorf, Samuel: *Gesammelte Werke*. Wilhelm Schmidt-Biggemann, (Ed.) Vol. 4.1. Berlin: Akademie Verlag.

Pufendorf, Samuel (1673): *De officio hominis et civis juxta legem naturalem libri duo*. Gerald Hartung (Ed.). In: Pufendorf, Samuel: *Gesammelte Werke*. Wilhelm Schmidt-Biggemann (Ed.). Vol. 2. Berlin: Akademie Verlag.

Reid, Thomas (2010): *Essays on the Active Powers of Man: A Critical Edition*. Knud Haakonssen and James Harris (Eds.). University Park, PA: Pennsylvania University Press.
Rousseau, Jean Jacques (1959 ff.): *Oeuvres completes*. Bernard Gagnebin/Marcel Raymond (Eds.). 5 vols. Paris: Gallimard.
Rousseau, Jean Jacques (1990 ff.): *Collected Writings*. Roger D. Masters/Christopher Kelly (Eds.). 13 vols. Dartmouth: University Press of New England.
Ross, William David (2002 [1930]): *The Right and the Good*. Stratton-Lake, P. (Ed.). Oxford: Clarendon Press.
Selden, John (1726): *Opera omnia*. David Wilkins (Ed.). London.
Shaftesbury, Ashley Anthony Cooper, third Earl (1999 [1711]): *Characteristics of Men, Manners, Opinions, Times, Etc.* Lawrence E. Klein (Ed.). Cambridge: Cambridge University Press.
Sidgwick, Henry (1981 [1907]): *The Methods of Ethics*. Indianapolis: Hackett Publishing Company.
Adam Smith. (1976 [1759]): *The Theory of Moral Sentiments*. D. D. Raphael/A. L. Mackfie (Eds.). Oxford: Oxford University Press.
Spinoza, Benedict (1926 [1677]): *Ethica ordine geometrico demonstrata*. In: *Opera*, im Auftrag der Heidelberger Akademie der Wissenschaften. Carl Gebhardt (Ed.). Vol. 2. Heidelberg.
Suarez, Francisco (1971 ff. [1612]): *Tractatus de legibus ac Deo legislatore*. Luciano Pereña Vicente et al. (Eds.). 8 vols. Madrid: Editorial C.S.I.C.
Wolff, C. (1976 [1720]): *Vernünftige Gedanken von der Menschen Thun und Lassen: Zu Beförderung ihrer Glückseligkeit*. Hildesheim: Georg Olms.

Secondary Literature

Ahnert, Thomas (2010): "Francis Hutcheson and the Heathen Moralists". In: *The Journal of Scottish Philosophy* 8, pp. 51–62.
Algra, Keimpe (2003): "The Mechanism of Stoic Appropriation and its Role in Hellenistic Ehics". In: *Oxford Studies in Ancient Philosophy* 25, pp. 265–296.
Allison, Henry (1990): *Kant's Theory of Freedom*. Cambridge: Cambridge University Press.
Allison, Henry (1996): *Idealism and Freedom: Essays on Kant's Theoretical and Practical Philosophy*. Cambridge: Cambridge University Press.
Allison, Henry (2007): "Comments on Guyer". In: *Inquiry* 50, pp. 480–488.
Allison, Henry (2011): *Kant's Groundwork for the Metaphysics of Morals: A Commentary*. Oxford: Oxford University Press.
Annas, Julia (1993): *The Morality of Happiness*. Oxford: Oxford University Press.
Annas, Julia (2006). "Virtue Ethics". In: Copp, D. (Ed.): *The Oxford Handbook of Ethical Theory*. Oxford: Oxford University Press, pp. 515–536.
Audi, Robert (2002): "Prospects for a Value-Based Intuitionism". In: Stratton-Lake, P. (Ed.): *Ethical Intuitionism: Re-evaluations*. Oxford: Clarendon Press, pp. 29–55.
Audi, Robert (2004): *The Good in the Right: A Theory of Intuition and Intrinsic Value*. Princeton: Princeton University Press.
Bagnoli, Carla (2002): "Moral Constructivism: a Phenomenological Argument". In: *Topoi* 21, pp. 125–138.

Baron, Marcia (1995): *Kantian Ethics Almost without Apology*. Ithaca NY: Cornell University Press.
Baron, Marcia (2006): "Acting from Duty". In: Christoph Horn and Dieter Schönecker (Eds.): *Groundwork of the Metaphysics of Morals*. Berlin, New York: De Gruyter, pp. 72–92.
Baron, Marcia (2013): "Moral Worth and Moral Rightness, Maxims and Actions". In: David Archard, Monique Deveaux, Neil Manson and Daniel Weinstock (Eds.): *Reading Onora O'Neill*. London: Routledge, pp. 11–16.
Baum, Manfred (1998): "Probleme der Begründung Kantischer Tugendpflichten". In: *Jahrbuch für Recht und Ethik/Annual Review of Law and Ethics* 6, pp. 41–56.
Baum, Manfred (2004): "Kant und Ciceros *De officiis*". In: *Studi Italo-Tedeschi / Deutsch-Italienische Studien*. Merano: Academia di Studi Italo-Tedeschi, pp. 17–32.
Baum, Manfred (2005a): "Freiheit und Verbindlichkeit in Kants Moralphilosophie". In: *Jahrbuch für Recht und Ethik/Annual Review of Law and Ethics* 13 (Philosophia Practica Universalis: Festschrift für Joachim Hruschka zum 70. Geburtstag), pp. 31–43.
Baum, Manfred (2005b): "Sittlichkeit und Freiheit in Kants *Grundlegung*". In: Kristina Engelhard/Dietmar Heidemann (Eds.): *Ethikbegründungen zwischen Universalismus und Relativismus*. Berlin, New York: De Gruyter, pp. 183–202.
Baum, Manfred (2006): "Gefühl, Begehren und Wollen in Kants praktischer Philosophie". In: *Jahrbuch für Recht und Ethik/Annual Review of Law and Ethics* 14, pp. 125–139.
Baum, Manfred (2013): "Prior Concepts of the Metaphysics of Morals (MS 6:221–228". In: Andreas Trampota/Oliver Sensen/Jens Timmermann (Eds.): *Kant's 'Tugendlehre': A Comprensive Commentary*. Berlin, Boston: De Gruyter, pp. 113–137.
Baxley, Ann Margaret (2010): *Kant's Theory of Virtue: The Value of Autocracy*. Cambridge: Cambridge University Press.
Beck, Lewis White (1960): *A Commentary on Kant's Critique of Practical Reason*. Chicago: University of Chicago Press.
Beck, Lewis White (1969): *Early German Philosophy*. Cambridge MA: Harvard University Press.
Beiner, Ronald/Booth, William James (1993): *Kant and Political Philosophy: The Contemporary Legacy*. New Haven, London: Yale University Press.
Beiser, Frederick (1996): *The Sovereignty of Reason: The Defense of Rationality in the Early English Englightenment*. Princeton: Princeton University Press.
Blackburn, Sim (1998): *Ruling Passions: A Theory of Practical Reasoning*. Oxford: Oxford University Press.
Blackburn, S. (2006): "Must We Weep for Sentimentalism?" In: James Dreier (Ed.): *Contemporary Debates in Moral Theory*. Oxford: Blackwell Publishing, pp. 144–159.
Bradley, Ben (2006): "Against Satisficing Consequentialism". In: *Utilitas* 18, pp. 97–108.
Brandt, Reinhard (1974): *Eigentumstheorien von Grotius bis Kant*. Stuttgart-Bad Cannstatt: Fromann-Holzboog.
Brandt, Reinhard (1999): *Kritischer Kommentar zu Kants Anthropologie in pragmatischer Hinsicht (1798)*, Hamburg: Meiner.
Brandt, Reinhard (2003): "Selbstbewußtsein und Selbstsorge: Zur Tradition der *oikeiôsis* in der Neuzeit". In: *Archiv für Geschichte der Philosophie* 85, pp. 179–197.
Brennan, Tad (2006): "Stoic Moral Psychology". In: Brad Inswood (Ed.): *The Cambridge Companion to the Stoics*. Cambridge: Cambridge University Press, pp. 257–294.
Brennan, Tad (2007): *The Stoic Life: Emotions, Duties, and Fate*. Oxford: Oxford Univeristy Press.

Brooke, Christopher (2012): *Philosophic Pride: Stoicism and Political Thought from Lipsius to Rousseau.* Princeton: Princeton University Press.
Brett, Anabel S. (1997): *Liberty, Right, and Nature: Individual Rights in Later Scholastic Thought.* Cambridge: Cambridge University Press.
Broadie, Sarah (1991): *Ethics with Aristotle.* Oxford: Oxford University Press.
Brocker, Manfred 1992: *Arbeit und Eigentum: Der Paradigmenwechsel in der neuzeitlichen Eigentumstheorie.* Darmstadt: Wissenschaftliche Buchgesellschaft.
Buckle, Stephen (1991): *Natural Law and the Theory of Property: Grotius to Hume.* Oxford: Oxford University Press.
Byrd, B. Sharon (2010): "Intelligible Possession of Objects of Choice". In: Lara Denis (Ed.): *Kant's Metaphysics of Morals: A Critical Guide.* Cambridge: Cambridge University Press, pp. 93–110.
Byrd, B. Sharon/Hruschka, Joachim (2006): "Der ursprünglich und a priori vereinigte Wille und seine Konsequenzen in Kants 'Rechtslehre'". In: *Jahrbuch für Recht und Ethik/Annual Review of Law and Ethics* 14, pp. 141–165.
Byrd, B. Sharon/Hruschka, Joachim (2006): *Kant and Law.* Aldershot, Burlington: Ashgate.
Byrd, B. Sharon/Hruschka, Joachim (2010): *Kant's Doctrine of Right: A Commentary.* Cambridge: Cambridge University Press.
Byrd, B. Sharon/Joachim Hruschka/Jan C. Joerden (Eds.) (2008): *Kants Metaphysik der Sitten im Kontext der Naturrechtslehre des 18. Jahrhunderts.* In: *Jahrbuch für Recht und Ethik/Annual Review of Law and Ethics* 16. Berlin: Duncker & Humblot.
Coady, C. A. J. (1992): *Testimony: A Philosophical Study,* Oxford: Clarendon Press.
Coady, C. A. J. (2004): "Reid and the Social Operations of the Mind". In: Terence Cuneo (Ed.): *The Cambridge Companion to Thomas Reid.* Cambridge: Cambridge University Press, pp. 180–203.
Cohen, G. A. (1995): *Self-Ownership, Freedom, and Equality.* Cambridge: Cambridge University Press.
Cohen, G. A. (2008): *Rescuing Justice and Equality.* Cambridge, MA: Harvard University Press.
Cohen, G. A. (2011): *On the Currency of Egalitarian Justice.* Michael Otsuka (Ed.). Princeton: Princeton University Press.
Cohen, Joshua (2010): *Rousseau: A Free Community of Equals.* Oxford: Oxford University Press.
Coleman, Janet (1988): "Property and Poverty". In: Burns, J. H. (Ed.): *The Cambridge History of Medieval Political Thought.* Cambridge: Cambridge University Press, pp. 607–648.
Cooper, John (2003): "Stoic Autonomy". In: *Social Policy and Philosophy* 20, pp. 1–29.
Cummiskey, David (1996): *Kantian Consequentialism.* Oxford: Oxford University Press.
Cummiskey, David (2008): "Dignity, Contractualism, and Consequentialism". In: *Utilitas* 20, pp. 383–408.
Cummiskey, David (2011): "Korsgaard's Rejection of Consequentialism". In: *Metaphilosophy* 42, pp. 360–367.
Cuneo, Terence (2004): "Reid's Moral Philosophy". In: Cuneo, T. (Ed.): *The Cambridge Companion to Thomas Reid.* Cambridge: Cambridge University Press, pp. 243–266.
Darwall, Stephen (2002): "Intuitionism and the Motivation Problem". In" Stratton-Lake, P. (Ed.): *Ethical Intuitionism: Re-evaluations.* Oxford: Clarendon Press, pp. 248–270.
Darwall, Stephen. (1995): *The British Moralists and the Internal 'Ought': 1640–1740.* Cambridge: Cambridge University Press.

Darwall, Stephen (2006): "The Value of Autonomy and Autonomy of the Will". In" *Ethics* 116, pp. 263–284.
Dean, Richard (2006): *The Value of Humanity in Kant's Moral Theory*. Oxford: Oxford University Press.
Debes, Remy (2007): "Humanity, Sympathy and the Puzzle Of Hume's Second Enquiry". In: *British Journal for the History of Philosophy* 15, pp. 27–57.
Denis, Lara (Ed.) (2010): *Kant's Metaphysics of Morals: A Critical Guide*. Cambridge: Cambridge University Press.
Denis, Lara (2013): "Virtue and Its Ends (TL 6:394–398)". In: Andreas Trampota/Oliver Sensen/Jens Timmermann (Eds.): *Kant's 'Tugendlehre': A Comprensive Commentary*. Berlin, Boston: De Gruyter, pp. 159–181.
Dieringer, Volker (2002): "Was erkennt die praktische Vernunft? Zu Kants Begriff des Guten in der Kritik der praktischen Vernunft". In: *Kant-Studien* 93, pp. 137–157.
Dreitzel, Horst (2003): "The Reception of Hobbes in the Political Philosophy of the Early German Enlightenment". In: *History of European Ideas* 29, pp. 255–289.
Douglas, Robin (2015): *Rousseau and Hobbes: Nature, Free Will, and the Passions*. Oxford: Oxford University Press.
Eagleton, Terry (2012): *Why Marx Was Right*. New Haven: Yale University Press.
Ebbinghaus, Julius (1988): "Die Idee des Rechts". In: Georg Geismann/Hariolf Oberer (Eds.): *Gesammelte Schriften*. Vol. 2. Bonn: Bouvier, pp. 144–198.
Edwards, Jeffrey (1998): "Disjunktiv- und kollektiv-allgemeiner Besitz: Überlegungen zu Kants Theorie der ursprünglichen Erwerbung". In: Dieter Hüning/Burkhard Tuschling (Eds.): *Recht, Staat, und Völkerrecht bei Immanuel Kant*. Berlin: Duncker & Humblot, pp. 121–140.
Edwards, Jeffrey (2000a): "Egoism and Formalism in the Development of Kant's Moral Philosophy". In: *Kant-Studien* 91, pp. 411–432.
Edwards, Jeffrey (2000b): "Self-love, Anthropology, and Universal Benevolence in Kant's Metaphysics of Morals". In: *The Review of Metaphysics* 53, pp. 887–914.
Edwards, Jeffrey (2000c): *Substance, Force, and the Possibility of Knowledge: On Kant's Philosophy of Material Nature*. Berkeley / Los Angeles / London: University of California Press.
Edwards, Jeffrey (2002): "Property and *communitas rerum*: Ockham, Suarez, Grotius, Hobbes". In: Dieter Hüning/Gideon Stiening/Ulrich Vogel (Eds.): *Societas rationis: Festschrift für Burkhard Tuschling zum 65. Geburtstag*. Berlin: Duncker & Humblot, pp. 41–60.
Edwards, Jeffrey (2004): "Universal Lawgiving and Material Determining Grounds in Kant's Moral Doctrine of Ends". In: Marion Heinz/Udo Rameil (Eds.): *Metaphysik und Kritik*. Berlin: De Gruyter, pp. 55–75.
Edwards, Jeffrey (2005a): "Natural Right and Acquisition in Grotius, Selden, and Hobbes". In Dieter Hüning (Ed.): *Der lange Schatten des Leviathan: Hobbes' politische Philosophie nach 350 Jahren*. Berlin: Duncker & Humblot, pp. 153–178.
Edwards, Jeffrey (2005b): "Reid vs. the Reidian Legacy". In: *Journal of Scottish Philosophy* 3, pp. 1–17.
Edwards, Jeffrey (2006): "Hutcheson's Sentimentalist Deontology?" In: *The Journal of Scottish Philosophy* 4, pp. 17–36.

Edwards, J. (2008): "Natural law and Obligation in Hutcheson and Kant". In: Ana Marta González, (Ed.): *Contemporary Perspectives on Natural Law: Natural Law as a Limiting Concept*. Aldershot: Ashgate, pp. 87–104.
Edwards, J. (2011a): "'The Unity of All Places on the Face of the Earth': Original Community, Acquisition, And Universal Will In Kant's Doctrine Of Right". In: Stuart Elden/Eduardo,Mendieta (Eds.): *Reading Kant's Physical Geography*. Albany: SUNY Press, 2011, pp. 233–263.
Edwards, Jeffrey (2011b): "Original Community, Possession, and Acquisition in Kant's Metaphysics of Morals". In: Charlton Payne/Lucas Thorpe (Eds.): *Kant and the Concept of Community*. Rochester: University of Rochester Press, 2011, pp. 152–182. (Expanded version of Edwards 2011a).
Edwards, Jeffrey (2013a): "Bemerkungen zu den englischen Übersetzungen von Kants *Rechtslehre*". In: Burkhard Tuschling/Werner Euler (Eds.): *Kants* Metaphysik der Sitten: *Editorische und Philosophische Probleme*. Berlin: Duncker & Humblot, pp. 21–24.
Edwards, Jeffrey (2013b): "A Tale of Two Ends: Obligatory Ends and Material Determining Grounds in Kant's *Metaphysik der Sitten*". In: Burkahrd Tuschling/Werner Euler (Eds.): *Kants* Metaphysik der Sitten: *Editorische und Philosophische Probleme*. Berlin: Duncker & Humblot, pp. 147–175.
Edwards, Jeffrey (2014a): "*Honestum* is as *Honestum* Does: Reid, Hume—and Mandeville?!". In: *The Journal of Scottish Philosophy* 12, pp. 119–141.
Edwards, Jeffrey (2014b): "Self-Love, Sociability, and Autonomy: Some Presuppositions of Kant's Account of Practical Law". In: Steven Hoeltzel/Halla Kim: *Kant, Fichte, and the Legacy of German Idealism*. Lanham, MD: Lexington Books, pp. 1–29.
Edwards, Jeffrey (2014c): "Squire Allworthy's Inclinations and Acting from Duty: On Moral Worth in Kant and Hume". In: Mario Egger (Ed.): *Philosophie nach Kant: Neue Wege zum Verständnis von Kants Transzendental- und Moralphilosophie*. Berlin: De Gruyter, pp. 251–277.
Edwards, Jeffrey (2017): "Hume and Hutcheson on Cicero's 'Proof against the Stoics'". In: *The Journal of Scottish Philosophy* 15, 175–195.
Edwards, Jeffrey (2018 [forthcoming]): "Imperfect Duties *Alone* are Duties of Virtue". In: Bernd Dörflinger/Dieter Hüning/Günter Kruck (Eds.): *Kant als Tugendethiker? Systematische und historische Perspectiven von Kants Tugendlehre*. Hildesheim, New York: Georg Olms Verlag.
Engberg-Pedersen, Troels (1990): *The Stoic Theory of Oikeiôsis: Moral Development and Social Interaction in Early Stoic Philosophy*. Aarhus: Aarhus University Press.
Engberg-Pedersen, Troels (2006): "Filling Pembroke's Lacuna in the *Oikeiôsis* Argument". In: *Archiv für Geschichte der Philosophie* 88, pp. 216–220.
Engstrom, Stephen (2009): *The Form of Practical Knowledge: A Study of the Categorical Imperative*. Cambridge MA / London: Harvard University Press.
Esser, Andrea Marlen (2004): *Eine Ethik für Endliche: Kants Tugendlehre in der Gegenwart*. Stuttgart-Bad Cannstatt: Fromann-Holzboog.
Feenstra, Robert (1978): "Der Eigentumsbegriff bei Hugo Grotius im Licht einiger mittelalterlicher und spätscholastischer Quellen". In: Okko Behrends/Malte Dießelhorst (Eds.): *Festschrift für Franz Wieacker*. Göttingen: Vandenhoek & Ruprecht, pp. 209–234.
Ferguson, Benjamin (2012): "Kant on Duty in the Groundwork". In: *Res Publica* 18, pp. 303–319.

Flikschuh, Katrin (2000): *Kant and Modern Political Philosophy*. Cambridge: Cambridge University Press.
Flikschuh, Katrin (2010): "Justice without Virtue". In: Denis, Lara (Ed.) (2010): *Kant's Metaphysics of Morals: A Critical Guide*. Cambridge: Cambridge University Press, pp. 51–70.
Forschler, Scott (2013): "Kantian and Consequentialist Ethics: the Gap Can Be Bridged". In: *Metaphilosophy* 44, pp. 88–104.
Forschner, Maximilian (1974): *Gesetz und Freiheit: Zum Problem der Autonomie bei I. Kant*. München, Salzburg: Verlag Anton Pustet.
Freudiger, Jüra (1993): *Kants Begründung der pratkischen Philosophie*. Bern, Stuttgart: Verlag Paul Haupt.
Friedrich, Rainer (2004): *Eigentum und Staatsbegründung in Kants 'Metaphysik der Sitten'*.Berlin, New York: De Gruyter.
Frierson, Patrick R. (2003): *Freedom and Anthropology in Kant's Moral Philosophy*. Cambridge: Cambridge University Press.
Frierson, Patrick R. (2014): *Kant's Empirical Psychology*. Cambridge: Cambridge University Press.
Fulda, Hans Friedrich (1997): "Kants Postulat des öffentlichen Rechts (*RL* §42)". In: *Jahrbuch für Recht und Ethik/Annual Review of Law and Ethics* 5, pp. 267–90.
Fulda, Hans Friedrich. (1998): "Zur Systematik des Privatrechts in Kants *Metaphysik der Sitten*". In: Dieter Hüning/Burkhard Tuschling (Eds.): *Recht, Staat, und Völkerrecht bei Immanuel Kant*. Berlin: Duncker & Humblot, pp. 141–156.
Garnsey, Peter (2007): *Thinking About Property: From Antiquity to the Age of Revolution*. Cambridge: Cambridge University Press.
Gauthier, David (2006): *Rousseau: The Sentiment of Existence*. Cambridge: Cambridge University Press.
Geismann, Georg (1974): *Ethik und Herrschaftsordnung: Ein Beitrag zum Problem der Legitimation*. Tübingen: Verlag Mohr.
Geismann, Georg (2002): "Die Formeln des kategorschen Imperativs nach H. J. Paton, N. N., Klaus Reich und Julius Ebbinghaus". In: *Kant-Studien* 93. No. 3, pp. 374–384.
Gibert, Carlos Melches (1994): *Der Einfluss von Christian Garves Übersetzung Ciceros* De officiis *auf Kants* Grundlegung zur Metaphysik der Sitten. Regensburg: S. Roderer Verlag.
Goy, Ina (2013): "Virtue and Sensibility (TL 6:399–409)". In: Andreas Trampota/Oliver Sensen/Jens Timmermann (Eds.): *Kant's 'Tugendlehre': A Comprensive Commentary*. Berlin, Boston: De Gruyter, pp. 183–206.
Gregor, Mary (1963): *Laws of Freedom: A Study of Kant's Applying the Categorical Imperative in the* Metaphysics of Morals.; Oxford: Blackwell.
Gregor, Mary (1993a): "Kant on Obligation, Rights and Virtue". In: *Jahrbuch für Recht & Ethik/Annual Review of Law & Ethics* 1, pp. 69–102.
Gregor, Mary (1993b): "Kant on 'Natural Rights'". In: *Kant and Political Philosophy: The Contemporary Legacy*. Ronald Beiner/William James Booth (Eds.). New Haven, London: Yale University Press.
Gregor, Mary (1997): "Natural Right or Natural law?". In: *Jahrbuch für Recht & Ethik/Annual Review of Law & Ethics* 3, pp. 11–35.
Gregor, Mary (2006): "Kant's Theory of Property". In: *Kant and Law*. B. Sharon Byrd/Joachim Hruschka. Aldershot, Burlington: Ashgate.

Guyer, Paul. (1998): "Life, Liberty, and Property: Rawls the reconstruction of Kant's political philosophy". In: Hüning, D. & B. Tuschling (Eds.): *Recht, Staat, und Völkerrecht bei Immanuel Kant*. Berlin: Duncker & Humblot, pp. 273–292.

Guyer, Paul. (2000): *Kant on Freedom, Law, and Happiness*. Cambridge: Cambridge University Press.

Guyer, Paul. (2002): "Kant's Deductions of the Principles of Right". In: Mark Timmons (Ed.): *Kant's Metaphysics of Morals: Interpretive Essays*. Oxford: Oxford University Press, pp. 23–64.

Guyer, Paul (2005): *Kant's System of Nature and Freedom: Selected Essays*. Oxford: Clarendon Press.

Guyer, Paul (2007): "Naturalistic and Transcendental Moments in Kant's Moral Philosophy". In: *Inquiry* 50, pp. 444–464.

Guyer, Paul (2010): "Moral Feelings in the *Metaphysics of Morals*". In: Lara Denis (Ed.): *Kant's Metaphysics of Morals: A Critical Guide*. Cambridge: Cambridge University Press, pp. 130–151.

Guyer, Paul (2012): "A Passion for Reason: Kant, Hume and the Motivation for Morality:. In: *Proceedings and Addresses of the American Philosophical Association* 86. No. 2, pp. 4–21.

Haakonssen, Knud (1996): *Natural Law and Moral Philosophy: From Grotius to the Scottish Enlightenment*, Cambridge: Cambridge University Press.

Haakonssen, Knud (2001): "The Character and Obligation of Natural Law according to Richard Cumberland". In M. A. Stewart (Ed.): *English Philosophy in the Age of Locke*. Oxford: Oxford University Press, pp. 29–47.

Haakonssen, Knud (2005): "The History of Eighteenth-Century Philosophy: History or Philosophy?" In: Knud Haakonssen (Ed.): *Cambridge History of Eighteenth-Century Philosophy*. Cambridge: Cambridge University Press, pp. 1–25.

Hare, R. M. (1997): *Sorting Out Ethics*. Oxford: Oxford University Press.

Harris, James (2009): "The Epicurean in Hume". In: *Studies on Voltaire and the Eighteenth Century* 12, pp. 161–181.

Harris, James (2010): "Reid and Hume on Justice". In: Sabine Roesser (Ed.): *Reid on Ethics*. London: Palgrave Macmillan, pp. 204–222.

Harrison, Jonathan (1981): *Hume's Theory of Justice*. Oxford: Clarendon Press.

Hartung, Gerald (1999): *Die Naturrechtsdebatte: Geschichte der Obligatio vom 17. Bis 20. Jahrhundert*. Freiburg, München: Verlag Karl Alber.

Herb, Karlfriedrich/Bernd Ludwig (1993): "Naturzustand, Eigentum und Staat". In: *Kant-Studien* 84, pp. 283–316.

Henrich, Dieter (1957–1958): "Hutcheson und Kant". In: *Kant-Studien* 49, pp. 49–69.

Henrich, Dieter (1963): "Über Kants früheste Ethik: Versuch einer Rekonstruktion". In: *Kant-Studien* 54, pp. 404–431.

Henrich, Dieter (1965): Über Kants Entwicklungsgeschichte". In: *Philosophische Rundschau* 13, pp. 252–263.

Henson, Richard (1979): "What Kant Might Have Said: Moral Worth and the Overdetermination of Dutiful Action". In: *Philosophical Review* 88, pp. 39–54.

Herman, B. (1993): *The Practice of Moral Judgment*. Cambridge MA: Harvard University Press.

Herman, Barbara (2006): "Reasoning to Obligation". In: *Inquiry* 49, pp. 44–61.

Herman, Barbara (2007): *Moral Literacy*. Cambridge MA: Harvard University Press.

Herman, Barbara (2011a): "A Mismatch of Methods". In: Derek Parfit: *On What Matters*. Vol. 2. Oxford: Oxford University Press, pp. 83–115.

Herman, Barbara (2011b): "Embracing Kant's Formalism". In: *Kantian Review* 16, pp. 49–66.

Herman, Barbara (2011c): "The Difference that Ends Make". In: Lawrence Jost/JulianWuerth (Eds.): *Perfecting Virtue: New Essays on Kantian Ethics and Virtue Ethics*. Cambridge: Cambridge University Press, pp. 92–115.

Hirschmann, Albert O. (1977): *The Passions and the Interests: Political Arguments for Capitalism before its Triumph*. Princeton: Princeton University Press.

Hochstrasser, Tim J. (2000): *Natural Law Theories in the Early Enlightenment*. Cambridge: Cambridge University Press.

Hochstrasser, Tim J./Schröder, Peter (Eds.) (2003): *Early Modern Natural Law Theories*. Dordrecht: Kluwer.

Höffe, Otfried (1987): *Politische Gerechtigkeit: Grundlegung einer kritischen Philosophie von Recht und Staat*. Frankfurt am Main: Suhrkamp.

Höffe, Otfried (1989): "Kant's Principle of Justice as Categorical Imperative of Law". In: Yirmiyahu Yovel (Ed.): *Kant's Practical Philosophy Reconsidered*. Dordrecht: Kluwer, pp. 149–167.

Höffe, Otfried (1990): *Kategorische Rechtsprinzipien. Ein Kontrapunkt der Moderne*. Frankfurt am Main: Suhrkamp.

Höffe, Otfried (2006): "'Gerne dien ich den Freunden, doch tue ich es leider mit Neigung …' — überwindet Schillers Gedanke der schönen Seele Kants Gegensatz von Pflicht und Neigung?" In: *Zeitschrift für philosophische Forschung* 60, pp. 1–20.

Honoré, Tony (2010): "Ulpian, Natural Law and Stoic Influence". In: *Tijdschrift voor Rechtsgeschiedenis* 78, pp. 199–208.

Hüning, Dieter (1998): "Zur Bedeutung des *suum cuique tribuere* bei Hobbes und Kant". In: Dieter Hüning/Burkhard Tuschling (Eds.): *Recht, Staat und Völkerrecht bei Immanuel Kant*. Berlin: Duncker & Humblot, pp. 53–70.

Hüning, Dieter (2002): "From the Virtue of Justice to the Concept of Legal Order: the Significance of the *Suum Cuique Tribuere* in Hobbes' Political Philosophy". In: Ian Hunter/David Saunders (Eds.): *Natural Law and Civil Sovereignty: Moral Right and State Authority in Early Modern Political Thought*. Basingstoke / New York: Palgrave MacMillan, pp. 139–152.

Hüning, Dieter (2007a): "Hobbes on the Right to Punish". In: Patricia Springbord (Ed.): *The Cambridge Companion to Hobbes' Leviathan*. Cambridge: Cambridge University Press, pp. 217–240.

Hüning, Dieter (2007b): "Die Begründung des *ius puniendi* in der Naturrechtslehre des 17. Jahrhunderts". In: Sylvia Kesper;Biermann/Diethelm Klippel (Eds.): *Kriminalität im Mittelalter und früher Neuzeit: Soziale, rechtliche, philosophische, und literarische Aspekte*. Wolfenbüttel: Herzog August Bibliotek, pp. 77–114.

Hüning, Dieter (Ed.) (2009): *Naturrecht und Staatstheorie bei Samuel Pufendorf*. Baden-Baden: Nomos.

Hüning, Dieter (2011): "'Diese sehr auffallende Verschiedenheit unter unsern Pflichten' — Johann Georg Sulzers Versuch, Recht und Ethik zu unterschieden". In: Frank Grunert/Gideon Stiening (Eds.): *Johann Georg Sulzer (1720–1779: Aufklärung zwichen Christian Wolff und David Hume*. Vol. 1. Berlin: Akademie Verlag, pp. 235–307.

Hüning, Dieter (2013): "'Rousseau set me aright'"—the Legacy of Rousseau in Kant's Legal and Political Philosophy and the Idealization of the *volonté générale*". In: *Estudos Kantianos* 1, pp. 107–120.

Hruschka, Joachim (1987): "Die Konkurrenz von Goldener Regel und Prinzip der Verallgemeinerung in der juristischen Diskussion des 17./18. Jahrhunderts als geschichtliche Wurzel von Kants kategorischm Imperativ". In: *Juristen Zeitung* 42, pp. 941–952.

Hruschka, Joachim (2006): "Kant and Human Dignity". In: B. Sharon Byrd/Joachim Hruschka: *Kant and Law*. Aldershot, Burlington: Ashgate.

Hurka, Thomas (1993): *Perfectionism*. Oxford: Clarendon Press.

Hurka, Thomas (2003): *Virtue, Vice, and Value*. Oxford: Oxford University Press.

Hursthouse, Rosalind (1999): *On Virtue Ethics*, Oxford: Oxford University Press.

Hursthouse, Rosalind (2006): "Are Virtues the Proper Starting Point for Morality?" In: James Dreier (Ed.): *Contemporary Debates in Moral Theory*. Oxford: Blackwell, pp. 99–112.

Hussain, Nadeem J. S./Nishi Shah (2006): "Misunderstanding Metaethics: Korsgaard's Rejection of Realism". In: Russ Schafer-Landau (Ed.): *Oxford Studies in Metaethics*. Vol. 1. Oxford: Clarendon Press, pp. 265–294.

Inwood, Brad (1985): *Ethics and Human Action in Early Stoicism*. Oxford: Oxford University Press.

Inwood, Brad (2002): "Comments on Professor Görgemann's Paper: The Two forms of *oikeiosis* in Arius and the Stoa". In: William Fortenbaugh (Ed.): *On Stoic and Peripatetic Ethics: The Work of Arius Didymus*. New Brunswick NJ: Rutgers University Press, pp. 190–201.

Inwood, Brad (2003): *The Cambridge Companion to the Stoics*. Cambridge: Cambridge University Press.

Irwin, Terence H. (1998): "Kant's Criticism of Eudaemonism". In: Stephen Engstrom/Jennifer Whiting (Eds.): *Aristotle, Kant and the Stoics: Rethinking Happiness and Duty*. Cambridge: Cambridge University Press, pp. 63–101.

Irwin, Terence H. (2007 ff.): *The Development of Ethics: A Historical and Critical Study*. 3 vols. Oxford: Oxford University Press.

Isawa, Noriaki (2011): "Hume's Alleged Success over Hutcheson". In: *British Journal for the History of Philosophy* 24, pp. 302–332.

James, David (2016): "Independence and Property in Kant's *Rechtslehre*". In: *British Journal for the History of Philosophy* 24, pp. 302–332.

Johnson, Robert N. (2010): "Duties to and Regarding Others". In: Lara Denis (Ed.): *Kant's Metaphysics of Morals: A Critical Guide*. Cambridge: Cambridge University Press.

Kagan, Shelly (1989): *The Limits of Morality*. Oxford: Clarendon Press.

Kagan, Shelly (1998): *Normative Ethics*. Boulder CO: Westview Press.

Kagan, Shelly (2002): "Kantianism for Consequentialists". In: Kant, Immanuel: *Groundwork for the Metaphysics of Morals*, Allen W. Wood (Ed.). New Haven: Yale University Press, pp. 111–156.

Kagan, Shelly (2012): *The Geometry of Desert*. Oxford: Oxford University Press.

Kain, Patrick (2004): "Self-Legislation in Kant's Moral Philosophy". In: *Archiv für Geschichte der Philosophie* 86, pp. 257–306.

Kaufman, Alexander (1999): *Welfare in the Kantian State*. Oxford: Oxford University Press.

Keohane, Nannerl O. (1980): *Philosophy and the State in France*. Princeton: Princeton University Press.
Kerstein, Samuel J. (2002): *Kant's Search for the Supreme Principle of Morality*. Cambridge: Cambridge University Press.
Kersting, Wolfgang (1982): "Das starke Gesetz der Schuldigkeit und das schwächere der Gütigkeit". In: *Studia Leibnitiana* 14, pp. 184–220.
Kersting, Wolfgang (1990): "Die Verbindlickeitstheoretischen Argumente der kantischen Rechtsphilosophie". In: Ralf Dreier (Ed.): *Positives Recht und Wertbezug des Rechts, ARSP-Beiheft 37*. Stuttgart: Steiner 1990, pp. 62–74.
Kersting, Wolfgang (1993): *Wohlgeordnete Freiheit: Immanuel Kants Rechts- und Staatsphilosophie*. Frankfurt am Main: Klostermann.
Kersting, Wolfgang (2013): "Die Vertragsidee des *Contrat Sociale* und Kant's *contractus originarius*". In: *Estudos Kantianos* 1, pp. 59–106.
Kippel, Diethelm (2001): "Kant im Kontext: Der naturrechtliche Diskurs um 1800". In: *Jahrbuch des historischen Kollegs 2001*, pp. 77–107.
Kirk, Linda (1987): *Richard Cumberland and Natural Law*, Cambridge: James Clark.
Korkman, Petter (2002): "Voluntarism and Moral Obligation: Barbeyrac's Defence of Pufendorf Revisited". In: Tim J. Hochstrasser/Peter Schröder (Eds.): *Early Modern Natural Law Theories*. Dordrecht: Kluwer, pp. 195–224.
Korsgaard, Christine (1996): *The Sources of Normativity*. Cambridge: Cambridge University Press.
Kriechbaum, Maximiliane (1996): *Actio, ius und dominium in den Rechtslehren des 13. und 14. Jahrhunderts* Ebelsbach: Activ Druck & Verlag.
Landau, Albert (Ed.). (1991): *Rezensionen zur Kantischen Philosophie*. Bebra: Albert Landau Verlag.
Lloyd, S. A. (2001): "Hobbes's Self-Effacing Natural Law Theory". In: *Pacific Philosophical Quarterly* 82, pp. 285–308.
Lloyd, S.A. (2007): *Morality in the Philosophy of Thomas Hobbes: Cases in the Law of Nature*. Cambridge: Cambridge University Press.
Long, Anthony A. (1996): *Stoic Studies*. Cambridge: Cambridge University Press. (2001 reprint by University of California Press.)
Long, Anthony A. (2003): "Stoicism in the Philosophical Tradition". In: Jon Miller/Brad Inwood (Eds.): *Hellenistic and Early Modern Philosophy*. Cambridge: Cambridge University Press, pp. 7–29.
Louden, Robert B. (2002): *Kant's Impure Ethics: From Rational Beings to Human Beings*. Oxford: Oxford University Press.
Louden, Robert B. (2011): *Kant's Human Being*. New York: Oxford University Press.
Ludwig, Bernd (1988): *Kants Rechtslehre*. Hamburg: Meiner.
Ludwig, Bernd (1998): *Die Wiederentdeckung des Epikureischen Naturrechts: Zu Thomas Hobbe's philosophischer Entwicklung von De cive zum Leviathan im Pariser Exil 1640–1651*. Frankfurt am Main: Klostermann.
Ludwig, Bernd (2001a): Arbeit, Geld, Gesetz: Eine Neubestimmung von Aufgabe und Ziel der Eigentumstheorie John Lockes. *Jahrbuch Politisches Denken* 10, pp. 69–104.
Ludwig, Bernd (2001b): "Auf dem Wege zu einer säkularen Moralwissenschaft: Von Hugo Grotius' *De Jure Belli ac Pacis* zu Thomas Hobbes' *Leviathan*". In: *JRE* 8, pp. 3–31.

Ludwig, Bernd (2007): "Kant, Garve, and the Motives or Moral Action". In: *Journal of Moral Philosophy* 4, pp. 183–193.
Ludwig, Bernd (2010): "Die 'consequente Denkungsart der speculativen Kritik': Kants radikale Umgestaltung seiner Freiheitslehre im Jahre 1786 und die Folgen für die Kritische Philosophy als Ganze'". In: *Deutsche Zeitschirft für Philosophie* 58, pp. 595–628.
Ludwig, Bernd (2013): "Die Einteilungen der *Metaphysik der Sitten* im allgemeinen und die der *Tugendlehre* im Besonderen (MS 6:218–221 und RL 6:239–242 und TL 6:388–394)". In: Andreas Trampota/Oliver Sensen/Jens Timmermann (Eds.): *Kant's 'Tugendlehre': A Comprensive Commentary*. Berlin, Boston: De Gruyter, pp. 59–84.
Lutterbeck, Klaus-Gert. (2002): *Staat und Gesellschaft bei Christian Thomasius und Christian Wolff: Eine historische Untersuchung in systematischer Absicht*. Stuttgart-Bad Cannstatt: Fromann-Holzboog.
Maikinnin, Viripi (2012): "Moral Psychological Aspects in William of Ockham's Theory of Natural Rights". In: *Catholic Philosophical Quarterly* 86, pp. 507–525.
Malcolm, Noel (2002): *Aspects of Hobbes*. Oxford: Oxford University Press.
Masters, Roger D. (1968): *The Political Philosophy of Rousseau*. Princeton: Princeton University Press.
Maurer, Christian (2010): "Hutcheson's Relation to Stoicism in the Light of His Moral Psychology". In: *The Journal of Scottish Philosophy* 8, pp. 33–49.
McCarty, Richard (2009): *Kant's Theory of Action*. Oxford, Oxford University Press.
Melzer, Arthur M. (1990): *The Natural Goodness of Man*. Chicago: University of Chicago Press.
McGregor, Rafe (2015): "Making Sense of Moral Perception". In: *Ethical Theory and Moral Practice* 18, pp. 745–758.
Miller, Jon (2015): *Spinoza and the Stoics*. Cambridge: Cambridge University Press.
Moore, James (1990): "The Two Systems of Francis Hutcheson: On the Origins of the Scottish Enlightenment". In: M. A. Stewart (Ed.): *Studies in the Philosophy of the Scottish Enlightenment*. Oxford: Oxford University Press, pp. 37–59.
Moore, James (2002): "Utility and Humanity: The Quest for the *Honestum* in Cicero, Hutcheson, and Hume". In: *Utilitas* 14, pp. 365–386.
Morgan, Seriliol (2009): "Can there be a Kantian Consequentialism?" In: *Ratio* 22, pp. 19–40.
Neuhouser, Frederick (2008): *Rousseau's Theodicy of Self-Love: Evil Rationality, and the Drive for Recognition*. Oxford: Oxford University Press.
Neuhouser, Frederick (2014): *Rousseau's Critique of Inequality: Reconstructing the Second Discourse*. Cambridge: Cambridge University Press.
Nguygen, Vinh-De (1991): *Le problème de l'homme chez Jean-Jacques Rousseau*. Quebec QC: Presses de l'Université de Quebec.
Niebling, Christian (2005): *Das Staatsrecht in der Rechtslehre Kants*. München: Martin Meidenbauer.
Oberer, Hariolf (2006): "Sittlichkeit, Ethik, und Recht bei Kant". In: *Jahrbuch für Recht und Ethik* 14, pp. 259–266.
Olsthoorn, Johan (2015): "Hobbes on Justice, Property Rights and Self-Ownership". In: *History of Polical Thought* 36, pp. 471–498.
O'Hagan, Timothy (1999): *Rousseau*. London: Routledge, 1999.

O'Neill, Onora (2002): "Instituting Principles: Between Duty and Action". In: Mark Timmons, (Ed.): *Kant's Metaphysics of Morals: Interpretive Essays*. Oxford: Oxford University Press, pp. 331–347.
O'Neill, Onora (2003): "Autonomy: The Emperor's New Clothes". In: *Proceedings and Addresses of the Aristotelian Society* 77, pp. 1–21.
O'Neill, Onora (2004a): "Self-legislation, Autonomy and the Form of Law". In: Harta Nagl-Docekal/Rudolf Langthaler (Eds.): *Recht, Geschichte, Religion: Die Bedeutung Kants für die Gegenwart, Deutschen Zeitschrift für Philosophie*, Supplement. Berlin: Akademie Verlag, pp. 13–26.
O'Neill, Onora (2004b): "Consequences for Non-Consequentialists". In: *Utilitas* 16, pp. 2–11.
Othmer, Sieglinde C. (1970: *Berlin und die Verbreitung des Naturrechts in Europa: Kultur- und sozialgeschichtliche Studien zu Jean Barbeyracs Pufendorf-Übersetzungen und eine Analyse seiner Leserschaft*. Berlin: De Gruyter.
Otsuka, Michael (2009): "The Kantian Argument for Consequentialism". In: *Ratio* 22, pp. 41–58.
Palladini, Fiametta (1990): *Samuel Pufendorf discepelo di Hobbes: Per una reinterpretazione del giusnaturalismo moderno*. Bologna: Il Mulino.
Palladini, Fiametta (2008): "Pufendorf Disciple of Hobbes: The Nature of Man and the State of Nature—The Docrine of *Socialitas*". In: *History of European Ideas* 34, pp. 26–60.
Paletta, Douglas R. (2011): "Francis Hutcheson: Why Be Moral?". In: *The Journal of Scottish Philosophy* 9, pp. 149–159.
Parfit, Derek (2011ff.): *On What Matters*. 3 vols. Oxford: Oxford University Press.
Parkin, Jon (1999): *Science, Religion and Politics in Restoration England: Richard Cumberland's* De Legibus Naturae. Woodbridge: Boydell.
Patzig, Günther (1996): "Cicero als Philosoph, am Beispiel der Schrift 'De finibus'". In: Günther Patzig (Ed.) *Gesammelte Schriften*. Vol. 3. Göttingen: Wallstein Verlag, pp. 251–272.
Piché, Claude (1990): "Rousseau et Kant". In: *Reveue philosophique de las France et de l'étranger* 80, pp. 625–635.
Pinheiro Walla, Alice (2013): "Virtue and Prudence in a Footnote of the *Metaphysics of Morals* (MS VI: 433n)". In: *Jahrbuch für Recht und Ethik/Annual Review of Law and Ethics* 21, pp. 307–322.
Pinheiro Walla, Alice (2014): "Human Nature and the Right to Coerce in Kant's *Doctrine of Right*". In: *Archiv für Geschichte der Philosophie* 14, 126–139.
Pinheiro Walla, Alice (2017): "Kant's Moral Theory and Demandingness". In: *Ethical Theory and Moral Practice* 18, pp. 731–743.
Radcliffe, Elizabeth S. (2004): "Love and Benevolence in Hutcheson's and Hume's Theories of the Passions". In: *British Journal for the History of Philosophy* 12, pp. 631–653.
Riley, Patrick (1986): *The General Will Before Rousseau: The Transformation of the Divine into the Civic*. Princeton, Princeton University Press.
Reiner, Hans (1974): *Die Grundlagen der Sittlichkeit*. Meisenheim am Glan: Anton Hain.
Reath, Andrews (1989): "Kant's Theory of Moral Sensibility: Respect for the Moral Law and the Influence of Inclination". In: *Kant-Studien* 80, pp. 284–302.
Reath, Andrews (2006): *Agency and Autonomy in Kant's Moral Theory*. Oxford: Clarendon Press.

Reich, Klaus (2001): "Kant und die Ethik der Griechen". In: Manfred Baum et al. (Eds.): *Gesammelte Schriften*. Hamburg: Meiner, pp. 113–146.
Reynolds, Susan (1994): *Fiefs and Vassals: The Medieval Evidence Reinterpreted*. Oxford: Clarendon Press.
Ridge, Michael (2009): "Consequentialist Kantianism". In: *Philosophical Perspectives* 23, pp. 421–438.
Ripstein, Arthur (2009): *Force and Freedom: Kant's Legal and Political Philosophy*. Cambridge MA: Harvard University Press.
Roberts, Tom Aerwyn (1973): *The Concept of Benevolence: Aspects of Eighteenth-Century Moral Philosophy*. London: MacMillan.
Robinson, Jonathan (2013): *William of Ockham's Early Theory of Property Rights in Context*. Boston, Leiden: Brill.
Rosen, Allen D. (1993): *Kant's Theory of Justice*. Ithaca, NY: Cornell University Press.
Ross, Jacob (2009): "Should Kantians be Consequentialists?" In: *Ratio* 22, pp. 126–135.
Rühl, Ulli F. H. (2010): *Kants Deduktion des Rechts als intelligibler Besitz. Kants ›Privatrecht‹ zwischen vernunftrechtlicher Notwendigkeit und juristischer Kontingenz*. Paderborn: Mentis.
Saatsmoinen, Kari (1995): "The Morality of the Fallen Man: Samuel Pufendorf on Natural Law". In: *Studia Historica* 52, pp. 95–110.
Schadow, Steffi (2013): "Recht und Ethik in Kant's *Metaphysik der Sitten* (MS 6:218–221 and TL 6:390f.)". In: Andreas Trampota/Oliver Sensen/Jens Timmermann (Eds.): *Kant's 'Tugendlehre': A Comprensive Commentary*. Berlin, Boston: De Gruyter, pp. 85–111.
Schaller, Walter E. (1987): "Kant on Virtue and Moral Worth". In: *The Southern Journal of Philosophy* 25, pp. 559–573.
Schmucker, Josef (1961): *Die Ursprünge der Ethik Kants*. Meisenheim am Glan: Anton Hain.
Schneewind, J. B. (1987): "Pufendorf's Place in the History of Ethics". In: *Synthese* 72, pp. 123–155.
Schneewind, Jerome B. (1993): "Kant and Natural Law Ethics". In: *Ethics* 104, pp. 185–207.
Schneewind, J. B. (1998): *The Invention of Autonomy: A History of Modern Moral Philosophy*. Cambridge: Cambridge University Press.
Schneiders, Werner (1971): *Naturrecht und Liebesethik*. Hildesheim: Georg Olms.
Schönecker, Dieter (2001): "What is the 'First Proposition' regarding Duty in Kant's *Grundlegung?*" In: Volker Gehrhardt/Rolf-Peter Horstmann/Ralph Schumacher (Eds.): *Akten des IX internationalen Kant-Kongresses*. Vol. 3. Berlin, New York: De Gruyter, pp. 89–95.
Schönecker, Dieter (2010): "Kant über die Menschenliebe als moralische Gemütsanlage". In: *Archiv für Geschichte der Philosophie* 92, pp. 133–175.
Schönecker, D. (2012): "Once Again: What is the 'First Proposition' in Kant's 'Groundwork'? Some Refinements, a New Proposal, and a Reply to Henry Allison". In: *Kantian Review* 17, pp. 281–296.
Schönecker, Dieter (2013): "Duties to Others from Love". In: Andreas Trampota/Oliver Sensen/Jens Timmermann (Eds.): *Kant's 'Tugendlehre': A Comprensive Commentary*. Berlin, Boston: De Gruyter, pp. 308–341.
Schönecker, Dieter/Wood, Allen W. (2004): *Kant's Grundlegung zur Metaphysik der Sitten: Ein einführender Kommentar*. Paderborn, München, Wien, Zürich: Ferdinand Schöningh.

Schönecker, Dieter/Wood, Allen W. (2015): *Immanuel Kant's Groundwork for the Metaphysics of Morals: A Commentary*. Cambridge MA: Harvard University Press.
Shaver, Robert (1996): "Grotius on Scepticism and Self-Interest". In: *Archiv für Geschichte der Philosophie* 78, pp. 27–47.
Silverstrini, Gabriella (2010): "Rousseau, Pufendorf and the Eighteenth-Century Natural Law Tradition". In: *History of European Ideas* 36, pp. 280–301.
Slote, Michael (1989): *Beyond Optimizing*. Cambridge MA: Harvard University Press.
Slote, Michael (2001): *Morals from Motives*. Oxford: Oxford University Press.
Slote, Michael (2010): *Essays on the History of Ethics*. Oxford: Oxford University Press.
Snedden, Andrew (2011): "A New Kantian Response to Maxim-Fiddling". In: *Kantian Review* 16, pp. 67–68.
Starobinski, Jean (1971): *Jean Jacques Rousseau: La transparence et l'obstacle, svivi de sept essais sur Rouseau*. Paris: Gallimard.
Stauman, Benjamin (2003/2004): "Appetitus Societatis and Oikeiôsis". In: *Grotiana* 24/25: pp. 41–66.
Stein, Peter (1993): "Donellus and Origins of the Modern Civil Law". In: J. A. Ankum et al. (Eds.): *Mélanges Felix Wubbe*. Fribourg: University Press, pp. 429–452.
Stewart, R. M. (1982): "John Clarke and Francis Hutcheson on Self-Love and Moral Motivation". In: *Journal of the History of Philosophy* 20, pp. 261–277.
Stratton-Lake, Philip (2000): *Kant, Duty and Moral Worth*. London and New York.
Straumann, Benjamin (2003–2004): "*Appetitus, societas* and *oikeiôsis*". In: *Grotiana* 24/25, pp. 41–66.
Street, Sharon (2010): "What is Constructivism in Ethics and Metaethics?" In: *Philosophy Compass* 5, pp. 363–385.
Striker, Gisela (1996): *Papers in Hellenistic Epistemology and Ethics*. Cambridge: Cambridge University Press.
Surprenant, Chris W. (2014): *Kant and the Cultivation of Virtue*. Abingdon, New York: Routledge.
Tierney, Brian (1997): *The Idea of Natural Rights: Studies on Natural Rights, Natural Law and Church Law 1150–1625*. Atlanta: Scholars Press.
Tierney, Brain (2000): "Medieval Rights and Powers: On a Recent Interpretation". In: *History of Political Thought* 21, pp. 327–338.
Tierney, Brian (2001a): "Kant on Property: The Problem of Permissive Law". In: *Journal of the History of Ideas* 62, pp. 389–406.
Tierney, Brian (2001b): "Permissive Natural Law and Property: Gratian to Kant". In: *Journal of the History of Ideas* 62, pp. 381–399.
Tierney, Brian (2002): "Natural Law and Natural Rights: Old Problems and Recent Approaches". In: *Review of Politics* 64, pp. 389–406.
Tierney, Brian (2011): "Response to S. Adam Seagrave's 'How Old are Modern Rights? On the Lockean Roots of Contemporary Human Rights Discourse'" In: *Journal of the History of Ideas* 72, pp. 461–468.
Tilley, John J. (2015): "John Clarke of Hull's Argument for Psychological Egoism". In: *British Journal for the History of Philosophy* 23, pp. 69–89.
Timmermann, Jens (2005): "Why Kant Could Not Have Been a Utilitarian". In: *Utilitas* 17, pp. 243–264.

Timmermann, Jens (2007): *Kant's Groundwork of the Metaphysics of Morals: A Commentary.* Cambridge: Cambridge University Press.
Timmermann, Jens (2009): "Acting from Duty: Inclination, Reason and Moral Worth". In: Jens Timmermann (Ed.): *Kant's Groundwork of the Metaphysics of Morals: A Critical Guide.* Cambridge: Cambridge University Press, pp. 45–62.
Timmons, Mark (Ed.): *Kant's Metaphysics of Morals: Interpretive Essays.* Oxford: Oxford University Press
Timmons, Mark (2006): "The Categorical Imperative and Universalizability". In: Christoph Horn/Dieter Schönecker (Eds.): *Groundwork for the Metaphysics of Morals.* Berlin, New York: De Gruyter, pp. 158–199.
Tuck, Richard (1993): *Philosophy and Government: 1572–1651.* Cambridge: Cambridge University Press.
Tuck, Richard (1999a): *The Rights of War and Peace: Political Thought and the International Order from Grotius to Kant.* Oxford: Oxford University Press.
Tuck, Richard (1999b): *The Law of War and Peace.* Oxford: Oxford University Press.
Turco, Luigi (1999): "Sympathy and Moral Sense: 1725–1740". In: *British Journal for the History of Philosophy* 7, pp. 79–101.
Uleman, Jennifer K. (2010): *An Introduction to Kant's Moral Philosophy.* Cambridge: Cambridge University Press.
Velkley, Richard (1989): *Freedom and the End of Reason: On the Moral Foundations of Kant's Critical Philosophy.* Chicago: University of Chicago Press.
Villey, Michel (1975): *La formation de la pensée juridique*, 4th edition. Paris: Éditions Montchrestien.
Vogt, Katja Maria (2008): *Law, Reason, and the Cosmic City: Political Philosophy in the Early Stoa*, Oxford: Oxford University Press.
Wagner, Hans (1994): "Kants Konzept von hypothetischen Imperativen". In: *Kant-Studien* 85, pp. 78–84.
Weber, Michael (2007): "More on the Motive of Duty". In: *The Journal of Ethics* 11: pp. 65–86.
Weinstock, Daniel M. (2000): "How Not to Bridge the Gap: Cummiskey on Kantian Consequentialism". In: *Canadian Journal of Philosophy* 30, pp. 315–339.
Westphal, Kenneth R. (1997): "Do Kant's Principles Justify Property or Usufruct?" In: *Jahrbuch für Recht und Ethik/Annual Review of Law and Ethics* 5, pp. 141–94.
Westphal, Kenneth R. (2013): "Natural Law, Social Contract and Moral Objectivity: Rousseau's Natural Law Constructivism". In: *Jurisprudence* 4, pp. 48–75.
Westphal, Kenneth R. (2015): "Kant: Vernunftkritik, Konstruktivismus and Besitzrecht". In: *Archiv für Rechts- und Sozialphilosophie—Beihefte (ARSP-B)* 143, pp. 57–100.
Willaschek, Marcus (1997): "Why the Doctrine of Right Does Not Belong in the *Metaphysics of Morals*". In: *Jahrbuch für Recht und Ethik/Annual Review of Law and Ethics* 5: 205–227.
Willaschek, Marcus (2002): "Which Imperatives for Right? On The Non-Prescriptive Character of Juridical Laws in Kant's *Metaphysics of Morals*". In: Mark Timmons (Ed.): *Kant's Metaphysics of Morals: Interpretive Essays.* Oxford: Oxford University Press, pp. 65–87.
Wilson, Eric Entrican (2015): "Kant and the Selfish Hypothesis". In: *Social Theory and Practice* 41, pp. 377–402.
Wokler, Robert (2012): *Rousseau, the Age of Enlightenment, and Their Legacies.* Princeton, Oxford: Princeton University Press.

Wood, Allen W. (1991): "Unsocial Sociability: The Anthropological Basis of Kantian Ethics". In: *Philosophical Topics* 19, pp. 325–391.
Wood, Alen W. (1996): "Self-Love, Self-Interest and Self-Conceit". In: Stephen Engstrom/Jennifer Whiting (Eds): *Aristotle and the Stoics: Rethinking Happiness and Duty*. Cambridge: Cambridge University Press, pp. 141–161.
Wood, Allen W. (1999): *Kant's Ethical Thought*. Cambridge: Cambridge University Press.
Wood, Allen W. (2008): *Kantian Ethics*. Cambridge: Cambridge University Press.
Wood, Allen W. (2014): *The Free Development of Each: Studies on Freedom, Right, and Ethics in Classical German Philosophy*. Oxford: Oxford University Press.
Yang, Xiaomei (2000): "The Problem of Overdetermination: The Metaphysical and Epistemological Criteria of Moral Worth of Right Action:. In: *Southwest Philosophy Review* 16, pp. 73–86.
Zagorin, Perez (2000): "Hobbes without Grotius: In: *History of Political Thought* 21, pp. 16–40.
Zurbuchen, Simone (2004): "Zum Prinzip des Naturrechts in der 'école romande du droit naturel'". In: *Jahrbuch für Recht und Ethik/Annual Review of Law and Ethics* 12, pp. 189–211.

Translations: Individual Works and Editions Containing Translations

Barbeyrac, Jean (2003 [1718]): "The Judgement of an Anonymous Writer on the Original of this Abridgment", David Saunders (Trans.). In: Samuel Pufendorf: *The Whole Duty of Man and Citizen According to the Law of Nature*. Ian Hunter/David Saunders (Eds.). Indianapolis: Liberty Fund, pp. 267–305.
Carr, Craig L. (Ed.)/Seidler, Michael J. (Trans.) (1994): *The Political Writings of Samuel Pufendorf*. (Contains partial translation of Pufendorf's DJN.) New York, Oxford: Oxford Univeristy Press.
Cicero, Marcus Tullius (1744): *Morals, containing the Conferences on Good and Evil, and the Academical Treatises*. William Guthrie (Trans.). London: T. Waller.
Grotius, Hugo (1724): *Le droit de la guerre et de la paix*, 3 vols. Jean Barbeyrac (Trans.). Amsterdam: Pierre de Coup.
Grotius, Hugo (2005): *The Rights of War and Peace*. Richard Tuck (Ed.). Liberty Fund: Indianapolis.
Hobbes, Thomas (1998): *On the Citizen*. Richard Tuck/MichaelSilverthorne (Eds.). Cambridge University Press.
The Institutes of Justinian (1987). Peter Birk/Grant McCleod (Trans.). Ithaca: Cornell University Press.
Kant, Immanuel (1992): *Theoretical Philosophy: 1755–1770*. David Walford (Ed.), in collaboration with Ralf Meerbote. Cambridge: Cambridge University Press.
Kant, Immanuel (1996): *Practical Philosophy*. Mary J. Gregor (Ed.). Cambridge: 1996.
Kant, Immanuel (2002): *Theoretical Philosophy after 1781*. Henry Allison et al (Eds.). Cambridge: Cambridge University Press.
Kilcullen, John/Scott, John (Trans.) (2001): *A Translation of William of Ockham's Work of Ninety Days*. Lewiston NY: E. Mellin Press.

Marx, K. (1996): *Later Political Writings*. Terell Carver, T. (Ed.). Cambridge: Cambridge University Press.
Pufendorf, Samuel (1703): *Of the Law of Nature and Nations*. Basil Kennett (Trans.). Oxford: L. Lichfield.
Pufendorf, Samuel (1706): *Le droit de la nature et des gens*. Jean Barbeyrac (Trans.). Amsterdam.
Pufendorf, Samuel (1707): *Les devoirs d'homme et du citoion*. Jean Barbeyrac (Trans.). Amsterdam.
Rousseau, Jean Jacques (1990 ff.): *Collected Writings*. Roger D. Masters/Christopher Kelly (Eds.). 13 vols. Dartmouth: University Press of New England.
Selden, John (1652): *Of the Dominion or, Ownership of the Sea*. Marchamount Nedham (Trans.). London.

Index

Achenwahl, Gottfried 150
Acquisition (original) 3–5, 7f., 10f., 127–129, 131, 135–142, 144–150, 152–155, 158–169, 171, 240, 271–275, 277–280, 284, 289–294, 307, 310–312, 314, 317, 319–321
– original acquisition/*prima occupatio* 3, 7, 150–159, 272, 289, 290
– provisional acquisition 141, 145
Affection 92, 94, 178, 188, 223, 250
– natural affection 93f., 266
Agreement 8, 68, 139, 153, 159, 162, 165, 181, 225f., 229, 235, 259, 271f., 285f.
– universal agreement 8, 153–156, 158f., 161f., 272, 274, 280
Allison, H. 46, 58, 77, 98f., 113, 115f., 178
Amour de Soi 9, 184, 196, 199, 201
Amour-Propre 184, 196, 200–202, 265
Annas, J. 82, 203f., 250f.
Anthropology 74, 195f., 198, 205, 236, 238, 269
– practical anthropology 14, 28, 72f., 75, 110
A priori 1f., 6f., 13, 15, 17, 28, 33, 35–37, 40f., 46, 54, 62, 73–75, 79, 92, 97, 110, 126, 129, 131, 133, 136, 140f., 161, 164f., 168, 182, 240, 298, 306, 320
– *a priori* given end 1, 40f., 240
– *a priori* united will 4, 7, 141, 144–146, 165, 168, 272, 290
Aristotle 203f., 320
Authority 38, 154, 156, 212, 224, 274, 289
Autonomy 2, 8, 63, 76, 118, 172f., 182f., 193, 196, 204f., 213, 238f., 267, 270
– autonomy of reason 184, 195, 239
– autonomy of the will 60, 173f., 196f., 213, 239

Balguy, John 248, 262
Barbeyrac, Jean 184, 204, 223
Baum, M. 21, 38, 46, 98, 120
Baxley, A.M. 39, 120
Beck, L.W. 58, 178

Beneficence 48, 88, 100, 104, 108f., 127, 201, 233f., 270, 297
Benevolence 10, 31–33, 46f., 67–70, 72, 88, 93–95, 104–106, 109, 176, 180, 206–213, 218f., 222f., 233f., 237f., 265–269, 295, 297–300, 302–305
Brett, A. 151, 161, 275
Broadie, S. 82, 296
Butler, Joseph 238, 255
Byrd, B.S. 123, 126, 131, 135, 146, 150, 167

Causality 76f., 191
– causality through freedom 63, 76
Cicero 154, 204, 242–245, 247, 249–256, 259, 262–267
Civil Condition 126f., 133f., 141, 144, 146f., 169, 287, 293
Civil Constitution 133f.
Clarke, S. 208, 248
Coercion 123, 125f., 306, 318
Cohen, G.A. 198, 315, 320
Common Good 201, 216, 218–222
Community 139f., 142f., 147, 153, 156–158, 160–162, 166f., 278, 281, 283–285, 287f., 290, 292
– original community 129, 135, 139–144, 147, 150, 153f., 159, 163, 165–167, 282–289, 291
– primitive community 155, 161f.
Compulsion 126, 213, 227, 233
Concept 1, 3–8, 10f., 13, 17f., 21–25, 27f., 30, 33–46, 48f., 52, 55, 67, 69, 71, 73f., 76f., 79–81, 83, 88, 90, 97f., 108, 110, 115, 119, 124–126, 129, 131–136, 138–141, 144–146, 151f., 159–161, 163–165, 173–176, 180–183, 185, 187, 189, 191, 195–197, 205, 213f., 226, 229, 231, 235–237, 239f., 249, 268, 272, 277f., 283, 285–287, 289f., 297f., 302–306, 309, 311, 314f., 318, 320
– concept of duty see Duty
Consequentialism 294–297
– Kantian consequentialism 5, 10, 294, 296, 298, 304, 306f.

Constraint 27f., 38–40, 126, 167, 210–212, 230, 232, 236, 296, 299–302, 304–306
- external constraint 22, 38, 123, 212f., 230
- self-constraint 38–40, 230, 318
Contentment 27, 32f., 88, 101, 105–109, 298, 304
Contract 146, 281, 288
- original contract 146f.
Crusius, Christian August 174f., 181, 248
Cumberland, Richard 9, 206, 208, 213–221, 224, 233–237, 242
Cumberland's Works
- *De legibus* 206, 214, 216
Cummiskey, D. 294

Darwall, S. 262
Denis, L. 21, 39
Deontology 219, 296
Desire 54f., 57, 60–63, 109, 177f., 191, 193, 195, 197, 201f., 215, 217f., 220, 227–229, 231, 237, 250f., 253–255, 281f., 287, 295
- faculty of desire 15, 23f., 52–58, 60–62, 66, 185
Dignity 188f.
Disposition 26, 30, 33, 87, 89–92, 100, 113, 122, 203, 207, 220–223, 267–270, 302
Distribution 4f., 8, 10f., 127, 145, 153, 158–160, 166–169, 283, 288f., 291, 293f., 307–321
- Principle of distribution 144f., 166–168, 272, 293
Dominium 129, 149–152, 155, 157–161, 272–280, 282–285, 290
Duty 1–4, 10, 16–30, 33–43, 45, 47–50, 52, 67f., 74, 79, 81–84, 86–92, 94–96, 98–104, 106, 111–116, 118f., 121–123, 177, 181f., 188f., 192, 196, 219, 234, 244–246, 248, 251, 253–258, 261, 264–268, 295, 297–304, 306, 318
- duty of right 39, 318
- duty of virtue 6, 10, 13, 37, 47f., 50, 294, 298
- external duty 18, 123
- imperfect/wide duty 31, 87–91, 195, 298f., 300, 305
- perfect/narrow duty 31
- principle of duty 19, 25f., 32, 43–45, 48f., 51, 71, 81, 83, 86, 181, 214, 221, 253–255

Edwards, J. 31, 43, 50, 95, 100, 106, 129, 143, 150, 152, 161, 169, 175, 196, 207, 219, 245, 257, 262, 289
Egoism 29, 56, 178, 187, 209, 238
End 1–3, 5–7, 10, 13–15, 20–50, 55f., 58, 62, 67, 71, 73, 79, 81, 83–89, 96, 98, 100, 102f., 108, 110f., 114, 118, 122–125, 145, 149, 158, 163, 168f., 174f., 180–183, 187, 190, 194f., 204, 218, 220–222, 228, 231, 236f., 240f., 250, 252, 260f., 268, 270, 272, 278, 281, 283, 289, 294, 297–306, 319
- a priori given end see A priori
- end in itself 21f., 189
- end that is also a duty 1–4, 6, 13, 21f., 24, 27–30, 35, 41f., 45–47, 49, 83–87, 237, 240, 301, 304f.
- objective end 22–24, 37, 45f.
- objectively necessary end 13, 21f., 24f., 35, 38–40, 79, 85, 303f.
- obligatory end 1–6, 9f., 13–15, 21f., 26–30, 33–35, 37, 40–43, 46–48, 50, 55, 77, 79–81, 83–89, 122f., 171, 182, 237, 240–242, 244, 268, 270, 294–298, 300–306, 318
- self-seeking end 6, 14, 48, 50, 79, 81, 85f., 240f.
- subjective end 22f., 26, 45f.
- Epicurean ethics 258, 261
Epicurus 172, 174f., 197
Essays on the Active Powers of Man (AP) 256–261
Esser, A. 18, 21, 120, 297
Ethics 1, 3, 5–7, 14, 18–20, 24f., 34, 36f., 39f., 43f., 47, 55, 79, 82f., 86, 97, 100, 102, 115, 121, 173, 175, 184f., 187, 190–193, 196f., 204, 240–242, 245, 247–252, 260, 262, 264, 269, 271, 294–298, 303–306
Etiology 81–84, 86
Eudaimonism/eudaimonistic ethics 83, 175, 179f., 182, 241, 249, 259f.

Exposition   9, 15, 40, 87, 89–91, 129, 195
– metaphysical exposition   6, 28 f., 144, 240

Facultas utendi   152 f., 157, 284
Faculty of Desire see Desire
Feenstra, R.   274
Fielding, Henry   102, 270
First Seizure/*prima occupatio* see Original Acquisition under Acquisition
Flikschuh, K.   131
Forschner, M.   187–190, 194
Freedom   4, 8, 10, 15, 18, 21, 23, 25, 33, 35 f., 39–44, 74, 76, 125 f., 131, 133, 136, 139–141, 145, 167, 191–193, 199, 235, 249, 272, 286, 290–294, 306 f., 311, 316, 319–321
– inner freedom   22, 36 f.
– law of freedom see Law
– outer freedom   18, 36, 39 f., 43 f., 135
– transcendental freedom   76 f.
Freudiger, J.   98
Friedrich, R.   126, 129, 131, 135, 167
Frierson, P.   73
Fulda, H.-F.   129

Garnsey, P.   275
Garve, Christian   83, 254
Gauthier, D.   103, 198
General Will see *Volonté Générale*
God   52, 61, 64, 180 f., 211, 213, 216–222, 224–236, 275–277, 279, 298
Good Will see Will
Goy, I.   39, 120
Gregor, M.   18, 21, 36, 38 f., 48, 50, 88 f., 98, 124, 129–131, 135, 167, 224, 297
Grotius, Hugo   8, 149–162, 184, 204, 272–275, 278–280, 284, 289–291
Grotius's Works
– *De jure belli ac pacis* (DJB)   151, 155, 158, 184, 274
– *De jure praedae commentaries* (DJP)   151, 214–216
– *Mare liberum* (ML)   149–151, 153, 160, 162, 273 f.
Ground   1, 6–8, 10, 13, 16 f., 23 f., 36–38, 43, 46 f., 49–51, 64, 71, 81 f., 84, 86, 90, 98, 115, 127, 131 f., 139, 141, 144, 151, 154, 159, 161, 165 f., 168, 174, 180–182, 185–188, 190 f., 195, 197, 204, 208 f., 211, 214 f., 219–221, 223 f., 227 f., 231, 234 f., 237, 239, 244, 247, 252 f., 255–258, 261, 265, 268, 270, 272, 274 f., 277–279, 285, 290–292, 294, 298, 300–306, 314, 319
– determining ground   2, 15, 17 f., 40, 47, 49, 53, 55–60, 63–66, 69, 71 f., 74, 106, 123, 165, 173–175, 181–183
– formal determining ground   13, 24, 40
– material determining ground   1 f., 13, 23–26, 33, 40, 47, 49 f., 53, 122, 172–175, 180, 182 f., 197, 205, 240 f., 268, 297, 306
– empirical ground   6, 14, 35–38, 41, 43, 48–50, 53, 57, 75, 79, 81, 91 f., 122, 165
– material ground   24 f., 48, 174
Guthrie, W.   250 f.
Guyer, P.   77, 99, 113, 120, 129, 168

Haakonssen, K.   216
Happiness   2, 7, 10, 13, 21, 24, 26–30, 32–34, 37, 41, 47, 49 f., 55–58, 61–73, 76, 79–88, 104, 106–114, 117–119, 173 f., 177–183, 185, 191, 193, 207 f., 211, 215–220, 222, 224, 234, 240, 269 f., 295, 297–305, 318 f.
– happiness of others   1, 6, 13 f., 24, 26 f., 29 f., 32–34, 37, 41, 45, 47–50, 54 f., 57 f., 61, 64–69, 72, 79, 81, 83–85, 87 f., 104, 109–111, 113 f., 117, 119, 177 f., 191, 207, 269, 297 f., 301 f., 318
– one's own happiness   6, 14, 27, 29, 31 f., 49 f., 53, 55–58, 60, 71, 79, 85 f., 106–108, 172 f., 175, 179, 183, 204 f., 236, 238, 240, 269, 300–302
– universal happiness   69–71, 173
Harris, J.   265–267
Hartung, G.   175, 223 f.
Hedonism   54, 178, 260, 305
Henrich, D.   175, 187, 190
Henson, R.   99
Herman, B.   21, 23, 99, 294
Heteronomy (of the power of choice)   60
Hobbes, Thomas   9 f., 159, 162, 206, 214 f., 223 f., 226–238, 242, 273, 279–293

Hobbes's Works
– *De cive*   206, 215, 224–227, 229–232, 235–237, 280–289
– *De homine*   237
– *Elements of Philosophy*   237
– *Leviathan*   215, 231, 236 f., 283, 287–289
Home, H/Lord Kames   267
Honestum   9, 121, 172, 239 f., 242, 244, 249–254, 256, 258–267
Hruschka, J.   21, 23, 123, 126, 131, 135, 146, 150, 167
Humanity   23, 31, 94, 144, 147, 155, 157, 159, 163, 167, 199, 202, 275–278, 280, 282, 284, 293, 299, 320
Human Nature see Nature
Hume, David   5, 7, 9, 79 f., 92–97, 100 f., 121, 187 f., 240–249, 251–264, 266–268, 318
Hume's Works
– *An Enquiry Concerning the Principles of Morals* (EPM)   94 f., 100, 260, 318
– *A Treatise of Human Nature* (THN)   92–96, 101, 243–245
– *The Letters of David Hume*   243, 245–247, 251 f. 263
Hüning, D.   224, 282
Hurka, T.   305
Hursthouse, R.   305
Hutcheson, Francis   8 f., 100, 172, 174, 176–180, 183–188, 190, 193, 195, 205–214, 219, 223, 235–247, 249, 251–253, 256, 262–269
Hutcheson's Works   177
– *An Essay on the Nature and Conduct of the Passions and Affections, with Illustrations on the Moral Sense* (ECI)   176–178
– *An Inquiry into the Original of Our Ideas of Beauty and Virtue* (IBV)   176–177, 193, 206–213, 263–265, 269
– *A System of Moral Philosophy* (SMP)   176
– *The Meditations of the Emperor Marcus Aurelius Antoninus*   213, 263

Imperative   16, 21, 38, 42, 45, 168, 174, 219
– categorical imperative   16, 18, 25, 42 f., 45, 49, 52, 113, 169, 174, 182 f.
– hypothetical imperative   219

Incentive   3 f., 7, 16–20, 27, 73, 81, 89–92, 97, 114 f., 118–123, 178 f., 218, 244, 268, 270 f.
– external incentive   17
– internal incentive   17–20, 22, 26
Inclination   1–4, 6, 13, 37 f., 40 f., 45, 48–50, 64 f., 67–69, 72 f., 77, 79, 84, 86, 97–107, 109–112, 114–116, 118–121, 188 f., 194 f., 207, 237 f., 240 f., 263, 268 f., 318
– benevolent inclination   9, 50, 68 f., 71, 79, 100 f., 103–106, 109 f., 172, 176, 206 f., 212 f., 235, 238
Inwood, B.   203
Irwin, T.H.   82, 175, 178, 238

James, D.   167–169, 198, 226, 263, 265 f.
Judgment   32, 69 f., 117, 299
– moral judgment   32, 262, 299
Juridical   11, 13, 18–20, 31, 43, 124–128, 130–139, 141, 145–148, 151, 160 f., 169, 195 f., 230, 240, 257, 280, 282, 285, 306, 314, 319
– juridical condition see Civil Condition
– juridical postulate of practical reason   129, 131, 135, 139, 291
– juridical right see Right
– juridical theory of right   4 f., 7, 10, 18 f., 39, 43 f., 115, 123, 190, 196, 240 f., 271, 294, 306 f.
Justice   5, 92 f., 129, 146, 172, 188 f., 200–202, 204, 211, 221, 224, 253, 257, 266, 281–283, 285 f., 307, 318, 320
– distributive justice   4 f., 10, 126, 128, 240, 293 f., 307, 315 f., 318
– natural justice 283, 285 f.

Kagan, S.   294, 296 f.
Kant, Immanuel   1–11, 13–77, 79–92, 96–142, 144, 146–150, 160–169, 171–197, 204–206, 213, 235, 238–242, 244, 254, 267–273, 280, 289–307, 317–320
Kant's Works   104
– *Bemerkungen in den »Beobachtungen über das Gefühl des Schönen und Erhabenen«* (BGSE)   190–196

- *Die Metaphysik der Sitten* (MS)/*Metaphysics of Morals* 15 – 25, 27, 31, 36 f., 39, 42 – 45, 49, 51 f., 66, 73 – 75, 8, 88, 89, 123 f., 126, 169, 176, 179, 182, 192 f., 195, 295, 306
  - *Rechtslehre* (RL)/Doctrine of Right 1, 3 – 6, 8, 13, 15, 18, 21, 35, 39 f., 42 – 44, 47, 115, 116, 123 – 149, 161 – 167, 169, 171, 272, 290 f., 293, 303, 306

  Tugendlehre (TL)/Doctrine of Virtue 1, 3 – 6, 8, 10, 13 – 15, 18 – 23, 25, 29, 31 f., 35 f., 38 – 49, 55, 67 f., 74, 79, 81 – 83, 86 – 91, 103 f., 110, 114 f., 122 f., 133, 169, 171, 179, 189, 197, 240 f., 268, 294 – 300, 302 f., 305 f., 319 f.
- *Die Metaphysik der Sitten Vigilantius* (V-MS/Vigil) 177, 179, 197
- *Die Religion innerhalb der Grenzen der bloßen Vernunft* (RGV) 24, 29, 83, 119, 175, 197
- *Grundlegung zur Metaphysik der Sitten* (GMS) 3, 7, 21 – 25, 29, 43, 51 f., 66, 73 f., 97 – 101, 103 – 107, 110 – 122, 179 f., 193, 197, 241, 294
- *Kritik der praktischen Vernunft* (KpV) 2 f., 6, 8, 14, 16, 21, 24, 27, 29, 49 – 54, 56 – 60, 63 f., 66, 68 – 71, 73 – 76, 79, 98, 103 – 107, 110, 117, 119 f., 172 – 179, 181 f., 185 f., 190, 192 f., 197, 241, 298
- *Kritik der reinen Vernunft* (KrV) 73, 142 f.
  - Third Analogy of Experience 143
- *Kritik der Urteilskraft* (KU) 33, 298
- *Metaphysische Anfangsgründe der Rechtslehre* (RL) see *Rechtslehre* (RL)/Doctrine of Right
- *Metaphysische Anfangsgründe der Tugendlehre* (TL) see *Tudgenlehre* (TL)/Doctrine of Virtue
- *Moral Mrongovius* (V-Mo/Mron) 110, 175, 179
- *Moralphilosophie Collins* (V-Mo/Collins) 110, 175, 176
- *Nachricht von der Einrichtung seiner Vorlesungen in dem Winterhalbenjahre von 1765–1766* (NEV) 187 f., 267
- *Opus Postumum* (Op) 142
- *Reflexionen* (Refl) 27, 110, 142, 179, 197
- *Träume eines Geistersehers, erläutert durch die Träume der Metaphysik* (TG) 194
- *Über den Gemeinspruch: Das mag in der Theorie richtig sein, taugt aber nicht für die Praxis* (TP) 83
- *Untersuchung über die Deutlichkeit der Grundsätze der natürlichen Theologie und der Moral* (UD) 184 – 189, 196
- *Vorarbeit zur Metaphysik der Sitten* (VAMS) 120
- *Vorarbeit zur Rechtslehre* (VARL) 136, 142 – 144, 166
- Kersting, W. 124, 126, 129, 137, 195

Labor 19, 153 f., 240, 307 – 314, 317, 319, 321
Law 2 f., 5, 8 f., 15 – 23, 25 – 28, 31 – 33, 35 – 38, 40, 42 – 47, 53 – 56, 58, 60 – 65, 67 – 69, 73 – 77, 87 – 92, 99, 103, 105, 108, 110 – 114, 117 – 127, 129, 132 – 135, 138 – 141, 144 f., 147, 150, 153 – 155, 160, 165, 168 f., 183 f., 194 – 196, 198, 200 f., 206 – 225, 231 f., 234 – 240, 242, 265, 268 – 271, 277, 282 f., 285 – 290, 293, 297 – 300, 302 – 304, 306, 319
- form of law 2
- juridical law 18, 123, 169, 303
- law of freedom 15 f., 21 f., 63, 77, 123, 191, 197
- law of right 4, 42, 126, 133, 140, 147, 160, 168 f., 291 – 293, 303, 306, 319
- moral law 15 f., 38, 60, 63, 69 – 71, 73, 113, 117, 120, 177, 192 f.
- natural law 117, 133, 148, 150, 156, 160, 172, 184, 196, 198, 201, 204, 206, 213 – 218, 220 – 222, 224, 227, 233 – 237, 281, 286 – 289
- permissive law/*lex permissiva* 132, 145, 156, 160
- practical law 2 – 4, 6, 10, 13, 16 – 21, 24 f., 32 f., 35, 37, 44, 46 – 49, 51, 53 – 56, 59 – 73, 75 – 77, 79, 81, 85, 87, 92, 99, 103 – 105, 107 f., 111 – 116, 118 – 120, 123, 172, 174, 182 f., 187, 197, 209 f., 219, 234 f., 238 – 241, 294 f., 297, 302, 306
- prescriptive law 15, 117, 210, 212, 214, 285, 288, 292

- prescriptive natural law 9, 197, 206, 214, 286
- property law 1, 3, 5, 7, 123, 127f., 132, 168, 272–274, 280
- universal law 2, 6f., 10, 14–16, 19, 22, 25, 29, 31f., 36–40, 43f., 46–50, 52, 56, 58–60, 62, 74, 83, 103f., 107f., 111f., 114, 117–121, 124–126, 133, 145, 218, 268, 272, 291, 298, 306
  - universal-law formula 25f.
  - universal law of right 44, 125, 133, 135
Lawgiver 17f., 123, 211f., 216, 218, 234, 237
- divine lawgiver 211, 215, 234
Lawgiving 2, 7f., 15–19, 20, 32, 39f., 59f., 63, 65–69, 71f., 76, 79, 92, 97, 110, 114, 119, 123f., 131, 134, 136–138, 141, 146, 164, 166, 169, 184, 195f., 206, 211f., 220, 222, 234f., 237, 239, 269
- ethical lawgiving 11, 13, 15, 17–20, 25, 32–34, 39, 123, 169, 240, 318f.
- juridical lawgiving 17–20, 25, 33, 44, 123, 321
- universal lawgiving 2, 13f., 16, 24f., 29, 31–33, 35, 37, 41, 44–50, 58–60, 62f., 67f., 71, 75f., 79, 84–87, 92, 104, 110, 113–115, 118, 120f., 137, 139, 141, 165, 168, 173, 182, 195f., 240, 268, 271
Legality 37, 90–92
Legislation see Lawgiving
Living in Accordance with Nature 249f., 252f.
Lloyd, S.A. 224, 289
Locke, John 154
Long, A.A. 183, 203f., 255
Ludwig, B. 18, 124, 126, 131, 137, 154, 235

Malcolm, N. 280
Mandeville, Bernard 174f., 262
Mare liberum/Mare clausum Controversy 149–160, 162
Marx, Karl 11, 135, 293f., 306–321
Marx's Works
- *Critique of the Gotha Program* 306–321
- *Grundrisse/Foundations of the Critique of Political Economy* 135
- *Marx/Engels Gesamtausgabe, Erste Abteilung* (MEGA) 307–321

Material Determining Ground see Ground
Material Equality 4f., 8, 10, 127f., 160, 168f., 272f., 289, 293f., 306f., 317, 319–321
Maxim 1–7, 11, 13–16, 19, 21–26, 29–33, 35–41, 43–72, 75f., 79, 81, 83f., 86–92, 97–99, 101–123, 125, 132, 169, 173f., 197, 199–202, 204, 214, 216, 240f., 247, 256–259, 268f., 271, 281f., 291, 293, 297, 299f., 302, 304, 306, 318
- empirically grounded maxim 6, 13f., 37, 41, 47–50, 73, 75f., 79–81, 85–87, 92, 110, 122, 240f., 268
- form of maxim 2, 60
- matter of maxim 25, 33, 46, 48, 71, 297
- Undoubted Maxim 92, 95f., 100f., 121, 241, 244–248, 256–259, 261, 266, 268
Means of Consumption 307–317, 320
Means of Production 284, 307, 309–311, 313, 315f., 319
Metaphysics 22, 74
metaphysics of morals 1, 3, 7, 13, 15f., 28, 35, 39, 43, 48, 52f., 73–77, 81, 97, 110, 115, 123f., 126, 131, 179, 189, 195, 303
Mill, John Stuart 203f., 262, 296
Montaigne, Michel de 174f.
Moore, J. 242, 263, 265
Moral Feeling 120, 176, 179f., 185, 187–195
Morality 26, 33f., 37, 69, 73, 87, 89–92, 95f., 101, 118, 172–177, 179f., 182–184, 188, 190, 196, 201, 205, 241, 245f., 248, 251, 256, 261, 265, 267, 298, 302
Moral Law see Law
Moral Permissibility 237, 295f.
Moral Sense 177, 193, 206, 209, 211, 213, 255
Moral Worth/Moral Value 2f., 5, 7, 9, 37, 77, 79–122, 172, 239, 241f., 244–249, 255f., 258–261, 264, 266–268, 270
Morgan, S. 294
Motivation 4–6, 28, 50, 58, 79, 81, 85, 97, 110f., 178, 184, 197, 206, 208, 213, 236, 267
- moral motivation 9, 83f., 86, 101, 176, 178, 193, 207, 239, 244, 246, 262, 266f.

Motive   4, 81, 83, 93–96, 101, 105, 109, 177, 181, 183, 194, 208, 243–246, 248 f., 252–258, 261, 263 f., 266

Natural Condition   10, 134, 144, 151, 153, 155–157, 161, 197, 277, 280, 282–285, 287
Natural Law see Law
Nature   6, 9, 23, 29 f., 33 f., 39, 61 f., 73 f., 87 f., 94, 100, 111, 116–118, 120, 140, 147, 153 f., 157, 163, 165, 169, 181, 184, 195 f., 198 f., 201 f., 205 f., 209 f., 214–222, 224–237, 239, 244, 249–253, 255, 260, 264 f., 267, 273–275, 279, 281–283, 285–290, 307, 311, 321
– human nature   7, 73 f., 92, 94 f., 100, 188 f., 194, 198, 220, 222, 236, 238, 245, 247, 256, 281 f.
– rational nature   23, 37, 225
– sensible nature   34, 38, 53, 63, 76, 239
– supersensible nature   63, 76
Necessitation   27, 38 f., 194
Necessity   16 f., 28 f., 31, 46, 60 f., 64, 72, 99, 115 f., 118 f., 126, 166, 168, 186, 193, 199, 215, 217–219, 234, 237, 253, 281
– objective necessity   54, 115
Neuhouser, F.   196, 198, 321
Nomothetic   97, 111, 114, 116, 121, 123, 212, 222
Norton, D.F.   251
Norton, M.J. 251
Noumenon   76 f., 131, 137, 163

Obligation   9, 16–21, 25, 29 f., 33, 89, 91, 94–96, 101, 115, 125, 132–135, 138–140, 145, 152–155, 164, 167 f., 172, 185–187, 189, 196, 206–224, 226–229, 231–235, 237–239, 241 f., 244, 246–248, 254–258, 261 f., 264–269, 272, 290 f., 295 f., 299–302, 305, 317–319, 321
– ethical obligation   20, 25 f., 31 f., 301
– form of obligation   20, 226
– juridical obligation   123, 152
– matter of obligation   18–22, 92, 123, 187, 304
– narrow obligation   31

– natural obligation   9, 206, 209, 214–216, 218, 220–224, 226 f., 229, 231–233, 235–238, 242
– obligatory end see End
– wide obligation   31 f., 87, 89, 91, 298–300
Occupation   4 f., 7, 88 f., 135 f., 141, 146 f., 150, 152–155, 157–163, 273
Ockham, William   10, 152, 273 f., 276–280, 289–292
Oikeiôsis   9, 184 f., 197, 202–205, 238 f., 241 f., 268 f.
Overall good   296–305

Pactum   8, 153, 158, 225
Palladini, F.   224, 235
Parfit, D.   294
Parkin, J.   216
Patzig, G.   250
Perfection   8, 13, 24, 26–30, 33, 54 f., 58, 61, 79–81, 85–92, 121 f., 172, 174 f., 180–183, 185–187, 189, 191–193, 197, 199, 205, 221, 241, 250, 268–270, 295, 297, 301 f., 305, 318 f.
– one's own perfection   1, 3, 6 f., 13 f., 21, 24, 26, 32, 55, 57, 62, 86 f., 90, 114, 182, 184, 240, 268, 297, 299, 302 f.
– others' perfection   30
– self-perfection   86, 91, 122, 199, 268, 305
Perfectionism   8, 175, 180, 184–187, 241, 305
– Stoic perfectionism   172, 176, 184
Philosophy   9, 15, 184, 242, 245, 261
– moral philosophy   1, 5, 8 f., 24, 37, 73 f., 102, 111, 171–173, 176, 180 f., 184–187, 194 f., 212, 214, 239, 242, 247, 260, 266, 303, 305
– practical philosophy   24, 68, 74
Piché, C.   190
Pinheiro Walla, A.   31, 126
Pistorius, Herman Andreas   98
Pity   199–202
Plato   204, 320
Pleasure   38, 54 f., 57–59, 102, 106–108, 177 f., 188, 190–193, 206–208, 211 f., 259–261, 270

Possession   4, 8, 127, 129–145, 147–149, 153, 156, 160–168, 272, 285, 290, 292 f., 319
– intelligible/rightful/rational possession   129–135, 137, 144, 147, 163, 169
– original possession 129, 139 f., 142, 167
– first possession   132, 134, 139 f., 145
– provisional rightful possession   133 f.
– sensible/physical/empirical possession   130–134, 137–139, 142, 153, 162
– universal possession   142–144, 166 f.
  – collective universal possession   142–144, 147, 166 f.
  – disjunctive/distributive universal possession   142–144, 147, 166 f.
Power of Choice   1 f., 4, 13, 15–19, 23–25, 33, 38–41, 44–50, 53, 57, 64, 74, 106, 122–125, 129, 132 f., 135, 138, 144–147, 162, 165 f., 168, 182, 191–194, 199 f., 240, 268, 291, 297, 306, 320
– matter of the power of choice   21–24, 26, 40, 45 f., 124, 127
– object of the power of choice   1, 40 f., 43, 46 f., 65, 70, 129, 131 f., 135, 137, 164, 166, 291, 306, 320
Practical Law see Law
Practical Love   31, 184, 189, 193, 202, 207, 297 f., 300
Practical Reason see Reason
Practical Rule   60–62, 64, 70, 181
Prescriptive Regress   91, 97, 111 f., 116, 121
Prescriptivity   59, 63, 77, 104
Price, R.   248, 262, 270
Prima Occupatio see Original Acquisition under Acquisition
Principle   2, 4–8, 10 f., 14–16, 18 f., 21–23, 26, 28 f., 32 f., 36 f., 42–46, 49, 51–58, 60–64, 68–77, 79, 82–84, 88, 90 f., 93–97, 100, 103, 106, 110, 116–118, 122–126, 128 f., 133, 135, 140, 144, 154, 159, 161–164, 166–169, 172–176, 178–189, 191–193, 196–202, 204 f., 207, 218 f., 227–229, 236, 238, 241, 243, 245–249, 251–255, 257–261, 265, 269 f., 272, 274, 280 f., 286 f., 289–297, 305–308, 310, 313–315, 317–321

– objective principle   52, 55, 59, 63, 68, 76, 104
– practical principle   2 f., 41 f., 45, 49–56, 58–60, 69, 75, 88 f., 106 f., 109, 111, 114, 173, 181–183, 204
  – empirical practical principle   73
  – material practical principle   4, 6, 8, 13 f., 51–57, 59 f., 63, 68–72, 75–77, 79 f., 92, 173, 176, 178 f., 183, 185–187, 189, 197, 204 f., 238 f., 241, 269
– principle of volition   37, 52, 81, 89, 103, 107, 122
  – objective principle of volition   52
  – subjective principle of volition   2, 41, 51 f., 103, 107 f., 125, 197
Private Right see Right
Property   3–5, 8, 10, 23, 59, 104, 108, 112, 114, 129, 150–158, 161, 169, 222, 272–279, 283–285, 287–289, 294, 308–310, 321
– property law see Law
Psychology   74
– moral psychology   73, 176, 179
  – empirical moral psychology   7, 28, 97, 110
Public Right see Right
Pufendorf, Samuel von   9, 152, 157, 161, 184, 204, 206, 208, 213 f., 219–224, 227–229, 231, 233–237, 242, 278
Pufendorf's Works
– *De jure naturae et gentium* (DJN)   152, 157, 206, 219–223, 227, 229, 233, 278
– *De officio hominis et civis*   234

Quintilian   154

Radcliffe, E.   94, 207
Rational Being   21 f., 24, 38, 52–64, 67 f., 70, 73 f., 76, 103, 107 f., 130, 147, 174, 194, 203, 213, 215–222, 225, 231 f., 234
Rationalism   9, 247
– rationalist ethics   9, 121, 172, 240, 242, 247, 261, 264
Rational Nature see Nature
Reason   2, 7 f., 13, 15, 17 f., 26, 29 f., 33, 39 f., 42, 47, 50–53, 55, 58, 63 f., 67, 69–73, 76 f., 79, 87–89, 93, 98, 108,

120, 122–125, 127, 131, 135, 137, 140, 146, 158f., 161f., 168, 171f., 177, 184, 191f., 197–202, 205, 208, 215, 217f., 220f., 223, 225–228, 231–233, 235–239, 241f., 247f., 252, 255, 258, 260–264, 266–271, 276–279, 281–283, 287f., 290–292, 316
- practical reason   1f., 6–8, 13–15, 17–22, 25, 28, 33–35, 37, 40–42, 46, 50–53, 58, 60, 63, 68, 75–77, 79, 86, 90, 126, 130, 132f., 135, 137, 141, 144, 146f., 163–166, 168f., 172–176, 186, 190, 195, 205, 213, 217, 234, 241, 268, 270, 272, 288, 290, 293, 299, 303, 306
  - empirically conditioned practical reason   53, 55, 58, 63, 71, 75, 174–176, 178, 187, 204, 238f., 241
  - juridical practical reason   44
  - morally practical reason   1f., 6, 9, 13, 15f., 21, 26–28, 31–33, 37, 41, 43, 48–50, 52, 55, 58f., 62f., 67–69, 72, 79, 85, 87, 97, 104, 107, 110–112, 114, 119, 173, 182, 187, 239f., 242, 244, 297f., 301–303, 318f.
  - pure practical reason   2, 13, 20, 40, 42, 46f., 49, 58, 64, 76f., 131, 163f., 174f., 179, 182, 240, 298
- pure reason   36, 39, 41, 43, 46, 63, 69, 73, 76, 143, 183
- reason's universal legislation   see Lawgiving
- right reason   214f., 225, 227, 231f., 235–237, 285, 287, 292
- theoretical reason   52
Reid, Thomas   9, 242, 244f., 247f., 256–261, 265f., 270
Representation   16f., 25f., 40, 45, 57, 59, 102, 117, 126, 141, 162, 164, 297, 304
Res nullius   132, 157–159, 277, 291
Respect   8, 10, 13, 15, 18f., 21, 30, 35f., 38, 44, 60f., 82, 84, 93f., 99, 102, 113, 118–120, 122f., 133, 137f., 140, 144f., 147, 154f., 158, 164, 167f., 180, 188, 198, 202, 212, 225, 232, 239f., 242f., 249f., 252–254, 260, 262, 267, 271–273, 278, 285, 291, 296, 301, 305, 308, 312, 314

- respect for law   2f., 7, 97, 99, 111, 113–116, 118–121, 244, 268, 270
Right   4, 8, 10, 13, 35, 40, 44f., 77, 115, 123–128, 132–136, 139, 144f., 147, 149–152, 154, 156–159, 166f., 169, 225–232, 235–237, 258, 271f., 276–280, 282–292, 294, 306f., 310–315, 317–321
- doctrine of right   1, 3, 5f., 8, 13, 15, 18, 35, 39f., 42–44, 47, 123f., 126f., 129, 131, 133, 135, 144f., 163, 166, 169, 171, 291, 303
- 'Doctrine of Right' see Kant's Works
- dominative right   151, 279f., 284, 289–291
- equal right   5, 11, 294, 306–315, 317–321
- law of right see Law
- natural right   5, 8, 10, 127, 151f., 154, 159, 169, 198–200, 225, 237, 272f., 278–280, 283–285, 287, 289–291
- positive right   124, 128
- private right   7, 10, 126f., 129, 133–136, 142, 147, 167
- public right   7, 126f., 293
- rights   8, 126, 130, 166, 169, 208, 272, 278, 286
- strict right/*jus strictum*   126–128, 145, 168f., 306
Ripstein, A.   128f., 167
Rischmüller, M.   190f., 194
Robinson, J.   161, 274f.
Ross, W.D.   30, 262, 294
Rousseau, Jean Jacques   8f., 102, 184f., 187, 190f., 194–200, 202–206, 238f., 241, 247, 269f., 321
Rousseau's Works
- *Discourse on the Origins of Inequality/Discourse II*   196–198, 205
- *Discourse on Political Economy*   197
- *Émile*   190, 196, 198, 200–202, 247
- *Julie, or the New Heloise*   102f., 196, 270
- *On the Social Contract*   200

Schadow, S.   18, 21, 31
Schmucker, J.   175, 187–191, 194
Schneewind, J.B.   175, 190, 223, 235, 255, 262

Schneiders, W.   195
Schönecker, D.   98, 297
Scottish Enlightenment   9, 242, 254
Selden, John   8, 149–151, 155–162, 272f., 279f., 284, 290f.
Selden's Works
– *Mare clausum*   149f., 155, 157f., 160, 162, 284
– *Opera omnia*   155f., 1580160, 284
Self-constraint see Constraint
Self-interest   34, 101, 105, 178f., 188, 193f., 208–210, 214, 223, 265
Self-legislation see Legislation
Self-love   6f., 9, 14, 29, 50, 53, 56–58, 60f., 64, 68f., 71–73, 75–77, 79–81, 86, 105–110, 172f., 175f., 178–180, 184, 196, 199–210, 213f., 219, 223, 235–238, 240f., 269f.
Self-preservation   184, 199f., 203, 214, 220, 223, 230f., 234, 236f., 269
Self-seeking end see End
Sensible nature see Nature
Sentimentalism   9, 96, 177, 247, 261f.
– sentimentalist ethics   5, 8, 95, 97, 100, 180, 185, 206, 242, 267
Shaftesbury, Earl of   100, 107, 176f., 1876f., 247
Sidgwick, H.   30, 33f., 260, 262
Silverthorne, M.   226, 232, 236, 263, 281, 286
Slote, M.   255, 262, 295
Smith, Adam   247
Sociability   197, 199f., 220–223
– natural sociability   184, 196, 204, 223
Socialitas Requirement   220f., 234
Square, Mr.   102, 251, 267
Squire Allworthy   97, 102, 105f., 109, 270
State of Nature   126, 134, 144, 149, 151, 159, 161, 200, 214f., 228f., 273f., 286, 288
– juridical state of nature   127, 144, 147, 169
– Stoic perfectionism see Perfectionism
Stratton-Lake, P.   120, 262
Striker, G.   203
Suarez, Francisco   151, 278
Sympathy   99–102, 104f., 107, 109, 111, 188, 190f.

Theonomous Ethics   174f., 180
Thwackum, Reverend   102
Tierney, B.   129, 151, 161, 274f., 278f., 289, 291
Timmermann, J.   98
Trampota, A.   21
Transcendental Freedom see Freedom
Tuck, R.   150, 155, 157, 159, 226, 232, 236, 281, 283, 286
Turco, L.   208

Undoubted Maxim see Maxim
Universal Agreement see Agreement
Universality   2, 16, 31f., 37, 41, 44, 49, 59–67, 69, 71f., 76f., 79, 104, 107f., 111, 117, 137, 141f., 144, 156, 159, 163, 165, 202, 217, 291f.
Universal Law see Law
Utilitarian ethics   235, 296f., 305
Utilitarianism   305

Virtue   2, 5f., 13, 15f., 20f., 24–26, 31–34, 37, 39, 42f., 46, 52, 55, 57, 59f., 63, 67, 76, 79, 81, 86f., 90, 93, 104, 109f., 112–114, 125, 127, 137, 142, 147, 151, 156f., 162, 166f., 176f., 180, 186, 188–191, 193, 195, 199, 201–203, 205, 207, 218, 221f., 226f., 232, 243–246, 248–255, 259–261, 263–265, 267, 283, 293, 295–298, 302f., 305, 318–320
– artificial virtue   92f.
– doctrine of virtue   1, 3–6, 10, 13f., 18f., 21–25, 29, 35, 38f., 41–44, 46, 48, 55, 74, 79, 81, 83, 86f., 115, 123, 171, 179, 240f., 294–298, 300, 303, 305f., 319
– 'Doctrine of Virtue' see Kant's Works
– natural virtue   92
Vogt, K.M.   203
Volition   16, 64–66, 68, 74, 76, 90, 98, 117f., 233, 285
– principle of volition see Principle
Volonté du tous   194
Volonté Générale   9, 184, 190, 194, 196f.
Voluntarism   181, 223f., 226, 234

Welfare   27, 30f., 87, 128, 295, 297

Will 1–6, 14, 28f., 31–33, 36–38, 41, 43–45, 48, 50–56, 58–75, 77, 81–86, 89, 92f., 97–101, 103–107, 109–115, 117–125, 127–129, 132, 134–142, 144–147, 149–152, 155f., 162–169, 172–177, 181–183, 185, 187, 190–197, 200–202, 204–206, 209, 211, 213f., 216–223, 226–228, 230, 232–235, 237–240, 242f., 245, 247, 249, 251, 258, 264–266, 268, 271, 273, 280–283, 293, 295–297, 300f., 303f., 307, 309–313, 315–318
– good Will 97f., 113
– omnilateral Will 136f., 141
– unilateral Will 138, 140, 142
– universal Will 134–136, 139–142, 190, 194f.
Westphal, K. 129
Willaschek; M. 169
Wilson, E.E. 56, 99
Wolff, Christian 174f., 185f., 248
Wolmar, Monsieur de 102f., 270
Wood, A. 39, 82, 98f., 128
Woolf, R. 251, 254

Zeno of Citium 250
Zurbuchen, S. 224

www.ingramcontent.com/pod-product-compliance
Lightning Source LLC
Chambersburg PA
CBHW030604230426
43661CB00053B/1834